Encyclopedia of American Political Reform

Encyclopedia of American Political Reform

Richard A. Clucas

ABC-CLIO
Santa Barbara, California
Denver, Colorado
Oxford, England

Library of Congress Cataloging-in-Publication Data

Clucas, Richard A.
Encyclopedia of American political reform / Richard A. Clucas.
p. cm.
Includes bibliographical references and index.
ISBN 0-87436-855-3 (alk. paper)
1. United States—Politics and government—1989– —Encyclopedias.
2. United States—Politics and government—1945–1989—Encyclopedias.
I. Title.
E839.5.C57 1996
320.973'09'045—dc20 96-26176
CIP

02 01 00 99 98 97 96 95 10 9 8 7 6 5 4 3 2 1

Cover photograph credits:
(*row one*) Vietnam veteran (AP/Wide World Photos);
(*row two*) Sandra Day O'Connor (U.S. Supreme Court), Jesse Jackson (AP/Wide World Photos);
(*row three*) gay rights activists (AP/Wide World Photos);
(*row four*) Newt Gingrich (The Bettmann Archive).

ABC-CLIO, Inc.
130 Cremona Drive, P.O. Box 1911
Santa Barbara, California 93116-1911

This book is printed on acid-free paper ♾.
Manufactured in the United States of America

To Elizabeth, Nathaniel, and Alexander

Contents

Preface

As the criticisms of the nation's political system have grown increasingly vehement in recent years, I have often been dismayed by how difficult it can be for my students to find simple explanations of the political reforms being bandied about on the nightly news, on radio talk shows, and over the Internet. A wealth of superb material that explains the various political reforms being debated in America today is available, yet this information is often difficult to track down unless you already know where to find it or are willing to spend considerable time looking.

This book is a simple guide to modern efforts to reform the American political system. The individual entries in the book explain terms, events, actors, issues, and concepts that are needed to understand the debates that have raged over political reform in America since the mid-1960s.

The number of reforms that have been offered over the years is so large that I had to decide what was important to include. For the most part, I limited my focus to reform proposals that seek to change either the structure or role of American government. I tried to keep away from narrow policy debates, fearing that to do otherwise would make my task unending. I have included some policy reforms, however, if I felt they represented fundamental change in the government's role in American society or the world. Although the book covers the period from the mid-1960s to the present, I also included a few older reform-related terms that I felt were important in understanding recent political debate.

Some scholars may be unhappy with how I have used the term *reform* in this text. Historically, the term has not meant simply change or revision, but it has often been associated with efforts to improve government and to bring about progress. Proposals that are designed to roll back the clock to an earlier time or to protect the status quo are not usually considered reform at all, but just its opposite. In compiling this book, however, I used a looser definition of reform in order to include concepts and ideas that I believe most nonspecialists would categorize as reform. Thus, not only did I include what might be called true reform proposals, but also innovations, counterreforms, and some important political firsts.

Given the broad scope of the book, some reforms had to be omitted and others not as fully explained as one might desire. But I believe the book provides a good starting point in understanding many of the most important political debates today in Washington, D.C., and around the country. To help readers fill in the missing details, each entry includes cross references to other related entries in the book and references to other works on the topic.

A number of individuals need to be thanked for their support in making this book a reality. The one person who deserves the most thanks is Beth Blenz-Clucas, who provided continual feedback on my work and aided me with specific parts of the project. She researched and wrote many of the entries on individual reformers, interest groups, education, and telecommunications; plus she helped put together the index. Of course, I could not have accomplished this task without her support at home.

Two students were particularly helpful. Patrick Brennan gathered research material on a wide array of topics and helped in fact-checking. I also gave him the unpleasant task of rechecking every entry in the reference list. Melissa Matczak helped research and write several of the entries that focus on ethics and minority politics. I want to thank Portland State University and the University of Wisconsin – Eau Claire for providing the financial support that allowed me to have the assistance of these two very able students.

I am grateful to both Gary Scott and Len Gambrell. As chairs of the political science departments at Portland State and the University of Wisconsin – Eau Claire, respectively, they have both been very supportive of my work on this project and in other areas.

In addition, many individuals have provided ideas and suggestions for the book. These include Michael Fine, Peter Myers, Jules Chan, and Tom Barth of the University of Wisconsin – Eau Claire; Keon S. Chi, Director, the Center for State Trends and Innovations, the Council of State Governments, Lexington, Kentucky; Joseph F. Zimmerman, Professor, State University of New York at Albany; Erick Low, Director, Library Services, National Center for State Courts, Williamsburg, Virginia; John Kincaid, Director, Meyner Center for the Study of State and Local Government at Lafayette College, Easton, Pennsylvania; Ronald D. Michaelson, Executive Director, Illinois State Board of Elections, Springfield, Illinois; and R. Steven Brown, Director, Centers for Environment and Safety, the Council of State Governments.

I would also like to thank the individuals at ABC-CLIO who worked on this project, especially the three editors with whom I had the pleasure to work: Todd Hallman, Mary Kay Kozyra, and Suzanne Chance.

Introduction

Riding high in public opinion polls after the successful Persian Gulf War, President George Bush appeared headed for certain reelection in the winter of 1991. Yet less than two years later, Bush was gone, removed by a disgruntled electorate that wanted change after 12 years of Republican leadership. The most revealing aspect of the nation's mood in the 1992 election was not Bush's defeat, but that a Texas billionaire, campaigning against the political system, received the largest presidential vote for an independent candidate since Theodore Roosevelt led the Bull Moose Party in 1912.[1] Two years after Bush's ouster, voters turned their wrath upon the Democratic Party, stripping the Democrats of their control of Congress for the first time in more than four decades.[2]

If there is one lesson to be learned from the tumultuous political events of the 1990s, it is that the American public has grown increasingly disillusioned with politics and politicians. With this disillusionment has come talk of political reform. Term limits, the line-item veto, devolution, privatization, welfare reform, a balanced budget amendment, school vouchers, and reinventing government are just a few of the reform proposals that have emerged as the focus of debate in the United States today.

Although the political turmoil of the early 1990s has helped propel reform back into the spotlight, the desire for change has played a fundamental role in shaping American politics since the nation was galvanized by political unrest in the 1960s. In retrospect, the past 30 years represent one of the most important reform eras in U.S. history. During this period, an impressive number of reforms have been enacted, opening up the political process, expanding the franchise, ensuring the election of racial minorities, regulating campaign finance and lobbying activities, restructuring government, changing the presidential selection process, redistributing power among governments, creating professional politicians, and then limiting their terms in office.

Despite the important role reform has played in recent U.S. politics, most Americans know little about the current proposals under debate among reformers, political leaders, and scholars. This book grew out of a desire to provide a guide to current reform proposals that have been put forward to change either the structure or the general role of American government. I quickly realized, however, that to explain current reform proposals I would have to expand the focus to cover the reform efforts of the past 30 years, because these efforts remain of critical importance in shaping political debate in the United States today. The war in Vietnam may be long over and the Watergate burglary a distant memory, but the reforms that were sparked by these and other events of the 1960s and 1970s continue to influence politics in the United States today, and in some important cases are themselves targets of current counterreform efforts.

Why have Americans been so unrelenting in seeking reform over these past 30 years? Although we can attribute the current upheavals in Washington to a general disillusionment with politics, a number of more specific underlying concerns have been motivating the demand for reform since the 1960s. Today, as in the past, the desire for reform reflects unmet social and political expectations. Americans want a government that protects and even furthers their interests, especially their economic position. They want a democratic system that offers them opportunities to participate. They want a government that can function. And they expect government officials to behave ethically. When the government appears unable or unwilling to meet these expectations, talk of reform arises.

These factors—the desires to protect economic interests, participate in governing, and obtain effective and honest government—are not the only motivations for modern reform efforts, but they have been continuously influential in shaping reform over the past 30 years, even though the political climate has turned from liberal to conservative. Instead of focusing on the changing political attitudes that have moved the nation to the right in the 1990s, it is important to look at these more enduring influences so as to understand the general nature of political reform in the United States.

Economic Concerns

Despite the noble rhetoric often espoused by political reformers, the motivation for political reform is often generated by a simple desire to protect personal interests, especially economic ones. The importance of economic interests is readily apparent in the battle over such current reform proposals as workfare, the balanced budget amendment, and restrictions on "takings." Yet the adoption of some reforms that appear to be economically neutral, such as those concerning term limits or voting rights, may affect political outcomes, which in turn could have significant economic ramifications. Although other factors have been important in recent reform debates, economic considerations have played a pivotal role in shaping the direction of political reform efforts over the past three decades.

The civil rights movement provides a good example of the importance of economic considerations in shaping demands for reform in the role played by the government in U.S. society. Although the movement was not triggered solely by economics, the desire to attain greater benefits from the nation's economic boom after the Second World War was certainly a major factor motivating African-Americans to seek change. As the postwar prosperity began to reach into the African-American community, expectations rose among poor and middle-class African-Americans, who then began to place greater demands on the federal government to remove racial barriers in the nation's economic system.[3]

By the mid-1960s, the civil rights movement had made impressive gains, ending legal segregation and opening up the political process. Even though these gains allowed African-Americans to register to vote and to sit where they wanted on city buses, a large number of African-Americans found that the reforms did little to improve their economic situation. In the latter part of the 1960s, many civil rights leaders turned their attention away from attaining equal rights and began to advocate a more active role for government to ensure economic justice, a decision that ultimately helped divide the movement and led to its decline.[4] Although many civil rights leaders became more radical in their economic proposals in those later years, the concern for African-Americans' economic well-being played a central role in motivating demands for political change throughout the movement's existence.

The economic prosperity of the postwar years not only helped stimulate the civil rights movement, it helped open the door to broader public acceptance of a more activist federal government in general. Immediately after the war, conservative reformers had a strong influence on public policy, as they tried to roll back the changes brought about by Roosevelt's New Deal. But by the early 1960s, the conservative backlash against a large and active federal government was replaced by a renewed commitment to using government to solve the nation's ills.[5]

President John Kennedy proposed a variety of new federal programs to overcome poverty, improve education, and strengthen health care, but it was not until Lyndon Johnson's administration that these reforms were enacted into law.[6] Through the passage of Johnson's Great Society programs and the introduction of Creative Federalism, political power became more centralized in the federal government. At the same time, federal spending soared.[7]

The renewed concentration of power in the federal government was reminiscent of Roosevelt's New Deal, yet unlike in the 1930s, the reforms of the 1960s came in a period of unparalleled economic growth.[8] From the late 1940s to 1973, median family income in the United States rose an average of 2.7 percent every year, inflation remained below 3 percent, and unemployment reached record lows.[9] Scholars differ in their opinions on Johnson's motivation for expanding the federal government, but with the nation's economy booming, opposition to his liberal political reforms was circumscribed.[10]

Over the next decade, there was broad acceptance of the liberal welfare state. Although Republican President Richard Nixon rewrote fiscal policy to increase the financial resources and powers of state governments, he continued to support an activist federal government. It was not until the late 1970s, when the economy began to stall under stagflation, that public support for the welfare state began to decline. With their own economic positions stagnating or even declining, many Americans became less willing to provide tax dollars to solve society's ills.

One of the watershed events in shaping political debate over the past two decades was the passage in 1978 of California's Proposition 13, which radically reduced the state's property tax rate. The success of the proposition spurred a nationwide property tax revolt that forced government officials to find policy solutions that did not raise taxes. The tightening of the economy in the late 1970s also helped spur a backlash toward various federal programs that were designed to improve employment and education opportunities for racial minorities and women, as working- and middle-class white males began to feel their own economic security threatened.[11]

With the election of Ronald Reagan as president in 1980, the American government moved further away from the activist role it had played in previous decades. A believer in limited government, Reagan slashed domestic spending, reduced the transfer of funds to state and local governments, cut taxes, and increased military spending.[12] The results of Reagan's actions were unprecedented federal budget deficits and a reduction in the federal government's role in U.S. society.[13]

Since Reagan's presidency, the nation has continued to become increasingly dissatisfied with the liberal policies of the past. Even though economic indicators showed sustained economic growth throughout the mid- to late 1980s, the economic positions of most Americans have not changed significantly since the early 1970s.[14] With their own pocketbooks continuing to feel pinched, many Americans have become unwilling to underwrite a large and activist government.

Expanding budget deficits and antitax sentiment have had profound effects on political reform in the United States, forcing much of the debate to revolve around how to reduce the role and size of government. These dual forces are not only shaping debate about the federal government, but state and local governments have similarly found themselves locked in a position where their budgets are constrained yet a majority of voters are unwilling to raise taxes.

Despite the attention that has been given to conservative reform efforts during the 1990s and the proposals of the new Republican majority in Congress, not all groups support a reduction in the role of government in society. Advocates for the poor, the elderly, minority groups, and others realize that conservative political reforms, from the balanced budget amendment to welfare reform, have consequences that will produce new economic winners and losers. They see their concerns as the probable losers if many of these reforms succeed.

Thus when Congress threatened to slash funding for Medicare and Medicaid in 1995, groups as diverse as the American Association of Retired Persons, the Children's Defense Fund, and the Consortium for Citizens with Disabilities began a concerted lobbying effort to protect these programs that help seniors, the poor, and children.[15] The battle over Medicare and Medicaid makes clear the importance of economic interests in the reform debate, in this case pitting conservatives who want to reduce their supporters' tax burden against the direct beneficiaries of these government programs.

Increased Democracy

The importance of economic concerns in shaping the debate over political reform since the 1960s should not be downplayed, yet other factors besides money have been instrumental in bringing about demands for change. None may be more significant than the pressure that has been put on the federal government to allow Americans to participate more fully in the political process. Since the mid-1960s, this demand to democratize the system has led to profound reforms in all aspects of U.S. politics, from forcing changes in voting registration laws to restructuring the internal workings of government itself. There is no other period in U.S. history in which the ideals of political equality have been extended so far and have had so much influence in driving political reform.

The civil rights activists who gathered in Mississippi for the Freedom Summer in 1964 and who braved the Edmund Pettus Bridge in Selma in 1965 wanted more than to be seated in all-white restaurants or to gain better jobs. They wanted African-Americans to be allowed to play a full and equitable role in the U.S. political system. Until the mid-1960s, African-Americans were essentially barred from participation by legal constraints, unethical electoral procedures, and threats of violence.[16]

In response to the mounting pressure for change, the federal government finally moved to overcome the political barriers that forced African-Americans outside the political system. In 1964, the Twenty-fourth Amendment to the U.S. Constitution was ratified; the amendment banned poll taxes, which had been used to prevent African-Americans and the poor from registering to vote. Then Congress adopted what may well have been the most important political reform of the past 30 years—the Voting Rights Act of 1965, a flexible yet forceful law that ensured African-Americans of their right to vote 100 years after they were promised this right with the passage of the Fifteenth Amendment.[17]

The success of the civil rights movement in bringing change for African-Americans emboldened other groups to push for additional reforms, both in economic matters and in expanding the nation's democratic principles. Beginning in the mid-1960s, Latinos, American Indians, women, students, homosexuals, the poor, the elderly, and the disabled began to organize and demand greater input into a political system that had historically denied them access.

The work of these groups changed the political process. Among the great success stories in democratizing the process were the amendments added to the Voting Rights Act in 1970, 1975, and 1982, which were passed through the concerted efforts of a large and well-organized coalition of civil rights organizations. These amendments expanded the law's scope to protect the voting rights of American Indians, Asian-Americans, Latinos, the disabled, and the illiterate.[18] In addition, the Twenty-second Amendment was ratified in 1971, extending the franchise to 18-year-olds. More recently, Congress enacted the so-called motor voter law to overcome restrictive voter registration procedures that have been used to deny citizens their right to vote.

Pressure to make the system more democratic has affected not only registration and voting but the entire electoral process, from the selection of candidates to the distribution of legislative seats. Some of the most important changes have come in party politics and the presidential selection process. After its tumultuous 1968 convention in Chicago, where Hubert Humphrey was nominated even though he had not participated in any primary elections, the Democratic Party was compelled to adopt a series of reforms to ensure that the party's decisions would be more representative of rank-and-file Democrats. The results included more proportional representation of women and minorities at the national nominating convention and the expanded use of primary elections to choose delegates. Although Democratic Party leaders scaled back the reforms after the disastrous nomination of George McGovern and the heavily criticized presidency of Jimmy Carter, the changes have made primaries the foundation of the presidential nomination process, ensuring broader participation of all party members in choosing nominees.[19]

The distribution of legislative seats has similarly been affected by the desire to make the system more democratic. As the 1960s opened, the U.S. Supreme Court announced its willingness to become involved in the political thicket of reapportionment in its decision in *Baker v. Carr.* Articulating the principle that all votes should carry the same weight, the Court ruled that legislative districts must have substantially equal populations. The Court's "one person, one vote" decision radically transformed legislative politics, improving the representation of cities while reducing the influence of sparsely populated rural areas.[20]

Turning its attention to the Voting Rights Act, the Court interpreted the scope of the act very broadly, ruling that the law covered more than simply the physical act of casting a ballot; rather, it covered "all action necessary to make a vote effective." The Supreme Court's stance, which was spelled out in a series of Court decisions beginning in the late 1960s, was that any type of voting procedure that reduced a minority group member's ability to influence election outcomes might violate the act's intent. This interpretation not only broke down barriers to registration and voting, but forced cities and states to reconsider all aspects of their electoral process, from the drawing of district boundaries to the types of electoral systems used.[21]

More recently, the Supreme Court's rulings, along with later revisions of the Voting Rights Act, have forced states to create what have been referred to as majority-minority districts to ensure the actual election of minorities. Despite the influence the act has had in helping minorities attain office, the debate on election reform has not ended. Many modern reformers, such as Lani Guinier, argue that the system will not be fair until some form of proportional representation is established.[22]

The concern to make the system more democratic has also influenced the internal structure of government itself. Among the best examples are the 1970 reforms in Congress, which were motivated by the desire to open up the system to give rank-and-file members more influence over policy matters. Until the 1970s, the congressional process was dominated by powerful committee chairs, who ruled their individual committees as if they were their own private kingdoms. Beginning with the Legislative Reorganization Act of 1970, Congress enacted a series of reforms to strip committee chairs of their power and allow all members greater influence in the policy-making process. By democratizing its internal structure in this manner, Congress was ensuring greater citizen input into the policy-making process.[23]

Effective Government

When the nation's founders gathered behind closed doors in Philadelphia during the sweltering summer of 1787, they constructed a constitution that was designed to embrace elements of democracy, but also to make government action difficult. The bicameral legislature, the separation of powers, and the federal system of government were meant to constrain government and, in so doing, protect the fundamental liberties of U.S. citizens. Although the nation's founders may have wanted to make the policy-making process cumbersome, most Americans expect the government to be able to perform its tasks effectively.

One main cause of political disillusion in the United States today and over the past three decades is the perception that government is simply not working. The desire to make government function more effectively has led to a variety of proposals, both to alter the distribution of power among governments and to change the internal structure of specific government bodies.

Reform in intergovernmental relations has been shaped in large part by shifting beliefs concerning which level of government is best able to deal with the nation's problems. During the 1960s, there was considerable optimism that the federal government could solve many of the nation's most pressing problems. Through Creative Federalism, President Johnson instituted the use of categorical grants to allow the federal government to work more closely with local governments to solve urban problems. The results were a strengthening in power of the national government and a decline in the role of the states.[24]

As the 1960s came to an end and many of the nation's perceived problems remained unsolved, Republican leaders began to argue with increasing success that state governments are better suited to handle many of those problems. When Nixon was elected president in 1968, he introduced revenue sharing and increased the use of block grants to channel more money to state governments as a way to give the states a greater role in solving the nation's problems with fewer federal strings attached.[25]

Although Nixon's New Federalism promised great changes in the relationship between governments, its effects were limited. It was not until Ronald Reagan's presidency that the relationship between the federal and state governments began to change, as Reagan cut federal spending and reduced the role of federal government, leaving the responsibilities for many policy areas to the states.[26]

Even though Reagan was considered very successful in restructuring federal-state relations, the federal government still plays a leading role in shaping public policy today through the use of unfunded mandates and direct federal action. Efforts to reduce the federal government's role further continue, however, with many reformers arguing that the federal government remains too large and that the nation would be better served if Congress were to give the states more power and flexibility in dealing with pressing social problems.

Aside from motivating reform in intergovernmental relations, the desire for more effective government has spurred reform within specific government bodies. Some of the most important structural reforms have come in legislative politics.

Despite the criticisms of gridlock in Washington that resonated throughout the 1992 presidential campaign, Congress has adopted a variety of reforms since the 1970s to make it function more effectively than in the past. Among the most significant reforms was the Congressional Budget and Impoundment Control Act of 1974, which was designed to reassert Congress's power against an increasingly imperial presidency.

Until the mid-1970s, there was little centralized control over the federal budget as it wound its way through the congressional process. Within the House, the Appropriations Committee had the greatest authority over the budget, yet its members tended to defer judgment to the committee's 13 subcommittees when they cast their budget votes. Moreover, a majority of federal expenditures did not go through the Appropriations Committee, but were controlled by the Ways and Means Committee or specific authorizing committees. Finally, there was no formal coordination between spending and taxing committees.[27]

The budget process had been criticized in the past, but Congress felt compelled to respond in 1974 as the budget grew out of control and President Nixon began to challenge Congress's power over the purse. The two specific turning points that persuaded Congress to enact budget reforms were the Pentagon's disclosure that it had used unauthorized funds to conduct the secret bombing of Cambodia and the president's refusal to spend federal money that had been duly appropriated by law.[28]

Facing a constitutional crisis over the president's actions, the members of Congress voted overwhelmingly to approve the 1974 budget act. Among its provisions, the act created separate budget committees in both houses, detailed budget procedures, and a legislative agency (the Congressional Budget Office) to provide members with expertise on budget and economic questions. The result of this reform, the large federal deficit notwithstanding, has been greater congressional control over the budgetary process.[29]

The desire to make government more effective has similarly influenced reforms in state legislatures. In the early years after the nation's founding, the state legislature was the preeminent branch in state politics, but by the mid-1940s, state legislatures were considered all but moribund. Meeting for only short periods every other year, with few resources and small staffs, most state legislatures were ill equipped to deal effectively with societal problems.

In the late 1960s, however, a legislative reform movement began to sweep the nation, bringing vast changes to state legislative politics. Supporters of the movement, who included California's powerful Assembly Speaker Jesse Unruh and members of the Citizens' Conference on State Legislatures (CCSL), argued that state legislatures needed to be modernized in order for them to be capable of dealing with state problems.[30]

The CCSL identified a set of criteria to assess state legislatures, and then it ranked all 50 state legislatures according to their operating capabilities. In developing its criteria, the CCSL argued that state legislatures need to have adequate staff, time, resources, and facilities in order to accomplish their tasks. After the CCSL's work was published, its ideas spread rapidly across the nation, encouraging state after state to improve the operation of its legislature. The results of this reform movement included increased capability of state legislatures as well as the rise of professional state legislators.[31]

I will end my discussion of reforms to improve government effectiveness here, although I could just as easily go on to mention similar movements to strengthen the roles of state governors and the president, to unify the judicial system, to reduce the backlog of cases confronting the courts, to experiment with new and better management techniques in government bureaucracies, and to privatize, downsize, devolve, and reinvent government itself. The desire to improve how government works has been unending.

Government Ethics

It is impossible to talk about political reform in the United States without recognizing the important role political scandals have played in stimulating demands for change. Watergate, Koreagate, Abscam, the Keating Five, the Iran-Contra affair, the resignation of House Speaker Jim Wright, the House banking scandal, and the controversial nomination of Clarence Thomas to the U.S. Supreme Court are only a handful of the political scandals that have dominated the press over the past 30 years and have led to calls for political reform.

Of these, no scandal has approached Watergate in its scope and relevance in shaping U.S. politics; Watergate led to the resignation of the president and the passage of several major pieces of reform legislation. The break-in at the Watergate Hotel and the subsequent cover-up were only part of the political abuses of the Nixon administration. As the events of Watergate were unveiled in congressional hearings, the nightly news was repeatedly filled with tales of illegal or unethical behavior associated with Nixon's reelection efforts, including laundered campaign contributions, the selling of ambassadorships, campaign "dirty tricks," and the use of the Internal Revenue Service against Nixon's opponents.[32]

Of the reforms enacted in the wake of Watergate and these other political scandals, the most important may have been the Federal Election Campaign Act (FECA) of 1971 and its revisions in 1974 and 1979. FECA represents the federal government's most impressive effort to date to regulate campaign finance and control the corrupting influences of campaign contributions. The act was initially designed to improve campaign finance disclosure and restrict the amount of money spent on media advertising, but it was substantially revised in 1974 as the abuses related to Watergate became known. Among its provisions, the act placed limits on campaign contributions and expenditures, created a federal agency to enforce the campaign finance regulations, and provided for public funding of presidential elections.[33]

The Watergate scandal also helped spawn the Ethics in Government Act of 1978, which was designed to reduce the potential for conflicts of interest among government officials. The most significant aspects of this act was that it required federal officials to file regular finance disclosure statements and created stricter guidelines regulating officials' financial holdings. The act also limited the lobbying activities of former government officials and created the Office of Government Ethics to administer the program.[34]

The Nixon presidency was exceptional in its unethical dealings, but other scandals have forced government officials to grapple with political reform repeatedly throughout the past three decades. Important congressional ethics reforms were adopted in 1977 in response to several political scandals that rocked the House during the 94th and 95th Congresses. One of the two primary scandals that generated pressure for the act was the disclosure that an employee of House Administration Committee Chair Wayne Hays was kept on the payroll for what appeared to be sexual favors. The second scandal involved several prominent House members who became entangled in an influence-peddling scheme with Tongsun Park, a lobbyist for the South Korean government. This scandal became known as Koreagate.[35] In response to the scandals, and to help soft-pedal a congressional pay raise, the House passed a stricter code of ethics, requiring regular financial disclosure statements, limiting income from outside activities, restricting the gifts received by House members, and regulating the use of frank mail.[36]

More recently, the Keating Five scandal compelled the Senate to rewrite a portion of its ethics code in 1992, and both the post office and banking scandals spurred the House to eliminate several of the perquisites available to legislators, including closing the House bank and ending subsidized medical care.[37]

Reform in the 1990s

The influence of political reform in the United States over the past 30 years has been immense, touching on all aspects of politics, from local neighborhood associations to the nation's role in the world. Many factors have been important in bringing about these reforms, including several I have not discussed here. Certainly, religion and philosophy have been important in motivating demands for reform, as they have since Puritan times. It is impossible to ignore the central role that southern churches played in spearheading the civil rights movement and that the Christian right has played in leading the crusade for conservative social reforms in more recent years. Yet, clearly, a large proportion of the reform efforts described above and in the pages that follow were motivated primarily by economic considerations or by the desire to make the political system more democratic, effective, and honest.

These four factors continue to explain much of the reform debate in the United States today, even though many of the political reforms coming out of Washington are far more conservative than those promoted in the 1960s. What has brought the conservative reform proposals to the top of the political agenda has not been a change in these expectations per se, but a combination of changes in Americans' attitudes toward specific policy solutions, shifts in political coalitions, and changes in the nature of the nation's problems.

Americans still want the government to protect their economic interests, but after two decades of limited economic growth, members of an important segment of American voters have grown increasingly reluctant to pay taxes for social programs in which they see little benefit for themselves. In reality, this conservative shift in Americans' attitudes toward government is not new; rather, it reflects a trend that has been growing in this country since the late 1960s and the beginning of the Nixon presidency. The Republican Party has been a major beneficiary of this trend, gaining supporters from among dissatisfied southerners and white males.[38]

Americans still want a political system that offers them the opportunity to participate, yet many feel increasingly detached from government and believe that their participation makes no difference in political outcomes. Thus they call for stronger lobbying and campaign finance laws, and seek a return to a citizen legislature that they believe will be more influenced by their concerns.

Americans still want a government that can function, yet they believe that government has become too large and bureaucratic, and that downsizing is in order. The one consistent finding that came out of public opinion polls conducted during the 1994 election campaigns was that voters were dissatisfied with the government's operation and size.[39] With the nation's social problems appearing to worsen and policy proposals repeatedly stymied by gridlock in Washington, it is only natural that Americans would want change.

Americans still expect government officials to behave ethically, yet with the relentless onslaught of news about political scandals coming out of Washington and state government, it is understandable that there continues to be demand for ethics reform. The apparent rise in the number of scandals is not illusionary. A 1992 Justice Department study found a tenfold increase in the number of federal indictments against public officials at all levels of government since 1970.[40]

As long as Americans' expectations of government remain unmet, reform will continue to look attractive. Since the 1970s, conservative reformers have been increasingly successful at changing the direction of political reform, yet their arguments continue to appeal to these underlying expectations. The reason is understandable: these concerns are at the heart of our democratic system of government.

Notes

1. Theodore J. Lowi and Benjamin Ginsberg, *Democrats Return to Power: Politics and Policy in the Clinton Era* (New York: W. W. Norton, 1994), 14.
2. Clyde Wilcox, *The Latest American Revolution? The 1994 Elections and Their Implication for Governance* (New York: St. Martin's Press, 1995), 1–7.
3. Charles T. Banner-Haley, *The Fruits of Integration: Black Middle-Class Ideology and Culture, 1960–1990* (Jackson: University of Mississippi Press, 1994), 28–34.
4. William H. Chafe, "The End of One Struggle, the Beginning of Another," in Charles W. Eagles, ed., *The Civil Rights Movement in America* (Jackson: University of Mississippi Press, 1986), 131–139.
5. Samuel H. Beer, "Foreword," in John William Ellwood, ed., *Reductions in U.S. Domestic Spending* (New Brunswick, NJ: Transaction, 1984), xvii–xviii.
6. Mark I. Gelfand, "The War on Poverty," in Robert A. Devine, ed., *Exploring the Johnson Years* (Austin: University of Texas Press, 1981), 127–129.
7. Beer, "Foreword," xviii.
8. Ibid.
9. Alice M. Rivlin, *Reviving the American Dream: The Economy, the States, and the Federal Government* (Washington, DC: Brookings Institution, 1992), 43–56; Juliet B. Schor, *The Overworked American: The Unexpected Decline of Leisure* (New York: Basic Books, 1991), 75.
10. Gelfand, "The War on Poverty," 127–129.
11. Thomas Byrne Edsall and Mary D. Edsall, *Chain Reaction: The Impact of Race, Rights, and Taxes on American Politics* (New York: W. W. Norton, 1992), 129–131.
12. Rivlin, *Reviving the American Dream,* 101–102.
13. Howard E. Shuman, *Politics and the Budget: The Struggle between the President and the Congress,* 3d ed. (Englewood Cliffs, NJ: Prentice Hall, 1992), 272–274.
14. Rivlin, *Reviving the American Dream,* 57–61.
15. Marilyn Werber Serafini, "No Strings Attached," *National Journal* 27 (20 May 1995): 1230–1234.
16. Chandler Davidson, "The Voting Rights Act: A Brief History," in Bernard Grofman and Chandler Davidson, eds., *Controversies in Minority Voting: The Voting Rights Perspective* (Washington, DC: Brookings Institution, 1992), 8–11.
17. Ibid., 7–51.
18. Ibid., 34–41.
19. Nelson W. Polsby, *Consequences of Party Reform* (New York: Oxford University Press, 1983).
20. Gordon E. Baker, *The Reapportionment Revolution: Representation, Political Power, and the Supreme Court* (New York: Random House, 1966).
21. Davidson, "The Voting Rights Act," 7–51.
22. Wilma Rule and Joseph F. Zimmerman, eds., *United States Electoral Systems: Their Impact on Women and Minorities* (New York: Praeger, 1992).
23. Leroy N. Rieselbach, *Congressional Reform: The Changing Modern Congress* (Washington, DC: Congressional Quarterly Press, 1994), 51–57.
24. Beer, "Foreword," xvii–xviii.
25. Laurence J. O'Toole, Jr., *American Intergovernmental Relations,* 2d ed. (Washington, DC: Congressional Quarterly Press, 1993), 18–21.
26. Ibid., 21–25.
27. John W. Ellwood and James A. Thurber, "The Politics of the Congressional Budget Process Re-examined," in Lawrence C. Dodd and Bruce I. Oppenheimer, eds., *Congress Reconsidered,* 2d ed. (Washington, DC: Congressional Quarterly Press, 1981), 247–253.
28. Shuman, *Politics and the Budget,* 220–230.
29. Ibid., 234–243.
30. Alan Rosenthal, *Governors and Legislatures: Contending Powers* (Washington, DC: Congressional Quarterly Press, 1990), 43.
31. Ibid., 39–64.
32. William J. Crotty, *Political Reform and the American Experience* (New York: Thomas Y. Crowell, 1977), 139–166.
33. Frank J. Sorauf, *Money in American Elections* (Glenview, IL: Scott, Foresman, 1988), 34–43.
34. Robert N. Roberts, *White House Ethics: The History of the Politics of Conflict of Interest Regulation* (Westport, CT: Greenwood, 1988), 161–163.
35. Allan J. Katz, "The Politics of Congressional Ethics," in Joseph Cooper and G. Calvin Mackenzie, eds., *The House at Work* (Austin: University of Texas Press, 1981), 97–118.
36. Ibid.
37. Rieselbach, *Congressional Reform,* 61.
38. Wilcox, *The Latest American Revolution?* 20.
39. Ibid., 24.
40. Lowi and Ginsberg, *Democrats Return to Power,* 35.

A

Abscam

In an attempt to expose corrupt federal officials, the Federal Bureau of Investigation (FBI) conducted a 23-month undercover investigation in the late 1970s known as Abscam, or Arab Scam. Following a few years after Watergate, the investigation and subsequent scandal heightened public disillusionment with government and focused attention on congressional ethics.

The Abscam operation began in 1979, when the FBI rented a house in Washington, D.C., and portrayed it as the home of a wealthy Middle Eastern businessman. FBI agents, posing as representatives of the businessman, were able to lure several members of Congress to the house. In the end, seven legislators or their aides were filmed accepting money in return for political favors. In perhaps the most lurid episode of the investigation, Representative Raymond Lederer, a Democrat from Pennsylvania, was taped accepting $50,000 in a paper bag. Prosecutions followed, and four legislators were sent to federal prison. The scandal also caused the first expulsion of a representative from Congress since the Civil War. Ultimately, all but one of the members involved were forced out of the House, through expulsion, resignation, or electoral defeat.

The Abscam scandal served as a prototype of sorts for future sting operations as similar investigations were conducted at the state and local levels repeatedly in the 1980s. More important, the scandal reduced public trust in Congress and kept the demand for ethics reform on the agenda.

See also Congress; Ethics.
References Amitai Etzioni, *Capital Corruption: The New Attack on American Democracy* (1988); Suzanne Garment, *Scandal: The Culture of Mistrust in American Politics* (1991); Dennis F. Thompson, *Ethics in Congress: From Individual to Institutional Corruption* (1995).

Absentee Voting

One reform that has been introduced by a number of states and the federal government to increase voter participation is a liberalization of absentee voting laws. The use of absentee ballots allows citizens to vote at places other than tradition polling places and at times other than election day.

The use of absentee ballots in the United States began in 1813, but was at first limited to members of the military. In 1896, Vermont became the first state to allow civilians to file absentee ballots. Since then, states have introduced a variety of laws permitting absentee voting under specified conditions. The use of absentee ballots has been constrained in many states, however, by strict laws requiring voters to show cause when requesting absentee ballots and to have their absentee applications notarized.

Since the 1940s, the federal government has become increasingly involved in forcing states to permit absentee balloting in federal elections. Among the government's most important acts was the 1955 Federal Voting Assistance Act, which required states to make absentee ballots available to U.S. citizens, and their families, who are serving in the military or working abroad as civilian employees of the U.S. government. The 1975 Overseas Citizens Voting Rights Act ensured all U.S. citizens living abroad that they could vote in federal elections. In 1986, Congress enacted the Uniformed and Overseas Citizens Absentee Voting Act, which consolidated the regulations of the 1955 and 1975 acts. Congress also eased the availability of absentee ballots to the disabled when it adopted the Voting Accessibility for the Elderly and Handicapped Act of 1984.

Many states have taken further steps to allow for greater use of absentee ballots in recent years. In particular, several states have expanded the categories of who is eligible to vote by absentee ballot and have removed the requirement that absentee ballot requests include notarized signatures. A few states have removed all restrictions on who is eligible to use absentee ballots.

See also All-Mail-Ballot Elections; Early Voting; Election-Day Holiday; Voter Registration.
References Edward D. Feigenbaum and James A. Palmer, *Absentee Voting: Issues and Options* (1987); Richard G. Smolka and Ronald D. Michaelson, "Election Legislation, 1992–93" (1994).

Act to Improve the Administration of Justice

The Act to Improve the Administration of Justice, which ended most of the U.S. Supreme Court's mandatory jurisdiction, was one of two major bills enacted by Congress in 1988 to help reduce the caseload burden confronting the federal courts.

See also Judicial Improvements and Access to Justice Act; Mandatory Appellate Jurisdiction; Supreme Court.

Administrative Reorganization

Almost all presidents since Lyndon Johnson have been associated with major proposals to reorganize the federal administration. These proposals have been designed to strengthen the president's control over the bureaucracy and to improve the bureaucracy's efficiency and effectiveness.

Johnson created two tasks forces on reorganization, the 1964 Task Force on Government Reorganization (the Price Task Force) and the 1967 Task Force on Government Organization (the Heineman Committee). The first called for a major reorganization of the cabinet, including the creation of three new departments (Transportation, Education, and Housing and Community Development) and the merger of others. The second task force considered proposals to create a Department of Housing, Education, and Welfare and to revamp the Office of Economic Opportunity to give it greater control over the War on Poverty.

Nixon's reorganization efforts grew out of proposals put forward by the Ash Council, which called for the creation of four "super departments" and the merger of the Bureau of the Budget into a new Office of Management and Budget. The President's Reorganization Project during the Carter administration called for the creation of the Senior Executive Service, the Office of Personnel Management, and two new departments: Education and Energy. There were two reorganization efforts associated with Reagan, the Grace Commission and Reform 88. Both sought to reduce waste, fraud, and abuse in the bureaucracy. Reagan also called for the elimination of the Department of Education. More recently, Clinton has begun to implement the recommendations of the National Performance Review for reinventing government.

Although these efforts resulted in the creation of five new cabinet-level departments (Transportation, Housing and Urban Development, Energy, Education, and Veterans Affairs) and some important new agencies (most notably the Office of Management and Budget), their effects have been mixed. Several of the reforms have strengthened the president's control of the bureaucracy, especially the creation of the Office of Management and Budget and the Senior Executive Service. However, many proposed reforms were never enacted, and the effects on the bureaucracy's efficiency and effectiveness of those that were have generally been minimal. Thus the desire for administrative reorganization remains an important goal of many reformers.

In addition to efforts at the federal level, most states have taken steps since the 1960s to reorganize the structure of state government. More than 20 have adopted broad, comprehensive reorganization of the executive branch. In general, state-level reforms have been designed to improve the governor's control over the bureaucracy by eliminating other statewide executive offices and reducing the bureaucracy's independence. Along with the legislative reform movement, these efforts to reorganize state government were central to the resurgence of state governments in the 1970s and 1980s.

See also Ash Council; Bureaucracy; Cabinet System, State; Constitutions, State; Fragmented Executive; Governors; Grace Commission; Gubernatorial Appointments; Legislative Reform Movement; National Performance Review; Office of Personnel Management; President's Reorganization Project; Reform 88; Reorganization Power; Senior Executive Service; State Renewal.

References Peri E. Arnold, Making the Managerial Presidency*: Comprehensive Reorganization Planning: 1905–1980* (1986); Peri E. Arnold, "Reform's Changing Role" (1995); William T. Gormley, Jr., *Taming the Bureaucracy: Muscles, Prayers, and Other Strategies* (1989); Patricia Ingraham and Carolyn Ban, eds., *Legislating Bureaucratic Change* (1984); Ronald N. Johnson and Gary D. Libecap, *The Federal Civil Service System and the Problem of Bureaucracy: The Economics and Politics of Institutional Change* (1994); Pan Suk Kim and Lance W. Wolff, "Improving Government Performance: Public Management Reform and the National Performance Review" (1994); Charles H. Levine, ed., *The Unfinished Agenda for Civil Service Reform: Implications of the Grace Commission Report* (1985); Larry J. Sabato, *Goodbye to Good-Time Charlie: The American Governorship Transformed* (1983); Donald J. Savoie, *Thatcher, Reagan, Mulroney: In Search of a New Bureaucracy* (1994); Carl E. Van Horn, ed., *The State of the States* (1993).

Affirmative Action

Affirmative action has been the focus of considerable debate concerning the role government should play in trying to overcome discrimination in U.S. society. Affirmative action is often compared with the idea of equal opportunity, which holds that employers and institutions should not discriminate against individuals because of their race, sex, religion, color, or national origin. But affirmative action goes one step further to deal with the problems of discrimination by directly trying to expand educational and employment opportunities for women and minorities.

Although the federal government has enacted nondiscriminatory rules in specific policy areas since the 1930s, the foundation of modern affirmative action laws is Title VII of the Civil Rights Act of 1964, which was passed by Congress with the strong support of President Lyndon Johnson. A few months after the passage of the act, President Johnson issued Executive Order 11246, which required federal contractors to take "affirmative action" to ensure the employment and fair treatment of minorities. Two years later, this order was expanded to protect women as well.

Proponents of affirmative action argue that a proactive orientation is necessary to eliminate past and present discrimination. Opponents argue, however, that it is unfair to discriminate against white males to obtain affirmative action goals. Moreover, they contend that affirmative action may promote "white backlash," hurt race relations, and do more harm than good regarding the economic position of minorities and women.

Support for affirmative action has declined in both the White House and the Supreme Court since the end of the 1970s. Presidents Ronald Reagan and George Bush both opposed quota systems in hiring and expressed support for lawsuits waged by white employees who claimed reverse discrimination. In addition, the Supreme Court issued a series of important rulings in the late 1980s that weakened the nation's affirmative action laws. The Civil Rights Act of 1991 was enacted in order to reverse many of these decisions.

The future of affirmative action is uncertain given its unpopularity among a large segment of the American public. In recent years, conservative members of Congress have been working to restrict or ban affirmative action programs altogether. With the election of a Republican majority to both houses of Congress in 1994, the prospect that these conservative reforms will succeed increased greatly.

Efforts to roll back affirmative action gained increased momentum in 1995 after the University of California moved to end its affirmative action programs and several California leaders began to champion a voter initiative to abolish all affirmative action programs in the state. Many political observers predicted that these events would push the battle over affirmative action onto the political agenda in other states and into the 1996 presidential race.

See also Civil Rights Act of 1964; Civil Rights Act of 1991; Civil Rights Movement; *Fullilove v. Klutznick; Regents of the University of California v. Bakke;* Reverse Discrimination; *United Steelworkers of America v. Weber; Wards Cove Packing Co. v. Frank Antonio;* Women's Movement.

References Susan D. Clayton and Faye J. Crosby, *Justice, Gender, and Affirmative Action* (1992); John Charles Daly and William B. Allen, *Affirmative Action and the Constitution* (1987); Christopher Jencks, *Rethinking Social Policy: Race, Poverty, and the Underclass* (1992); Kirsten Mangold, "Affirmative Action and the UC Vote" (1995); Peter Schrag, "Son of 187" (1995); Steve Shulman and William Darity, Jr., eds., *The Question of Discrimination: Racial Inequality in the U.S. Labor Market* (1989); Jared Taylor, *Paved with Good Intentions: The Failure of Race Relations in Contemporary America* (1992).

Agency Registration

Recent reform proposals concerning voter registration include requiring that state and local governments make voter registration materials available through government offices or agencies serving the public. This requirement is referred to as agency registration.

See also National Voter Registration Act; Voter Registration.

Reference Francis Fox Piven and Richard A. Cloward, *Why Americans Don't Vote* (1988).

Aid to Families with Dependent Children (AFDC)

Aid to Families with Dependent Children is the nation's largest social welfare program and a focal point of recent debate between conservatives and liberals on the proper role of American government in society. AFDC was created by the Social Security Act of 1935 to provide support to children whose fathers had died. In recent years, however, the primary recipients of AFDC have been single-parent families headed by divorced or never-married women, not widows. The program is jointly funded by national and state governments, with specific benefit levels determined by the individual states.

Conservative critics of AFDC argue that the program has created a culture of dependency, led to a decline in social mores, and spurred the proliferation of out-of-wedlock births. These critics have championed reforms to reduce the availability of AFDC and to force recipients to take responsibility for their own actions. Three of the most prominent reforms discussed are a requirement that recipients must work in order to receive benefits (workfare), a limitation on the number of years recipients can be eligible for AFDC, and the denial of additional benefits to recipients who have additional children while receiving AFDC. All three of these reform proposals were incorporated into the Republican Party's Contract with America in 1994. Moreover, many of these reforms have been written into state rules over the past few years. In 1995 alone, 17 states approved major changes in their AFDC programs, adopting many of these proposals to reform the welfare system.

Supporters of AFDC argue that there is no evidence that AFDC is causing these social ills, and that the proposed reforms will hurt recipients, particularly children, without solving the problems of poverty in the United States.

See also Big Swap; Bridefare; Contract with America; Learnfare; Personal Responsibility Act; Welfare; Workfare.

References Patrick M. Cunningham, *Welfare Reform: A Response to Unemployed Two Parent Families* (1993); Steven D. Gold, *The Fiscal Crisis of the States: Lessons for the Future* (1995); Christopher Jencks, *Rethinking Social Policy: Race, Poverty, and the Underclass* (1992); Joseph A. Pechman and Michael S. McPherson, *Fulfilling America's Promise: Social Policies for the 1990s* (1992); Jack Tweedie, "Changing the Face of Welfare" (1995).

Airline Deregulation Act

The Airline Deregulation Act of 1978, which completely deregulated the airline industry, is considered to be one of the first victories by reformers seeking to roll back government regulation of the economy in the mid-1970s. The act was designed to remove government barriers that were limiting competition within the airline industry. These barriers, reformers argued, kept new airlines from entering the market, created unnecessarily high prices for airline tickets, and led to poor service to consumers. The act is generally considered to have reduced prices and created a more efficient market, though some smaller communities have lost airline services or have had to pay higher ticket prices.

See also Deregulation.

Reference Paul L. Joskow and Roger G. Noll, "Economic Regulation" (1994).

Allen v. State Board of Elections

Allen v. State Board of Elections was a key case in shaping the scope of the Voting Rights Act of 1965. The Voting Rights Act was originally designed to ensure that African-Americans would be allowed to register and vote in southern elections. After the act was adopted, however, a number of southern states began to introduce changes in their electoral laws that allowed African-Americans to vote but made it difficult for them to influence elections.

In *Allen v. State Board of Elections,* the U.S.

Supreme Court considered the legality of a Mississippi law that changed the method of selecting county supervisors from district elections to at-large ones. Although the law did not deny African-Americans the franchise, it was challenged by civil rights lawyers because it diluted the votes of African-Americans, reducing their influence on county elections.

The Supreme Court threw out the Mississippi law and, in deciding the case, gave a very broad interpretation to the scope of the Voting Rights Act. In the Court's decision, Chief Justice Earl Warren wrote that the act recognizes voting to include "all action necessary to make a vote effective." The Court's interpretation meant that the act would cover not only the franchise, but a wide range of practices and procedures that affect the ability of African-Americans to elect candidates of their choice.

See also *City of Mobile v. Bolden;* Electoral Discrimination; *Shaw v. Reno; South Carolina v. Katzenbach; Thornburg v. Gingles;* Voting Rights Act; *White v. Regester.*
References Chandler Davidson, ed., *Minority Vote Dilution* (1989); Bernard Grofman and Chandler Davidson, eds., *Controversies in Minority Voting: The Voting Rights Act in Perspective* (1992).

All-Mail-Ballot Elections

All-mail-ballot elections, or elections in which all voting is done by mail, represent an alternative approach to conducting elections. All-mail-ballot elections have been tried by local governments in 16 states since they were first introduced in California in 1977. In late 1995 and early 1996, Oregon became the first state to use this approach for a higher office, conducting the primary and general elections for an open U.S. Senate seat entirely by mail. The approach is often compared with absentee balloting, but it is broader in scope, entirely replacing precinct polling places with mail ballots.

Supporters of this electoral innovation argue that it increases voter participation and thus makes elections more representative of public sentiment. Moreover, the all-mail method is promoted as being less expensive than traditional elections. Critics argue that all-mail-ballot elections have greater potential for fraud and voter coercion than traditional-style elections, and that they reduce the public character of elections.

See also Absentee Voting; Early Voting; Election-Day Holiday; Voter Registration.
Reference Margaret Rosenfield, *All-Mail-Ballot Elections* (1995).

Alternative Dispute Resolution (ADR)

Alternative dispute resolution is a procedure to settle legal disputes without going through formal court proceedings. It has been one of the most popular types of court reforms introduced over the past decade to reduce the growing caseload in state courts.

There are several different types of ADR programs, but the process generally involves the use of a mediator or arbitrator to help resolve the conflict. The most common form of ADR is mediation, in which an impartial third party acts as intermediary to help resolve the dispute. The mediator does not have the formal power to make a final decision, but works with all the parties involved to help find an acceptable solution. Arbitration is another common method of ADR; it involves the use of a third party who considers the arguments involved and then issues a decision resolving the dispute. Before entering arbitration, all the parties involved agree to be bound by the arbitrator's actions. By the late 1980s, arbitration programs were being used by courts in 24 states.

Advocates of ADR argue that it offers

methods to resolve disputes that are cheaper, more efficient, less intimidating, and less destructive to the relationship between litigants than going through a court of law. However, some judicial experts question the claim that ADR methods are cheaper and more efficient than formal court proceedings. In addition, some observers argue that ADR may be unfair to poor litigants.

See also Caseload; Civil Justice Reform Act; Courts; Judicial Access; Judicial Improvements and Access to Justice Act.
References Carl F. Bianchi, "Alternative Dispute Resolution: Is the Jury Still Out?" (1988); Robert A. Carp and Ronald Stidham, *Judicial Process in America* (1993); Linda R. Singer, *Settling Disputes: Conflict Resolution in Business, Families, and the Legal System* (1990).

Alternative Service Delivery

The delivery of government services through means other than traditional bureaucracies is referred to as alternative service delivery. Some examples include privatization, contracting for services, contracting out, and vouchers.

See also Contracting for Services; Contracting Out; Privatization; Public Service Deregulation.
Reference Rowan Miranda and Karlyn Andersen, "Alternative Service Delivery in Local Government, 1982–1992" (1994).

Amateur Politicians

Amateur politicians are candidates, elected officeholders, and other political actors who have little to no previous political experience. In recent years, amateur politicians have been replaced for the most part by professionals, a trend that many reformers, though not all, see as a source of many of the problems in American government today.

See also Professional Politicians.
References David T. Canon, *Actors, Athletes, and Astronauts: Political Amateurs in the United States Congress* (1990); Alan Ehrenhalt, *The United States of Ambition: Politicians, Power, and the Pursuit of Office* (1991); James Q. Wilson, *The Amateur Democrat* (1966).

American Civil Liberties Union (ACLU)

The American Civil Liberties Union (ACLU) is a public law firm and the nation's leading champion of civil liberties, using litigation, lobbying, and education campaigns to protect and expand the freedoms guaranteed in the Bill of Rights. The ACLU was founded in 1920 by Roger Baldwin and today is led by executive director Ira Glasser. It is a nonprofit, nonpartisan organization with 270,000 members. Some of the issues it has been involved with include government censorship, education reform, national security, voting rights, and corrections.

American Dream Restoration Act

The American Dream Restoration Act was one of the ten proposals in the Republican Party's Contract with America. The proposed act called for a $500 per child tax credit, a change in federal income tax to eliminate the federal penalty on married couples, and the creation of a new kind of Individual Retirement Account (IRA) to encourage saving. As of late 1995, both houses of Congress had passed separate bills supporting the act, but none of the bills had been enacted into law.

See also Contract with America; Taxes.
References George Hager, "Harsh Rhetoric on Budget Spells a Dismal Outlook" (1995); "Republicans' Initial Promise: 100-Day Debate on 'Contract'" (1994); Clyde Wilcox, *The Latest American Revolution? The 1994 Elections and Their Implication for Governance* (1995).

American Enterprise Institute for Public Policy Research (AEI)

The American Enterprise Institute for Public Policy Research is a conservative research foundation that supports studies that "preserve and improve open and competitive enterprise, limited and public-oriented government, defense and foreign policies," as well as traditional social values. The research published by this group influenced the policies and reforms of the Reagan administration, and continued to affect the reform ideas of Republican leaders into the 1990s. Founded in 1943 and based in Washington, D.C., the AEI has a $12 million budget devoted to public educational projects and an "Election Watch" project during national election years that highlights candidates who espouse conservative policies.

American Indians

In the 1960s, American Indians began to play a more active role in politics than they had previously, to force the federal government to address Indian problems and to reaffirm treaty rights. The increased politicization of American Indians is often traced to the federal government's efforts to terminate the reservation system and force the relocation of Indians in the 1950s, which brought thousands of Indians together in the nation's urban centers. Spurred on by the successes of the civil rights movement, Indians' efforts to improve their position intensified in the late 1960s, with the rise of new Indian interest groups and more radical tactics.

As a result of these activities, Indian tribes gained some significant victories in the courts and in Congress that have strengthened their position in the American political system. The first important victory came in the U.S. Supreme Court case of *Williams v. Lee* in 1959, when the Court ruled that a Navajo tribal court had jurisdiction in a debt dispute that arose on the Navajo reservation between two Indians and a non-Indian. In deciding the case, the Court recognized that Indian tribes retain some inherent sovereignty, a ruling that opened the door to a flood of cases involving Indian tribal rights. Although the Court has identified some limitations, the decisions in these cases have generally expanded the power of tribes to exercise self-government.

In addition, the courts have also reaffirmed the legality of specific provisions spelled out in Indian treaties with the U.S. government. Among other consequences, this has allowed tribes to reclaim lost land and to enjoy greater access to the natural resources promised in the treaties. Some of the most controversial cases have allowed Indian tribes to exercise their hunting and fishing rights, which has generated considerable criticism from sportsmen and others who argue that Indians should not be given special treatment.

Along with these victories in the courts, American Indians have also benefited from several pieces of legislation that have been enacted by Congress over the past 25 years. One of the most important of these is the Indian Self-Determination and Education Assistance Act of 1975, which provided for greater tribal self-government and more influence by Indians in the management of the Bureau of Indian Affairs. Other legislation included the Alaskan Native Claims Act of 1971, the Indian Health Care and Improvement Act of 1976, and the Indian Finance Act of 1976.

In recent years, the most prominent issue relating to American Indians has been the emergence of gambling operations on reservations across the United States. As of

1994, Indian tribes in 19 states operated gambling facilities. It has been estimated that the gross revenue from these operations in 1992 was $1.5 billion. The rise of Indian gambling is the result of a 1987 Supreme Court case (*California v. Cabazon Band of Mission Indians*) in which the Court ruled that Indian tribes have the right to conduct gambling operations. The following year, Congress enacted the Indian Gaming Regulatory Act to regulate reservation gambling. The rise of reservation gambling has helped many tribes improve their economic conditions, but it has also generated considerable criticism from state officials and private citizens who object to the tribes being permitted to operate these facilities with minimal government regulation and without having to pay taxes on their earnings.

See also Civil Rights Movement; Gambling; *Seminole Tribe of Florida v. Florida.*

References Stephen Cornell, *The Return of the Native: American Indian Political Resurgence* (1988); Leonard Dinnerstein et al., *Natives and Strangers: Blacks, Indians, and Immigrants in America* (1990); U.S. Commission on Civil Rights, *Indian Tribes: A Continuing Quest for Survival* (1981); Charles F. Wilkinson, *American Indians, Time, and the Law: Native Societies in a Modern Constitutional Democracy* (1987); Richard L. Worsnop, "Gambling Boom: Will the Gaming Industry's Growth Hurt Society?" (1994).

Americans for Limited Terms

Americans for Limited Terms is a group that supports term limit reform efforts through telephone campaigns and advertising aimed at voters. Targeting political candidates who refuse to sign a pledge to serve no more than two terms, Americans for Limited Terms spent $1.4 million in the 1994 congressional election and helped defeat many Democratic candidates in that Republican landslide year.

See also Term Limits.

Americans with Disabilities Act

The Americans with Disabilities Act of 1990 protects individuals with physical and mental disabilities against discrimination. It is the nation's most sweeping civil rights law since the passage of the Civil Rights Act of 1964. The law forbids discrimination in employment and government programs and also requires that public accommodations be made accessible to the disabled.

See also Civil Rights Act of 1964; Mandates, Federal.

References Sy DuBow and Sarah Geer, *Legal Rights: The Guide for Deaf and Hard of Hearing People* (1992); Joseph P. Shapiro, *No Pity: People with Disabilities Forging a New Civil Rights Movement* (1993).

Annexation

Annexation is a legal action in which a government body expands its physical boundaries to absorb adjacent land. Many political reformers recommend the use of annexation by big cities as a solution to the problems of metropolitan fragmentation. By annexing suburbs and other outlying areas, the central city is able to expand its influence and more adequately address regional problems. Although annexation may improve metropolitan government, it is often opposed by suburban residents, town governments, and others who are the target of annexation. These groups argue that annexation deprives them of their ability to address particular problems and concerns where they live, and that it reduces local input into government activities.

See also Consolidation; Metropolitan Fragmentation; Regional Government.

References Terry Christensen, *Local Politics: Governing at the Grassroots* (1995); David B. Walker, *The Rebirth of Federalism: Slouching toward Washington* (1995).

Approval Voting

Approval voting is an alternative election system that supporters argue will produce election outcomes that more accurately reflect voter sentiments than do current election procedures. Under approval voting, voters are allowed to vote for as many candidates as there are running for a particular office. The candidate who receives the most votes wins. Advocates of this reform argue that it allows voters to state their approval of multiple candidates and, in so doing, ensures the election of the most widely supported candidate. Approval voting has not been adopted in any state, but one of its creators, Professor Steven Brams of New York University, has lobbied extensively for it across the nation.

See also Election Systems.
References Steven J. Brams and Peter C. Fishburn, *Approval Voting* (1983); Bernard Grofman and Arend Lijphart, eds., *Electoral Laws and Their Political Consequences* (1986).

Ash Council

The Ash Council was a commission created by President Richard Nixon to develop reform proposals to make the federal bureaucracy work more efficiently and effectively. Two of the primary proposals put forward by the council were the creation of four super cabinet-level departments and the merger of the Bureau of the Budget into a new Office of Management and Budget (OMB). Congress rejected the cabinet proposal, but in 1970 the OMB was established. Some political analysts argue that the creation of the OMB was the most important bureaucratic reform in the past several decades. Since 1970, the OMB has emerged as one of the most powerful actors in the executive branch.

The formal title of the Ash Council was the Advisory Council on Government Organization; it was known by the name of its chair, businessman Roy Ash.

See also Administrative Reorganization; Office of Management and Budget.
References Eliza Newlin Carney, "Still Trying To Reinvent Government" (1994); William T. Gormley, Jr., *Taming the Bureaucracy: Muscles, Prayers, and Other Strategies* (1989); Stephen Hess, *Organizing the Presidency* (1988).

Aspin, Les (1938–1995)

As chairman of the House Armed Services Committee and later secretary of defense under President Clinton, Les Aspin built his career out of military reform. Aspin worked as an economist under Defense Secretary Robert McNamara during the Vietnam War, and then served as a Wisconsin representative to Congress. There, he lambasted the close relationship between veteran Congress members and the Pentagon, saying that it led to overspending and insider agreements. Aspin continued his critique of military wastefulness as chair of the Armed Services Committee from 1985 to 1992. In late 1992, after the Cold War had ended, President Clinton appointed Aspin to his cabinet. Aspin was charged with cutting the U.S. military budget by $10 billion and restructuring the defense apparatus. Aspin began a scaled-back defense plan in which military action would take place as a support to diplomacy. Conflicts with the military leadership and lack of a clear administration military policy prevented implementation of the reforms, however. A series of embarrassments over the proposal to allow homosexuals to serve openly in the military, along with a series of bungles regarding the conflicts in Haiti and Somalia, led to Aspin's resignation in 1993. He died following a heart attack in May 1995.

See also Clinton, William J.

References John Barry, "The Collapse of Les Aspin" (1993); "Les Aspin" (1995).

At-Large Elections

Historically, at-large elections have been the primary electoral system used by cities across the United States. Since the passage of the Voting Rights Act of 1965, however, many cities have begun to do away with this electoral system under pressure from the U.S. Justice Department and the federal courts. Civil rights organizations have challenged at-large elections, arguing that they make it difficult for African-Americans and other minorities to elect candidates of their choice.

Under an at-large system, all candidates for city council run in a citywide election, instead of by district or ward. The result is that in a city with a large minority population, a white majority may control the entire city council. Under pressure to ensure minority representation, many cities have begun to adopt single-member districts or mixed systems that include both district and citywide elections.

See also Election Systems; Electoral Discrimination; Multimember Districts; Single-Member Districts; Voting Rights Act.
References Chandler Davidson, ed., *Minority Vote Dilution* (1989); Wilma Rule and Joseph F. Zimmerman, eds., *United States Electoral Systems: Their Impact on Women and Minorities* (1992).

B

Backdoor Spending

Expenditures that are approved by Congress outside the regular appropriations process are referred to as backdoor spending. The two primary types of backdoor spending are contract authority and borrowing authority. Contract authority comes from legislation that allows federal agencies to enter into contracts to provide necessary services, whereas borrowing authority comes from legislation that allows agencies to borrow money from the federal government or the public. Unlike traditional appropriations, these types of expenditures are written into law by congressional authorization committees and are not overseen by appropriations committees. Some congressional observers also refer to entitlements and permanent authorizations as types of backdoor spending, because these also fall outside the traditional appropriations process.

Backdoor appropriations are criticized because they make it more difficult for Congress to control the budget process and federal spending. The Congressional Budget and Impoundment Control Act of 1974 restricted the use of backdoor spending by requiring appropriations approval before new contract or borrowing authority is adopted. To control entitlement spending, the Budget Enforcement Act of 1990 included a pay-as-you-go provision requiring that all congressionally approved increases in spending be offset by corresponding decreases in spending elsewhere or by increases in taxes. Despite these reforms, backdoor spending remains a concern for budget reformers.

See also Budget Deficit, Federal; Budget Enforcement Act of 1990; Congressional Budget and Impoundment Control Act; Entitlements; Pay-as-You-Go Budgeting.

References Roger H. Davidson and Walter J. Oleszek, *Congress and Its Members* (1994); Howard E. Shuman, *Politics and the Budget: The Struggle between the President and the Congress* (1992).

Baker v. Carr

In the landmark 1962 case of *Baker v. Carr,* the U.S. Supreme Court ruled that legislative apportionment was justiciable, opening up a floodgate of lawsuits over the past three decades to force states to adopt equitable redistricting plans.

Prior to *Baker v. Carr,* the Court maintained that apportionment was a political question, and therefore not appropriate for judicial review. The precedent-setting case had been *Colegrove v. Green.* In this 1946 decision, the Court decided it "ought not to enter this political thicket." The Court reversed its position in *Baker v. Carr,* arguing that under the

Fourteenth Amendment voters could seek redress from the federal court to protect themselves from unfair redistricting plans.

Although the Court's decision acknowledged that disparities in district population could violate the equal protection clause, it did not offer any specification on what factors are essential to a fair redistricting plan, leaving that question for future cases. The case had a profound effect on redistricting reform, moving the battle from Congress and state legislatures to the courts.

See also *Davis v. Bandemer;* Electoral Discrimination; Gerrymandering; Reapportionment Revolution; *Reynolds v. Sims; Shaw v. Reno; Thornburg v. Gingles; Wesberry v. Sanders; White v. Regester.*
References Gordon E. Baker, *The Reapportionment Revolution: Representation, Political Power, and the Supreme Court* (1966); William J. Keefe and Morris S. Ogul, *The American Legislative Process: Congress and the States* (1993); National Conference of State Legislatures Reapportionment Task Force, *Reapportionment Law: The 1990s* (1989).

Bakke, Alan (b. 1940)

See *Regents of the University of California v. Bakke.*

Balanced Budget Amendment

This proposed amendment to the U.S. Constitution would require the federal government to balance the federal budget every fiscal year, except under extraordinary circumstances. Until the 1930s, most economists and politicians believed it was economically wise to have federal revenues correspond to expenditures. With the rise of Keynesian economics and the appearance of repeated budget deficits during the Great Depression and the Second World War, the concern for a balanced budget declined, though it did not entirely disappear. Since the early 1980s, however, public support for a balanced budget has grown, as the federal budget deficit reached record heights and the government seemed unwilling or unable to control it. This support has brought proposals for a balanced budget amendment to the forefront of political debate in the United States today.

Several different balanced budget amendments have been proposed, but their differences are minimal. In general, most would require federal expenditures to be equal to federal revenues, except in periods of war or when a supermajority of both houses of Congress votes to suspend this rule. In addition, most would give the government a period of several years to achieve a balanced budget before the requirement of balancing expenditures and revenues would take effect.

Supporters of a balanced budget amendment argue that a change in the Constitution is necessary because that is the only way in which Congress can be forced to balance the budget. A balanced budget is needed, many economists argue, because the large federal deficit requires the federal government to borrow massive amounts of private and public funds, thus absorbing a large portion of the nation's savings, which otherwise could be used by business for investment and to enhance productivity. The result is poor economic growth. Moreover, many supporters argue that since 48 states have some type of balanced budget requirement, the federal government should have one too.

Opponents offer a litany of criticisms against a balanced budget amendment, but two of the most common are that it will not work and that it is bad policy. An amendment will not work, opponents argue, because Congress would simply find loopholes in it to circumvent the law's intent. One way in which Congress might do this would be to declare some types of expenditures "off budget," which it has done in the past to circumvent previous deficit reduction laws. This is also what happens at the state level. Most states routinely categorize certain expenditures as being off budget, especially capital expenditures. Thus most states do not balance their budgets, despite constitutional requirements that they do so.

Alternatively, instead of moving expenditures off budget, the federal government may increase its use of unfunded mandates to attain policy objectives, without having to find the money to pay for these programs. This is a major concern among state leaders, who do not want the states to have to carry the financial burden of balancing the federal budget. Thus many state governors have declared that a balanced budget amendment should not be adopted unless it includes provisions banning unfunded federal mandates. In a similar vein, some business leaders fear that Congress will circumvent any balanced budget amendment by requiring businesses to provide services the government had handled in the past.

Many opponents argue that a balanced budget amendment is bad policy because it places balancing the budget above other social concerns. Among urban leaders and many liberal politicians, the deficit is a secondary concern compared with such problems as crime, poverty, homelessness, inadequate education, and drug abuse. Requiring a balanced budget may reduce the government's ability to deal with such problems. Others assert that a balanced budget amendment would restrict the federal government's ability to use fiscal policies to stimulate economic growth. Thus, in a recession, the federal government may have fewer options for reviving the economy. Finally, critics argue that such an amendment could move budgeting away from Congress and into the courts.

Proposals for a balanced budget amendment have been introduced repeatedly in Congress since the early 1980s, but have not been able to receive the two-thirds vote necessary from both houses for the amendment to be sent to the states for adoption.

The Republican Party's Contract with America included a balanced budget amendment, and when the Republicans took control of both houses after the 1994 election, it was rapidly brought to the forefront of debate. After easily passing the House, the proposal was defeated in the Senate by two votes. The Senate rejected the proposal again in 1996.

See also Budget Deficit, Federal; Fiscal Policy; Fiscal Responsibility Act; Keynesian Economics; Mandates, Federal; Supermajorities.

References Daniel P. Franklin, *Making Ends Meet: Congressional Budgeting in the Age of Deficits* (1993); Donald F. Kettl, *Deficit Politics: Public Budgeting in Its Institutional and Historical Context* (1992); "Special Report: A Summary of Legislative Action: Economics and Finance" (1995); Clyde Wilcox, *The Latest American Revolution? The 1994 Elections and Their Implications for Governance* (1995).

Balanced Budget and Emergency Deficit Control Act

See Gramm-Rudman-Hollings.

Ballot Access

The ability of interested candidates and political parties to appear on the ballot is a fundamental aspect of a democracy. A democracy provides citizens not simply the right to vote, but the opportunity to vote for candidates of their choice. The rules and regulations governing the rights of candidates and parties to appear on the ballot are all elements of ballot access.

Historically, many states have placed burdensome restrictions on ballot access to deny third-party candidates, less well-known challengers, and minorities the opportunity to appear on the ballot. In recent years, however, many states have rewritten their ballot access laws to make it easier for both parties and candidates to gain access, primarily by lowering the numbers of signatures needed for candidates and parties to qualify and by reducing or eliminating filing fees.

See also Third Parties.
References Edward D. Feigenbaum and James A. Palmer, *Ballot Access 1: Issues and Options* (1988); Richard G. Smolka and Ronald D. Michaelson, "Election Legislation, 1992–93" (1994).

Benefit Principle

The benefit principle is the political principle that tax rates should be higher for those who receive more benefits from government. This principle is different from that underlying both progressive taxes and supply-side economics. Supporters of progressive taxes argue that tax rates should be based on individuals' ability to pay. Supply-side economists support more regressive tax plans, based on the belief that these plans are more effective at encouraging savings, investments, and economic growth. The benefit principle underlies support for user fees.

See also Progressive Tax; Reaganomics; Regressive Tax; User Fees.
References Ann O'M. Bowman and Richard C. Kearney, *State and Local Government* (1993); Werner Z. Hirsch and Anthony M. Rufolo, *Public Finance and Expenditure in a Federal System* (1990).

Bennett, William J. (b. 1943)

William J. Bennett served as secretary of education under President Reagan, and in that position he sought sweeping reforms of education, primarily to make it more academically rigorous and traditionally moral. His aggressive tactics alienated many educational and political leaders, and led to few policy victories. Bennett is credited, however, with attracting broad attention to the need for reform in the nation's schools. After stepping aside as secretary of education, he served as "drug czar" in the Bush administration. He also made a brief bid for the presidency during the 1992 primaries.

See also Education.
References Charles Moritz, ed., *Current Biography Yearbook 1985* (1985); Robin Wilson, "Bennett's Tenure: Prominence for the Education Dept., but Alienation on Capitol Hill and the Campuses" (1988).

Big Swap

In 1982, President Ronald Reagan proposed a restructuring of federal-state relations to provide a more rational and effective distribution of domestic policy responsibilities. The cornerstone of his proposal was an exchange in which the states would assume full control over Aid to Families with Dependent Children and food stamps, and the federal government would assume full financial responsibility for Medicaid. Reagan also proposed a devolution of 43 federal programs to the states, along with the creation of a federal trust fund to help the states cover the cost of these programs. The trust fund was to be phased out slowly by 1991. This proposal met with considerable resistance from governors, who feared that it would adversely affect states' already tight fiscal position, and was soon dropped by the Reagan administration. The proposal has been referred to by various political observers as the Big Swap, the Great Swap, and simply Reagan's swap proposal.

See also Aid to Families with Dependent Children; Devolution; Federal-State Relations; Medicaid; New Federalism; Reagan, Ronald Wilson; Reaganomics; Sorting Out.
References Timothy J. Conlan, *New Federalism: Intergovernmental Reform from Nixon to Reagan* (1988); Alice M. Rivlin, *Reviving the American Dream: The Economy, the States, and the Federal Government* (1992); David B. Walker, *The Rebirth of Federalism: Slouching toward Washington* (1995).

Bill Introduction Limit

One reform that has been proposed to improve the quality of public policy and reduce the flow of new legislation is a limitation on the number of bills individual legislators can introduce each session. Currently, legislatures in more than ten states have bill introduction limits.

See also Legislative Reform Movement.
Reference Rich Jones, "State Legislatures" (1994).

Blanket Primary

See Open Primary.

Block Grants

Block grants are a type of federal grant that state and local governments can use for broader purposes and with fewer strings attached than is true of categorical grants, with which they are often compared. Since the Nixon administration, the federal government has made some effort to replace many categorical grant programs with block grants as a way to give state and local governments more power and greater flexibility in solving social problems. By the early 1990s, the federal government oversaw 15 block grant programs, providing funds for such different purposes as job training, mental health programs, and transportation projects. Although the number of block grant programs has increased over the past 20 years, such grants still represent a much smaller proportion of aid to state and local governments than do categorical grants.

See also Categorical Grants; Creative Federalism; Federal-State Relations; General Revenue Sharing; New Federalism.
References Timothy J. Conlan, *New Federalism: Intergovernmental Reform from Nixon to Reagan* (1988); David B. Walker, *The Rebirth of Federalism: Slouching toward Washington* (1995).

Bolling Committee

The Bolling Committee was one of the first in a series of congressional committees created in the 1970s to propose reforms for democratizing the House committee structure. The committee arose in 1973 out of discontent among liberal Democrats, who found themselves with little influence because of the dominating role played by southern Democrats as committee chairs. The Bolling Committee proposed a reorganization of the committee structure that offered a more rational and equitable breakdown of committee jurisdictions. The committee's proposals met strong opposition in the Democratic Party caucus, however, and eventually the House voted to approve only some of the least controversial elements of the Bolling plan, which were included as part of a weaker substitute proposed by the House Committee on Organization, Study, and Review (the Hansen Committee). These House reforms are known as the Committee Reform Amendments of 1974. The Bolling Committee was officially called the House Select Committee on Committees, and was chaired by Missouri Representative Richard Bolling.

See also Congress; Hansen Committee; Multiple Referrals.
References Roger H. Davidson, "Two Avenues of Change: House and Senate Committee

Reorganization" (1981); Leroy N. Rieselbach, *Congressional Reform: The Changing Modern Congress* (1994).

Bridefare

Bridefare is the name attached to a welfare reform introduced in Wisconsin in 1994 to encourage teenage parents to marry or to remain married by providing greater benefits if they do so.

See also Learnfare; Thompson, Tommy G.; Welfare; Workfare.
Reference Rodney Atkins, "Governor Get-a-Job: Tommy Thompson" (1995).

Brookings Institution

The Brookings Institution is a nonpartisan, influential Washington, D.C.-based research group that supports studies on various public policy matters, particularly problem areas that need reform. The institution avoids taking sides on issues; rather, it publishes scholarly treatises that are approved by experts in the particular policy fields discussed.

Brown, Edmund "Jerry" Gerald, Jr. (b. 1938)

The son of a powerful California governor (Edmund G. "Pat" Brown), Jerry Brown began his own political career locally in Los Angeles and served as California's secretary of state before winning two terms as governor in the 1970s. Always regarded as a maverick who eschewed ostentation and perks among government officials, Brown captured the popular sentiment of the 1970s and implemented expanded social and environmental programs in California. A fierce proponent of election and voter reform, Brown championed Spanish-language ballots and strict campaign finance laws as secretary of state and as governor, including the sweeping Political Reform Act of 1974. His later attempts to win a U.S. Senate seat and to gain his party's nomination for the presidency during the 1980s failed, though he attracted loyal supporters for his populist message of campaign and structural reforms. As a private citizen, he continues his calls for government reform through a syndicated call-in radio show.

See also Campaign Finance; Lobbying; Political Reform Act of 1974.
References Charles G. Bell and Charles M. Price, *California Government Today: Politics of Reform?* (1988); "Is This a Bunch of Lollipops?" (1992); Charles Moritz, ed., *Current Biography Yearbook 1975* (1975).

Buchanan, Patrick J. (b. 1938)

Patrick Buchanan, a two-time candidate for nomination as the Republican Party's presidential candidate, has represented the far-right constituencies of his party. He is one of the nation's most outspoken neo-isolationists and a strong proponent of reduced federal support for social programs such as welfare. Buchanan has a long history in Republican party politics. He was hired as an executive assistant in Richard Nixon's law firm in 1969, and then became an assistant to Nixon in the White House. After a brief stint in the Ford administration, Buchanan spent the 1970s as a popular television political commentator. In the 1980s, he served as Ronald Reagan's communications director.

Buchanan's 1992 presidential bid divided Republican voters, as his outspoken positions alienated the party's more moderate wing. Though he lost the nomination, some observers maintain that his campaign may have helped deny President Bush's reelection. Buchanan's 1996 presidential campaign again divided the party as he stole the important New Hampshire primary vote from party favorite Bob Dole. His campaign centered largely on economic nationalism and populist harangues against corporate greed.

See also Isolationism.
References Patrick J. Buchanan, *Right from the Beginning: An Autobiography* (1988); Peverill Squire et al., *Dynamics of Democracy* (1995).

Buckley v. Valeo

The landmark 1976 case of *Buckley v. Valeo* resulted in the principal U.S. Supreme Court decision regarding government regulation of campaign finance. The key element of the decision is the Court's ruling that any limitations on campaign spending are an infringement of the First Amendment right of free expression. The decision severely restricts campaign finance reform because it prevents government from directly limiting campaign expenditures.

The *Buckley* case came in response to a set of amendments to the Federal Election Campaign Act (FECA) that were passed by Congress in 1974. These amendments placed limits on campaign contributions and expenditures, created the Federal Election Commission to monitor the act, and set up public financing of presidential campaigns. The amendments also established campaign disclosure requirements. After passage of the amendments, a broad coalition of liberals and conservatives, including New York Senator James Buckley, joined together to challenge the law's constitutionality. Francis R. Valeo, the secretary of the Senate, was the lead defendant.

The case moved rapidly through the lower courts before reaching the U.S. Supreme Court in 1975. In its January 1976 decision, the Court struck down the expenditure limits and the Federal Election Commission, but upheld the other components of the law. The Court recognized campaign spending as a form of free speech and, in so doing, said that the government could not limit an individual candidate's expenditures, what candidates spend out of their own pockets, or independent expenditures by individuals not affiliated with candidates' campaigns. The one exception to this ruling was that the government could place expenditure limits on individual campaigns as a condition for candidates to receive public financing. In striking down the Federal Election Commission, the Court ruled that the law's provision for allowing Congress to appoint members to the commission violated the Constitution's separation of powers.

Congress moved quickly to restore the Federal Election Commission in spring 1976, but the Court's decision left it powerless to regulate expenditures. Critics of the ruling argue that the decision has made it impossible for federal and state governments to control the rising costs of political campaigns, the unequal distribution of campaign funds, the unfair advantages held by wealthy candidates, and the corrupting influence of campaign contributions. On the legal side, critics argue that the Court gave special protection to campaign spending, whereas in other areas it has restricted free speech. By doing this, the Court has allowed wealthy campaigns to drown out the speech of poorer competitors. Some observers believe the act may face challenges in the future based on the argument that disproportionate campaign spending violates the Equal Protection Clause of the Fourteenth Amendment to the Constitution because it denies poorer candidates their right to be heard.

See also Campaign Finance Disclosure; Contribution Limits; Federal Election Campaign Act; Federal Election Commission; Public Financing; Spending Limits.
References Herbert E. Alexander, *Financing*

Politics: Money, Elections, and Political Reform (1992); Jamin B. Raskin and John Bonifaz, *The Wealth Primary: Campaign Fundraising and the Constitution* (1994); Frank J. Sorauf, *Money in American Elections* (1988).

Budget Deficit, Federal

In every fiscal year since 1969, the federal government has spent more money than it has brought in through income taxes and other revenue sources. The size of these yearly budget deficits soared in the early 1980s, causing them to emerge as one of the most important political issues in the nation and consequently generating demands for reform.

A federal budget deficit occurs when total federal revenues fall below outlays for a fiscal year. The federal government rarely produced a budget deficit until the 1930s, but during the Great Depression and the Second World War federal spending far exceeded revenues. Deficits grew more common over the next three decades, but their size generally was limited. In 1968 and then again in the early 1970s, these deficits reached new heights, but they remained far below the level experienced in the 1980s and 1990s, when the deficit soared above $200 billion.

The initial jump in the deficit in the 1980s was caused primarily by two factors: the passage of the Economic Recovery Tax Act of 1981 and the dramatic rise in defense spending during the Reagan administration. Budget expert Howard Shuman refers to the passage of the 1981 act as the "watershed event" in creating the fiscal crisis of the 1980s, reducing federal revenues by $750 billion over the next five years and by as much as $2 trillion by the 1990s. At the same time the act was reducing revenues, the military buildup was adding another $115 billion to federal expenditures. The result of these two events, as well as a number of lesser factors, was a budget deficit of $207 billion in 1983 and continued large deficits over the next several years.

Although the tax and spending decisions made during the Reagan administration may have spurred the initial rise in budget deficits, a number of other factors have continued to push the federal budget into the red. Both the savings and loan bailout and the Persian Gulf War incurred considerable costs, which helped compound the budget problems in the early 1990s. The savings and loan bailout alone added $61 billion in 1991 and $115 billion in 1992.

A more critical problem in recent years has been the continuing rise in costs of Medicare, Medicaid, and interest payments on the national debt. Between 1981 and 1991, federal expenditures in each of these three categories increased on average more than 16 percent a year. As of 1990, Medicare, Medicaid, Social Security, and other entitlement programs constituted two-thirds of the federal budget. Payment on the interest from the debt represented another 15 percent.

Many economists and political reformers argue that the deficit must be reduced because it is detrimental to the nation and the economy. In particular, they argue that the deficit harms the economy because it requires the federal government to borrow massive amounts of private and public funds, thus absorbing a large proportion of the nation's savings that otherwise could be used by business for investment and to enhance productivity. In addition, the recurring deficits have caused the nation's debt to mount, which in turn has caused a greater proportion of federal funds to go toward interest payments. With more funds going to pay off the debt, there is less money for the federal government to use to address the nation's problems. Finally, some economists argue that the government's continued inability to reduce the deficit is so damaging that it may eventually lead to a massive decline in private investments, a precipitous drop in the dollar's value, and ultimately a severe economic crisis.

Some economists and political activists are not as fearful of the continuing deficit, and see it as having only minimal effects on the economy and government spending. Many caution that the absolute dollar amount of the deficit is not as important as is its size in relation to the nation's economy. When compared with the gross national product over time, the current deficits are not extraordinarily acute. Finally, many urban leaders also see the deficit as a secondary problem; they argue that the nation should be more concerned about such issues as crime, poverty, racism, and the quality of education.

The rise in federal deficits in the late 1960s, early 1970s and during the past decade has generated a variety of reform efforts. The large jump in deficit spending during the early Nixon administration was one of the key factors spurring the passage of the Congressional Budget and Impoundment Control Act of 1974. This act included a variety of structural and procedural reforms that were designed to improve Congress's control over the budget. As deficits soared in the 1980s, Congress enacted the Gramm-Rudman-Hollings Act specifically to provide a mechanism to control deficit spending. When Gramm-Rudman-Hollings failed to achieve this goal, Congress and President George Bush adopted the Budget Enforcement Act of 1990, which offered new mechanisms for reducing the deficit. Although the deficit has declined a bit during the Clinton administration, it has continued to remain quite large from a historical perspective. Moreover, many economic estimates indicate that it will grow in the latter part of the 1990s as spending on Medicare, Medicaid, and the debt continue to grow.

The continued presence of large deficits has kept budget reform a major political issue. Given that discretionary spending has already been cut markedly, much of the attention in reducing the deficit has begun to focus on entitlements, particularly Medicare and Medicaid. The balanced budget amendment, the line-item veto, and an increased devolution of responsibilities to the states have all been offered as steps in broader efforts to reform the system.

Despite the political concern over deficit spending, many political scientists and economists are skeptical about whether these proposals will actually solve the problem, or even be enacted into law.

See also Backdoor Spending; Balanced Budget Amendment; Budget, Federal; Budget Enforcement Act of 1990; Congressional Budget and Impoundment Control Act; Deficit Reduction Act; Devolution; Discretionary Spending; Economic Recovery Tax Act; Entitlements; Federal-State Relations; Finance, State; Gramm-Latta; Line-Item Veto; Medicaid; Medicare; National Debt; Reaganomics; Savings and Loan Crisis; Social Security; Tax Equity and Fiscal Responsibility Act; Uncontrollable Spending.

References Daniel P. Franklin, *Making Ends Meet: Congressional Budgeting in the Age of Deficits* (1993); Donald F. Kettl, *Deficit Politics: Public Budgeting in Its Institutional and Historical Context* (1992); Alice M. Rivlin, *Reviving the American Dream: The Economy, the States, and the Federal Government* (1992); Howard E. Shuman, *Politics and the Budget: The Struggle between the President and the Congress* (1992).

Budget Enforcement Act of 1990

The Budget Enforcement Act of 1990 was one of a series of reforms enacted over the past two decades to reduce the federal budget deficit. The act, which was included as Chapter XIII of the Omnibus Reconciliation Act of 1990, was designed to close several of the loopholes in the Gramm-Rudman-Hollings Act and to introduce some restraints on entitlement spending.

Gramm-Rudman-Hollings had been introduced in the mid-1980s as a means to force the federal government to reduce the growing budget deficit by requiring automatic across-the-board spending cuts if the deficit exceeded preestablished limits. The act, however, quickly proved incapable of attaining that goal. One of the main problems in enforcing the act was that the president used overly optimistic economic and fiscal forecasts in developing the budget, which made the budget deficit appear to be smaller than it actually was. In addition, members of Congress began to put off approval of some legislation until after the legal date in which the budget deficit was to be estimated, thus ensuring that these figures were not included in the calculation.

To overcome optimistic estimates, the Budget Enforcement Act focused on spending levels instead of deficits. The act divided discretionary spending into three categories (domestic, defense, and international) and then set spending levels for each of the next three fiscal years. If the spending level in a category went above its cap, the act required an across-the-board cut within the category to bring it into compliance. By dividing the budget into these separate categories, the act ensured that domestic spending would not suffer reductions because of overspending on defense programs, and vice versa. The act removed these divisions for the 1994 and 1995 fiscal years, and replaced them with an overall spending cap. In order to force Congress to reduce late-year funding, the act required that these expenditures be included in the following year's fiscal budget.

In addition, the act offered one of the first efforts to gain control over entitlement spending, which is one of the primary causes for the large federal budget deficit. The act required that if Congress decides to create new entitlement programs, it must cut other entitlement programs (except Social Security) or find additional revenues to make these changes. Similarly, if Congress decides to reduce taxes, it must make corresponding cuts in expenditures or raise other taxes so that the tax reduction does not expand the deficit. These "pay-as-you-go" provisions (or PAYGO) were included in the budget in order to make budget changes deficit neutral.

Although the act was more effective than its predecessors, it did little to control the budget deficits in the early 1990s, as spending on such entitlement programs as Medicare, Medicaid, and farm price supports soared. In 1993, President Clinton affirmed his commitment to the components of the act, though most of the budget debate has since moved on to finding ways to control the cost of entitlement programs.

See also Budget Deficit, Federal; Discretionary Spending; Entitlements; Gramm-Rudman-Hollings; Medicaid; Medicare; Pay-as-You-Go Budgeting; Sequestration.

References Leroy N. Rieselbach, *Congressional Politics: The Evolving Legislative System* (1995); Howard E. Shuman, *Politics and the Budget: The Struggle between the President and the Congress* (1992); James A. Thurber, "New Rules for an Old Game: Zero-Sum Budgeting in the Postreform Congress" (1992).

Budget, Federal

The federal budget has been central to much of the nation's political debate and reform efforts since the early 1980s, as the budget began to experience record deficits. The appearance of these unprecedented deficits has forced reforms in the congressional budget process, caused political leaders to reevaluate the government's role in society, helped redefine the federal government's relationship with the states, generated change in many of the nation's policies and programs, and raised cries for constitutional reform, including the passage of a balanced budget amendment and the line-item veto.

The federal budget is the nation's financial plan for each fiscal year, authorizing expenditures for government programs and outlining expected revenues. Since the passage of the Budget and Accounting Act of 1921, the president has been responsible for preparing the budget, which must be submitted to Congress each January. The fiscal year runs from October 1 to September 30. If the budget has not been approved by the start of the fiscal year, Congress must enact a continuing resolution for the government to keep operating until the budget is approved.

See also Balanced Budget Amendment; Budget Deficit, Federal; Budget Enforcement Act of 1990; Congressional Budget and Impoundment Control Act; Discretionary Spending; Economic Policy; Entitlements; Finance, State; Fiscal Policy; Gramm-Latta; Gramm-Rudman-Hollings; Line-Item Veto; Mandates, Federal; Taxes; Two-Year Budget Cycle; Uncontrollable Spending.

Budgeting Techniques

Traditionally, most governments in the United States have relied on an incremental approach to budgeting, in which one year's expenditures are used as a baseline in developing the next year's budget allocations. This approach has been criticized as ineffective for dealing with societal problems and for making needed changes in the bureaucracy. Over the past three decades, a number of alternative budgeting techniques have been introduced at all levels of government that are designed to produce more rational budgeting decisions. These include cost-benefit analysis, performance budgeting, program budgeting, and zero-base budgeting. All of these programs are tied together in their intent to encourage administrators and budget writers to focus more attention on improving the programs and services provided by government agencies. Although each of these proposals has received praise from reformers, all of them have enough problems that none has emerged as the universal standard.

See also Cost-Benefit Analysis; Incrementalism; Management by Objectives; Performance Budgeting; Program Budgeting; Total Quality Management; Zero-Base Budgeting.

Bundling

Bundling is a method of channeling campaign contributions to candidates in which individual contributions are presented together by a group in a package, or bundle, in order to increase the group's influence. The practice is criticized because it allows the group channeling the money to circumvent contribution limits. Campaign finance reformers have proposed amendments to the Federal Election Campaign Act to ban bundling, though opponents of this reform argue that it would reduce electoral competition.

See also Campaign Finance; Federal Election Campaign Act; Political Action Committees; Soft Money.

References David B. Magleby and Candice J. Nelson, *The Money Chase: Congressional Campaign Finance Reform* (1990); Frank J. Sorauf, *Money in American Elections* (1988).

Bureaucracy

The federal bureaucracy has been a repeated target of reform efforts since the

1960s, as each new president has attempted to offer his own solution on how to make the bureaucracy more efficient, effective, and accountable. Two of the primary types of reforms proposed have been administrative reorganizations and the introduction of new types of budgeting or management techniques. Almost every president since the 1960s has been associated with a major proposal to reorganize the administration, from Lyndon Johnson's 1964 Task Force on Government Reorganization to Bill Clinton's National Performance Review. Along with these reorganization efforts, a variety of new budgeting and management techniques have been introduced, including planning-programming-budgeting systems, management by objectives, performance budgeting, and zero-base budgeting. Finally, there have been numerous efforts to reform other specific problems within the bureaucracy, including efforts to open the bureaucratic process to closer public scrutiny and to weed out fraud and unethical behavior.

The effects of these reforms have been limited, and today many reformers continue to advocate additional changes in the bureaucracy's structure and management. There are considerable differences of opinion, however, on what form these changes should take, from those who advocate the imposition of a single broad sweeping reform, such as total quality management or cost-benefit analysis, to those who argue that individual reforms need to be tailored to fit specific parts of the bureaucracy. The most extreme reform proposals call for a reduction in the role of the bureaucracy and greater dependence on alternative forms of service delivery, including privatization and contracting out. These proposals are designed to solve bureaucratic problems by removing the bureaucracy from the picture altogether.

Similar concerns over the bureaucracy have arisen at the state level during the past 30 years. Since the 1960s, more than 20 states have adopted broad, comprehensive reforms of the executive branch, and many others have made partial reorganizations.

See also Administrative Reorganization; Alternative Service Delivery; Ash Council; Budgeting Techniques; Civil Service Reform Act of 1978; Contracting Out; Cost-Benefit Analysis; Deregulation; Downsizing; Empowerment; Grace Commission; Inspector General Act; Management by Objectives; National Performance Review; Office of Management And Budget; Ombudsman; Open Record Laws; Oversight; Paperwork; Performance Budgeting; President's Reorganization Project; Privatization; Program Budgeting; Public Service Deregulation; Reform 88; Reinventing Government; Sunshine Rules; Total Quality Management; Whistle-Blowing; Zero-Base Budgeting.

References Peri E. Arnold, *Making the Managerial Presidency: Comprehensive Reorganization Planning: 1905–1980* (1986); William T. Gormley, Jr., *Taming the Bureaucracy: Muscles, Prayers, and Other Strategies* (1989); Patricia Ingraham and Carolyn Ban, eds., *Legislating Bureaucratic Change* (1984); Ronald N. Johnson and Gary D. Libecap, *The Federal Civil Service System and the Problem of Bureaucracy: The Economics and Politics of Institutional Change* (1994); Charles H. Levine, ed., *The Unfinished Agenda for Civil Service Reform: Implications of the Grace Commission Report* (1985); Larry J. Sabato, *Goodbye to Good-Time Charlie: The American Governorship Transformed* (1983); Donald J. Savoie, *Thatcher, Reagan, Mulroney: In Search of a New Bureaucracy* (1994); Carl E. Van Horn, ed., *The State of the States* (1993).

Burger, Warren (1907–1995)

Warren Burger, who served as chief justice of the U.S. Supreme Court, was appointed to the Court in 1969 by President Richard M. Nixon, who hoped Burger would hold a more conservative line than his predecessor, Earl Warren. Even though several important civil rights decisions were rendered during Burger's tenure, including the abortion rights case *Roe v. Wade*, the Burger

Court is generally considered to have been more conservative than the Warren Court, especially in the 1980s. Burger was also known for his work in bringing court reform onto the political agenda through his public speeches, his efforts in organizing both the Freund Committee and the Pound Conference, and his support for such groups as the National Center for State Courts and the Institute for Court Management.

See also Courts; Freund Committee; Institute for Court Management; National Center for State Courts; Pound Conference; Supreme Court.
References Robert A. Carp and Ronald Stidham, *Judicial Process in America* (1993); William C. Louthan, *The United States Supreme Court: Lawmaking in the Third Branch* (1991); Bruce Miroff et al., *The Democratic Debate: An Introduction to American Politics* (1995).

Bush, George Herbert Walker (b. 1924) (41st U.S. President, 1989–1993)

When George Bush was elected president in 1988, he promised to "stay the course" of the Reagan administration, although with a "kinder, gentler" attitude toward social problems. Despite his promises to address such issues as the growing budget deficit and the need for stronger family values, Bush failed to win reelection in 1992 as the deficit climbed to over $200 billion and social problems continued.

Following the Reagan era, Bush inherited a $3 trillion national debt and an economy that was beginning to slide after several years of growth. Bush's famous 1988 campaign promise, "Read my lips! No new taxes!" became difficult to fulfill in the face of the snowballing budget deficit. Two years into his tenure, Bush was instrumental in the passage of the Budget Enforcement Act of 1990, which introduced new mechanisms for balancing the federal budget. In May 1990, he called a summit with the Democratic-controlled Congress, stating "no preconditions" for the process of reducing the deficit. After weeks of late-night squabbling, both Bush administration officials and congressional participants in the summit admitted that increased taxation was inevitable, and a compromise measure led to some increased taxes, along with spending caps outlined in the Budget Enforcement Act.

Bush's popularity rode high as he took a hard-line position against Iraq's invasion of Kuwait in 1990. His decision to deploy American forces against Saddam Hussein's troops led to quick and flashy victory, and Bush's policy of cooperation with other U.N. member nations during the conflict set new precedent for foreign policy in the post-Vietnam era. Bush also claimed a victory for Republican military buildups as the Soviet Union collapsed in 1989. Still, the continuing economic malaise proved a more important impetus for reform, and voters turned away from Bush in the 1992 elections.

See also Budget Enforcement Act of 1990; Capital Gains Tax; Education; Foreign Policy; Multilateralism.
References Donald F. Kettl, *Deficit Politics: Public Budgeting in Its Institutional and Historical Context* (1992); Theodore J. Lowi and Benjamin Ginsberg, *Democrats Return to Power: Politics and Policy in the Clinton Era* (1994); Sidney M. Milkis and Michael Nelson, *The American Presidency: Origins and Development, 1776–1993* (1994).

C

Cabinet System, State

As part of the reform movement to reorganize the structure of state government, many states have introduced some type of cabinet system within the executive branch during the past three decades in order to improve the governor's control over the bureaucracy. During the 1970s alone, some 14 states introduced a traditional cabinet system. Under such a system, the cabinet is composed of the heads of the major state agencies and departments, who meet together with the governor to provide advice, share information, and receive direction. Some 25 states have also introduced a subcabinet system in which the governor meets formally with the directors of related agencies to coordinate activities in particular policy areas.

See also Administrative Reorganization; Governors.
References Ann O'M. Bowman and Richard C. Kearney, *The Resurgence of the States* (1986); James L. Garnett, "Organizing and Reorganizing State and Local Government" (1993); William T. Gormley, Jr., "Accountability Battles in State Administration" (1993); Larry J. Sabato, *Goodbye to Good-Time Charlie: The American Governorship Transformed* (1983).

Cabinet (United States)

As part of their efforts to reorganize the executive branch, most recent presidents have pursued change in their cabinets. In the 1960s, President Johnson pushed successfully for the creation of both the Department of Transportation and the Department of Housing and Urban Development. In the 1970s, President Nixon unsuccessfully advocated the creation of four super departments. Under Carter's urging, Congress created the Department of Energy in 1977 and the Department of Education in 1980. Reagan moved to eliminate the Department of Education upon taking office, but eventually abandoned the effort. The Department of Veterans Affairs was created in 1988 during the final year of the Reagan administration. More recently, both presidents Bush and Clinton have proposed elevating the Environmental Protection Agency to a cabinet-level position. Several Republican members of the House proposed legislation in 1995 to eliminate the Departments of Commerce, Education, and Energy.

Despite the attention recent presidents have given to restructuring the cabinet, cabinet members tend to play a far less important role today in providing advice to presidents than they did before the Nixon administration. A few department secretaries remain influential, but in general, since the late 1960s presidents have relied more on top advisers within the White House staff for advice than on cabinet members.

See also Administrative Reorganization; Bureaucracy; President.

References George C. Edwards III and Stephen J. Wayne, *Presidential Leadership: Politics and Policy Making* (1990); William T. Gormley, Jr., *Taming the Bureaucracy: Muscles, Prayers, and Other Strategies* (1989).

California Plan

See Judicial Selection; Merit Plan.

Campaign Finance

The federal government has made several attempts to reform the nation's campaign finance system since the beginning of this century, yet the desire for further change remains one of the most prominent goals among political reformers in the United States today. Many problems have been identified in the current finance system, but the underlying goals of most reformers are to improve electoral competition, control campaign costs, and reduce the harmful effects of campaign contributions on the political system.

The first major wave of campaign finance reform in the United States came in the early 1900s, as Congress tried to reduce the role of businesses and corporations in the electoral process. The first federal campaign finance law was the Tillman Act of 1907, which prohibited contributions to campaigns from corporations and national banks. In 1910, Congress enacted the Federal Corrupt Practices Act, requiring the disclosure of campaign contributions to House candidates from multistate political organizations. In 1911, Congress extended the act's requirements to Senate campaigns and made its first effort to limit campaign spending in congressional elections, restricting the amount House candidates could spend to $5,000 and Senate candidates to $10,000.

When the Teapot Dome scandal broke in the early 1920s, revealing the use of campaign contributions in what appeared to be a political payoff, Congress once again turned to the question of campaign finance reform, passing the Corrupt Practices Act of 1925. This act, which attempted to tighten regulations on campaign spending and improve financial disclosure, was the nation's most comprehensive campaign finance law until the passage of the Federal Election Campaign Act of 1971 (FECA). The act had many loopholes, however, allowing candidates to circumvent its spending and disclosure requirements easily.

A third wave of reform occurred in the late 1930s and the 1940s, when Congress passed several laws regulating the campaign activities of federal employees, federal contractors, labor unions, and other groups. The Hatch Act of 1939 (also known as the Clean Politics Act) prohibited federal employees from active involvement in politics and made it illegal to solicit contributions from individuals receiving federal relief funds. The act was revised the following year, with new amendments banning campaign contributions from federal contractors and placing the first contribution limits on federal campaigns. In 1947, Congress passed the Labor-Management Relations Act, prohibiting labor unions from contributing to federal campaigns. This act is also known as the Taft-Hartley Act.

The Federal Corrupt Practices Act, the Hatch Act, and the Taft-Hartley Act were the primary laws regulating federal campaign finance until the 1970s, but they did little to control the problems associated with campaign money. The inadequacies of these laws became clear in the late 1960s and early 1970s, when revelations about Watergate and President Nixon's receipt of thousands of dollars of illegal campaign contributions reached the public. In response to these scandals and the growing costs of federal campaigns, Congress passed the Federal Election Campaign Act in 1971. This act, which was revised three times in the 1970s, is the primary law governing campaign finances in federal elections today. FECA regulates campaign contributions, requires campaign committees to file extensive finance disclosure reports, provides for the public funding of presidential campaigns, and authorizes the Federal Election Commission to administer the act.

Although the act represents the nation's most serious effort to regulate campaign financing, many of its goals have been unmet, owing to U.S. Supreme Court action and aspects of the law itself. In the *Buckley v. Valeo* decision, the Court threw out several of the key components of the act. The Court's most devastating ruling for campaign finance reform was the decision that the government could not place limits on campaign spending. Such limits, the Court held, violate the First Amendment right to free speech. The Court's ruling removed the government's ability to cap the rising costs of campaigns, while creating a loophole allowing individuals and groups to spend unlimited amounts of money on campaigns, the sole requirement being that this money be spent "independently" from funds spent by candidates.

Two of the major problems seen with the act are that it gave legal recognition to political action committees (PACs) and it included a number of harmful loopholes. Given legal recognition, the number of PACs grew rapidly in the 1970s and 1980s, becoming increasingly important players in electoral politics. The most harmful loophole was an amendment passed in 1979 that allows state and local political parties to spend unlimited amounts of money on "party-building" activities. This amendment has allowed individuals, corporations, labor unions, the national parties, and others to channel unlimited funds, or what is called soft money, to state and local parties, which then use the funds to help candidates attain office. Since the last amendments were added to FECA in 1979, Congress has considered several major reform proposals, but has adopted none.

Political reformers seek a number of different changes in federal law, from restrictions on soft money and bundling to a comprehensive overhaul of the current campaign finance system. A variety of proposals have been considered by Congress over the past few years to control campaign finance, including expanded public funding, tighter restrictions on campaign contributions, and greater limits on the role of PACs. Congress has been unable to pass new legislation, in large part because of partisan differences and the divided control of the federal government.

The history of campaign finance reform is similar at the state level, though there is considerable variations among the states. Like their federal counterparts, state campaign finance laws have often been enacted after major scandals. In the early 1900s, most states adopted some form of campaign disclosure rules in response to the growing electoral role of businesses and corporations. Over the next half century, many states enacted campaign contribution and spending limits, though the effectiveness of these laws was limited. The campaign finance controversies of the Nixon administration brought rapid change in state laws, causing many states to adopt stricter contribution limits and reporting requirements, as well as public funding of elections. In the early 1990s, campaign finance reform reemerged on the political agenda, with many states again moving to tighten their campaign finance rules, expand public financing, and introduce stronger penalties for violators.

See also *Buckley v. Valeo;* Bundling; Campaign Finance Disclosure; Contribution Limits; Federal Election Campaign Act; Federal Election Commission; Federal Employees Political Activities Act; Heard Commission; Independent Expenditures; In-Kind Contributions; Off-Year Fund-Raising; Out-of-District Money; Political Action Committees; Political Reform Act of 1974; Public Financing; Revenue Act of 1971; Soft Money; Spending Limits; Watergate.

References Herbert E. Alexander, *Financing Politics: Money, Elections, and Political Reform* (1992); *Congressional Campaign Finances: History, Facts, and Controversy* (1992); Frederick M. Herrmann and Ronald D. Michaelson, "Financing State and Local Elections: Recent Developments" (1994); David B. Magleby and Candice J. Nelson, *The Money Chase: Congressional Campaign Finance Reform* (1990); Jamin B. Raskin and John Bonifaz, *The Wealth Primary: Campaign Fundraising and the Constitution* (1994); Frank J. Sorauf, *Money in American Elections* (1988).

Campaign Finance Disclosure

A central goal of campaign reform has been to open up the campaign finance system to permit closer scrutiny of the flow of campaign contributions and expenditures. The first federal law requiring disclosure of campaign finances was the Federal Corrupt Practices Act in 1910, which required campaign finance reports from organizations and individuals that attempted to influence the results of congressional races in more than one state.

Today, candidates and political committees that receive or spend more than $5,000 in federal election campaigns are required by the Federal Election Campaign Act (FECA) to file periodic reports identifying the sources of their receipts and detailing all expenditures of more than $200. In addition, all states have laws requiring campaign finance disclosure, though there are considerable differences over who needs to file reports, what needs to be reported, and the frequency with which reports need to filed.

Although these laws have made it easier to scrutinize campaign finances, many reformers argue that they need to be strengthened. At the federal level, reformers are particularly critical of the 1979 amendments to the Federal Election Campaign Act, which exempted state and local political parties from reporting money used for "party-building" purposes. The result of this amendment has been the increased flow of funds, or what is called soft money, to these parties from individuals, businesses, political action committees, and other groups, none of which is disclosed. Reformers argue that FECA should be tightened to require disclosure of these funds. Reformers also advocate clearer identification of the sponsors of campaign advertisements paid for through independent expenditures.

At the state level, reformers are trying to improve disclosure requirements, expanding who must file reports and what must be reported. There is also a growing effort to make reporting requirements uniform for all political committees within a state. Finally, a number of states, including Connecticut and Michigan, are attempting to computerize campaign finance records to make it easier to file disclosure reports and improve public scrutiny.

See also Bundling; Campaign Finance; Federal Election Campaign Act; Independent Expenditures; Political Reform Act of 1974; Soft Money.

References *Congressional Campaign Finances: History, Facts, and Controversy* (1992); Frederick M. Herrmann and Ronald D. Michaelson, "Financing

State and Local Elections: Recent Developments" (1994); David B. Magleby and Candice J. Nelson, *The Money Chase: Congressional Campaign Finance Reform* (1990); Michael J. Malbin, ed., *Money and Politics in the United States: Financing Elections in the 1980s* (1984); Frank J. Sorauf, *Money in American Elections* (1988).

Candidate Diminution

See Electoral Discrimination.

Candidate-Centered Campaigns

An important trend in American politics over the past four decades has been the increased importance of individual candidates, rather than political parties, in running election campaigns. In the past, parties played a dominant role in all aspects of electoral politics, from recruiting candidates to overseeing the day-to-day operation of campaigns. Today, however, most candidates decide on their own to run, and then put together their own campaign organizations to help them get elected to office. Candidate-centered campaigns are those in which candidates play this entrepreneurial role.

The emergence of candidate-centered campaigns was caused in large part by the progressive reforms at the turn of the century, which weakened the hold of political parties on the nomination process. The recent rise in professional politicians has further encouraged this trend, as the pressure to win has caused politicians to focus increased attention on developing their own personal campaign organizations. Finally, the 1970 Democratic Party reforms also helped expand the importance of candidate-centered campaigns to presidential races by making primary elections central to the nomination process.

Critics argue that the rise in candidate-centered campaigns has created a political system in which the candidates who are nominated by their parties or elected to office are unrepresentative of the public or incapable of governing. Critics often point to Jimmy Carter's success in 1976 as an example of how modern candidates create their own campaigns, but are incapable of governing.

The main reform that has been offered to overcome candidate-centered campaigns is to increase the role of political parties in elections at all levels of government. At the national level, the Democratic Party has attempted to give a greater role to party leaders in the presidential selection process since the late 1970s in order to improve the party's prospects for winning and to ensure that the nominees who are chosen have the ability to govern the country.

The rise of candidate-centered campaigns is supported by some political observers, however, who argue that it has opened up the political process, increased electoral competition, and actually improved representation.

See also McGovern-Fraser Commission; Party-Centered Campaigns; Political Parties; Presidential Selection; Primary Elections; Professional Politicians; Responsible Parties.

References Alan Ehrenhalt, *The United States of Ambition: Politicians, Power, and the Pursuit of Office* (1991); Barbara G. Salmore and Stephen A. Salmore, *Candidates, Parties, and Campaigns: Electoral Politics in America* (1989).

Capital Gains Tax

Capital gains taxes are taxes placed on the sale of real estate, securities, and other forms of capital investments. A reduction in capital gains taxes has been a major goal of conservative economic reformers since the passage of the Tax Reform Act of 1986, which raised the tax rate on capital gains to the same as that on other income.

President George Bush and other conservatives argue that low capital gains taxes encourage investments and stimulate economic growth. Opponents argue that a cut in these taxes would make the tax system more unfair, benefiting the most wealthy members of U.S. society. Despite Bush's strong support, the Democratic-controlled Congress refused to cut the capital gains tax rate during his administration. The Republican Party's Contract with America in 1994 included a proposal to reduce the capital gains tax rate by 50 percent.

See also Contract with America; Economic Recovery Tax Act; Job Creation and Wage Enhancement Act; Supply-Side Economics; Tax Reform Act.
References Daniel P. Franklin, *Making Ends Meet: Congressional Budgeting in the Age of Deficits* (1993); Donald F. Kettl, *Deficit Politics: Public Budgeting in Its Institutional and Historical Context* (1992); Howard E. Shuman, *Politics and the Budget: The Struggle between the President and the Congress* (1992).

Career Legislators

Career legislators are those who devote their work lives to legislative service, making it their sole occupation. Supporters of the legislative reform movement of the 1960s and 1970s specifically tried to encourage longer legislative service, arguing that longer tenure produces more competent and informed legislators. Since the 1960s, there has been a large increase in the number of career legislators across the nation, and this has generated much criticism, especially from supporters of term limits, who argue that these careerists are too powerful and unrepresentative of voters. Career legislators are also referred to as professional legislators or professional politicians.

See also Amateur Politicians; Citizen Legislators; Legislative Reform Movement; Professional Legislature; Professional Politicians; Term Limits.
References Citizens' Conference on State Legislatures, *The Sometime Governments: A Critical Study of the 50 American Legislatures* (1973); Alan Ehrenhalt, *The United States of Ambition: Politicians, Power, and the Pursuit of Office* (1991); Gary F. Moncrief and Joel A. Thompson, eds., *Changing Patterns in State Legislative Careers* (1992).

Carter, James E. (Jimmy) (b. 1924) (39th U.S. President, 1977–1981)

A former governor of Georgia and a prosperous peanut farmer, Jimmy Carter became president in 1976, as the nation was emerging from the cloud of Watergate. His outsider status helped him win voter favor, but hindered his efforts at building bridges with Congress and other Washington insiders. Despite this conflict, Carter helped champion a number of important reforms in American government and its role both at home and in the world.

Many reforms associated with the Reagan era actually had their roots in the Carter administration. After the massive growth of regulations during the Nixon administration, Carter led the first efforts to deregulate industry, bringing important changes in the government's control over airlines, banking, and trucking. In addition, Carter appointed Paul Volcker to the Federal Reserve Board, and Volcker introduced the use of conservative monetarist policies to address the nation's worsening inflation.

Like other presidents, Carter introduced reforms to reorganize the bureaucracy. He created the Departments of Energy and Education and championed the Civil Service Reform Act of 1978, which established the Senior Executive Service, the Office of Personnel Management, and the Merit Systems Protection Board. One of his most praised victories was the passage of the Ethics in Government Act of 1978, which, among other actions, required federal officials for the first time to file comprehensive annual reports on their personal finances. In foreign affairs, Carter was the first president to make human rights a central concern in the nation's foreign policy.

See also Bureaucracy; Civil Service Reform Act of 1978; Deregulation; Human Rights; Monetary Policy; Watergate.
References Colin Campbell, *Managing the Presidency: Carter, Reagan, and the Search for Executive Harmony* (1986); George C. Edwards III and Stephen J. Wayne, *Presidential Leadership: Politics and Policy Making* (1990).

Case Act

The Case Act was one of several laws enacted by Congress in the 1970s to limit the power of the president. This 1972 act attempted to restrain the president's use of executive agreements with other nations by requiring the secretary of state to submit all executive agreements to Congress within 60 days of their signing. Critics argue that the act was not strong enough, and that presidents can continue to make international agreements without fully informing Congress of their actions.

See also Congress; Congressional Budget and Impoundment Control Act; National Emergencies Act; Nixon, Richard M.; President; War Powers Resolution.
References Lance T. Leloup and Steve A. Shull, *Congress and the President: The Policy Connection* (1993); Robert J. Spitzer, *President and Congress: Executive Hegemony at the Crossroads of American Government* (1993).

Caseload

One of the most pressing problems confronting state and federal courts today is the growing backlog of cases that await hearing. The increase in caseload has been particularly dramatically in the state courts, which currently handle more than ten times the number of cases they did three decades ago. Today, state courts handle more than 100 million cases a year. The federal courts have also seen their caseload grow, and today they confront more than 250,000 cases each year. This rise in caseload has been blamed for the long delays in the court system and for a reduction in the quality of the nation's justice system.

Numerous reforms have been proposed to reduce the backlog of cases waiting to be heard and to provide long-range protection of the court system. Possibly the most popular reform of the past decade has been the introduction of different types of alternative dispute resolution (ADR), procedures that allow conflicts to be settled without going through formal court proceedings. There are several different approaches to ADR, but the process generally involves the use of an arbitrator or mediator to help resolve a conflict.

Alternatively, some reformers have advocated changes in the structure of the court system itself to make it possible for the courts to handle the caseload. At the state level, this has usually meant the consolidation of courts into a more unified system, with an administrator at the top to manage the court docket and oversee more administrative aspects of the court system. At the national level, the Federal Magistrates Act of 1968 established the Office of U.S. Magistrate to help reduce the backlog of cases. In addition, some reformers have advocated the creation of a new national court of appeals just below the Supreme Court, to help reduce the burden on the Supreme Court. Even without these structural changes, many reformers argue that the caseload could be reduced if the court system were better managed.

Additional proposals have been made concerning changes in state and federal laws that would reduce the number of cases that reach the courtroom and would shorten legal proceedings. These proposals include the introduction of no-fault insurance laws, simplified divorce rules, and the decriminalization of some illegal drugs. Many states and the federal government have passed laws instituting "loser pays" rules and allowing judges to impose sanctions on individuals who bring frivolous lawsuits. Finally, some reform proposals focus on judges, calling for more positions, higher pay, and simplified rules to discipline and remove those who are unfit to serve on the bench.

Despite the concern increased judicial caseloads have created, none of the proposed reforms has unanimous support. Some observers argue that ADR can be unfair to poorer litigants. Changes in court structure and administration often meet with resistance from senior court members. Moreover, many proposed legal changes are opposed by voters. Finally, some court analysts question whether these reforms would make any real difference in the courts' backlog of cases.

See also Act to Improve the Administration of Justice; Alternative Dispute Resolution; Burger, Warren; Civil Justice Reform Act; Court Centralization; Courts; Federal Magistrates Act; Judicial Improvements and Access to Justice Act; Loser Pays Rules; National Court of Appeals; Plea Bargaining; Rule of Four; Supreme Court.

References Samuel Estreicher and John Sexton, *Redefining the Supreme Court's Role: A Theory of Managing the Federal Judicial Process* (1986); Henry R. Glick, "The Politics of Court Reform: In a Nutshell" (1982); William P. McLauchlan, "Courts and Caseloads" (1991); Richard A. Posner, *The Federal Courts: Crisis and Reform* (1985); Henry J. Reske, "Long-Range Plan Would Cut Federal Cases" (1995); Linda R. Singer, *Settling Disputes: Conflict Resolution in Business, Families, and the Legal System* (1990).

Casework

With the growing involvement of the federal government in all aspects of society, members of Congress have become increasingly involved in helping constituents deal with the federal bureaucracy. Each day, members of Congress receive a variety of requests for assistance from citizens, from such minor concerns as requests for particular federal publications to more serious problems, including help in resolving personal conflicts with the bureaucracy. The assistance legislators provide to their constituents who request it is referred to as casework.

Some legislative observers have criticized the growing emphasis legislators place on casework, arguing that it has stimulated the growth in legislative staff, turned legislators away from more important tasks, and helped cause the increase in the reelection rate of incumbents. Reformers argue that an independent office should be created within Congress to handle such requests, removing this responsibility from the individual members.

See also Congress; Constituency Service; Incumbency Advantage; Ombudsman.

Reference Roger H. Davidson and Walter J. Oleszek, *Congress and Its Members* (1994).

Categorical Grants

Categorical grants are federal grants given to state and local governments for specific, well-defined projects. These grants are awarded with strict regulations on how they are used, which allows the federal government to monitor closely the activities of state and local governments. Lyndon Johnson greatly expanded the use of categorical grants during his presidency as part of his Creative Federalism program. Presidents Richard M. Nixon and Ronald Reagan attempted to reduce the number of categorical grants with some success during the 1970s and 1980s, but today categorical grants still represent the largest share of federal aid to states and local governments.

See also Block Grants; Creative Federalism; Federal-State Relations; General Revenue Sharing; New Federalism.
References Timothy J. Conlan, *New Federalism: Intergovernmental Reform from Nixon to Reagan* (1988); David B. Walker, *The Rebirth of Federalism: Slouching toward Washington* (1995).

Cato Institute

The Cato Institute, a conservative public policy research foundation, was created in 1977 to promote public debate on "the options the institute believes are consistent with traditional American principles of limited government, individual liberty, and peace." The institute had philosophical influence over Republican leaders during the 1980s, and particularly swayed the economic and foreign policies of President Reagan's administration.

See also Reaganomics.

Center for Public Integrity

The Center for Public Integrity, founded in 1989, is a watchdog organization intended to promote ethical behavior among government officials and throughout the political process. The center provides support to leading journalists who conduct in-depth investigations on national political issues and then makes the results of these investigations available to the public, press, and government. Some of the center's studies have focused on campaign finance, lobbying, the government's employment of women and minorities, and the hiring of former U.S. trade officials as lobbyists by foreign interests.

Center for Responsive Politics

The Center for Responsive Politics, based in Washington, D.C., acts as a congressional watchdog, focusing reform efforts on campaign finance, ethics in government, and "the inner workings of Congress." The center supports research on issues affecting Congress and its operations, such as the rising costs of political campaigns, voter registration, and political action committees.

See also Campaign Finance; Congress; Independent Expenditures.

Checkoff Funds

There are several ways in which federal and state governments generate revenue for the public financing of election campaigns, one of the most common of which is through the use of the tax checkoff system. Under this system, taxpayers can check a box on their income tax returns designating that a portion of their tax liability go toward the public financing program.

The Revenue Act of 1971 created a checkoff system that allowed taxpayers to earmark one dollar of their federal income taxes for presidential campaigns. As of the mid-1990s, a dozen states had checkoff plans through which taxpayers could, depending on the state, designate one or two dollars to candidates or parties.

Instead of using tax checkoffs, some states use tax add-on systems through which taxpayers can voluntarily contribute part of their tax refunds to a public financing program. Add-ons, however, tend to generate far less revenue than tax checkoff plans. Other states rely on general revenue funds and special fees to pay for these programs.

See also Campaign Finance; Federal Election Campaign Act; Public Financing; Revenue Act of 1971.

References *Congressional Campaign Finances: History, Facts, and Controversy* (1992); Frederick M. Herrmann and Ronald D. Michaelson, "Financing State and Local Elections: Recent Developments" (1994); David B. Magleby and Candice J. Nelson, *The Money Chase: Congressional Campaign Finance Reform* (1990); Michael J. Malbin, ed., *Money and Politics in the United States: Financing Elections in the 1980s* (1984); Frank J. Sorauf, *Money in American Elections* (1988).

Chicano Movement

The efforts of Mexican-American activists in the 1960s and 1970s to end discrimination against them and to obtain full and equal participation in U.S. society are referred to collectively as the Chicano movement. The movement grew in large part out of the success of the civil rights movement, which encouraged Mexican-Americans to seek similar political and social reforms.

The Chicano movement included a wide variety of groups, many of which were quite radical in their tactics and goals. One of the movement's primary concerns was to reform the education system in the United States to make it more responsive to the needs of Mexican-American children. By the mid-1970s, the movement began to decline, as the radical groups disappeared and more traditional interest groups became dominant in representing Mexican-American interests.

Although its policy successes are generally considered limited, the Chicano movement is credited with playing an important role in mobilizing Mexican-Americans to seek political and social reform and with helping to spur Congress to adopt the 1975 revisions of the Voting Rights Act that protect language minorities.

See also Civil Rights Movement; Mexican American Legal Defense and Educational Fund; Southwest Voter Registration Education Project; Voting Rights Act.

References Rodolfo Acuña, *Occupied America: A History of Chicanos* (1988); F. Chris Garcia, *Latinos and the Political System* (1988); Bernard Grofman and Chandler Davidson, eds., *Controversies in Minority Voting: The Voting Rights Act in Perspective* (1992).

Christian Coalition

Organized in 1989 to fight back against liberalization in American culture and politics, the Christian Coalition works to "stop the moral decay of government" by lobbying for conservative social legislation and supporting both national and local candidates who share coalition members' fundamentalist Christian beliefs. The coalition is based in Virginia and is closely allied with television evangelist Pat Robertson. Its executive director is Ralph Reed, who is considered one of the strongest voices in the new conservative Christian movement. The group monitors educational reforms closely, scrutinizing textbooks and criticizing sex education and liberal social studies curricula. Believing that social programs instituted in the 1960s and 1970s were misguided, the Christian Coalition advocates limited government involvement and a return to stronger individual responsibility and family values. The organization currently has 350,000 members and boasts of a $10 million budget to promote its causes.

Reference Ted Jelen and Clyde Wilcox, "The Christian Right in the 1990s" (1993).

Circuit Judge Nominating Commission

The Circuit Judge Nominating Commission was created by President Jimmy Carter to evaluate and make recommendations for open judgeships on the U.S. Court of Appeals. The commission was championed as a means of removing undue political pressure from the selection process and allowing decisions to be made based more firmly on merit. The effectiveness of the commission at reaching these goals has been debated, though it has been credited with increasing the number of women and minorities appointed to the courts. The commission was dismantled in 1981.

See also Judicial Selection.
References Henry J. Abraham, *The Judicial Process: An Introductory Analysis of the Courts of the United States, England, and France* (1993); Larry Charles Berkson and Susan B. Carbon, *The United States Circuit Judge Nominating Commission: Its Members, Procedures, and Candidates* (1980).

Citizen Legislators

Legislators who do not make careers out of legislative service, but serve only briefly in office before returning to their private occupations, are known as citizen legislators, amateur legislators, or amateur politicians. During the nation's first 100 years, most legislators at both national and state levels were citizen legislators. Around the beginning of the twentieth century, however, citizen legislators began to disappear from Congress, replaced by more professional ones. State legislatures experienced similar changes in the 1970s and 1980s.

Supporters of the legislative reform movement of the 1970s argued that if state legislators were to acquire the political expertise needed to perform their functions, citizen legislators should be replaced by individuals who are willing to remain in office for many years. In more recent years, however, supporters of term limits have argued that professional legislators are out of touch with the voters, and that the best way to improve representation is to bring back citizen legislators.

See also Amateur Politicians; Career Legislators; Legislative Reform Movement; Professional Politicians; Term Limits.
References Gary F. Moncrief and Joel A. Thompson, eds., *Changing Patterns in State Legislative Careers* (1992); Alan Rosenthal, "The Legislative Institution: In Transition and at Risk" (1993).

Citizen Legislature Act

The final proposal in the Republican Party's Contract with America, the Citizen Legislature Act called for a congressional vote on term limits within the first 100 days of the new session. In March 1995, after a spirited debate, the House voted against a constitutional amendment to limit members' terms in office.

See also Contract with America; Term Limits.
References Jennifer Babson, "House Rejects Term Limits: GOP Blames Democrats" (1995); "Republicans' Initial Promise: 100-Day Debate on 'Contract'" (1994); Clyde Wilcox, *The Latest American Revolution? The 1994 Elections and Their Implication for Governance* (1995).

Citizens against Waste

Citizens against Waste is a grassroots organization that was created by businessman J. Peter Grace and newspaper columnist Jack Anderson in 1984 to reduce waste and improve management in the government. The organization currently has 600,000 members. Its president is Thomas A. Schatz.

See also Grace Commission.
Reference Donald J. Savoie, *Thatcher, Reagan, Mulroney: In Search of a New Bureaucracy* (1994).

Citizens' Conference on State Legislatures

The Citizens' Conference on State Legislatures was one of the leading advocates of state legislative reform in the late 1960s and early 1970s. The organization's book *The Sometimes Governments,* which was first published in 1971, helped spawn a nationwide effort to modernize state legislatures. The book identified a variety of different characteristics that the conference argued were essential for legislatures to perform their tasks. It then ranked state legislatures based on how closely they matched these characteristics.

See also Legislative Reform Movement.
Reference Citizens' Conference on State Legislatures, *The Sometimes Governments: A Critical Study of the 50 American Legislatures* (1973).

Citizens for Tax Justice

Citizens for Tax Justice, founded in 1979, is a coalition of labor unions and other citizens' organizations that promotes income tax policies that lessen the burden on working people and the poor. The group opposes reforms that favor the rich and large corporations, or that bring additional taxes on middle-class families. Led by Robert S. McIntyre, Citizens for Tax Justice was vocal during the 1996 presidential primaries against the Republican candidates' push for a flat income tax.

Reference R. A. Saldivar, "Trashing the Tax Code" (1996).

City Commission

The city commission is an unusual form of city government that emerged in the early 1900s and grew in popularity in the 1920s and 1930s, but is now on the verge of disappearing. Under this form of government, political power is vested in a city commission composed of the heads of the city's major departments. These department heads are elected by voters in citywide elections.

When the first city commission governments were created in Texas and elsewhere, they worked fairly well, and the concept soon became popular among reformers in many states. Over a period of time, however, it became apparent in many cities that there were problems with the system's unusual mix of legislative and administrative functions. Some department heads proved to be poor administrators, whereas others used their positions as commission members solely to advance their departments' interests. During the 1970 and 1980s, a large proportion of the cities using the commission form of government replaced it with other types.

See also Council-Manager; Strong Mayor; Weak Mayor.
References Ann O'M. Bowman and Richard C. Kearney, *State and Local Government* (1993); Terry Christensen, *Local Politics: Governing at the Grassroots* (1995); John J. Harrigan, *Political Change in the Metropolis* (1993).

City Government

See City Commission; Council-Manager; Finance, Local; Home Rule; Metropolitan Fragmentation; Model City Charter; Regional Government; Strong Mayor; Weak Mayor.

City of Mobile v. Bolden

In the 1980 case *City of Mobile v. Bolden,* the U.S. Supreme Court ruled that for an election practice to be found in violation of the Voting Rights Act of 1965, the plaintiff had to show that the intent of the practice was to discriminate. This was a reversal of the decision in *White v. Regester,* in which the Court ruled that a plaintiff had to demonstrate only that the practice gave minority voters less opportunity "to participate in the process and to elect representatives of their choice." After intensive lobbying by civil rights groups in 1982, when the Voting Rights Act came up for readoption, Congress removed the intent requirement and replaced it with the criteria spelled out in the *White* case.

See also Voting Rights Act; *White v. Regester.*
References Chandler Davidson, ed., *Minority Vote Dilution* (1989); Bernard Grofman and

Chandler Davidson, eds., *Controversies in Minority Voting: The Voting Rights Act in Perspective* (1992).

City-County Consolidation

See Consolidation.

Civil Justice Reform Act

The 1990 Civil Justice Reform Act was enacted by Congress to reduce costs and delays in the federal court system while improving judicial access. The act required all federal court districts to work with local advisory groups to develop plans for reducing costs and delays within their districts. The act was championed by Delaware Senator Joseph Biden and has been referred to as the Biden bill. Most of the plans developed by the district courts in response to this act have focused on developing alternative forms of dispute resolution.

See also Alternative Dispute Resolution; Caseload; Courts; Judicial Access.
References Jeffrey J. Peck, "'Users United': The Civil Justice Reform Act of 1990" (1991); Judith Resnik, "Finding the Factfinders" (1993); Carl Tobias, "Improving the 1988 and 1990 Judicial Improvements Acts" (1994).

Civil Rights Act of 1964

Enacted during the height of the civil rights movement, the Civil Rights Act of 1964 is the nation's most important law protecting Americans' civil rights. The passage of the act transformed U.S. society, bringing an end to legal discrimination and providing greater legal equity for African-Americans and other minorities.

Several sections of the act have been particularly important in reshaping American society. Title II barred discrimination in public accommodations, giving African-Americans greater access to restaurants, motels, theaters, and other services that had previously been denied them. Titles III and IV required the desegregation of public facilities and public education. Title VI banned discrimination in federally assisted programs, providing the federal government with a mechanism to force equal treatment in private schools and elsewhere. Title VII prohibited discrimination in employment on the basis not only of race, but also of gender. This section also created the Equal Employment Opportunity Commission to investigate allegations of discrimination in the workplace and to seek solutions when discrimination is found. More important than these specific provisions, however, is that the act made the federal government an active participant in the fight for civil rights.

Although the act helped move the nation one step closer to ensuring equality, it has not been as successful in eliminating discrimination in the workforce as supporters hoped, nor has it solved the ills confronting the nation's minority populations. The result is that even though the act is considered one of the most important pieces of legislation in U.S. history, many liberal reformers argue that more needs to be done to address the social and economic problems confronting African-Americans and other minorities.

See also Affirmative Action; Americans with Disabilities Act; Civil Rights Act of 1991; Civil Rights Movement; Great Society; Johnson, Lyndon B.; Voting Rights Act.
References Hugh Davis Graham, *Civil Rights and the Presidency: Race and Gender in American Politics, 1960-1972* (1992); Herbert Hill and James E. Jones, Jr., *Race in America: The Struggle for Equality* (1993); Laughlin McDonald and John A. Powell, *The Rights of Racial Minorities: The Basic ACLU Guide to Racial Minority Rights* (1993); Charles Whalen and Barbara Whalen, *The Longest Debate: A Legislative History of the 1964 Civil Rights Act* (1985).

Civil Rights Act of 1991

The Civil Rights Act of 1991 was enacted by Congress to reverse a series of Supreme

Court decisions in the late 1980s that had weakened the nation's affirmative action policies and made it more difficult for minorities and women to fight discrimination in the workplace. Of particular importance, the act reversed the court's decision in *Wards Cove Packing Co. v. Frank Antonio,* which had placed a greater burden on individuals charging discrimination in the workplace to prove that their treatment was unfair. The act also allows workers to sue for monetary damages in cases of sexual harassment and other forms of intentional discrimination based on sex, religion, or disability. The passage of the act was attributed in part to the public attention given to the sexual harassment charges leveled against Supreme Court nominee Clarence Thomas.

See also Affirmative Action; Hill, Anita; Thomas, Clarence; *Wards Cove Packing Co. v. Frank Antonio.*
References Joan Biskupic, "Civil Rights Act of 1991" (1991); Julia C. Ross, "New Civil Rights Law" (1992).

Civil Rights Lobby

The civil rights lobby comprises a large coalition of interest groups that fight for civil rights legislation in the nation's capital. The term is often used to refer specifically to the Leadership Conference on Civil Rights, a 185-member organization that includes most of the major civil rights organizations in the United States, such as the National Association for the Advancement of Colored People, the League of Women Voters, and the Mexican American Legal Defense and Educational Fund. The lobby has played a preeminent role in most of the major civil rights reform efforts since the 1960s, including the Voting Rights Act of 1965 and its extensions.

See also Leadership Conference on Civil Rights.
Reference Karen McGill Arrington and William L. Taylor, eds., *Voting Rights in America: Continuing the Quest for Full Participation* (1992).

Civil Rights Movement

The civil rights movement refers to the concerted efforts of African-Americans in the 1950s and 1960s to obtain equal rights and to be allowed to participate fully in U.S. society. This movement had profound effects on the United States, radically changing the position of African-Americans, altering the nation's political and social structure, and stimulating other groups to seek reform. The movement may have been, as Professor William H. Chafe of Duke University has put it, "the most important domestic event of the 20th century."

The starting point for the civil rights movement is often tied to the 1954 U.S. Supreme Court case *Brown v. Board of Education,* which banned segregation in public schools. The Court's decision in *Brown* emboldened African-Americans in the South and elsewhere, encouraging them to push more actively for full and equal participation in American society. There were a number of earlier events, however, that are also perceived as beginning points, including African-American experiences in the Second World War, the 1944 publication of Gunnar Myrdal's *An American Dilemma,* and the Supreme Court's banning of white primaries in *Smith v. Allwright* that same year.

The movement gained considerable momentum in the late 1950s and early 1960s, before reaching its peak in the period between 1963 and 1965, when it achieved its greatest successes, including the passage of the Civil Rights Act of 1964 and the Voting Rights Act of 1965. These two acts banned discrimination in public accommodations and worked to allow

African-Americans to exercise their right to vote. Other major legislation attributed to the effects of the civil rights movement are the 1957 Civil Rights Act, the 1963 Equal Pay Act, and the 1968 Fair Housing Act.

After the passage of these major reforms, the civil rights movement began to dissipate in the late 1960s, when civil rights groups began to disagree over the direction of the movement. A visible segment of the movement became much more radicalized, using more militant tactics to seek more dramatic changes in U.S. society. The results were splits within and among civil rights groups and losses in popular support for further reform.

The civil rights movement is considered to have ended in the late 1960s, but its success is credited with stimulating the rise of later reform movements, including the Chicano movement, the women's movement, and the gay rights movement.

See also American Indians; Chicano Movement; Civil Rights Act of 1964; Civil Rights Lobby; Congress of Racial Equality; Gay Rights Movement; King, Martin Luther, Jr.; Leadership Conference on Civil Rights; Marshall, Thurgood; National Association for the Advancement of Colored People; National Urban League; Southern Christian Leadership Conference; Student Nonviolent Coordinating Committee; Voting Rights Act; Women's Movement.

References Denise L. Baer and David A. Bositis, *Politics and Linkage in a Democratic Society* (1993); William H. Chafe, "The End of One Struggle, The Beginning of Another" (1986); Charles W. Eagles, ed., *The Civil Rights Movement in America* (1986); Armstead L. Robinson and Patricia Sullivan, eds., *New Directions in Civil Rights Studies* (1991).

Civil Service Reform Act of 1978

The Civil Service Reform Act of 1978 was the centerpiece of President Jimmy Carter's efforts to reform the civil service. One of the main components of the act was the creation of the Senior Executive Service, which was designed to help increase the efficiency and effectiveness of the federal bureaucracy by creating an elite group of top-level managers who were to be more active in policy making and who would be paid based on their performance. The act provided simple procedures to allow the president to reassign these managers to other agencies if their skills were needed elsewhere or if they were not performing satisfactorily. In addition, the act created the Office of Personnel Management to oversee nonmilitary federal personnel and the Merit Systems Protection Board to monitor the treatment of federal employees.

Although the act was designed to use performance to improve the bureaucracy's output, the Reagan administration used the new procedures to place political allies in key positions and to gain greater ideological control over the bureaucracy, thus defeating what some analysts considered the act's intent. Reagan's use of the act to politicize the bureaucracy was one of several key factors blamed for a morale crisis in civil service in the 1980s, when many talented supervisors were forced to leave the federal bureaucracy. Moreover, the introduction of performance pay is considered to have had little effect on the bureaucracy's performance.

See also Bureaucracy; Merit Systems Protection Board; Office of Personnel Management; Senior Executive Service; Whistle-Blowing.

References William T. Gormley, Jr., *Taming the Bureaucracy: Muscles, Prayers, and Other Strategies* (1989); Patricia Ingraham and Carolyn Ban, eds., *Legislating Bureaucratic Change* (1984); Ronald N. Johnson and Gary D. Libecap, *The Federal Civil Service System and the Problem of Bureaucracy: The Economics and Politics of Institutional Change* (1994); Charles H. Levine, ed., *The Unfinished Agenda for Civil Service Reform: Implications of the Grace Commission Report* (1985); Donald J. Savoie, *Thatcher,*

Reagan, Mulroney: In Search of a New Bureaucracy (1994).

Clinton, Hillary Rodham (b. 1947)

Hillary Rodham Clinton, Yale Law School graduate and former lawyer as well as wife of President Bill Clinton, is considered by many to have redefined the role of First Lady with the unusually active part she has played in the Clinton administration. After her husband took office in 1993, she was placed in charge of the Task Force on National Health Care Reform, which was assigned responsibility for drafting the president's national health care plan. When her work on the task force ended, she began to play a less visible role in the administration, though she is still considered an important adviser to the president.

See also Clinton, William J.; Health Care.

Clinton, William J. (Bill) (b. 1946) (42d U.S. President, 1993–)

Bill Clinton, former governor of Arkansas, became the 42d U.S. president in 1993, following 12 years of Republican White House leadership. Clinton's promises of "change" during the 1992 presidential election appealed to many voters who had suffered under recession and who had grown disillusioned with the government's commitment to confronting the nation's problems. Known for his ability to win compromises with opposing factions, Clinton began his term of office with an appeal to Congress and Republican leaders that they work together for various reforms; his record, however, like that of many other presidents, has been mixed.

Clinton's most noteworthy reform proposal—to enact a comprehensive national health care plan—died in Congress. Opposition to his efforts to allow homosexuals to serve openly in the military forced him to accept a compromise policy known as "Don't ask, don't tell." His highly touted National Performance Review produced myriad reform proposals to reduce government costs and improve efficiency. Although many of these proposals were quickly adopted, political observers have been skeptical of their value.

On education and trade, Clinton has been more successful, signing a comprehensive education reform bill into law in 1994 and compelling Congress to enact the controversial North American Free Trade Agreement (NAFTA). Both of these legislative acts, however, had their roots in earlier administrations.

With the election of a Republican majority to Congress in the November 1994 election, many reform proposals became stymied by partisan differences. Despite this conflict, Clinton and the Republican Congress agreed to several important reforms, including restrictions on unfunded mandates, stricter lobbying disclosure rules, and deregulation of the telecommunications industry.

See also Education; Health Care; Lobbying; Mandates, Federal; National Information Infrastructure; National Performance Review; North American Free Trade Agreement; Telecommunications.

References Judith Graham, ed., *Current Biography Yearbook 1994* (1994); Sidney M. Milkis and Michael Nelson, *The American Presidency: Origins and Development, 1776-1993* (1994); Bruce Miroff et al., *The Democratic Debate: An Introduction to American Politics* (1995); William Schneider, "Clinton: The Reason Why" (1994).

Closed Primary

A closed primary is a type of primary election in which only voters who are registered party members are allowed to vote on potential party nominees. Some scholars also use this term to refer to primary elections in which voters simply have to declare their party affiliation at the voting place before being given a ballot, they do not have to be formally registered to the party.

Some reformers criticize closed primaries for excluding voters from a fundamental part of the electoral process. The problem with closed primaries is seen as being particularly acute in districts where one party dominates elections, since the primary election in these districts is usually the most important vote in determining who is elected to office. Critics argue that by limiting the primary only to party members in these districts, voters who are registered with other parties or as independents are denied a meaningful opportunity to participate in the election. Reformers also argue that closed primaries encourage the nomination of extremist candidates. Supporters of strong parties maintain, however, that closed primaries are essential to ensuring that party nominees best represent the party's interest.

One of the most important political battles in recent years over closed primaries occurred in California in March 1996, when state voters were asked to consider a ballot initiative that would allow voters in future primary elections to switch between parties as they vote on nominees for each office. The initiative (Proposition 198) was approved after receiving nearly 60 percent of the vote.

With the change in California law, 26 states currently use closed primaries that restrict participation to preregistered party members, while another 11 require voters to declare their affiliation at the polling place.

See also Open Primary; Political Parties; Primary Elections; Responsible Parties; Winograd Commission.
References John F. Bibby and Thomas M. Holbrook, "Parties and Elections" (1996); William J. Keefe, *Parties, Politics, and Public Policy in America* (1994); Charles Price, "The Virtual Primary" (1995).

Coercive Federalism

The modern relationship between the federal government and the states is often described as coercive federalism. Before the 1930s, the federal government played only a minor role in domestic policy making, as most social programs were created and overseen by the states. The Great Depression and the New Deal radically increased the federal government's role in U.S. society and altered the relationship between the different levels of government. Some scholars refer to the post-1930s relationship as cooperative federalism, because most federal programs require joint effort by the national government and the states. Other scholars prefer the term *coercive federalism* because of the dominant role the federal government plays in dictating the nature of the relationship. The term has grown more popular in recent years as the federal government has made greater demands on the states through preemptions and federal mandates. Conservative reformers and state leaders have put increased pressure on the federal government in recent years to reduce the government's demands on states and communities.

See also Cooperative Federalism; Federal-State Relations; Mandates, Federal; New Deal; Preemption.
Reference Thomas R. Dye, *Politics in States and Communities* (1994).

Collective Security

See Multilateralism.

Committee on the Constitutional System

The Committee on the Constitutional System, which is composed of leading former government officials and academics, was created in 1981 to study ways to improve how the federal government functions. The committee has proposed a variety of constitutional reforms to improve the government's ability to address the nation's problems, including proposals to strengthen the party system and to overcome divided government.

See also Divided Government; Term Expansion.
Reference James L. Sundquist, *Constitutional Reform and Effective Government* (1992).

Committee Reform Amendments

See Bolling Committee; Congress; Hansen Committee.

Common Cause

Common Cause is a liberal public interest organization that lobbies for open and accountable government, using a network of veteran lobbyists and a $10 million annual budget. Some reforms Common Cause has proposed include public financing of congressional election campaigns, nuclear arms control, stricter oversight of defense spending, and more equitable taxation. Other projects include "People against PACs," which seeks to reduce the power of political action committees in Congress, and "Clean Up Congress," which promotes stronger ethical standards for Congress members. Common Cause was founded in 1970 by liberal Republican John Gardner and rapidly became one of the preeminent "good government" groups in the United States. Its former name was the Urban Coalition Action Council.

See also Gardner, John W.
References Michael W. McCann, *Taking Reform Seriously: Perspectives on Public Interest Liberalism* (1986).

Common Sense Legal Reform Act

The Common Sense Legal Reform Act was one of the ten proposals put forward in the Republican Party's Contract with America. It called for limitations on punitive damage awards in product liability and medical malpractice cases in order to discourage litigation and reduce business costs. The act also called for a new federal law requiring losers to pay the legal fees for both sides in civil lawsuits. In March 1996, Congress passed legislation placing limits on damage awards, but the act was vetoed by President Clinton.

See also Contract with America; Courts; Loser Pays Rules.
References "Republicans' Initial Promise: 100-Day Debate on 'Contract'" (1994); Andrew Taylor, "Bill Curbing Investor Lawsuits OK'd by Veto-Proof Margins" (1995); Clyde Wilcox, *The Latest American Revolution? The 1994 Elections and Their Implication for Governance* (1995).

Common Shared Tax

A common shared tax is a proposed tax that would be levied nationally but provide funds to state governments. This type of tax has been advocated by economist Alice Rivlin and others as a way to increase state revenues, simplify the tax structure, and reduce the detrimental effects of disproportionate tax rates across the states. The tax could be imposed in a variety of forms, such as through a national sales tax, a value-added tax, or increased corporate income taxes.

See also Corporate Income Tax; Finance, State; Rivlin, Alice M.; Sales Tax; Taxes; Value-Added Tax.
Reference Alice M. Rivlin, *Reviving the American*

Dream: The Economy, the States, and the Federal Government (1992).

Community Action Agencies

Among its other provisions, the Economic Opportunity Act of 1965 called for the creation of neighborhood organizations that would help oversee federal welfare programs at the local level. The community action agencies, as they were called, were designed not only as an innovative approach to fight poverty, but as a means of improving the political participation of the poor. With some exceptions, these agencies were unsuccessful in reducing poverty. However, they have been credited with building political leadership within the African-American community.

See also Great Society.
References Eli Ginzberg and Robert M. Solow, *The Great Society: Lessons for the Future* (1974); William T. Gormley, Jr., *Taming the Bureaucracy: Muscles, Prayers, and Other Strategies* (1989).

Concurrent Budget Resolution

One of the key procedural changes of the Congressional Budget and Impoundment Control Act of 1974 was the creation of the Concurrent Budget Resolution, which sets spending and tax guidelines for upcoming fiscal years. Prior to the passage of the act, the congressional budget process was highly decentralized, with little coordination in spending and tax decisions. The concurrent resolution was introduced to establish limits and set priorities in these decisions. The resolution is initially drawn up by the House and Senate Budget Committees and must be approved by both houses. Like any concurrent resolution, it does not have the force of law.

Originally, there were two congressional budget resolutions. The first was adopted at the outset of the budget process, making recommendations on appropriate spending and tax levels. The second resolution, which was passed near the end of the process, established final and binding guidelines. The second resolution also gave instructions to each congressional committee, identifying the amount of money the committee needed to cut in order to meet these guidelines. In 1982, Congress discontinued using the second concurrent resolution and made the first resolution binding.

See also Congressional Budget and Impoundment Control Act; Reconciliation.
References Roger H. Davidson, ed., *The Postreform Congress* (1992); Howard E. Shuman, *Politics and the Budget: The Struggle between the President and the Congress* (1992).

Conflict of Interest Laws

Conflict of interest laws are designed to prevent government officials from making decisions that benefit themselves personally rather than the public. The most important recent reform in federal conflict of interest laws was the passage of the Ethics in Government Act in 1978. Until the passage of this act, most federal conflict of interest rules dated to the Civil War era. Although these laws were revised in the early 1960s, they were viewed as increasingly inadequate in the wake of Watergate and the growing mistrust of government in the 1970s. The Ethics in Government Act required high-ranking government officials for the first time to file comprehensive financial disclosure statements every year. In addition, it established rules on the handling of financial holdings that could create potential conflicts of interest. It also created "revolving-door" policies regulating the activities of government officials after they have left public office.

After several prominent officials in the Reagan administration moved directly from government positions into lucrative lobbying positions in the mid-1980s, pressure mounted on Congress to tighten the federal government's conflict of interest laws. The result was that Congress enacted the Ethics Reform Act in 1989. This act expanded the federal government's revolving-door policies, established limits on outside income, and placed restrictions on gifts, honoraria, and other perquisites flowing to government officials. This act was also noteworthy because it extended these conflict of interest rules to members of Congress and their staffs. Until the 1989 law was passed, most of the conflict of interest regulations for Congress were confined to those in the House and Senate rules.

Most states also strengthened their conflict of interest laws in reaction to the Watergate scandal in the 1970s and to more recent ethics violations. In the past few years alone, several states have introduced financial disclosure reports, placed restrictions on gifts and honoraria, and established rules regulating employment after government service.

See also Congress; Ethics; Ethics in Government Act; Ethics Reform Act of 1989; Lobbying; Revolving-Door Restrictions; Watergate.

References Thad L. Beyle, "The Executive Branch: Organization and Issues, 1992-93" (1994); Joyce Bullock, "State Lobby Laws in the 1990s" (1994); Suzanne Garment, *Scandal: The Culture of Mistrust in American Politics* (1991); Jerald A. Jacobs, ed., *Federal Lobbying* (1989); Robert N. Roberts, *White House Ethics: The History of the Politics of Conflict of Interest Regulation* (1988); Robert G. Vaughn, *Conflict-of-Interest Regulation in the Federal Executive Branch* (1979).

Congress

The U.S. Congress has been the target of a variety of reform efforts during the past 30 years in response to changing political demands, unmet social expectations, and institutional crises. The reform efforts reached a peak in the 1970s, though growing public dissatisfaction helped propel congressional reform back onto the political agenda in the early 1990s. The reforms that have been adopted vary widely, but much of the reform effort has focused on trying to democratize Congress and improve its capacity to govern.

Efforts to democratize Congress emerged initially in the late 1950s and early 1960s after the House experienced a large influx of northern liberal Democrats. Despite their gains in seats, these liberal representatives found their influence was limited by congressional rules that concentrated power in the hands of committee chairs and senior members. In the early 1970s, the liberal Democrats achieved some success in reforming the House with the passage of the Legislative Reform Act of 1970 and the Hansen Committee reforms. Among other consequences, these reforms stripped the committee chairs of their power, reduced the importance of seniority, and gave rank-and-file members greater say in the policy-making process. These reforms have had a profound effect on Congress, making its internal structure more democratic and its decisions more representative of the views of the American public.

The desire to improve Congress's capacity to govern emerged in the late 1960s and early 1970s in response to the growing dominance of the executive branch and the misuse of power by the president. In particular, many legislators believed that Congress needed to reassert its authority against a president who was defying its will and violating federal law in his handling of the war in Southeast Asia and in his control of the federal budget. Two of the most important acts to emerge in the 1970s were the War Powers Resolution of 1973 and the Congressional Budget and Impoundment Control Act of 1974. These acts were designed to reassert congressional control over U.S. involvement in foreign wars and the president's handling of the budget. The War Powers Resolution is generally seen as having done little to strengthen Congress's position vis-à-vis the president on military matters. However, the Budget and Impoundment Control Act has provided Congress with greater expertise and more independence in developing the federal budget. In addition to these acts, the Hansen Committee reforms strengthened the position of the House Speaker, which helped centralize power in the House and has allowed Congress to become more effective in confronting the nation's problems and in responding to the president.

Other major reforms to emerge in the 1960s and 1970s focused on improving elections, tightening congressional ethics, and opening up the political process to greater public scrutiny. Efforts to reform congressional elections focused primarily on improving representation and reducing the influence of money. One of the most important pieces of legislation enacted during the past 30 years was the Voting Rights Act of 1965. Although this act was not specifically designed to address congressional elections, it has had a profound effect on congressional politics, expanding the number of minority voters and increasing the number of minorities within Congress itself. The Federal Election Campaign Act of 1971, along with its later amendments, set limits on the amount of money that individuals and groups could contribute to congressional candidates and established campaign reporting requirements for both contributors and recipients.

Congressional ethics reforms have generally arisen in response to political scandals. Watergate, the Wayne Hays affair, Koreagate, Abscam, and other scandals in the 1970s encouraged Congress to establish stricter ethics rules, limit lobbying activities, and require members to file financial disclosure statements. Some of the most important reforms were included in the Obey Commission proposals, which were adopted in 1977. These reforms required House members to file annual financial disclosure statements and set limits on members' outside income, the size of gifts members could accept from lobbyists, and the use of frank mail. In 1995, Congress established the strictest rules in its history governing the gifts that members can receive from individuals other than their family and friends. The Senate banned individual gifts of more than $50 and set a $100 annual limit on the amount of gifts senators and their staffs can receive. These limitations include meals and entertainment. The House went even further, banning all gifts to House members except for some small home-state goods.

Finally, Congress took steps in the 1970s to open up the legislative process to closer public scrutiny. The Legislative Reorganization Act of 1970 required committee roll call votes to be made public, permitted recorded votes in the Committee on the Whole, and made provisions allowing television and radio into committee chambers. In the mid-1970s, both the House and the Senate passed reforms requiring that most committee hearings be made open to the press and the public. Public access to congressional floor activity was improved in 1979 when the House allowed C-SPAN to begin television coverage of its general sessions. The Senate opened its doors to C-SPAN in 1986.

After the successes of the 1970s, the

desire for further reform of Congress slowed during the Reagan administration. The primary exception was that Congress began to consider ways in which it could force itself to gain control over the federal budget deficit. The Gramm-Rudman-Hollings Act of 1985 established new budget procedures and attempted to force Congress to balance the budget by threatening across-the-board budget cuts if Congress failed to act. Two years later, Congress enacted a second Gramm-Rudman-Hollings bill with revised deficit targets. In 1990, Congress scrapped the law entirely, and created a new institutional framework for forcing Congress to bring the budget deficit down as part of the Budget Enforcement Act.

The desire for reform reemerged in the late 1980s and early 1990s, when a series of scandals and growing public disillusionment rocked Congress. The Keating Five, the resignation of House Speaker Jim Wright, the House banking scandal, and the controversial hearings over Supreme Court nominee Clarence Thomas generated increased public dissatisfaction with Congress. Moreover, by the end of the Bush administration there was a growing sense within the public that the government was unwilling or unable to deal with many of the nation's most pressing problems. These events encouraged Congress to rewrite its ethics rules, to limit legislative perquisites, to reexamine the process of examining Supreme Court nominees, and to establish a Joint Committee on the Organization of Congress to consider further reform.

These actions did little to improve Congress's image, and the desire for broader change remained widespread into the mid-1990s. Many members of the new Republican majority in both houses of Congress in 1995 advocated a number of more sweeping reforms, many of which have received considerable public support. These include limitations on legislators' terms, stricter lobbying and campaign finance laws, new internal procedures and structures, and a balanced budget amendment to force Congress to come to grips with the budget deficit. By the end of 1995, Congress had made some changes in its procedures and structure, eliminated additional legislative perquisites, and required Congress to abide by several federal laws from which it had previously been exempt. Two of the more important internal House reforms were limitations on the number of terms members can serve as committee chairs or as Speaker and the imposition of a supermajority requirement to raise taxes. Most of the Republican Party's broader reform proposal, however, had not been enacted.

See also Abscam; Bolling Committee; Budget Deficit, Federal; Budget Enforcement Act of 1990; Campaign Finance; Casework; Congressional Accountability Act; Congressional Budget and Impoundment Control Act; Constituency Service; Contract with America; C-SPAN; Franking; Gingrich, Newt; Gramm-Rudman-Hollings; Hansen Committee; Hays, Wayne; House Banking Scandal; House Post Office Scandal; Joint Committee on the Organization of Congress; Keating Five; Koreagate; Legislative Veto; Lobbying; Nixon, Richard M.; Obey Commission; Omnibus Legislation; Oversight; Renewing Congress Project; Stevenson Committee; Subgovernments; Sunshine Rules; Supermajorities; Term Limits; Thomas, Clarence; Twenty-seventh Amendment; Voting Rights Act; War Powers Resolution; Watergate; Wright, James C., Jr.

References Roger H. Davidson, ed., *The Postreform Congress* (1992); Lawrence C. Dodd and Bruce I. Oppenheimer, "The House in Transition: Change and Consolidation" (1981); Leroy N. Rieselbach, *Congressional Reform: The Changing Modern Congress* (1994); David W. Rohde, *Parties and Leaders in the Postreform House* (1991); James L. Sundquist, *The Decline and Resurgence of Congress* (1981); Dennis F. Thompson, *Ethics in Congress: From Individual to Institutional Corruption* (1995); James A. Thurber and Roger H. Davidson, *Remaking Congress: Change and*

Stability in the 1990s (1995); Clyde Wilcox, *The Latest American Revolution? The 1994 Elections and Their Implication for Governance* (1995).

Congress of Racial Equality (CORE)

The Congress of Racial Equality was one of the leading organizations in the civil rights movement from the 1940s to the 1960s. CORE has been credited with introducing the movement's use of nonviolent protest, which became one of its hallmarks. In the late 1960s, CORE adopted a black nationalist orientation, a decision that eventually led to its decline. Although the organization's activities are not as visible today as in the past, it continues to work to encourage black enterprise.

See also Civil Rights Movement.
References Charles W. Eagles, ed., *The Civil Rights Movement in America* (1986); August Meier and Elliott Rudwick, *CORE: A Study in the Civil Rights Movement* (1973).

Congress Watch

Congress Watch is a watchdog group that publishes the voting records of Congress members on consumer issues. Its staff also lobbies the members themselves on issues such as health care and product safety. The group has supported campaign finance reform and rejected such trade reforms as the General Agreement on Tariffs and Trade (GATT) and the North American Free Trade Agreement (NAFTA). Congress Watch is affiliated with Ralph Nader's Public Citizen.

Congressional Accountability Act

The 1995 Congressional Accountability Act extended several important federal laws governing the workplace to Congress. Until the passage of this act, Congress had routinely exempted itself from federal work laws out of concern that the executive branch would use these laws to interfere with congressional politics. A series of political scandals in the early 1990s put increased pressure on Congress to remove these exemptions. When the new Republican majority took control of both houses after the 1994 election, it moved quickly to enact reforms, making the Congressional Accountability Act the first bill it enacted into law. Among the laws extended to members of Congress through this act are the Family and Medical Leave Act, the Occupational Safety and Health Act, and the Civil Rights Act. The law allows congressional employees to file suit against their employers when they violate these acts.

See also Congress.
Reference Richard Scammon, "GOP Counts a 'Contract' Win as Compliance Bill Clears" (1995).

Congressional Budget and Impoundment Control Act

Until the 1970s, there was little structure to the congressional budget process, which made it difficult for Congress to control the federal purse. When the president's budget was introduced, it was referred to the House and Senate appropriations committees, where it was then divided up for consideration among 13 subcommittees. The two full appropriations committees provided some centralization to the process, but it was limited. The problem with the process was that most of the major decisions were made independently by the subcommittees, without anyone looking at the budget in its entirety. Moreover, a large part of the budget did not go through the appropriations committees at all, but was determined by "substantive" committees.

This was especially true for Social Security and other entitlements, which fell under the jurisdiction of the House Ways and Means Committee.

As the nation's economy slowed in the late 1960s and federal deficits reached record heights, pressure grew on Congress to institute reforms that would give it greater control over the budgeting process. Congress was eventually spurred to make reforms in 1974 after President Richard M. Nixon directly challenged Congress's control over the purse. The key turning point was Nixon's refusal to spend money allocated by law to a variety of domestic programs. Enraged by Nixon's "impoundment" of these funds, Congress enacted the Congressional Budget and Impoundment Control Act. This 1974 act is considered the most important budgetary reform in U.S. history since the Budget and Accounting Act of 1921, when Congress gave the president the responsibility for developing the federal budget.

The act established clearer budgetary procedures, created a timetable for completing each task, placed controls on the president's use of impoundment, and moved the start of the fiscal year to October 1. The act also created House and Senate budget committees to oversee the entire budget and the Congressional Budget Office to provide Congress with independent professional expertise in analyzing the budget and other economic matters.

The act has generally been credited with strengthening Congress's role in the budget process and, at least initially, creating a more coherent budget. The act did not, however, solve all of the budget problems, as the growing budget deficits of the 1980s made clear. Although the act created more centralization, major parts of the budget remained outside the control of the new process, including entitlement programs. By the early 1980s, the budget process was again in disarray, as deadlines were repeatedly missed and budget deficits soared. Beginning in the mid-1980s, Congress began to enact alternative budgetary reforms, including Gramm-Rudman-Hollings, to improve Congress's control over the budget.

See also Backdoor Spending; Budget Deficit, Federal; Concurrent Budget Resolution; Congressional Budget Office; Deferral; Entitlements; Gramm-Rudman-Hollings; Impoundment; Nixon, Richard M.; Recission.

References Roger H. Davidson, ed., *The Postreform Congress* (1992); Howard E. Shuman, *Politics and the Budget: The Struggle between the President and the Congress* (1992).

Congressional Budget Office

In order to strengthen its role in the federal budget process, Congress created the Congressional Budget Office as part of the Congressional Budget and Impoundment Control Act of 1974. This research agency conducts budgetary, fiscal, and other economic analyses for members of Congress. The office is nonpartisan and is often considered the most reliable source of economic analysis in the federal government. Its creation has improved Congress's ability to analyze the budget and has made Congress more independent of the president.

See also Congress; Congressional Budget and Impoundment Control Act; Oversight; Rivlin, Alice M.

References Daniel P. Franklin, *Making Ends Meet: Congressional Budgeting in the Age of Deficits* (1993); Leroy N. Rieselbach, *Congressional Reform: The Changing Modern Congress* (1994).

Congressional Campaign Committees

See Legislative Caucus Campaign Committees.

Congressional Pay Raise

See Twenty-seventh Amendment.

Consolidation

The merger of one or more local governments to form a single government is called consolidation. There are two types: one is the merger of two cities into one larger city, and the other is the merger of a county and the cities within its boundaries into one governmental entity. Reformers see consolidation as a way for metropolitan areas to address the problems created by the fragmentation of governments, by allowing one larger, central government to handle the problems.

See also Annexation; Metropolitan Fragmentation; Regional Government.

References Terry Christensen, *Local Politics: Governing at the Grassroots* (1995); John J. Harrigan, *Political Change in the Metropolis* (1993).

Constituency Service

The activities that legislators undertake to produce goods and services that benefit specifically the voters in their districts are referred to as constituency service. Two of the most notable types of constituency service are casework and pork-barrel legislation. Critics argue that the growing emphasis among legislators on constituency service is one of the main reasons for the growth in legislative staff, the nation's continued budget problems, and the increased reelection rate for incumbents. Supporters of constituency service argue that these activities are expected by voters and are needed to deal with legitimate local and personal problems that would otherwise go unaddressed.

See also Budget Deficit, Federal; Casework; Congress; Incumbency Advantage; Oversight; Pork-Barrel Legislation.

References Roger H. Davidson and Walter J. Oleszek, *Congress and Its Members* (1994); Leroy N. Rieselbach, *Congressional Politics: The Evolving Legislative System* (1995).

Constitution, U.S.

Many different proposals have been advocated over the past 30 years to alter the U.S. Constitution to reform the political system. These proposals range from the simple 24-word proposal to ensure equal rights for women to elaborate plans to redesign the national government. Since 1967, however, only three constitutional amendment have been adopted. These amendments have established new procedures for handling presidential succession and disability, lowered the voting age to 18, and placed restrictions on congressional pay raises.

See also Balanced Budget Amendment; Divided Government; Equal Rights Amendment; Line-Item Veto; National Initiative; National Primary; Official English Movement; Term Expansion; Term Limits; Twenty-fifth Amendment; Twenty-seventh Amendment; Twenty-sixth Amendment.

Constitutions, State

Unlike the federal Constitution, which is a short 8,700 words, most state constitutions provide long and detailed rules for the operation of state government, with the most extreme exceeding 170,000 words. These constitutions have received considerable criticism since the 1940s from political observers who argue that they are too specific, outdated, overly wordy, and often contradictory. Many reformers have called for vast revisions in these constitutions to reduce their size, improve their coherence, and limit their content to fundamental law. In addition, reformers have repeatedly called for constitutional changes over the past 30 years to restructure state government. Some of the most important constitutional changes enacted have been designed to strengthen the positions of governors and state legislatures.

Since the 1960s, many states have made efforts to reduce the size of their constitutions, including 11 that have rewritten their constitutions entirely. In many cases, these states relied on the National Civic League's Model State Constitution as a guide for their reform efforts. Despite these efforts, state constitutions continue to include far more details than many observers consider appropriate. Moreover, many constitutions have experienced renewed growth because of the ease with which amendments can be added. These problems have helped keep constitutional change an important political goal for state reformers.

See also Administrative Reorganization; Fragmented Executive; Governors; Legislative Reform Movement; Model State Constitution; National Civic League; Short Ballot; Unicameralism.
References Ann O'M. Bowman and Richard C. Kearney, *State and Local Government* (1993); Thomas R. Dye, *Politics in States and Communities* (1994); John J. Harrigan, *Politics and Policy in States and Communities* (1994).

Consumed-Income Tax

The consumed-income tax is a type of consumption tax that has been promoted as one of the most manageable alternatives to the current federal income tax system. The primary feature that distinguishes the consumed-income tax from the traditional income tax is that it does not require any taxes to be paid on income that is placed in savings or investments. By exempting savings and investments from taxation, the tax is effectively applied only to income that is used for consumption. This form of tax is considered one of the most manageable alternatives to the current income tax because it would require only minimal changes in reporting requirements and would leave the structure of the current system intact.

The consumed-income tax has never been instituted in the United States or elsewhere, but during the mid-1980s it was seriously considered by economists within the Reagan administration as one possible avenue for reform. After the Republicans gained control of both houses of Congress in 1994, a proposal for a consumed-income tax was put forward in the U.S. Senate.

Like other types of consumption taxes, the consumed-income tax is praised by supporters for encouraging investments and, in turn, economic growth. Opponents criticize it as being regressive and as potentially allowing a vast concentration of wealth in the hands of a few.

See also Consumption Taxes; Personal Income Tax; Taxes.
References Timothy J. Conlan et al., *Taxing Choices: The Politics of Tax Reform* (1990); Joseph J. Minarik, *Making Tax Choices* (1985); Christopher Zimmerman, "Flat Tax, Sales Tax, or VAT?" (1995).

Consumption Tax

A consumption tax is any type of tax that is applied to the consumption of goods or services. The most common type of consumption tax is the sales tax, which is used in 45 states. Several different types of consumption taxes have been proposed in recent years as alternatives to the current federal tax system. These include the value-added tax, the consumed-income tax, and the national sales tax. Supporters of consumption taxes argue that they encourage savings and investments, which are needed to stimulate economic growth. Opponents criticize consumption taxes because they are regressive, requiring that the poor pay a higher percentage of their income in taxes than the wealthy.

See also Consumed-Income Tax; Progressive Tax; Regressive Tax; Sales Tax; Taxes; Value-Added Tax.
References Joseph J. Minarik, *Making Tax Choices* (1985); Charls E. Walker and Mark A. Bloomfield, eds., *The Consumption Tax: A Better Alternative?* (1987).

Containment

The determination to contain the spread of communism was the cornerstone of U.S. foreign policy from the 1940s to the collapse of the Soviet Union in the early 1990s. Discontent over the war in Vietnam generated criticism of the nation's containment policy, however, and helped lead to important changes in America's relationships with other nations. While remaining committed to containment, President Nixon tried to reduce tensions between the United States and the Soviet Union in the 1970s through a new foreign policy referred to as détente. President Carter followed by focusing on other nations' human rights policies in helping to shape America's foreign relations. Ultimately, the collapse of the Soviet Union made containment less relevant in defining U.S. foreign policy. No single policy focus has emerged, however, to take its place.

See also Détente; Foreign Policy; Human Rights; Vietnam War.
References Charles W. Kegley, Jr. and Eugene R. Wittkopf, *American Foreign Policy: Pattern and Process* (1991); James A. Nathan and James K. Oliver, *United States Foreign Policy and World Order* (1989).

Contract with America

The Contract with America was a broad list of political reforms put forward by Republican congressional candidates during the 1994 election campaign as an agenda for what the party would do in its first 100 days of power if it gained control of Congress. Most political scientists downplay the importance of the contract in shaping the election results, but after the Republicans gained control of both houses in the election they immediately set to work to pass the contract's proposals. By the end of 1995, however, few of the provisions of the contract had been adopted into law.

The Contract with America consisted of ten separate sections that called for, among other proposals, massive changes in U.S. welfare policy, the passage of a balanced budget amendment and the line-item veto, reduction in taxes, and the imposition of term limits.

See also American Dream Restoration Act; Citizen Legislature Act; Common Sense Legal Reform Act; Family Reinforcement Act; Fiscal Responsibility Act; Gingrich, Newt; Job Creation and Wage Enhancement Act; National Security Restoration Act; Personal Responsibility Act; Senior Citizens Fairness Act; Taking Back Our Streets Act.
References "Republicans' Initial Promise: 100-Day Debate on 'Contract'" (1994); Clyde Wilcox, *The Latest American Revolution? The 1994 Elections and Their Implication for Governance* (1995).

Contracting for Services

One approach used by local governments to provide services at the lowest possible cost is to contract with one or more other local governments to handle the services together. Alternatively, some local governments simply pay larger, neighboring governments to provide some services for them. Some reformers see contracting for services in either of these manners as a way to overcome the fragmentation of metropolitan governments by expanding certain types of services, such as police protection, throughout larger regions. Others argue that contracting for services may actually increase fragmentation because it allows smaller governments to remain in existence. Contracting for services is often referred to as the Lakewood Plan.

See also Metropolitan Fragmentation; Regional Government.
References Terry Christensen, *Local Politics: Governing at the Grassroots* (1995); David B. Walker, *The Rebirth of Federalism: Slouching toward Washington* (1995).

Contracting Out

The government's hiring of private companies to provide specific public services is referred to as contracting out. Since the 1970s, state and local governments have relied increasingly on contracting out as a means of improving government efficiency while lowering costs.

Advocates for contracting out argue that many types of government services, from trash pickup to prison management, can be better handled by private companies than through government bureaucracy. Contracting out forces the delivery of services into the marketplace, which improves their efficiency and causes their costs to come down. Moreover, private firms do not have to conform to civil service requirements, and they rarely provide the same level of employee benefits as do civil service agencies, which allows them to operate with lower costs.

Opponents argue that private business can be just as inefficient as government agencies in fulfilling service responsibilities, and many assert that it is inappropriate to turn some government functions over to the private sector, even if it would reduce costs. These opponents argue that governments should not only be concerned with costs, but with other goals as well, such as equity in treatment of recipients, citizen involvement in service decisions, and the protection of individuals' rights. For instance, proposals to allow private businesses to run state prisons have stirred interest in recent years, but they have also been severely criticized as an inappropriate role for the private sector.

See also Alternative Service Delivery; Bureaucracy; Crime; Privatization; School Choice.
References Joan W. Allen, *Private Sector in State Service Delivery: Examples of Innovative Practices* (1989); John J. Harrigan, *Politics and Policy in States and Communities* (1994); John R. Miller and Christopher R. Tufts, "Privatization Is a Means to 'More with Less'" (1993); E. S. Savas, *Privatization: The Key to Better Government* (1987); Linda Wagar, "The Tricky Path to Going Private" (1995).

Contribution Limits

One of the most common reforms that has been offered to overcome the adverse effects of campaign contributions on politics in the United States has been to place limits on campaign contributions. Since the beginning of the twentieth century, federal and state governments have used contribution limits to try to reduce the political influence of particular groups and to control campaign costs.

The first federal effort to limit campaign contributions came in 1907, when Congress passed the Tillman Act, which prohibited contributions from corporations or national banks. Since then, Congress has passed laws banning contributions from federal employees, federal contractors, labor unions, and other groups. The Federal Election Campaign Act, which is the primary federal law regulating campaign finances today, places specific limits on the total amount of money that individuals, political action committees, and parties can contribute to campaigns. Most states have also enacted limits of one type or another on campaign contributions, though the regulations vary considerably.

See also Campaign Finance; Federal Election Campaign Act; Independent Expenditures.
References Herbert E. Alexander, *Financing Politics: Money, Elections, and Political Reform* (1992);

Congressional Campaign Finances: History, Facts, and Controversy (1992); David B. Magleby and Candice J. Nelson, *The Money Chase: Congressional Campaign Finance Reform* (1990); Frank J. Sorauf, *Money in American Elections* (1988).

Cooperative Federalism

The political relationship between the federal government and the states from the 1930s until the mid-1960s is referred to as cooperative federalism. The term *cooperative* is used in reference to the joint nature in which both levels of government worked together to solve the nation's problems. Cooperative federalism is often compared with dual federalism, which is the type of federalism that existed prior to the expansion of the federal government in the 1930s. Under dual federalism, the federal and state governments did not work together, but instead concentrated their attention on entirely separate policy concerns, with the federal government playing only a minor role in domestic policy matters.

Cooperative federalism was replaced by Creative Federalism during the Johnson administration, and later by different forms of New Federalism in the 1970s and 1980s. Some scholars view Creative and New Federalism as simply different types of cooperative federalism, and not entirely distinct structures. Cooperative federalism is often referred to as marble-cake federalism, because it was characterized by an intermingling of the different levels of government; dual federalism, conversely, is often called layer-cake federalism.

See also Coercive Federalism; Creative Federalism; New Deal; New Federalism.
References Ann O'M. Bowman and Richard C. Kearney, *State and Local Government* (1993); Laurence J. O'Toole, Jr., *American Intergovernmental Relations: Foundations, Perspectives, and Issues* (1993); David B. Walker, *The Rebirth of Federalism: Slouching toward Washington* (1995).

Coordinated Spending

Political parties will often purchase goods and services directly to help a candidate attain office, instead of contributing funds to the candidate's campaign coffers. This form of campaign assistance, which is done with a candidate's knowledge and approval, is referred to as coordinated spending. The 1974 amendments to the Federal Election Campaign Act established a formula for the amount of money that parties could spend in coordinated spending on individual candidates.

See also Campaign Finance; Federal Election Campaign Act.
References *Congressional Campaign Finances: History, Facts, and Controversy* (1992); David B. Magleby and Candice J. Nelson, *The Money Chase: Congressional Campaign Finance Reform* (1990); Frank J. Sorauf, *Money in American Elections* (1988).

Corporate Income Tax

The corporate income tax is a type of government levy applied to a corporation's net earnings. It is the third-largest source of revenue for the federal government, behind the personal income and social security taxes. Corporate income taxes are also used in 46 states, though states depend far more on sales and personal income tax for revenue.

Federal corporate income taxes were reduced markedly during the 1980s as part of conservatives' efforts to introduce supply-side economic principles into the nation's tax policies. Supply-side economists argued that reducing corporate taxes would increase the amount of money available for investment, which in turn would lead to economic growth. The Economic Recovery Tax Act of 1981 (ERTA) applied these principles to the federal tax structure by establishing more generous depreciation rules (the Accelerated Cost

Recovery System) and introducing a new Investment Tax Credit. Combined, these two parts of ERTA are estimated to have reduced federal corporate taxes by $46 billion over the next three years. The changes in the law effectively allowed many corporations to avoid paying any income taxes.

Responding to growing criticism of these corporate tax benefits, Congress tightened the depreciation rules and eliminated the tax credit in the Tax Reform Act of 1986. At the same time, it lowered the corporate tax rate from a maximum of 46 percent to 34 percent. These changes reduced the tax loopholes that allowed corporations to avoid paying taxes, spread the tax burden more fairly among corporations, and promised an increase in corporate tax revenue of $120 billion over the next four years.

State governments have often been reluctant to impose or raise corporate income taxes out of fear that a robust corporate tax will drive businesses to other states. Some states raised their corporate income taxes in the late 1980s and early 1990s, however, to help overcome fiscal crises. These increases were much smaller, however, than those imposed on sales and personal income tax.

See also Economic Recovery Tax Act; Personal Income Tax; Progressive Tax; Regressive Tax; Sales Tax; Supply-Side Economics; Tax Reform Act; Taxes.

References Timothy Conlan et al., *Taxing Choices: The Politics of Tax Reform* (1990); Werner Z. Hirsch and Anthony M. Rufolo, *Public Finance and Expenditure in a Federal System* (1990); Henry J. Raimondo, "State Budgeting in the Nineties" (1993); Howard E. Shuman, *Politics and the Budget: The Struggle between the President and the Congress* (1992).

Corrections

See Crime; Plea Bargaining; Sentencing.

Cost-Benefit Analysis

Cost-benefit analysis is a type of appraisal used by some government agencies to help decide whether particular projects should be undertaken. This approach requires an agency to quantify the anticipated costs and benefits of a project to determine if it is justified. Efforts to expand the use of cost-benefit analysis have increased in recent years, led by conservative reformers who argue that the spate of new regulations coming out of Washington over the past two decades has been too costly for the economy. In particular, many of these reformers have advocated using cost-benefit analysis to shape environmental policy. Opponents argue, however, that it is difficult, and even inappropriate, to try to quantify the costs and benefits associated with clean air, good health, and a sound environment.

Closely associated with the debate over cost-benefit analysis is the proposed use of risk assessment. With risk assessment, government agencies would be required to conduct extensive scientific tests of perceived health or safety concerns before introducing new regulations. Supporters of risk assessment argue that such tests are needed to reduce unnecessary regulation and produce better policy. Opponents argue that many of the risk assessment proposals being debated today set demands for justifying government regulations too high and would harm the nation's environmental and health laws if enacted.

The Job Creation and Wage Enhancement Act, which was one of ten provisions in the Republican Party's Contract with America, called for the use of both cost-benefit analysis and risk assessment.

See also Deregulation; Environmental Policy; Job Creation and Wage Enhancement Act.

References Mary H. Cooper, "Environmental

Movement at 25: Will Congress Weaken Environmental Regulations?" (1995); Maureen L. Cropper and Wallace E. Oates, "Environmental Economics: A Survey" (1992).

Council-Manager

Under the council-manager form of city government, formal political power is vested in a city council, but the day-to-day operation of the city is left to a professional administrator. Some council-manager systems also have a mayor who serves on the council, but this person usually has no more power than other council members.

Since the beginning of the twentieth century, the council-manager system has been the preferred political system of most municipal reformers. It is often championed as a means of improving representation, making city government more effective, and reducing corruption. Under this system, the city council provides representation and policy guidance, and the administrator brings professional knowledge to the city's operation. City managers are often given considerable responsibilities, including preparation of the city budget, policy initiation, and hiring and firing of city employees. Critics argue that this system of government gives too much political power to an individual who is not elected by voters, and does not offer strong enough leadership to deal with many of the most pressing problems confronting U.S. cities.

The council-manager system is the most popular form of city government in the United States.

See also City Commission; Model City Charter; Strong Mayor; Weak Mayor.

References David N. Ammons and Charldean Newell, "'City Managers Don't Make Policy': A Lie; Let's Face It" (1988); Terrell Blodgett, "Beware the Lure of the 'Strong' Mayor" (1994); Ann O'M. Bowman and Richard C. Kearney, *State and Local Government* (1993); Terry Christensen, *Local Politics: Governing at the Grassroots* (1995); Rob Gurwitt, "The Lure of the Strong Mayor" (1993); John J. Harrigan, *Political Change in the Metropolis* (1993).

Councils of Government (COGs)

One proposal that has been offered to overcome the problems of metropolitan fragmentation is the increased use of voluntary councils of government. Composed of representatives of neighboring cities and counties, these councils provide local governments with a vehicle to coordinate policy in such areas as zoning, transportation, and criminal justice.

The role and prominence of COGs have changed considerably over the past 30 years. In the early 1960s, few COGs existed across the nation. However, the passage of the Model Cities Act of 1966, which required regional review of many federal grant applications, spurred their growth. The number of COGs is estimated to have increased from 20 to almost 700 between the early 1960s and 1980. Not only did their numbers grow, but so did their power, as the Model Cities Act gave them some influence over regional planning decisions. The power to review grant applications was taken away from COGs during the Reagan administration, as the Republican president attempted to reduce the federal government's role in local government affairs, leading to the demise of some 125 COGs.

Today, a few councils of government have a formal role in overseeing some state activities, but for the most part they primarily provide clearinghouses for information and opportunities for local government to coordinate activities. Supporters argue that COGs offer a politically viable solution to the problems of metropolitan fragmentation because they do not pose a threat to the power of local governments. Opponents argue that although the COGs may be politically acceptable, their voluntary status makes them incapable of dealing with many of the major problems confronting the nation's urban centers.

See also Metropolitan Fragmentation; Model Cities Program; Regional Government.
References Terry Christensen, *Local Politics: Governing at the Grassroots* (1995); John J. Harrigan, *Political Change in the Metropolis* (1993); David B. Walker, *The Rebirth of Federalism: Slouching toward Washington* (1995).

Court Centralization

One of the primary proposals put forward by reformers to reduce the backlog of state court cases, improve court management, and provide more consistent application of the law is the centralization of state court systems. Under this proposal, a state's supreme court and chief justice would be given more control over the administration of all state courts, taking responsibility for such duties as personnel management, case assignment, budgeting, court rules and procedures, and the reassignment of judges to positions where they are needed.

Over the past three decades, many states have moved to centralize their court systems, placing many of these responsibilities, though rarely all, in the hands of the supreme court. To help the court handle these tasks, the states have appointed court administrators to oversee the day-to-day management of their court systems.

See also Caseload; Court Consolidation; Courts.
References Larry Charles Berkson and Susan B. Carbon, *Court Unification: History, Politics, and Implementation* (1978); Henry R. Glick, "The Politics of Court Reform: In a Nutshell" (1982).

Court Consolidation

State court reformers have repeatedly called for a consolidation of state court systems since the 1960s in order to reduce judicial overlap, improve court administration, and produce more uniform decisions. Such court consolidation proposals usually call for two- or three-tiered systems, with a supreme court, one main type of trial court, and possibly an intermediary court of appeals. Most consolidation proposals retain a few specialized courts, but eliminate the use of other minor trial courts. This kind of reform is also referred to as court unification.

See also Caseload; Court Centralization; Courts.
References Larry Charles Berkson and Susan B. Carbon, *Court Unification: History, Politics, and Implementation* (1978); Robert A. Carp and Ronald Stidham, *Judicial Process in America* (1993); Henry R. Glick, "The Politics of Court Reform: In a Nutshell" (1982).

Court of Appeals for the Federal Circuit

The Court of Appeals for the Federal Circuit was created by Congress in 1982 to handle specialized appellate cases involving patents, trademarks, copyrights, and international trade. The court was formed by merging the Court of Claims and the Court of Customs and Patent Appeals.

See also Courts; Specialized Courts; Supreme Court.
Reference Henry J. Abraham, *The Judicial Process: An Introductory Analysis of the Courts of the United States, England and France* (1993).

Courts

The American court system has been the focus of considerable public attention in the 1990s, with the controversial nomination of Clarence Thomas to the U.S. Supreme Court and the unexpected verdicts in both the trial of the police officers accused of beating Rodney King and the trial of O. J. Simpson. Although these events helped build awareness of problems in the courts, political activists have been pushing court reform for several decades.

The movement to reform state courts is often traced to the release of a report by the President's Commission on Law Enforcement and Administration of Justice in 1967, which called for the consolidation and centralization of state courts. Since then, court reformers have actively sought solutions for a number of critical problems confronting the court system. Among their goals, court reformers have tried to improve the selection and conduct of judges, to increase access to the judicial system, to reduce the massive caseload confronting the courts, to improve the treatment received by women and minorities in the court system, and to ensure fairer application of the law. Considerable gains have been made in centralizing court administration, but most of the other problems remain of concern to reformers, especially the continued backlog of cases.

One of the first modern efforts to reform the federal courts also occurred in 1967, with the creation of the Federal Judicial Center. In the 1970s, interest in reforming the federal courts intensified, helped along by the work of Supreme Court Chief Justice Warren Burger, who repeatedly spoke out on the problems confronting the court system, especially its mounting caseload. Burger organized the Freund Committee and the Pound Conference, both of which stirred important debate on how best to address the problems confronting the Supreme Court and the federal court system. As at the state level, some of the major concerns confronting the federal court have been its growing caseload, constraints on access, and unfair application of the law.

The most important efforts to help the federal courts occurred in the late 1980s and early 1990s, when Congress passed legislation all but ending the Supreme Court's mandatory jurisdiction, limiting the federal court's jurisdiction over some types of state disputes, and requiring all federal court districts to develop plans to reduce costs and delays.

One of the primary solutions being championed today to solve the problems confronting both the federal and state court systems is the increased use of alternative forms of dispute resolution, which supporters argue can reduce caseloads and improve access to the judicial system.

See also Act to Improve the Administration of Justice; Alternative Dispute Resolution; Caseload; Civil Justice Reform Act; Crime; Federal Judicial Center; Freund Committee; Hill, Anita; Hruska Commission; Institute for Court Management; Judicial Access; Judicial Activism; Judicial Conduct; Judicial Improvements and Access to Justice Act; Judicial Selection; Jury Trials; National Center for State Courts; New Judicial Federalism; Pound Conference; Sentencing; Supreme Court; Thomas, Clarence.

References Henry J. Abraham, *The Judicial Process: An Introductory Analysis of the Courts of the United States, England, and France* (1993); Robert A. Carp and Ronald Stidham, *Judicial Process in America* (1993).

Creative Federalism

The relationship between the federal government and the states since the 1930s has often been referred to as cooperative federalism, because of the way in which both levels of government have worked jointly to solve the nation's problems. In the 1960s, however, President Johnson introduced a variety of new federal programs that gave the federal government a larger and more dominant role in dealing with societal problems while considerably reducing the importance of the states. Johnson's efforts to restructure federal-state relations to strengthen the federal government's role is known as Creative Federalism.

The heart of Johnson's efforts was the creation of more than 200 new federal grants that were made available to states, local governments, and nonprofit groups to address specific social problems. These grants-in-aid, which included such well-known programs as Medicaid and Head Start, came with considerable strings attached to ensure that they were used in accordance with the federal government's expectations.

With the election of Richard Nixon as president in 1968, Johnson's Creative Federalism was replaced by New Federalism, which attempted to reduce the federal government's role in solving society problems while strengthening the position of the states. Although there are important differences between Creative and New Federalism, they are considered by some scholars to be simply different types of cooperative federalism.

See also Coercive Federalism; Cooperative Federalism; Federal-State Relations; Johnson, Lyndon B.; New Federalism; Nixon, Richard M.
References Laurence J. O'Toole, Jr., *American Intergovernmental Relations: Foundations, Perspectives, and Issues* (1993); David B. Walker, *The Rebirth of Federalism: Slouching toward Washington* (1995).

Crime

Federal and state policies regarding crime and criminals have become less tolerant over the past 20 years, as the public has grown increasingly frustrated with the nation's crime rate. The effect of this get-tough attitude on crime is debated, but the changes have had profound effects on the U.S. criminal justice system and on state governments.

The concern over crime emerged as an important political issue in the 1960s, encouraging President Johnson to declare a "war on crime" and President Nixon to campaign for "law and order." Despite this rhetoric, the concern over crime only intensified in the late 1970s and 1980s. One of the primary ways that federal and state governments responded was by introducing harsher penalties on criminals. At both levels of government, there was a move throughout the 1980s to replace indeterminate sentencing rules with determinate ones to ensure that convicted criminals did not return quickly to the streets. In addition, penalties for many types of crimes were strengthened, especially drug violations.

The pressure to crack down on criminals continued into the 1990s, and led many states to enact tough mandatory sentences for repeat offenders. One of the best-known reforms was the introduction of "three strikes and you're out" policy, which imposes life sentences on individuals found guilty of their third felony offenses. Three-strikes policy was also incorporated into the Federal Crime Control Act of 1994. Many states also enacted "victims' bills of rights" that focused on giving greater attention during criminal proceedings to the plight of crime victims.

The result of these policies has been an explosion in the number of persons incarcerated in U.S. prisons, with some studies estimating that the total number of people imprisoned has tripled over the past 15 years, reaching close to a million prisoners today. The growth in the prison population has in turned forced a massive increase in spending on corrections. From 1975 to 1994, the total amount of money spent by federal, state, and local governments on corrections rose from $4 billion to $30 billion. The increase has been particularly difficult for state governments, which have been forced to channel larger proportions of their budgets to corrections despite economic hard times. A large share of this money has gone to the construction of new prisons. The state of California, for instance, has built 18 new prisons since the mid-1980s. The number of federal prisons has risen from 43 to 77 since 1982.

Despite the building boom, the pace of prison construction has not kept up with the growing incarceration rate. The result is that many state prisons have become increasingly overcrowded. Although states continue to build new prisons, the costs associated with corrections have assumed such a large percentage of state budgets that many states are beginning to consider ways to reform the criminal justice system.

Proposals for reforming the system vary considerably, from increased police presence in the community to the decriminalization of some drugs. Some reformers also call for more spending on education and social welfare programs as a way to reduce the social problems that lead to crime. One of the most popular reform proposals to reduce costs and overcrowding in the prisons is the introduction of alternative types of sentencing that allow criminals to remain in the community, but requires them to be closely monitored. Finally, many advocates argue that states should allow private companies to run their prisons as a means to reduce costs.

See also Contracting Out; Courts; Privatization; Sentencing; Taking Back Our Streets Act.
References John J. DiIulio, Jr., "Punishing Smarter: Penal Reforms for the 1990s" (1989); Steven A. Holmes, "The Boom in Jails Is Locking Up Lots of Loot" (1994); Penelope Lemov, "The Next Best Thing to Prison" (1991); Wesley G. Skogan, "Crime and Punishment" (1996).

Criminal Justice

See Courts; Crime.

C-SPAN

Providing a link between the U.S. government and the public, C-SPAN (the Cable-Satellite Public Affairs Network) began televising congressional proceedings to the public in 1979. This television network was created to help counter the public's growing mistrust of Congress after a series of scandals in the 1970s tarnished the legislature's image. The Legislative Reorganization Act of 1970 first opened the doors of Congress to the public by allowing the televising and broadcasting of committee proceedings. Then in March of 1979, C-SPAN began broadcasting formal floor sessions live into America's living rooms.

Supporters argue that C-SPAN allows Americans to view congressional sessions, thereby demystifying the activities of Congress and making them more accessible to the public. Unlike the sound bites of most television daily news, C-SPAN's telecasts are unedited and extended. The presence of cameras in congressional proceedings also helps to hold the lawmakers accountable for their actions during sessions. However, some critics argue that C-SPAN encourages legislators to engage in political rhetoric rather than to concentrate on the heart of legislative matters.

See also Congress; Legislative Reorganization Act; Sunshine Rules.
References Brian Lamb, *C-SPAN: America's Town Hall* (1988); Leroy N. Rieselbach, *Congressional Reform: The Changing Modern Congress* (1994).

Cumulative Voting

Cumulative voting is an alternative election system that has been proposed to improve the representation of minority political parties and racial minorities. Under such a system, voters are allowed to cast the same number of votes as there are seats to be filled in a multimember district. Voters can cast all their votes for one candidate or divide their votes among candidates. By concentrating their votes on one candidate, minority parties and racial groups are more likely to elect representatives of their choice than they are in traditional multimember district elections.

A cumulative voting system was introduced by the Illinois House of Representatives in 1870 to ensure the election of Republicans from the heavily Democratic southern part of the state and Democrats from the Republican north. Illinois voters replaced the system in 1980 with single-member districts. The process was adopted by a handful of local governments in Alabama in the late 1980s to increase the representation of African-Americans.

See also Election Systems; Guinier, Lani; Multimember Districts; Single-Member Districts.
Reference Wilma Rule and Joseph F. Zimmerman, eds., *United States Electoral Systems: Their Impact on Women and Minorities* (1992).

D

Davis v. Bandemer

The U.S. Supreme Court historically has been reluctant to become involved in the "political thicket" of legislative redistricting cases. The Court's position changed, however, in the 1962 case of *Baker v. Carr,* when it decided that redistricting was open to judicial redress.

Despite the sweeping effects of the *Baker* ruling, the Court limited most of its subsequent action to cases involving disparities in district population and racial gerrymandering. On questions dealing with political gerrymandering, the Court remained reluctant to become involved. This reluctance ended in 1986, when the Court ruled in *Davis v. Bandemer* that partisan gerrymandering was a justiciable concern because it has the potential to violate the equal protection clause of the Constitution. The Court's decision is significant because it allows political parties to seek redress if they believe that their members' right to influence elections has been denied because of partisan gerrymandering.

See also *Baker v. Carr;* Gerrymandering; Reapportionment Revolution; Redistricting; *Reynolds v. Sims; Wesberry v. Sanders.*

References Charles Backstrom et al., "Partisan Gerrymandering in the Post-Bandemer Era" (1987); National Conference of State Legislatures Reapportionment Task Force, *Reapportionment Law: The 1990s* (1989).

Deferral

Deferrals are one of two types of presidential impoundments defined by the Congressional Budget and Impoundment Control Act of 1974. A president may decide to defer, or delay temporarily, the spending of funds previously approved by law. The Congressional Budget Act limits the length of time the president may defer expenditures to within the same fiscal year. The act also gives Congress the power to overturn a deferral if either house votes against it.

See also Congressional Budget and Impoundment Control Act; Impoundment; Legislative Veto; Recission.

References John W. Ellwood and James A. Thurber, "The Politics of the Congressional Budget Process Re-examined" (1981); Howard E. Shuman, *Politics and the Budget: The Struggle between the President and the Congress* (1992).

Deficit Reduction Act (DEFRA)

The Deficit Reduction Act was one of several tax bills enacted in the 1980s to overcome the federal budget deficit that had been created by the tax cuts in the Economic Recovery Tax Act of 1981. The act raised a handful of excise and corporate taxes while establishing new regulations on tax shelters.

See also Budget Deficit, Federal; Economic

Recovery Tax Act; Tax Equity and Fiscal Responsibility Act; Tax Reform Act.
References Howard E. Shuman, *Politics and the Budget: The Struggle between the President and the Congress* (1992); C. Eugene Steuerle, *The Tax Decade: How Taxes Came To Dominate the Political Agenda* (1992).

Democratic Leadership Council

The Democratic Leadership Council (DLC), an association of elected Democrats, was created in 1985 to provide a counter to the leftward drift of the Democratic Party among such interest groups as Jesse Jackson's Rainbow Coalition. The members believe that "Democrats should be the party that embraces change," meaning that more conservative fiscal and social policies should be part of the Democratic agenda. Senator Sam Nunn of Georgia and Representative Richard Gephart of Missouri are among the members of the DLC. The council was a strong supporter of Bill Clinton's presidential campaign in 1992.

See also National Rainbow Coalition; Political Parties.
Reference Karen O'Connor and Larry J. Sabato, *American Government: Roots and Reform* (1995).

Democratic Party

See Fairness Commission; Hughes Commission; Hunt Commission; McGovern-Fraser Commission; Mikulski Commission; Mississippi Freedom Democratic Party; Political Parties; Presidential Primaries; Winograd Commission.

Democratic Study Group

The Democratic Study Group is an organization created by Democrats in the U.S. House of Representatives in 1959 to increase the political power of the House's expanding liberal membership. One of the major problems confronting liberal Democrats in the 1950s and 1960s was that the House was dominated by conservative southern Democrats, who controlled the powerful committee chair positions because of the seniority rule. A large influx of liberal northern Democrats in 1958 helped spur the creation of the Democratic Study Group as a means to overcome the southern Democrats' dominance. In the 1970s, the group played an instrumental role in the passage of a variety of reforms designed to democratize Congress, including the Legislative Reorganization Act of 1970 and the Hansen Committee reforms.

See also Congress; Hansen Committee; Legislative Reorganization Act; Seniority Rule.
References Lawrence C. Dodd and Bruce I. Oppenheimer, "The House in Transition: Change and Consolidation" (1981); David W. Rohde, *Parties and Leaders in the Postreform House* (1991).

Depository Institutions Deregulation and Monetary Control Act

The Depository Institutions Deregulation and Monetary Control Act of 1980 partially deregulated the savings and loan industry, introducing a phaseout of interest rate ceilings, expanding the coverage of federal deposit insurance on savings accounts from $40,000 to $100,000, and allowing savings institutions to expand the types of loans and accounts they could offer. These changes were designed to strengthen the savings industry during a time in which high interest rates were encouraging investors to redirect their funds away from savings deposits into more profitable accounts, particularly money market mutual funds. The act was one of several efforts in the late 1970s and early 1980s to reduce the federal government's involvement in the economy. It is considered to have been partially responsible for the savings and loan crisis of the 1980s.

See also Deregulation; Financial Institutions Reform, Recovery, and Enforcement Act; Garn-St. Germaine Depository Institutions Act; Savings and Loan Crisis.

References Anthony S. Campagna, *The Economy in the Reagan Years: The Economic Consequences of the Reagan Administrations* (1994); Robert E. Litan, "Financial Regulation" (1994); William A. Niskanen, *Reaganomics: An Insider's Account of the Policies and People* (1988).

Deregulation

Deregulation is the reduction or elimination of government regulations on business and industry. Since the late 1970s, many reformers have advocated deregulation as a means of improving the nation's economic performance and reducing the government's role in society.

The recent support for deregulation has grown out of the rapid expansion of federal regulations on the economy and society in the 1960s and 1970s. This expansion was particularly great during the Nixon administration, which is considered to have introduced more new regulations than any other administration in U.S. history. In general, the regulations adopted during this period were less concerned with controlling the marketplace than with addressing social problems. The new regulations focused particularly on improving the environment, strengthening health and safety laws, and protecting consumer interests. New federal laws created such regulatory bodies as the Consumer Protection Agency, the Environmental Protection Agency, the Occupational Safety and Health Administration, and the National Transportation and Safety Administration.

When the nation's economy stalled under the weight of stagflation in the mid- to late 1970s, many conservative economists and political reformers began to argue that the economic problems were the result of too much government regulation. The imposition of these regulations, the reformers argued, had placed too great an economic burden on business, causing profits to decline, wasting resources that could be better spent on investment, forcing prices to rise, and undermining the market economy. Reformers called for a reduction in economic and social regulations and, at the extreme, complete deregulation of some industries.

By the late 1970s, the effort to roll back government regulations began to fall on receptive ears in the nation's capital. Senator Edward Kennedy of Massachusetts is considered to have helped spawn interest within Congress for regulatory relief when he sponsored hearings on deregulation of the airline industry in 1974. Two years later, the first major effort to roll back federal government regulations was adopted with the Railroad Revitalization and Reform Act of 1976, which loosened restrictions on the railroad industry. Jimmy Carter is considered to be the first president to try to slow and even reduce federal regulation on business since the concern for regulatory relief emerged in the 1970s. During Carter's administration, legislation was enacted reducing regulations on airlines, banking, natural gas, and trucking. In most of these cases, regulations were simply reduced or modified, but the Airline Deregulation Act of 1978 completely deregulated the airline industry. Despite these efforts to reduce government regulation, Carter's record in championing deregulation was mixed, as he also pushed through several important laws increasing government regulation elsewhere, particularly in protecting the environment.

With a conservative Republican president newly installed in the White House in 1981, the efforts to reduce the government's regulation of business and industry gained new momentum. Regulatory relief was one of the primary goals of the economic program Ronald Reagan proposed in 1981, which became known as Reaganomics. Within the first two months of his administration, Reagan took steps to give the White House greater power to control the flow of regulation coming out of the bureaucracy. He issued orders requiring agencies to conduct cost-benefit analyses before adopting new regulations and when evaluating older ones, and to submit their proposals to the Office of Management and Budget for prior review. He then appointed several conservative opponents of government regulation to head key federal agencies and departments, including the Department of Interior, the Environmental Protection Agency, and the Federal Communications Commission. These actions helped slow the increase in regulations during the outset of Reagan's tenure.

Besides trying to slow the rise of new regulation, Reagan pushed Congress and the heads of the federal bureaucracy to roll back regulations on selected industries. Several major reforms in government regulations were adopted in the early 1980s, through changes in agency policies, executive orders, or new laws. In 1981, the Reagan administration removed most of the regulations on commercial radio stations and removed oil price controls. In 1982, Congress enacted the Garn-St. Germaine Depository Institutions Act, which deregulated the savings and loan industry, and the Bus Regulatory Reform Act, which significantly reduced regulations on commercial bus lines. Two years later, Congress adopted the Shipping Act of 1984, reducing the regulations on the rates and services provided by shipping companies.

Like Carter, however, Reagan had a mixed overall record in reducing government regulation. Within three years after Reagan entered office, the movement to roll back government regulations declined as he began to concentrate on other matters. After 1984, the Reagan administration floated a variety of other regulatory reforms, but made little serious effort to see them enacted. Political support for deregulation also declined as the deregulation of the savings and loan industry helped spur a crisis in the industry. During Reagan's second term, the federal government ultimately returned to its traditional pattern of increased regulation.

Interest in regulatory relief and deregulation rose again in the mid-1990s with the election of a Republican majority to both houses of Congress. Many of these Republicans have argued strongly that government regulation needs to be reduced in order to improve the nation's economy. In 1995, Congress considered several proposals to scale back federal regulations. Then, in 1996, it passed a major reform bill to deregulate local television service and cable television. How successful the Republicans will be in reducing other regulation is uncertain, however. Although deregulation has been found to improve economic performance in some situations, many of the social regulations on business enjoy widespread popular support, and thus may be difficult to remove.

See also Airline Deregulation Act; Carter, James E.; Cost-Benefit Analysis; Depository Institutions Deregulation and Monetary Control Act; Financial Institutions Reform, Recovery, and Enforcement Act; Garn-St. Germaine Depository Institutions Act; Railroad Revitalization and Reform Act of 1976; Reaganomics; Savings and Loan Crisis; Takings; Telecommunications.

References Bob Benenson, "Procedural Overhaul Fails after Three Tough Votes" (1995); Anthony S. Campagna, *The Economy in the Reagan Years: The Economic Consequences of the Reagan Administrations* (1994); Martin Feldstein, ed., *American Economic Policy in the 1980s* (1994); Gary

Mucciaroni, *Reversals of Fortune: Public Policy and Private Interests* (1995); William A. Niskanen, *Reaganomics: An Insider's Account of the Policies and People* (1988); Anandi P. Sahu and Ronald L. Tracy, *The Economic Legacy of the Reagan Years: Euphoria or Chaos?* (1991).

Détente

Détente was the foreign policy introduced by President Richard Nixon in the 1970s that called for an improvement in relations between the United States and the Soviet Union. Prior to the emphasis on détente, the nation's foreign policy had been dominated by the determination to contain the spread of communism. Nixon's efforts led to the formal recognition of Eastern Europe's boundaries through the Helsinki Accords, the signing of the first arms limitation agreement with the Soviet Union (SALT I), and the start of relations with the People's Republic of China.

See also Containment; Foreign Policy; Human Rights; Nixon, Richard M.

References John Robert Greene, *The Limits of Power: The Nixon and Ford Administrations* (1992); Robert D. Schulzinger, *Henry Kissinger: Doctor of Diplomacy* (1989).

Devolution

The redistribution of political power and responsibility from the national government to state and local governments is referred to as devolution. Since the 1960s, when there was increased concentration of political power at the national level, the demand for devolution has become a prominent part of the political agenda for many conservative reformers. President Richard M. Nixon made some effort to strengthen the states' role through his New Federalism program, which reduced the number of strings attached to federal funds flowing to the states. Nixon's devolution efforts were continued by President Ronald Reagan, though in slightly different form. Whereas Nixon supported an active state government, Reagan was skeptical of all government involvement in society. Thus in advocating devolution, he not only proposed a redistribution of responsibilities to the state level, but he also wanted the states to find their own sources of funding.

Despite the strong rhetoric used by both these presidents in support of devolution, the federal government has continued to play a leading role in the federal system. The result is that the demand for devolution has remained an important goal for many conservative reformers. The Republican Party's Contract with America in 1994 proposed the devolution of some federal programs, including most welfare programs. During the 1995 budget debate, the Republicans advocated a devolution of Medicaid to the states.

Supporters of devolution argue that the federal government has become too large and too distant from the people to identify and solve society's problems. Opponents argue that the states have neither the ability nor the resources to handle many of the nation's most pressing concerns.

Some advocates of devolution acknowledge that the states are not well suited to handle all government functions, and thus do not call for complete devolution of power to the states. Instead, they advocate a more rational distribution of responsibilities, with the states playing a more active role in the functions they handle best. Economist Alice M. Rivlin, the budget director in the Clinton administration, is one of the most prominent supporters of the redistribution of responsibilities. She has called for "dividing the job," with the states given control of economic development and public services, including education, job training, infrastructure, and housing.

The federal government, in turn, would concentrate on international affairs, health care, and some social welfare programs.

See also Big Swap; Contract with America; Creative Federalism; Federal-State Relations; New Federalism; Rivlin, Alice M.; Sorting Out.
References Timothy J. Conlan, *New Federalism: Intergovernmental Reform from Nixon to Reagan* (1988); Alice M. Rivlin, *Reviving the American Dream: The Economy, the States, and the Federal Government* (1992); David B. Walker, *The Rebirth of Federalism: Slouching toward Washington* (1995); Christopher Zimmerman, "A Devolution Revolution?" (1995).

Direct Primaries
See Primary Elections.

Discretionary Spending
The part of federal spending that is controlled by the annual budget process is referred to as discretionary spending. It excludes entitlement programs, multiyear government contracts, interest payments on the debt, and other ongoing expenditures required by law. The amount of money spent on discretionary programs was reduced dramatically during the 1980s under the Reagan administration, and today totals less than 25 percent of the federal budget. Although discretionary spending represents a smaller portion of the budget than nondiscretionary spending, it is often the focus of reform because appropriations for these programs must be reapproved every year.

See also Backdoor Spending; Budget Deficit, Federal; Budget Enforcement Act of 1990; Entitlements; Uncontrollable Spending.
References Daniel P. Franklin, *Making Ends Meet: Congressional Budgeting in the Age of Deficits* (1993); Donald F. Kettl, *Deficit Politics: Public Budgeting in Its Institutional and Historical Context* (1992); Howard E. Shuman, *Politics and the Budget: The Struggle between the President and the Congress* (1992).

Disenfranchisement
See Electoral Discrimination.

Divided Government
In a divided government, one political party controls the executive branch and another party holds a majority in one or both houses of the legislature. In recent decades, divided government has become much more common at both federal and state levels than at any other time in U.S. history. The federal government has had a divided government in every year since 1968, except for during the Carter administration and the first two years of President Clinton's tenure, when the Democratic Party controlled both branches. The number of states with divided government rose from approximately 30 percent in 1962 to more than 55 percent in 1986.

Many political observers criticize the development of divided government, arguing that it is ineffective, inefficient, and unaccountable. Reformers advocate strengthening the party system and making changes in the electoral process. The Committee on the Constitutional System has proposed several different reforms for the problem of divided government at the national level, including electing the president and members of Congress on the same ticket, requiring states to design ballots so that it is easier to vote a straight party line, and scheduling congressional elections two weeks after the presidential vote to encourage greater support for the president's party. The committee has also suggested giving bonus seats in Congress to the president's party.

Some political observers argue that the problem of divided government is not as severe as critics maintain, and that the government works just as well when it is divided as it does when it is unified.

See also Committee on the Constitutional System; President; Responsible Parties; Term Expansion.
References Morris P. Fiorina, *Divided Government* (1992); David Mayhew, *Divided We Govern: Party Control, Lawmaking, and Investigations, 1946–1990* (1991); James L. Sundquist, *Constitutional Reform and Effective Government* (1992).

Downsizing

Government downsizing is a reduction in the size of the government bureaucracy in order to provide public services at lower costs without sacrificing efficiency. Interest in downsizing emerged initially in the private sector in the late 1980s, as corporate leaders pondered how to make their companies more competitive with Japanese firms. Many of the nation's largest corporations decided to lay off thousands of employees in order to bring their costs down. As corporations began to downsize, interest in downsizing spread to government operations. Several state governments announced intentions to lay off employees in the early 1990s as a way to reduce costs in the face of mounting fiscal stress. In 1993, President Clinton's National Performance Review unveiled its report on reinventing government, which called for a 12 percent reduction in federal government jobs. Despite promises to downsize, however, the numbers of layoffs have not been as severe as suggested. Several studies have found that most states looked for alternatives to bring in more revenue or reduce costs instead of cutting back employees. As for the National Performance Review proposal, it does require a major reduction in the size of the federal bureaucracy, but it spreads the reduction out until end of the century.

Although downsizing may reduce costs, opponents argue that individual downsizing plans can have bad side effects, including reducing service levels and causing an exodus of a bureaucracy's better employees. In order to avoid these problems, supporters maintain that downsizing should be done selectively and usually in tandem with bureaucratic reorganization.

Recently, many management reformers have begun to talk about "rightsizing" instead of downsizing. Although the term is often seen as simply a euphemism for downsizing, supporters of rightsizing argue that it is a distinct management technique. Rightsizing, they maintain, is more concerned than downsizing with establishing priorities in government services and selectively restructuring government programs to meet the public's needs as it cuts costs.

See also Bureaucracy; Finance, State; National Performance Review; Privatization.
References Daniel P. Franklin, "Downsizing: Is It Aimed at the Right Targets?" (1994); Wayne W. Hall, Jr., "State Management and Administration: Doing More with Less" (1992); Penelope Lemov, "Tailoring Local Government to the 1990s" (1992); Jonathan Walters, "The Downsizing Myth" (1994).

E

Early Voting

A recent proposal adopted in a number of states to increase voter participation is early voting, an election procedure that allows voters to cast their ballots during a designated period prior to election day. The process has similarities to both traditional election-day voting and absentee voting, but it is distinct.

In early voting, extra days or extended hours are provided to allow registered voters to cast their ballots, thus allowing individuals who cannot arrive at their polling places during normal voting hours an opportunity to vote. As in traditional election-day voting, voters show up at designated polling places, sign poll books, have their eligibility verified from registration lists, and then cast their ballots. Unlike traditional election-day voting, however, voters can choose from more than one polling place to cast their ballots.

As in the use of absentee ballots, voters are allowed to cast their ballots at times other than the election day. However, there are typically no eligibility requirements for early voting. In addition, early voting usually does not allow for mail voting, which can be done through absentee ballots.

The first early voting law was passed by the state of Texas in 1991. Since then, early voting laws have been adopted by Arizona, Colorado, Iowa, Nevada, and Virginia.

See also Absentee Voting; All-Mail-Ballot Elections; Election-Day Holiday; Voter Registration.
Reference Margaret Rosenfield, *Early Voting* (1994).

Economic Policy

The passage of the Employment Act of 1946 gave the president formal responsibility for producing policy to guide the nation's economy. For the first three decades after the passage of the act, the federal government's economic policies were rooted in Keynesian economic theories. In the late 1970s, however, a combination of high inflation and unemployment rates led to growing disillusionment with many Keynesian ideas. One of the most important reform efforts of the Reagan administration was its attempt to introduce the use of supply-side economics into the making of economic policy.

The cornerstone of Reagan's supply-side approach was the Economic Recovery Tax Act of 1981, which drastically cut federal taxes on corporations and the nation's wealthiest citizens. The advocates of supply-side economics argued that these tax cuts would encourage savings and investments, which in turn would lead to economic growth. Instead of economic growth, however, the nation experienced a deep recession in 1982 and unprecedented federal budget deficits. Political outrage over the deficit led the Reagan administration to put aside the principles of supply-side economics and to focus instead on bringing the deficit under control. By 1982, the nation's fiscal policies began to concentrate primarily on developing changes in the tax structure and federal spending to achieve the politically desirable goal of deficit reduction, with little attention given to broader economic concerns. Since then, the president's ability to use fiscal policy to influence the economy has been severely constrained by the public's conflicting demands on the federal government to reduce the deficit, keep taxes low, and protect popular programs.

The one aspect of federal government policy that has remained focused on the economy has been the nation's monetary policy, which is controlled by the Federal Reserve Board. This strong reliance on monetary policy to manipulate the economy, which began in 1979, represents an important change from the past. Until the late 1970s, the Federal Reserve used the money supply primarily as a means to regulate interest rates. In 1979, however, the board began to use the money supply more directly to control demand and, consequently, the nation's economy growth. The Federal Reserve introduced the use of monetarist economic policy in guiding its actions, restricting the money supply in 1979 as a means of bringing the nation's skyrocketing inflation rate under control. The board stayed with this monetarist policy until 1982, when the recession put pressure on the Federal Reserve to stimulate the economy by loosening the money supply. Since then, the federal government has relied extensively on manipulating the money supply and interest rates to achieve its economic policy goals, using a more flexible approach than it did during the monetarist experiment from 1979 to 1982.

During President Bill Clinton's first year in office, he pushed for a more active role of the federal government in the economy than had his two Republican predecessors. However, the two core aspects of his economic plan—health care reform and an economic stimulus package—were not approved by Congress. The election of a Republican majority to both houses of Congress brought renewed attention to supply-side economic principles, but with the federal budget deficit remaining a dominant political concern among voters, it appears unlikely that there will be a profound change in the direction of economic policy in the near future.

See also Budget Deficit, Federal; Economic Recovery Tax Act; Federal Reserve System; Fiscal Policy; Free Market Economy; Humphrey-Hawkins Act of 1978; Industrial Policy; Keynesian Economics; Monetary Policy; Reaganomics; Stagflation; Supply-Side Economics; Taxes.

References William A. Niskanen, *Reaganomics: An Insider's Account of the Policies and People* (1988); Howard E. Shuman, *Politics and the Budget: The Struggle between the President and the Congress* (1992); Herbert Stein, *Presidential Economics: The Making of Economic Policy from Roosevelt to Clinton* (1994).

Economic Recovery Tax Act

The Economic Recovery Tax Act of 1981 was the cornerstone of President Ronald Reagan's use of supply-side economics to stimulate economic growth in the early 1980s. The act, which included one of the largest tax cuts in U.S. history, made the tax system more regressive and helped create the massive budget deficits of the 1980s.

The Economic Recovery Tax Act grew out of support within the Reagan administration for conservative supply-side economic theory. The underlying argument in this theory is that the economy will prosper if taxes on the wealthy are reduced, because this will encourage these individuals to work harder and provide more funds for investments. The result will be strong economic growth that benefits everyone and, paradoxically, increases tax revenues.

Among its other provisions, the act slashed the individual tax rate by 23 percent, reduced taxes on the highest wage earners from 70 percent to 50 percent, lowered the capital gains tax, and all but eliminated corporate tax.

Although the act was successful in reducing the tax burden of the wealthiest members of U.S. society, it did not generate the economic growth promised by its supporters; instead, the economy suffered a severe downturn in 1981–1982.

The Economic Recovery Tax Act is also considered one of the primary causes of the growth in federal budget deficits in the 1980s. Enacted at the same time that Reagan was increasing military spending, the act helped propel the budget deficit from $78.9 million in 1981 to $127.9 million in 1982 and $208 million in 1983.

See also Budget Deficit, Federal; Capital Gains Tax; Corporate Income Tax; Laffer Curve; Progressive Tax; Reaganomics; Regressive Tax; Supply-Side Economics; Tax Reform Act.

References Donald F. Kettl, *Deficit Politics: Public Budgeting in Its Institutional and Historical Context* (1992); Howard E. Shuman, *Politics and the Budget: The Struggle between the President and the Congress* (1992).

Education

Education has long been the focus of reform efforts in the United States, but policy makers' ideas about what should be changed have shifted along with popular trends. Most educational reforms during the 1970s focused on bringing greater equity to the schools, through increased federal funding in poorer school districts, busing, and efforts to expand opportunities for minorities and people with disabilities. These efforts to increase equality of opportunity in the schools extended the federal mandates of the Elementary and Secondary Education Act of 1965.

By the mid-1980s, as students' scores on standardized tests declined and traditional notions about education were revived, reformers grew more concerned about the economic future of the country than about issues of equity. In 1983, the National Commission on Excellence in Education reported in *A Nation at Risk*: "Our once unchallenged preeminence in commerce, industry, science, and technological innovation is being overtaken by competitors around the world." Educational policy makers at the national and state levels placed greater emphasis on going "back to basics," with revised curricula emphasizing math, reading, and science. When reports showed that some classroom teachers lacked basic skills themselves, public outcries for more stringent teacher training and certification arose in many states, notably Kentucky in 1990. Some states and municipalities instituted "school choice" policies whereby parents could choose their children's schools rather than their being assigned to specific ones—the idea being that greater competition would increase the drive for excellence in all schools. Especially in cities where schools were clearly failing, many advocated the establishment of a federal voucher program that would provide government subsidies to allow parents to send their children to private schools. Finally, a few school districts, including the Los Angeles Unified School District, introduced site-based management techniques to give individual schools greater control in making policy decisions.

A Nation at Risk was a crucial topic of debate among the National Governors Association at an education summit meeting in 1989 chaired by President George Bush. Bill Clinton (then governor of Arkansas) and other governors called for sweeping national standards for education in key curricular areas. The following January, Bush unveiled plans to establish national goals for education, and by April 1991 his administration introduced "America 2000" legislation to implement voluntary national school standards and achievement tests.

In March 1994, with Clinton as president, the Goals 2000: Educate America Act was passed by Congress. The act committed the nation to eight educational goals to be achieved by the year 2000 and provided funding to communities and states that would sign up for its comprehensive educational reforms. The provisions of Goals 2000 included the establishment of various commissions to create curriculum guidelines and assessment tools to achieve greater "outcomes" from students, as well as to deal with issues of increased technology, school safety, and a more focused "school to work" curriculum.

Republican legislators disliked the idea of increased federal oversight of state education systems, and liberals criticized the heavy emphasis on vocational training and "market-driven" competition among schools and the constrictive demands of a standardized curriculum that did not address local needs. Some of the standards that were developed were deemed unworkable and politically biased, notably those for history. Still, despite continued controversy over the scope and content of Goals 2000, 46 states were participating in the effort by mid-1995.

Some interest group calls for privatization of education have been heeded. In 1992, the city of Baltimore contracted with a private company, Education Alternatives, Inc., to run nine of the city's most troubled schools. Despite promises to increase academic excellence, student scores on standardized tests did not improve, and in 1995 the city terminated the contract, ending its experiment with school privatization.

At the college and university level, the relatively free-flowing federal funding of the 1970s was stymied during the economic recessions of the 1980s. By the 1990s, state budgeting for higher education was crippled by hard times and tax-cutting reforms. Most states were forced to implement unprecedented budget cuts and to increase student fees at state universities and colleges. In some states, notably California, deep cuts in spending resulted in faculty and staff layoffs. Amid the belt-tightening, some state governments began to scrutinize faculty workloads and to direct college administrations to cut spending. Affirmative action policies that had brought greater numbers of minorities to college campuses were also criticized, and a state college education once again seemed an expensive proposition as student fees increased dramatically.

See also Affirmative Action; Bennett, William J.; Family Reinforcement Act; Privatization; Public Service Deregulation; School Finance.

References Stanley Aronowitz and Henry A. Giroux, *Education Still under Siege* (1993); Leslie A. Lawrence and Cynthia D. Prince, "The National Education Goals Panel: State and National Partnerships in Education Reform" (1994); National Commission on Excellence in Education, *A Nation at Risk: The Imperative for Educational Reform* (1983); "Struggling for Standards" (1995).

Election Administration

Growing advances in technology and problems in conducting elections have encouraged local and state governments, as well as the Federal Election Commission (FEC), to pursue changes in how elections are administered. One of the most impressive innovations is the introduction of computerized electronic systems in all aspects of election administration, including registration, signature verification, balloting, campaign finance, and general record keeping.

In addition, the FEC began investigating and developing nationwide standards in the mid-1980s for different types of voting systems. It completed its investigation and released a proposed set of standards for punch cards and electronic devices in 1990. Although states and local governments are not required to adopt these standards, they are recommended as ways to increase accountability and reliability in voting.

See also Federal Election Commission.
References Arthur Young and Company, *Computerizing Elections Administration,* Vol. 1, *Current Applications* (1985); Federal Election Commission, *Voting Systems Standards* (1990); Richard G. Smolka and Ronald D. Michaelson, "Election Legislation, 1992–93" (1994).

Election Systems

Most elected officials in the United States are chosen through the use of single-member districts, though a few are elected in multimember districts and at-large elections. None of these methods, however, produces election results that are entirely representative of the American public. Racial and ethnic minorities, voters living in districts dominated by an opposing political party, and members of minor parties often find that the winner-take-all character of these elections leaves them without representatives who reflect their viewpoints.

A number of political reformers and scholars argue that the government would be more representative if alternative types of election systems were used. Several alternative systems have been proposed, including cumulative voting, limited voting, and single-transferable vote. The mechanics of these systems differ, but the underlying argument used to justify all is that they produce election results that are more representative of the distribution of opinion and groups in society. These systems promise greater proportional representation of interests than is provided by the current system.

The unsuccessful nomination of Lani Guinier to the post of assistant attorney general for civil rights in 1993 brought attention to these alternative systems because of her advocacy of them, but few have actually been adopted by states and communities. The U.S. Supreme Court's decision in *Shaw v. Reno,* which questioned the use of racial gerrymandering to ensure minority representation, has led some advocates to see these election systems as a means to meet the requirements of the Voting Rights Act without the color-conscious remedies that are currently being used, including the creation of majority-minority districts.

See also Approval Voting; At-Large Elections; Cumulative Voting; Electoral Discrimination; Guinier, Lani; Limited Voting; Majority-Minority Districts; Multimember Districts; Proportional Representation; *Shaw v. Reno;* Single-Member Districts; Voting Rights Act.
References Bernard Grofman and Arend Lijphart, eds., *Electoral Laws and Their Political Consequences* (1986); Wilma Rule and Joseph F. Zimmerman, eds., *United States Electoral Systems: Their Impact on Women and Minorities* (1992).

Election-Day Holiday

One proposal to increase voting turnout that is often discussed among reformers but has received little serious legislative consideration is to make election day a state or national holiday. Supporters of this proposal argue that one of the major causes of poor voter turnout is that many voters cannot easily leave their jobs while the polls are open to cast their ballots. If election day were made a holiday, or if elections were moved to weekend days, voters would conceivably be better able to reach the polls, and voting turnout would rise. A variety of alternative proposals have been put forward to attain the same end that have received more serious attention, such as extending voting hours, increased use of absentee ballots, and the introduction of early voting.

See also Absentee Voting; All-Mail-Ballot Elections; Early Voting; Voter Registration.
References M. Margaret Conway, *Political Participation in the United States* (1991); Ruy A. Teixeira, *The Disappearing American Voter* (1992).

Elections

The changes in elections over the past 35 years may constitute the most impressive set of political reforms in U.S. history. In the early 1960s, African-Americans and many other minority group members were effectively denied the right to vote, presidential nominees were chosen in a closed party process, state legislative districts were drawn to favor rural areas, and campaign finance rules were all but nonexistent. The Voting Rights Act of 1965, the McGovern-Fraser Commission, *Baker v. Carr,* and the Federal Election Campaign Act transformed the electoral process and, in so doing, the American political system. Above all else, these and other recent election reforms have helped open up the political process, allowing more people to participate and making the system more democratic.

Although these changes have been applauded, many political observers note that not all the reforms were effective, and many had undesirable consequences. The process may be more open, but participation rates are at record lows. Moreover, along with the benefits, the reforms have also helped spur the rise of candidate-centered campaigns, the dominance of professional politicians, and the proliferation of political action committees. Even the Voting Rights Act, which has probably generated the most praise, has led to a profound debate on how best to ensure the representation of African-Americans and other minorities. As a result, the demand for more reforms remains present.

Of the reforms being discussed today, the most popular is the proposal to limit the number of terms elected officials can serve in given offices. Although term limits enjoy widespread public support, a variety of other reforms have also been championed in the past few years as ways to make the process more representative of the people, from campaign finance reform to motor voter laws to proportional representation. Efforts to enact term limits and motor voter laws have enjoyed some success, but the outlook for more comprehensive reform is doubtful.

See also *Baker v. Carr;* Campaign Finance; Candidate-Centered Campaigns; Election Administration; Election Systems; Electoral Discrimination; Federal Election Campaign Act; McGovern-Fraser Commission; National Voter Registration Act; Political Action Committees; Political Parties; Presidential Selection; Professional Politicians; Term Limits; Voter Registration; Voting Rights Act.

Electoral College

American voters elect a president and vice president indirectly through a unique political institution called the electoral college. Because the electoral college has the potential to produce a winner who has not received a majority of popular votes, it is frequently the focus of reform proposals.

On election day in November, voters do not technically cast their ballots for presidential candidates, but rather for slates of electors who are pledged to support particular candidates in the electoral college. All states except Maine and Nebraska use a winner-take-all method for choosing electors, so that the one slate of electors that receives the plurality of votes is elected. Maine and Nebraska elect some of their electors from congressional districts. On the first Monday after the second Wednesday of December, the electors meet in their state capitols to cast their ballots. On January 6, the House and Senate meet in joint session to count the electoral ballots and announce the election's winner.

Several criticisms have been leveled against the electoral college. One of the most persistent is that it can produce a winner who has not received a majority of the popular vote. This can occur, for example, if one candidate receives overwhelming popular support in states with few electors, but loses by a close margin in states with many electors. Because of the winner-take-all nature of choosing electors, the popular vote winner could in such a situation receive fewer electoral college votes than the other candidate.

Although this has not occurred in the twentieth century, there were three elections in the 1800s in which the popular vote winner was denied the presidency. The most recent was in 1888, when Benjamin Harrison was elected president even though he received 100,000 votes fewer than Grover Cleveland. Both Andrew Jackson in 1824 and Samuel Tilden in 1876 lost the presidency even though they had received the most votes. In addition, there have been several elections in the twentieth century in which the popular vote winner could have lost if the voting had turned out slightly differently in a handful of states, including the Kennedy-Nixon race in 1960 and the Carter-Ford campaign in 1976.

A second criticism of the electoral college is that it could create a situation in which a geographically concentrated third party could secure enough electoral votes to force the election into the House of Representatives, where the outcome would be uncertain. Another criticism is that because electors are not bound by the Constitution to vote for the candidates to whom they are pledged, they can be unfaithful and vote for whomever they please. Finally, the system is criticized for giving large and small states greater influence than others in selecting the president.

A number of different proposals have been offered to overcome these problems and improve the presidential election process. The most sweeping is the replacement of the electoral college with the direct election of the president, which reformers argue would solve all these problems at once as well as make the process more democratic. Alternative plans include retaining the college but replacing the winner-take-all system with district elections, making the distribution of electors in each state proportional to the number of votes each candidate receives, and requiring electors to vote for the candidates to whom they are pledged.

See also Presidential Selection.
References David W. Abbott and James P. Levine, *Wrong Winner: The Coming Debacle in the Electoral College* (1991); Walter Berns, ed., *After the People Vote: A Guide to the Electoral College* (1992); Lawrence D. Longley and Alan G. Braun, *The Politics of Electoral College Reform* (1972).

Electoral Discrimination

Professor Chandler Davidson of Rice University identifies three types of electoral discrimination that have been the focus of voting rights reform efforts since the 1960s: disenfranchisement, candidate diminution, and vote dilution.

Disenfranchisement takes place when legal procedures and practices are used to bar or discourage particular groups from voting. The Fifteenth Amendment ended *de jure* disenfranchisement based on race or color, but alternative means have since been used to attain this same end, including poll taxes, literacy tests, arduous registration requirements, and threats of violence.

Candidate diminution occurs when favored candidates are prevented from running, denying particular groups the right to select the candidates of their choice. Candidate diminution has been accomplished through threats of violence, unreasonable filing requirements, and the changing of elected offices to appointed ones.

Vote dilution takes place through a variety of different types of practices that reduce particular groups' voting strength, making it difficult for them to affect election outcomes. Vote dilution can occur through the gerrymandering of district lines, the replacement of single-member districts with at-large ones, the use of runoff elections, and other means.

The Voting Rights Act of 1965 was originally aimed at forcing southern states to enfranchise African-Americans. Over time, however, the act has been revised by Congress and the Supreme Court so that it now addresses these other forms of electoral discrimination as well. These changes have been made to ensure not only that members of minority groups have the right to cast their ballots, but that their votes can have meaningful effects on election outcomes.

See also At-Large Elections; Ballot Access; Election Systems; Elections; Gerrymandering; Literacy Tests; Multimember Districts; Poll Tax; Runoff Elections; Single-Member Districts; Voter Registration; Voting Rights Act.

References Chandler Davidson, ed., *Minority Vote Dilution* (1989); Bernard Grofman and Chandler Davidson, eds., *Controversies in Minority Voting: The Voting Rights Act in Perspective* (1992).

Electronic Town Meeting

A recent concept for revitalizing American politics and government is the electronic town meeting, which uses modern telecommunications equipment to bring groups of citizens together to discuss major political issues and possibly to vote directly on policy measures. There have been several electronic town meeting experiments conducted in different areas of the country. One of the most discussed was a project in Hawaii in the late 1970s that was called Televote. The term *electronic town meeting* has been attributed to Theodore Becker, who helped create the Hawaiian Televote project. Electronic town meetings are often discussed as one of several ways in which modern technology can be used to allow Americans to participate more directly in the political system; some writers have called such use of technology for political participation "teledemocracy."

See also National Initiative.

References F. Christopher Arterton, *Teledemocracy: Can Technology Protect Democracy?* (1987); Lawrence K. Grossman, *The Electronic Republic: Reshaping Democracy in the Information Age* (1995); Christa Daryl Slaton, *Televote: Expanding Citizen Participation in the Quantum Age* (1992).

Elrod v. Burns

Elrod v. Burns was the first of a series of U.S. Supreme Court cases over the past two decades that have severely restricted the use of political patronage. In this 1976 case, the Court ruled that state and local employees cannot be fired because of their party affiliations. Such action, the Court argued, violates employees' First Amendment rights. Four years later, the Court reaffirmed this decision in *Branti v. Finkel.* The Court expanded on this decision in *Rutan v. Republican Party of Illinois* in 1989, ruling that no type of government employment decision can be made on partisan grounds.

See also Merit System; Party Machines; Patronage; *Rutan v. Republican Party of Illinois.*
References Ronald N. Johnson and Gary D. Libecap, *The Federal Civil Service System and the Problem of Bureaucracy: The Economics and Politics of Institutional Change* (1994); Larry J. Sabato, *Goodbye to Good-Time Charlie: The American Governorship Transformed* (1983).

Empowerment (Bureaucratic)

One proposed type of management reform that is designed to improve the delivery of government services involves empowering midlevel managers to make more decisions on their own. Decentralizing control, advocates of such empowerment assert, promotes innovation and gives managers opportunities to contribute meaningfully to the bureaucracy's operation, which is essential for a bureaucracy to succeed. The movement to empower managers has grown increasingly popular at the state and national levels since the 1980s.

See also Budgeting Techniques; Bureaucracy; Management by Objects; Performance Budgeting; Program Budgeting; Reinventing Government; Total Quality Management.
References Peter Block, *The Empowered Manager: Positive Political Skills at Work* (1987); Donald J. Savoie, *Thatcher, Reagan, Mulroney: In Search of a New Bureaucracy* (1994).

Empowerment Zones

See Enterprise Zones.

English-Only Laws

See Official English Movement.

Enterprise Zones

Enterprise zones are urban areas that have been given reduced tax rates and other government incentives in order to attract business investments. They were proposed in the early 1980s by conservative economists as a way to encourage growth in the nation's troubled cities, but without extensive government intervention. The proposal rapidly gained popularity among city and state governments, and by 1994, more than 3,000 enterprise zones had been created nationwide. Despite their popularity, many critics argue that these zones have been ineffective in attracting business to urban areas, generating economic growth, and solving the nation's urban woes.

In 1993, President Bill Clinton built on the popularity of enterprise zones by targeting nine separate areas across the nation as "empowerment zones." Like enterprise zones, these areas were to receive tax breaks and other economic incentives. Clinton, however, also included federal assistance for housing, crime prevention, and other social programs in his proposal. Moreover, the plan not only targeted urban centers, but included three rural areas.

See also Economic Policy.
References William Fulton and Morris Newman, "The Strange Career of Enterprise Zones" (1994); Roy E. Green, *Enterprise Zones: New Directions in Economic Development* (1991); Robert Guskind, "Zeal for the Zones" (1989).

Entitlements

Government programs that provide benefits directly to individuals who meet preestablished eligibility requirements are referred to as entitlement programs. Some of the more prominent of these are Social

Security, Medicare, Medicaid, veterans' benefits, and farm price supports. Since the 1960s, entitlement programs have been the fastest-growing part of the federal budget; they represent more than 75 percent of all outlays today. The growing importance of these expenditures in expanding the budget deficit have made them a target of reform efforts, though with only limited success.

Entitlements create problems for the federal budget because the total amount of money expended in any entitlement program depends on the number of people who become eligible. The only way to reduce the costs of an entitlement program is to rewrite the laws governing eligibility requirements, which is politically difficult to accomplish. Because changes in entitlement spending require changes in law, entitlements are often referred to as a type of uncontrollable spending. To reduce spending on discretionary programs, on the other hand, Congress simply has to reduce the amount allocated within the federal budget. Members of Congress find it difficult to rewrite the laws governing entitlement programs because many of these programs enjoy widespread popular support.

In an attempt to control entitlement spending, Congress included provisions in the 1990 Budget Enforcement Act requiring that all new increases in entitlement spending be offset by decreases elsewhere. Congress has also considered, and in some cases approved, specific changes to individual entitlement programs, including tightening eligibility requirements and reducing benefits.

See also Budget Deficit, Federal; Budget Enforcement Act of 1990; Discretionary Spending; Medicaid; Medicare; Pay-as-You-Go Budgeting; Social Security; Uncontrollable Spending.

References Daniel P. Franklin, *Making Ends Meet: Congressional Budgeting in the Age of Deficits* (1993); Donald F. Kettl, *Deficit Politics: Public Budgeting in Its Institutional and Historical Context* (1992); Leroy N. Rieselbach, *Congressional Politics: The Evolving Legislative System* (1995); Howard E. Shuman, *Politics and the Budget: The Struggle between the President and the Congress* (1992).

Environmental Movement

A desire to protect and conserve the nation's vast natural resources has had a long tradition in U.S. history. In the 1960s and 1970s, however, Americans' concerns about the environment escalated, spawning what is referred to as the environmental movement. Led by a coalition of diverse interest groups, the movement pushed the federal government into taking a more active role in protecting the environment. The birth of the movement is often dated to the first Earth Day, on 22 April 1970, though some observers trace its rise to the publication of Rachel Carson's *Silent Spring* in 1962.

The environmental movement achieved its greatest success in the 1970s, as the federal government passed a broad array of new regulations on such diverse issues as clean air, endangered species, toxic substances, and strip mining. Some of the legislation associated with the movement during this period includes the Clean Air Act of 1970, the Endangered Species Act of 1973, the Toxic Substance Act of 1976, the Surface Mining Control and Reclamation Act of 1977, and the Alaskan National Interest Lands Conservation Act of 1980. Although these laws have been highly praised by environmentalist, many business leaders and conservative politicians have criticized them as placing too great a burden on business. Since the late 1970s, many of these rules and regulations have been the focus of conservative efforts to roll back the size of the federal government.

See also Deregulation; Environmental Policy; Sagebrush Rebellion.
References Charles L. Cochran and Eloise F. Malone, *Public Policy: Perspectives and Choices* (1995); Nancy Lammers, ed., *The Washington Lobby* (1982); Roderick Nash, *Wilderness and the American Mind* (1982).

Environmental Policy

Although the federal government enacted some important legislation to conserve natural resources and control pollution in the past, it played only a minor role at best in protecting the environment until the 1960s. Since then, the federal government has enacted a broad variety of laws designed to protect and improve the nation's environment. These include the Wilderness Act of 1964, the Wild and Scenic Rivers Act of 1968, the National Environmental Policy Act of 1970, the Clean Air Act of 1970, the Endangered Species Act of 1973, the Federal Land Policy and Management Act of 1976, and many more.

These laws have been highly praised by environmentalists, but not everyone supports the federal government's new role of guarding the environment. In particular, many business leaders and conservative politicians argue that the increase in environmental regulations has placed too great a burden on American business. Since the late 1970s, these probusiness forces have waged a strong campaign to obtain relief from environmental regulations and to change the federal government's land use policies. Many believed that the election of Ronald Reagan to the presidency in 1980 would bring about a profound reversal in the nation's environmental policies, as Reagan promised to reduce the environmental constraints on business. Despite his efforts to roll back environmental regulation and cut funding for environmental protection, Reagan was not as successful as many conservatives had hoped in reshaping environmental policy. Moreover, many environmental groups began to target their efforts on state governments, where the lawmakers were more receptive to environmentalists' concerns.

The election of Bill Clinton as president in 1992 led to increased optimism among environmentalists about the future of environmental laws, yet Clinton was less supportive of environmental policy in his first three years in office than many environmentalists had hoped he would be. With the election of a Republican majority to both houses of Congress in 1994, the nation's environmental policies once again appeared threatened by an alternative perspective on the proper role of government in regulating environmental concerns. Many members of this new Republican majority have been particularly adamant in advocating the greater use of cost-benefit analysis and risk assessment in setting environmental rules as a way to ensure that these rules do not place an undue burden on the economy.

See also Cost-Benefit Analysis; Deregulation; Environmental Movement; Property Rights Movement; Sagebrush Rebellion; Takings.
References Charles L. Cochran and Eloise F. Malone, *Public Policy: Perspectives and Choices* (1995); Mary H. Cooper, "Environmental Movement at 25: Will Congress Weaken Environmental Regulations?" (1995); Nancy Lammers, ed., *The Washington Lobby* (1982); Roderick Nash, *Wilderness and the American Mind* (1982).

Equal Rights Amendment

Stating, "Equality of rights under the law shall not be denied or abridged by the United States or by any state on account of sex," the proposed constitutional amendment known as the Equal Rights Amendment (ERA) failed to be enacted by its 1982 deadline after decades of debate. The effort to amend the Constitution to secure equal rights for women emerged initially in the early 1920s, but despite the work of several women's organizations, the proposal repeatedly failed to pass Congress. For some time, the ERA remained a controversial subject, even within and among feminist organizations. Many professional and well-educated women perceived the amendment to be a means of ensuring gender equality in the workforce and supported the ERA. Others, however, thought it was important to maintain special legal distinctions between the sexes to ensure legal protections for women. Some claimed the amendment was unnecessary because the Fifth and Fourteenth Amendments already protected women's rights.

In the wake of the civil rights movement, many women's organizations began to make more concerted efforts to get the ERA enacted. By 1972, the amendment managed to pass through Congress and move to state legislatures for approval. However, due to the traditional view of women that prevailed in the South, state legislatures in that area of the country blocked the amendment's passage. Although the amendment was not enacted, the struggle to see it through helped to promote women's rights and garnered support for issues of gender equality for years to come.

See also Civil Rights Movement; Constitution, U.S.; Women's Movement.
Reference Susan M. Hartmann, *From Margin to Mainstream: American Women and Politics since 1960* (1989).

Ethics

Efforts to strengthen state and federal regulations regarding government ethics have enjoyed considerable success over the past 30 years. In general, most of these reforms have come in response to specific political scandals, from the Watergate affair in the 1970s to the more recent House banking scandal, as the government has looked for ways to regain public confidence.

Some of the most important reform efforts have attempted to reduce the potential for conflicts of interest by requiring government officials to file regular financial disclosure statements; placing limits on outside income, gifts, and honoraria; and restricting post-government employment. Federal and state governments have also adopted regulations on campaign finance to reduce the influence of money in the decision-making process. Sunshine laws have been introduced to open up the political process to greater scrutiny by the press and the public, and other laws have been enacted to protect the government whistle-blowers. More recently, such political events as the nomination of Clarence Thomas to the Supreme Court and the abuses of the House bank have led to greater attention to the problems of sexual harassment, new restrictions on perquisites and gifts given to government officials, and the extension of federal workplace laws to Congress. Finally, federal and state governments have created a variety of agencies to administer these various ethics laws.

The most important federal law governing ethics is the Ethics in Government Act of 1978, which was adopted in the wake of the Watergate scandal. This act strengthened the federal government's conflict of interest rules, created a government ethics office, and established rules for the use of special prosecutors to investigate allegations of government misconduct. The Ethics Reform Act of 1989 further tightened many of these rules, and expanded their scope to include members of Congress. In addition, both the House and the Senate have specific rules governing ethics, and these have been repeatedly revised since the mid-1970s.

At the state level, one of the most comprehensive reform efforts that has taken place was the passage of the Political Reform Act of 1974 in California, which established new conflict of interest rules in the state as well as regulations on both lobbying and campaign finance.

Despite these successes, many reformers remain dissatisfied with government ethics rules, arguing that loopholes in the law allow unethical behavior to continue. Reformers continue to advocate stronger conflict of interest rules, tighter campaign finance restrictions, and additional regulation of lobbying. Support for stronger ethics laws is not universal, however. Some critics argue that many of these laws, particularly financial disclosure requirements and limitations on outside income, keep talented individuals from entering government service.

See also Abscam; Campaign Finance; Conflict of Interest Laws; Congress; Congressional Accountability Act; Ethics in Government Act; Ethics Reform Act of 1989; Federal Election Campaign Act; Hays,Wayne; Hill, Anita; House Banking Scandal; House Post Office Scandal; Independent Counsel; Inspector General Act; Keating Five; Koreagate; Lobbying; Nixon, Richard M.; Obey Commission; Political Reform Act of 1974; Revolving-Door Restrictions; Sunshine Rules; Thomas, Clarence; Watergate; Whistle-Blowing; Wright, James C., Jr.

References Thad L. Beyle, "The Executive Branch: Organization and Issues, 1992–93" (1994); Joyce Bullock, "State Lobby Laws in the 1990s" (1994); Suzanne Garment, *Scandal: The Culture of Mistrust in American Politics* (1991); Jerald A. Jacobs, ed., *Federal Lobbying* (1989); Alfred S. Neely IV, *Ethics-in-Government Laws: Are They Too 'Ethical'?* (1984); Robert N. Roberts, *White House Ethics: The History of the Politics of Conflict of Interest Regulation* (1988); Dennis F. Thompson, *Ethics in Congress: From Individual to Institutional Corruption* (1995); Robert G. Vaughn, *Conflict-of-Interest Regulation in the Federal Executive Branch* (1979).

Ethics in Government Act

Enacted in the aftermath of the Watergate scandal, the Ethics in Government Act of 1978 was designed to restrain government officials from participating in activities that would present conflicts of interest with their duty to serve the American public. The most significant aspect of the act was that it required federal officials for the first time to file comprehensive annual reports on their personal finances. The act also created stricter guidelines on how federal officials must handle their financial holdings to eliminate any potential conflicts of interest, including specifying when these holdings must be sold or put into blind trusts; established "revolving-door" restrictions on the lobbying activities of former government officials; and created the Office of Government Ethics to administer the law's various regulations.

Finally, the act created an Office of Special Prosecutor to investigate allegations of government misconduct. Until the act was passed, the Justice Department had been responsible for investigating unlawful activities by government officials. This procedure was criticized, however, because the head of the justice department (the attorney general) is a presidential appointee and often would have direct political and personal ties to those under investigation. The act now requires the attorney general to hold a brief investigation of alleged misconduct and then to hand the case over to a special prosecutor appointed by a federal court if there is evidence that misconduct occurred. When the act was revised in 1983, the term "special prosecutor" was replaced with "independent counsel."

The act has been both favored and opposed by presidential administrations. Wary of potential conflicts of interest, President Carter implemented rigid guidelines for selecting his top-level employees. His actions subsequently aided the law's passage. President Reagan, however, was critical of the act, contending that it hindered the recruitment of qualified and trustworthy officials. The Reagan administration supported a more minimal disclosure of financial statements. With Republicans in control of both the Senate and the White House, the law was amended in 1983, with several changes reflecting Reagan's concerns. The 1983 amendments decreased the number of executive branch officials to which the law applied and gave the attorney general more leeway when selecting cases to investigate. In 1987, the Democratic-controlled Congress strengthened the law by making it more difficult for an attorney general to halt the investigation of an official before an independent counsel is appointed.

See also Conflict of Interest Laws; Congress; Ethics; Independent Counsel; Lobbying; Revolving-Door Restrictions.
References Suzanne Garment, *Scandal: The Culture of Mistrust in American Politics* (1991); Jerald A. Jacobs, ed., *Federal Lobbying* (1989); Stanley I. Kutler, *The Wars of Watergate: The Last Crisis of Richard M. Nixon* (1990).

Ethics Reform Act of 1989

The Ethics Reform Act of 1989 created new ethics rules for members of Congress and the executive branch, while at the same time raising their pay by 30 percent. The act prohibited federal officials from accepting honoraria for speeches and public appearances, placed limits on outside income, restricted the value of gifts these officials can receive, broadened the revolving-door restrictions on the executive branch, and established similar revolving-door restrictions on members of Congress and their staffs. In addition, the act banned members of Congress from converting unused campaign funds into private use when they retired, beginning in 1993.

Supporters argued that the act was an important step in strengthening federal ethics rules, but critics maintained that the ethics aspect of the act was a subterfuge to allow members of Congress to raise their pay.

See also Congress; Ethics; Lobbying; Revolving-Door Restrictions.
References William T. Bianco, "Representatives and Constituents in the Postreform Congress: The Problem of Persuasion" (1992); Jerald A. Jacobs, ed., *Federal Lobbying* (1989); Christopher Madison, "Ethics as Usual?" (1989).

Executive Reorganization

See Administrative Reorganization

Extraterritorial Jurisdiction

Under the practice of extraterritorial jurisdiction, local governments are given the power to regulate activities in unincorporated areas outside their boundaries. Extraterritorial jurisdiction is seen by many reformers as a means through which cities can address the problems created by the fragmentation of government in metropolitan areas. Currently, 35 states permit cities to exercise some form of extraterritorial jurisdiction, including such activities as zoning and other forms of subdivision regulation.

See also Metropolitan Fragmentation; Regional Government.
References Terry Christensen, *Local Politics: Governing at the Grassroots* (1995); Thomas R. Dye, *Politics in States and Communities* (1994); John J. Harrigan, *Political Change in the Metropolis* (1993); David B. Walker, *The Rebirth of Federalism: Slouching toward Washington* (1995).

F

Fair Tax

In 1982, Senator Bill Bradley of New Jersey and Representative Richard Gephardt of Missouri called for the elimination of numerous tax loopholes and a reduction in the number of tax brackets through a proposal called the Fair Tax bill. Although the bill to establish this relatively flat tax was defeated, it is considered an important forerunner to the Tax Reform Act of 1986. The Fair Tax is often referred to as the Bradley-Gephardt plan.

See also FAST; Flat Tax; Tax Reform Act.
References Timothy J. Conlan et al., *Taxing Choices: The Politics of Tax Reform* (1990); Howard E. Shuman, *Politics and the Budget: The Struggle between the President and the Congress* (1992).

Fairness Commission

The Democratic Party created the Fairness Commission in 1984 to consider reforms for the 1986 Democratic Party National Convention. The commission generally followed the same proposals put forward by the Hunt Commission four years earlier, but it increased the number of superdelegates to the convention to 650. The Fairness Commission's reforms were adopted by the Democratic National Committee in 1986.

See also Hughes Commission; Hunt Commission; McGovern-Fraser Commission; Mikulski Commission; National Primary; Presidential Primaries; Winograd Commission.
Reference William J. Keefe, *Parties, Politics, and Public Policy in America* (1994).

Family Reinforcement Act

The Family Reinforcement Act was one of the ten proposals set forth in the Republican Party's Contract with America. It called for a new federal effort to enforce child support payments, the creation of tax benefits to encourage adoption and to help individuals who care for elderly family members, and the strengthening of child pornography laws. The act also called for the use of vouchers in the nation's education system. Legislation creating adoption tax benefits and strengthening child pornography laws had passed both houses of Congress by December of 1995.

See also Contract with America; Education.
References "Child Pornography Bill Heads Back to House" (1995); George Hager, "Harsh Rhetoric on Budget Spells a Dismal Outlook" (1995); "Republicans' Initial Promise: 100-Day Debate on 'Contract'" (1994); Clyde Wilcox, *The Latest American Revolution? The 1994 Elections and Their Implication for Governance* (1995).

FAST

Representative Jack Kemp of New York and Senator Robert Kasten of Wisconsin proposed a tax reform in 1984 that was very similar to the Fair Tax reform proposal considered by Congress two years earlier, but it was more conservative in tone. As with the Fair Tax proposal, Kemp and Kasten's plan, which was called FAST (Fair and Simple Tax), sought to eliminate tax loopholes and reduce the number of tax brackets. The tax rate for the highest income earners and for corporations was much lower under the FAST proposal, however. In addition, the FAST proposal retained more tax exemptions and deductions. Although the bill was not enacted into law, it is considered an important forerunner of the Tax Reform Act of 1986. The FAST proposal is often referred to as the Kemp-Kasten plan.

See also Fair Tax; Flat Tax; Tax Reform Act.
References Timothy J. Conlan et al., *Taxing Choices: The Politics of Tax Reform* (1990); Howard E. Shuman, *Politics and the Budget: The Struggle between the President and the Congress* (1992).

Federal Election Campaign Act

The 1971 Federal Election Campaign Act (FECA), along with its later revisions, is considered the nation's most important legislation governing campaign finance in federal elections. Passed in response to spiraling campaign costs and the growing size of individual contributions, FECA was initially designed to improve campaign finance disclosure and restrict the amounts of money spent on media advertising. The act was substantially revised in 1974 in the wake of Watergate and other scandals, and the revisions placed limits on campaign contributions and expenditures, created a federal agency to enforce the act, and provided for public funding of presidential elections. Additional amendments were adopted in 1976 and 1979.

As originally enacted, FECA required candidates in federal campaigns who received more than $1,000 in contributions to file regular campaign disclosure statements reporting all expenditures over $100 and the sources of all contributions over $100. The act restricted the amount of money that could be contributed by candidates and their families to the candidates' own campaigns. It also established a formula that limited the total amount candidates could spend on media advertising. Finally, the act established rules governing political action committees and, in so doing, gave legal recognition to these groups.

In 1974, Congress adopted sweeping changes to FECA to try to control campaign finance further. Two of the primary reforms were restrictions on campaign contributions and expenditures. The act limited contributions from individuals to $1,000 and from political action committees and parties to $5,000. These limits were per candidate per election. The act also placed a ceiling on the amount that individuals could contribute to federal campaigns each year. As for expenditures, the act established specific limits on the total amount that individual candidates could spend in primary and general elections. It also limited what individuals or groups could spend independently to help a candidate get elected, as well as the amount that party committees could spend on behalf of a candidate through coordinated spending.

In addition to establishing these limits, the 1974 amendments strengthened FECA's campaign disclosure requirements, created the Federal Election Commission to administer the act, and removed the spending limits on media advertising. Finally, the amendments provided for the partial public funding of presidential primary campaigns and full public funding for general election campaigns. The money for the presidential campaigns was to come from a voluntary tax checkoff plan established in the Revenue Act of 1971. Congress also considered including public financing of congressional campaigns in the act, but this was rejected by the House.

Shortly after the passage of the 1974 amendments, a broad coalition of liberals and conservatives, including Senator James Buckley of New York, joined together to challenge the law's constitutionality. In *Buckley v. Valeo,* the U.S. Supreme Court struck down the act's assorted limitations on campaign expenditures, arguing that they violated the First Amendment right to free speech. The Court also struck down the Federal Election Commission, ruling that the law's provision for allowing Congress to appoint members violated the Constitution's separation of powers.

In response to the Court's decision, Congress revised FECA again in 1976, reconstituting the Federal Election Commission and making a number of minor changes. These changes included the establishment of a $5,000 limit on the amount that individuals can contribute to political action committees, as well as a $25,000 limit on contributions to political parties. The amendments also further strengthened reporting requirements and established new rules regarding PAC fund-raising.

In 1979, Congress made a few more alterations in the act. Most of these were fairly minor and concerned reducing the paperwork requirements of filing campaign disclosure reports. One addition was quite important, however, and that was a change in the law to allow state and local parties to spend unlimited amounts of money in party-building activities, including voter registration and get-out-the-vote drives. This change has spurred the growth of what is called soft money, or the channeling of unregulated campaign funds from individuals, businesses, political action committees, and other groups to state and local party organizations.

Although FECA is considered the nation's most important legislation governing campaign finance, reformers argue that it has failed to solve the problems in campaign financing and that many aspects of act itself were flawed. The one element of the act that has received the most praise is the disclosure requirements, which have allowed closer public scrutiny of campaign financing. Reformers criticize FECA for making PACs major players in election campaigns, and for its loopholes, which have allowed the spread of soft money, bundling, and other techniques that are used to circumvent the law's intent.

See also *Buckley v. Valeo;* Bundling; Campaign Finance; Contribution Limits; Coordinated Spending; Federal Election Commission; Political Action Committees; Political Parties; Revenue Act of 1971; Soft Money; Spending Limits; Sun-PAC Decision; Watergate.

References Herbert E. Alexander, *Financing Politics: Money, Elections, and Political Reform* (1992); *Congressional Campaign Finances: History, Facts, and Controversy* (1992); Jamin B. Raskin and John Bonifaz, *The Wealth Primary: Campaign Fundraising and the Constitution* (1994); Frank J. Sorauf, *Money in American Elections* (1988).

Federal Election Commission

Originally created by the 1974 amendments to the Federal Election Campaign Act (FECA), the six-member Federal Election Commission (FEC) is responsible for administering federal election laws. The commission was declared unconstitutional in 1976 when the U.S. Supreme Court ruled that the commission's selection process, which allowed Congress to appoint two-thirds of the members, violated the Constitution's separation of powers. The commission was reconstituted in 1976, giving the president the power to appoint all members with Senate confirmation.

Since its creation, the FEC has been the focus of considerable criticism. Most observers praise the commission's record-keeping activities, but many are critical of its work in regulating campaign finance. Three of the primary criticisms of the commission are that it is underfunded, that it is too slow in conducting investigations, and that it is too constrained by its close ties to Congress to exercise adequate enforcement of campaign finance laws. Reformers argue that the commission would do a better job in regulating campaign finance with a larger budget, more streamlined rules, a more effective structure, and greater independence from Congress.

See also Campaign Finance; Federal Election Campaign Act.
References *Congressional Campaign Finances: History, Facts, and Controversy* (1992); Brooks Jackson, *Broken Promise: Why the Federal Election Commission Failed* (1990); Frank J. Sorauf, *Money in American Elections* (1988).

Federal Employees Political Activities Act

Under the Hatch Act of 1939, federal employees were barred from participating in a variety of political activities, including making campaign contributions, working on campaigns, and running for partisan office. The Federal Employees Political Activities Act of 1993 liberalized many of these restrictions, allowing federal workers to participate more fully in campaigns and elections. However, federal workers are still barred from running in partisan elections and from soliciting contributions from their underlings.

See also Campaign Finance.
Reference Ronald N. Johnson and Gary D. Libecap, *The Federal Civil Service System and the Problem of Bureaucracy: The Economics and Politics of Institutional Change* (1994).

Federal Judicial Center

The Federal Judicial Center is an independent federal office created in 1967 to conduct research on the federal judiciary and to propose reforms to improve the courts' operations and administration. The center also conducts training programs for judicial personnel.

See also Courts; Institute for Court Management; National Center for State Courts.
References Henry J. Abraham, *The Judicial Process: An Introductory Analysis of the Courts of the United States, England, and France.* (1993); Robert A. Carp and Ronald Stidham, *Judicial Process in America* (1993).

Federal Magistrates Act

The 1968 Federal Magistrates Act established the Office of U.S. Magistrate to help reduce the caseload confronting federal trial courts. Amended in 1976 and 1979, the act empowers individual federal magistrates to handle some pretrial activities, to recommend motions to the court, and, in some circumstances, to try civil court cases and misdemeanors. The name of the magistrate position was changed to U.S. magistrate judge in 1990. There are more than 450 magistrate judges in the United States today.

See also Caseload; Courts.
References Henry J. Abraham, *The Judicial Process: An Introductory Analysis of the Courts of the United States, England, and France.* (1993); Robert A. Carp and Ronald Stidham, *Judicial Process in America* (1993).

Federal Reserve System

The Federal Reserve System is the federal body that serves as the nation's bank. It consists of 12 regional Federal Reserve

Banks, a Board of Governors, and the Federal Open Market Committee (FOMC).

The Board of Governors and the FOMC are technically the central decision-making bodies for the system, but the chairman of the Board of Governor wields considerable influence over the board's decisions. The Federal Reserve System controls the nation's money supply, interest rates, and credit. Its control over these policy matters makes it one of the most powerful bodies in the world, and its independent position in the nation's political system makes it a frequent target of reform.

Reformers argue that the system needs to be put under greater control of either Congress or the president and made more responsive to public expectations. As it is now, the only way either branch of government can dictate decisions to the Federal Reserve is if Congress enacts legislation doing so. Thus the Federal Reserve has considerable freedom to shape monetary policy however it wants, regardless of public opinion or the desires of the nation's elected officials. This situation has caused some reformers to argue that the Federal Reserve's independent status should be removed, and that it should be made into an administrative agency that is directly answerable to the president. Opponents of this reform argue that the Federal Reserve's independence allows it to focus on longer-term economic considerations than would be possible if it were directly answerable to the president.

During the 1970s, Congress enacted some minor reforms requiring the Federal Reserve to report policy goals to Congress on a regular basis as a means to make the Reserve more responsive to congressional concerns, though this was a far cry from removing its independent status. Finally, some reformers argue that some of the Federal Reserve's more bureaucratic activities should be given to other agencies, so that the Reserve can focus solely on monetary matters.

See also Economic Policy; Monetary Policy.
References Paul A. Samuelson and William D. Nordhaus, *Economics* (1992); Herbert Stein, *Presidential Economics: The Making of Economic Policy from Roosevelt to Clinton* (1994).

Federalism

See Federal-State Relations.

Federal-State Relations

The relationship between the national government and the states has been the focus of considerable reform efforts over the past 30 years, as advocates of a strong national government have fought with those who support the states to determine how the nation's federal system of government will be shaped. In the 1960s, the federal government emerged as a much more dominant player in American politics than ever before. Since then, conservative reformers have continuously advocated a greater role for the states, yet despite their efforts, the federal government remains the dominant figure in this relationship.

The relationship between the federal government and the states from the 1930s to the 1960s has often been referred to as cooperative federalism, because both levels of governments worked together jointly to solve the nation's problems. The first major effort to alter this relationship occurred in the 1960s, when President Lyndon Johnson introduced a variety of new federal programs to give the federal government a more direct role in dealing with societal problems. These programs, which were labeled Creative Federalism, called for the federal government to work more closely with local governments, bypassing the states. The heart of Johnson's efforts was the creation of more than 200 new federal grants that were made available to states, local governments, and nonprofit groups to address specific social programs. These grants-in-aid came with considerable strings attached to ensure that they were used in accordance with the federal government's expectations.

The election of Richard M. Nixon to the presidency in 1968 brought a new wave of reform. Opposed to the centralization of power that developed under Johnson's Creative Federalism, Nixon advocated a program he called New Federalism, which was designed to strengthen the position of the states. The centerpiece of New Federalism was an increase in the flow of federal money to the states with fewer strings attached. This money was to be made available through general revenue sharing and the increased use of block grants. Although these reforms helped strengthen the states' position, Nixon also oversaw a profound expansion in the federal regulation of state and local governments. Thus, by the time he left office, the states continued to find themselves playing a secondary role to the federal government.

In the early 1980s, President Ronald Reagan talked again about strengthening the position of the states and introduced his own version of New Federalism. Unlike Nixon, however, Reagan also attempted to reduce the flow of federal money to the states, which meant that if the states wanted to address a particular social problem they would have to find the money themselves. Many political scientists argue that Reagan was less concerned with devolving power to the states than he was with simply reducing the role of government in U.S. society.

As during the Nixon administration, the changes during the 1980s in federal-state relations were mixed. On the one hand, Reagan's cutbacks in domestic spending and the continued presence of large budget deficits led to some decline in the federal government's domestic activities. Also, increased activism on the part of the states themselves and the professionalization of state government institutions allowed the states to emerge as much more important players than they were in the 1960s and 1970s. On the other hand, several trends have helped ensure the continued strong presence of the federal government in dominating federal-state relations. In particular, Congress began to rely more extensively on the use of mandates and preemptions in the mid- to late 1980s to force state governments to address specific social problems. In addition, federal regulations continued to expand in the mid-1980s after a brief slowdown during the first few years of the Reagan administration.

Since Reagan left office, neither of his successors nor Congress has taken serious steps to alter the relationship between the two levels of government. The success of the Republican Party in the 1994 congressional elections, however, suggests that this relationship is likely to become a major focus of reform efforts once again. Many of the members of the new Republican majority in both houses are strong advocates of a devolution of power to the states. This support for devolution was embedded in parts of the Republican Party's Contract with America in 1994, which, among other recommendations, proposed turning over most welfare programs to state control. As of late 1995, however, few changes had been made. The one exception is that Congress and the president agreed in 1995 to a bill that would try to limit unfunded federal mandates.

The U.S. Supreme Court has also played a significant role in redefining federal-state relations over the past 30 years. During Earl Warren's tenure as chief justice in the 1960s, the Court took an active role in forcing state and local governments to adhere to the Constitution's principles of liberty and equality. At the same time, the Court upheld the federal government's growing intrusion into state and local affairs. Under Warren Burger's leadership, however, the Court slowly began to adopt a more conservative stance on issues of civil rights and civil liberties, which led to less Court intervention in state policy matters. The Court's most important action, however, was its ruling in *National League of Cities v. Usery* (1976). In this case, the court ruled that the federal government did not have the power to force state and city governments to abide by federal minimum wage laws. In making this decision, the Court indicated a willingness to draw a line on the federal government's involvement in state and local matters.

The *National League of Cities* decision did not survive for long, however. In 1985, the Supreme Court overturned the decision in *Garcia v. San Antonio Metropolitan Transit Authority* (1985) and, in so doing, profoundly strengthened the federal government's position. In the *Garcia* case, the Court ruled that the Constitution does not set a specific limit on the national government's power to become involved in traditional state government functions, and that if states are dissatisfied with the federal government's actions they should seek redress from Congress, and not the courts. The Court's decision has generated considerable criticism from supporters of states' rights, who argue that it ignored the reserved powers clause of the Tenth Amendment and dramatically reduced state government power.

Whether the *Garcia* decision will stand is uncertain, though the Supreme Court under Chief Justice William H. Rehnquist has shown signs that it is willing to reassert some constitutional protection for the states. In *Gregory v. Ashcroft* (1991), for instance, the Court ruled that the Tenth Amendment can protect state laws governing the formation of state governments. In *United States v. Lopez* (1995), the Court took steps to restrict the federal government's use of the commerce clause to supersede state authority, throwing out a federal law that had banned the possession of firearms near public schools. In *Seminole Tribe of Florida v. Florida* (1996), the Court ruled that Congress did not have the power to authorize private lawsuits against state governments, citing the Eleventh Amendment.

In addition to these challenges to the federal government's dominance of the states, the Court in recent years has continued to play a lesser role in championing civil rights and liberties than did the Warren Court. In so doing, the Supreme Court has demonstrated some willingness to protect the authority of state governments. These actions have been limited, however, and in general the Court has continued to reassert the federal government's power over state governments.

Although these trends in federal-state relations have allowed the federal government to emerge as the dominant force, the federal government has not become involved in all elements of state and local policy making. Many types of policy matters remain almost entirely controlled by state and local governments, including education, criminal justice, and the delivery of most public services. Moreover, even in the areas where the federal government plays an active role, state governments are often able to exercise considerable influence of their own, either because of flexibility in the federal government's demands or through the states' innovative efforts in creating separate programs that go beyond what the federal government dictates.

See also Budget Deficit, Federal; Coercive Federalism; Creative Federalism; Devolution; *Garcia v. San Antonio Metropolitan Transit Authority;* Johnson, Lyndon B.; Mandates, Federal; *National League of Cities v. Usery;* New Federalism; New Judicial Federalism; Nixon, Richard M.; Preemption; Reagan, Ronald W.; *Seminole Tribe of Florida v. Florida;* Sorting Out; *United States. v. Lopez.*

References Timothy J. Conlan, *New Federalism: Intergovernmental Reform from Nixon to Reagan* (1988); Martha Fabricus, "More Dictates from the Feds" (1991); Laurence J. O'Toole, Jr., *American Intergovernmental Relations* (1993); Michael A. Pagano and Ann O'M. Bowman, "The State of American Federalism, 1994–1995" (1995); David B. Walker, *The Rebirth of Federalism: Slouching toward Washington* (1995); Christopher Zimmerman, "A Devolution Revolution?" (1995).

Ferraro, Geraldine (b. 1935)

Geraldine Ferraro was the first woman to be nominated for the vice presidency by one of the nation's major political parties. Ferraro was chosen at the 1984 Democratic Party's national convention to be Walter Mondale's running mate in his efforts to unseat President Ronald Reagan. At the time of the nomination, Ferraro was a member of the U.S. House of Representatives representing Queens, New York. Prior to that she had been a practicing attorney, and then worked in the New York District Attorney's Office. Many political scientists argue that Ferraro's presence on the ballot had little effect on the election outcome, though her nomination has been credited with improving the opportunities for women candidates.

See also Women's Movement.

References Michael Barone and Grant Ujifusa, *The Almanac of American Politics 1984* (1983); Michael Nelson, ed., *The Elections of 1984* (1985).

Filibuster

The filibuster is a practice in which a U.S. senator (or senators) speaks indefinitely on the Senate floor to force a compromise on or the defeat of pending legislation. The filibuster is defended as a mechanism to protect minority rights, but its increased use in the past few decades has led to calls for reform. Most reform efforts have focused on the rules governing cloture, which is the procedure for ending debate. In 1975, the Senate reduced the threshold of votes needed to invoke cloture from two-thirds of those present and voting to three-fifths of the entire Senate membership. The Senate also placed stricter limits on the amount of debate allowed after cloture has been approved. Despite these changes, many senators remain dissatisfied with the rules governing filibusters and have called for additional reforms. These include reducing the threshold for invoking cloture to a simple majority and further limiting the amount of time for postcloture debate.

See also Congress.

References Roger H. Davidson and Walter J. Oleszek, *Congress and Its Members* (1994); William J. Keefe and Morris S. Ogul, *The American Legislative Process: Congress and the States* (1993); Steven S. Smith, *Call to Order: Floor Politics in the House and the Senate* (1989).

Finance, Local

Like state and federal governments, local governments across the United States have experienced severe financial problems during the past two decades. These problems have forced local governments to make important reforms in the services they offer and to look for alternative sources of revenue.

Several different factors have contributed to the financial problems confronting local governments. One of the first was the property tax revolt that began with the passage of California's Proposition 13 in 1978. The revolt led more than 40 states to adopt limitations on property taxes or to enact property tax relief plans over the following few years and put pressure on government officials to reduce other forms of taxation as well. Because property taxes have historically been the primary source of funds for local governments, the tax revolt put considerable stress on local government finances.

The decline in revenue brought on by the tax revolt was compounded in the 1980s by a slowdown in the flow of federal aid to local governments during the Reagan administration. From 1980 to 1987, numerous federal grants-in-aid programs were scaled back, and others were eliminated entirely. This cutback in federal grants placed particular stress on many of the nation's largest cities, reducing the proportion of funds provided by the federal government in many city budgets by more than half. Conversely, the end of revenue sharing in 1986 is seen as having been particularly harmful to small cities and rural towns, because many of these governments relied extensively on federal money to fund their programs.

Finally, demographic changes have also led to revenue problems in many cities, as businesses have moved from the central cities to the suburbs and from the Snowbelt to the Sunbelt, causing reductions in many cities' tax bases.

At the same time that local governments have been confronted by these reductions in revenue, they have been met by growing demands for services. Many of these demands have come from local residents who have grown increasingly disturbed by crime, deteriorating schools, traffic problems, and environmental concerns. In addition, federal and state mandates have placed increased burdens on local governments to provide services without providing the funds for them to do so.

These trends have led to severe financial problems among the nation's cities, counties, and other local governments as they try to provide increased services with fewer resources. In order to overcome these problems, many local governments have been forced to turn to alternative sources of revenue to bring in funds, the most popular of which have been user fees and increased sales taxes. In addition, some state governments have begun to channel more funds to local governments to compensate for reductions in other revenues.

Financial problems have also forced local governments to reexamine the services they provide, causing many to cut programs, downsize their operations, and turn to the private sector to provide many of their functions. Moreover, in some severe instances of fiscal stress, state governments have been forced to assume entirely the responsibilities of some local governments.

See also Alternative Service Delivery; Budget Deficit, Federal; Categorical Grants; Contracting for Services; Contracting Out; Downsizing; Federal-State Relations; Finance, State; Mandates, State; New Federalism; Privatization; Property Tax; Proposition 13; Sales Tax; Service Taxes; Tax Revolt; User Fees.
References David R. Berman, "Takeovers of Local Governments: An Overview and Evaluation of State Policies" (1995); Terry Christensen, *Local Politics: Governing at the Grassroots* (1995); Richard L. Cole et al., "American Cities and the 1980s: The Legacy of the Reagan Years" (1994); Werner Z. Hirsch and Anthony M. Rufolo, *Public Finance and Expenditure in a Federal System* (1990); W. John Moore, "Cutoff at Town Hall" (1987); David O. Sears and Jack Citrin, *Tax Revolt: Something for Nothing in California* (1985).

Finance, State

State governments have experienced considerable change in their fiscal position over the past 30 years, causing them to make important reforms in the services they provide and in their tax policies.

The nation's strong economic growth and the increased flow of federal funds to the states during the 1960s and 1970s meant that most states maintained a healthy financial position throughout this period. In the late 1970s, however, state governments began to confront budgeting problems as the nationwide taxpayers' revolt made it increasingly difficult for states to raise taxes. In some cases, moreover, the tax revolt actually led to declines in state tax revenue. States found themselves with new problems in the early 1980s as a recession battered state finances, forcing many to reduce services and lay off employees. The recession was then followed by a reduction in the flow of federal funds, as the Reagan administration ended general revenue sharing and cut back on other forms of federal aid.

Despite these trends, most states rebounded after the recession in the early 1980s and were able to maintain their fiscal health throughout the decade by expanding their own revenue bases. The economic downturn of the early 1990s, however, put renewed financial stress on state governments, forcing welfare program costs to soar and tax revenue to decline. The fiscal stress was compounded by the federal government's increased use of unfunded mandates in the late 1980s that required states to provide additional services but without providing any federal funds.

The fiscal stress forced many states to cut back drastically on their activities, raise tax rates, and look for new forms of taxation, including state lotteries, other forms of gambling, and service taxes. The stress also caused many states to force local governments to take over some traditional state programs but without providing state funds to help them.

With the end of the recession in 1992, the fiscal position of state governments began to improve. By 1995, state finances had improved enough that for the first time in ten years there was a net reduction in state taxes. Despite these recent gains, financial concerns continue to dominate much of the political debate in state government, especially as federal officials ponder ways to reduce the federal budget deficit and return more responsibilities to the states. These concerns have caused state leaders to push for an end to unfunded mandates and to continue to look for alternative revenue sources.

See also Budget Deficit, Federal; Common Shared Tax; Creative Federalism; Crime; Federal-State Relations; Finance, Local; Gambling; General Revenue Sharing; Lotteries; Mandates, Federal; Mandates, State; Medicaid; New Federalism; Proposition 13; Sales Tax; Service Tax; Sorting Out; Tax Revolt; Taxes.

References "Fiscally Speaking, a Very Good Year" (1995); Steven D. Gold, *The Fiscal Crisis of the States: Lessons for the Future* (1995); Henry J. Raimondo, "State Budgeting in the Nineties" (1993); Alice M. Rivlin, *Reviving the American Dream: The Economy, the States, and the Federal Government* (1992); David B. Walker, *The Rebirth of Federalism: Slouching toward Washington* (1995).

Financial Institutions Reform, Recovery, and Enforcement Act

The Financial Institutions Reform, Recovery, and Enforcement Act was adopted in 1989 to help the federal government gain control over the savings and loan crisis that had plagued the nation since the early to mid-1980s. The act set aside funds to help dispose of some 700 ailing savings institutions, abolished the Federal Home Loan Bank Board and the Federal Savings and Loan Insurance Corporation, created a new agency to handle the bailout (the Resolution Trust Corporation), and instituted new regulations on savings practices. The law brought to a close the federal government's deregulation of the savings industry.

See also Depository Institutions Deregulation and Monetary Control Act; Deregulation; Garn-St. Germaine Depository Institutions Act; Savings and Loan Crisis.

References Anthony S. Campagna, *The Economy in the Reagan Years: The Economic Consequences of the Reagan Administrations* (1994); Robert E. Litan, "Financial Regulation" (1994); William A. Niskanen, *Reaganomics: An Insider's Account of the Policies and People* (1988); Bruce C. Wolpe, *Lobbying Congress: How the System Works* (1990).

Fine-Tuning

The practice of making minor adjustments in fiscal policy to try to reduce unemployment and promote economic stability is often referred to as fine-tuning. This practice was originally associated with the Kennedy and Johnson administrations, though fine-tuning was still used into the 1970s. In the late 1970s, this type of Keynesian economic approach lost favor as the economy became stymied by stagflation and conservative economic theories grew in popularity.

See also Economic Policy; Fiscal Policy; Keynesian Economics; Supply-Side Economics.

Reference Herbert Stein, *Presidential Economics: The Making of Economic Policy from Roosevelt to Clinton* (1994).

Fiscal Policy

The federal government's use of taxes and expenditures to influence the overall health of the nation's economy is referred to as its fiscal policy. Since the federal government began to play a more active role in the economy during the Great Depression, the nation's fiscal policies have been shaped primarily by Keynesian economic theories. The core principle of these theories is that when the economy is in a recession, the federal government should increase spending and reduce taxes to stimulate demand and, consequently, economic growth. Conversely, when the economy is experiencing inflation, the government should reduce spending and increase taxes to reduce demand.

During the late 1970s, the U.S. economy experienced a combination of both economic stagnation and inflation, which led to disillusionment with many Keynesian ideas. After Ronald Reagan was elected president in 1980, he attempted to use supply-side economics to guide the nation's fiscal policy. The supply-siders argued that reducing business and income taxes, particularly for the wealthy, would encourage people to work harder and provide more funds for investments. The result would be economic growth.

The cornerstone of the supply-side effort was the Economic Recovery Tax Act of 1981, which drastically cut federal taxes for corporations and the nation's wealthiest citizens. Instead of economic growth, however, the nation experienced a recession in 1982 and unprecedented federal budget deficits. Political outrage over the deficit forced the president to abandon the supply-side theories and turn his attention to deficit reduction. Since then, the federal government has been restrained in its ability to use fiscal policy to shape the economy because of the pressure to balance the budget.

See also Budget Deficit, Federal; Economic Policy; Economic Recovery Tax Act; Keynesian Economics; Supply-Side Economics; Taxes.

References Howard E. Shuman, *Politics and the Budget: The Struggle between the President and the Congress* (1992); Herbert Stein, *Presidential Economics:*

The Making of Economic Policy from Roosevelt to Clinton (1994).

Fiscal Responsibility Act

The first of ten proposals in the Republican Party's Contract with America, the Fiscal Responsibility Act called for the passage of a balanced budget amendment and the presidential line-item veto. The balanced budget amendment was voted down in the Senate in 1995, and then again in 1996 when it was put to a second vote. The line-item veto was signed into law in April 1996, though many scholars believe it will be declared unconstitutional.

See also Balanced Budget Amendment; Contract with America; Line-Item Veto.
References David S. Cloud, "GOP's Balancing Act Gets Tricky as Budget Amendment Sinks" (1995); "Republicans' Initial Promise: 100-Day Debate on 'Contract'" (1994); Andrew Taylor, "Congress Hands President a Budgetary Scalpel" (1996); Clyde Wilcox, *The Latest American Revolution? The 1994 Elections and Their Implication for Governance* (1995).

Flat Tax

The flat tax is a type of government levy in which, in theory, the same tax rate is applied to all income levels, though most specific proposals include provisions allowing the poor to forgo paying any taxes. Most flat tax proposals also call for ending or reducing most tax deductions and exemptions.

The flat tax is championed by many conservative reformers as a fairer form of taxation than is currently in place because it applies a uniform rate that treats all taxpayers the same and closes egregious tax loopholes. Moreover, the flat tax would reduce the tax burden on the wealthy, which could make more money available for investments. Opponents argue that the flat tax is not as fair as a progressive tax because low-wage earners have less ability to pay than do high-wage earners. In addition, if the flat tax were introduced today, it would cause an increase in the amount of taxes paid by members of the middle class.

During the 1980s, several tax reform proposals were debated in Congress that were designed to make the tax rates more flat, including Senator Bill Bradley's Fair Tax in 1982 and Senator Jack Kemp's FAST plan two years later. Although neither of these was enacted into law, the nation's tax system did move a little closer to a flat tax when Congress passed the Tax Reform Act of 1986, which reduced the number of tax brackets from 15 to 3 and closed many important tax loopholes.

Interest in a flat tax remained strong in the early and mid-1990s. Former California Governor Jerry Brown championed the flat tax proposal as part of his 1992 bid for the Democratic Party's presidential nomination, as did publishing heir Steve Forbes in his campaign for the Republican nomination four years later. In addition, several of the leaders of the new Republican majority in Congress in 1995 were strong advocates of a flat tax, including House Majority Leader Richard Armey.

See also Brown, Edmund "Jerry" Gerald, Jr.; Fair Tax; FAST; Kemp, Jack R.; Progressive Tax; Proportional Tax; Regressive Tax; Tax Reform Act; Taxes.
References Timothy J. Conlan et al., *Taxing Choices: The Politics of Tax Reform* (1990); Joseph J. Minarik, *Making Tax Choices* (1985); Christopher Zimmerman, "Flat Tax, Sales Tax, or VAT?" (1995).

Ford, Gerald R. (b. 1913) (38th U.S. President, 1974–1977)

Taking office in the shadow of Watergate, President Gerald Ford spent little more than two years in office, and hence had little time to institute reforms, though he is credited with trying to reduce the office's regal trappings after the excesses of the Nixon administration. Ford was the first nonelected president in U.S. history, reaching office under the provisions of the Presidential Succession Act and the Twenty-fifth Amendment. Ford was appointed vice president by Congress in 1973 after the resignation of Spiro Agnew, and when President Nixon resigned in 1974, Ford became president. Ford's most noteworthy action was his decision to pardon Nixon for all crimes related to Watergate, a move that helped lead to his defeat when he ran for election two years later and to further public disillusionment with government.

See also Nixon, Richard M.; Twenty-fifth Amendment; Watergate.

References George C. Edwards III and Stephen J. Wayne, *Presidential Leadership: Politics and Policy Making* (1990); Sidney M. Milkis and Michael Nelson, *The American Presidency: Origins and Development, 1776–1993* (1994); Bruce Miroff et al., *The Democratic Debate: An Introduction to American Politics* (1995).

Foreign Policy

The cornerstone of U.S. foreign policy from the 1940s to the end of the 1980s was the determination to prevent the territorial expansion of communist countries, especially the Soviet Union. This emphasis on containment, as the policy is known, compelled the United States to help rebuild Western Europe through the Marshall Plan in the late 1940s, to commit troops to North Korea in the 1950s and Vietnam in the 1960s, and to provide support to noncommunist countries throughout the period.

The war in Vietnam led many Americans and foreign policy experts to question the wisdom of the nation's containment policy. Although containment remained of importance for two more decades, President Richard Nixon began to broaden U.S. foreign policy in the 1970s, as he attempted to build more cordial relations with communist nations through a policy called détente. Nixon's efforts led to the formal recognition of Eastern Europe's boundaries through the Helsinki Accords, the signing of the first arms limitation agreement with the Soviet Union (SALT I), and the start of relations with the People's Republic of China. In the late 1970s, President Jimmy Carter also brought a concern for human rights into U.S. foreign policy; he criticized other nations, both friends and foes of the United States, for any inhumane treatment of their citizens. Calling the Soviet Union an "evil empire" and pressing for massive increases in defense spending, President Ronald Reagan initially attempted to focus U.S. foreign policy once again on the perceived Soviet threat. Later in his administration, however, Reagan's rhetoric became less harsh and he began to work with Soviet President Mikhail Gorbachev.

Since the collapse of the Soviet Union in the late 1980s and early 1990s, containment has no longer been as relevant in defining U.S. foreign policy. As a result, the direction of foreign policy has become the focus of considerable political debate. The unpopularity of the war in Vietnam has made the government reluctant to commit American troops abroad, yet some foreign policy experts and political leaders argue that the United States must continue to play a leading role in world affairs. Others argue, however, that the world has become too complex, nations too interdependent, and America's economy too weak for the United States to continue to dominate world politics as it once did. Instead, it must work jointly with other nations to resolve the world's problems. Finally, some individuals call for a reduction in the military role of the United States in the world and greater emphasis on solving domestic problems and strengthening the economy.

See also Carter, James E.; Containment; Détente; General Agreement on Tariffs and Trade; Gold Convertibility; Human Rights; Isolationism; Multilateralism; National Security Restoration Act; North American Free Trade Agreement; Nixon, Richard M.; Trade Policy; Vietnam War; War Powers Resolution.

References Doug Bandow, "Avoiding War" (1992–1993); Charles W. Kegley, Jr., and Eugene R. Wittkopf, *American Foreign Policy: Pattern and Process* (1991); Edward C. Luck, "Making Peace" (1992–1993); James A. Nathan and James K. Oliver, *United States Foreign Policy and World Order* (1989); George Weigel, *Idealism without Illusion* (1994).

Fragmentation (Legislative)

One of the preeminent problems that makes it difficult for Congress and state legislatures to enact comprehensive and coherent policy is that most legislatures are highly fragmented bodies. The primary factor causing this fragmentation is the independent manner in which legislators are elected to office from single-member districts. The result of this independence is that when legislators consider major policy proposals, their first concerns are usually focused on how the proposals will affect their own constituencies, and not the broader public interest.

Initially, the congressional reforms of the 1970s, including those proposed by the Hansen Committee, helped increase this fragmentation, as they spread power to the House subcommittees and strengthened the position of rank-and-file members. In the 1980s, however, there was some decline in this fragmentation, as the two parties began to square off against each other during the Reagan administration. The newfound cohesion of the parties in the 1980s is generally considered to have been caused by the increased political homogeneity within the congressional parties and the 1970s reforms that increased the power of the House Speaker.

During the first year of Republican control of Congress in 1995, the House Republicans worked more cohesively than before in any modern Congress, yet many scholars remain skeptical that this trend will continue. Members of the Republican majority have committed themselves to championing conservative reforms, but their reelection depends on their ability to satisfy voters back home. Thus it may prove difficult for many members to continue to pursue comprehensive policy changes if those changes threaten local interests.

In state legislatures, the problem of fragmentation has increased in recent years as legislatures have become more professional and legislators more career-minded. The growth of personal staffs, the explosion of interest groups in the states, and the rise of career politicians have all encouraged state legislators to act more independently and thus state legislatures have become more fragmented.

Reformers argue that the primary way to overcome legislative fragmentation is either to increase the power of legislative leaders or to strengthen the role of political parties in elections. Many political observers argue, however, that the problem of fragmentation is not as severe or as important as critics maintain. The problem is not that the government is fragmented, they argue, but that there is considerable disagreement in the public concerning the direction public policy should take. As long as there is no agreement among the voters, the legislature cannot be expected to produce coherent and comprehensive solutions. When consensus develops, however,

Congress and state legislatures are quite capable of enacting major legislation, as they have done in the past.

See also Candidate-Centered Campaigns; Career Legislators; Congress; Hansen Committee; Legislative Reform Movement; Political Parties; Responsible Parties.

References Alan Ehrenhalt, *The United States of Ambition: Politicians, Power, and the Pursuit of Office* (1991); Leroy N. Rieselbach, *Congressional Reform: The Changing Modern Congress* (1994); David W. Rohde, *Parties and Leaders in the Postreform House* (1991); Alan Rosenthal, *Governors and Legislatures: Contending Powers* (1990).

Fragmented Executive

Since the Jacksonian era, most states have elected several statewide executives in addition to the governor. These officials often include a lieutenant governor, attorney general, auditor, secretary of state, and treasurer. The presence of a large number of these independently elected executives in many states has been criticized by state constitutional reformers, who argue that it creates a fragmented executive branch that is less accountable and effective than one in which there are fewer independent executives. These reformers argue for a shortening of the state ballot in order to reduce the number of statewide elected officials and to consolidate power in the hands of the governor. Efforts to reduce the number of these executives have enjoyed some success over the past four decades, but nearly 500 statewide executives besides governors are still elected in the United States. The continued fragmentation of the executive branch into these different offices is considered one of the most important structural problems confronting the executive branch of state government today.

See also Administrative Reorganization; Constitutions, State; Governors; Short Ballot.

References Thad Beyle, "Being Governor" (1993); Terry Christensen, *Local Politics: Governing at the Grassroots* (1995); Larry J. Sabato, *Goodbye to Good-Time Charlie: The American Governorship Transformed* (1983); David C. Saffell, *State and Local Government: Politics and Public Policies* (1993).

Franking

Franking privileges, or free mailing privileges, enable members of Congress to send mass mailings to their constituents that are paid for by taxpayers. Most of these mailings take the form of newsletters that inform constituents of members' activities and often solicit their opinions. Since the 1970s, there has been a profound rise in the amount of franked mail sent by members of Congress, and many scholars argue that this has been a major factor in the increased reelection rate of incumbents. Reform groups, including Common Cause, argue that franking privileges need to be reduced in order to improve electoral competition.

See also Congress; Incumbency Advantage.

References Roger H. Davidson and Walter J. Oleszek, *Congress and Its Members* (1994); Gary C. Jacobson, *The Politics of Congressional Elections* (1992).

Fraser, Donald (b. 1924)

Donald Fraser is a Democratic Party leader who was one of two chairs of the McGovern-Fraser Commission, which rewrote the party's nomination rules prior to the 1972 national convention. The party reforms led to profound changes in the presidential selection process, increasing the importance of presidential primaries and encouraging the emergence of more candidate-centered campaigns. A former mayor of Minneapolis, Fraser served during the 88th to the 95th Congresses.

See also McGovern-Fraser Commission; Political Parties; Presidential Primaries.

Free Market Economy

A free market economy is one in which there is little to no government intervention in the marketplace. Until the 1930s, the federal government played only a minimal role in the U.S. economy, occasionally helping some major economic interests, but generally relying on a free market system. Since the devastation of the Great Depression, however, the federal government has played a more active role in trying to bolster the nation's economy and in regulating business activities. When the nation experienced a period of economic stagflation in the 1970s, however, many economists and political leaders began to question the ability of the government to solve the nation's economic woes. The economic downturn spurred a renewed interest in free market economic ideas, generating support for supply-side economics, monetarism, and deregulation. The intellectual foundation of free market economics is traced to the publication of Adam Smith's *An Inquiry into the Nature and Causes of the Wealth of Nations* in 1776. More recent advocates include Milton Friedman and Arthur Laffer.

See also Deregulation; Economic Policy; Friedman, Milton; Laffer, Arthur B.; Keynesian Economics; Laissez-Faire Economics; Monetarism; Reaganomics; Supply-Side Economics.
References Milton Friedman and Rose Friedman, *Free To Choose* (1980); Robert Lekachman, *Greed Is Not Enough: Reaganomics* (1983).

Free Trade

Under an economic policy of free trade, restrictions and tariffs on foreign-made goods are removed to allow businesses to compete in the international market without government barriers. Since the 1940s, the federal government has generally supported free trade to stimulate economic growth in the United States and other countries. As the U.S. economy began to decline in the 1970s and foreign businesses began to compete more effectively with American firms, pressure mounted on the federal government to combat what many saw as unfair trade practices by other nations. The result was that the government turned its attention from "free trade" to "fair trade," and began to impose a variety of restrictions and tariffs on specific foreign goods. These recent restrictions in trade are seen as minimal, however, in comparison to the protectionist policies the government supported prior to the 1930s. Since the end of the 1980s, the federal government has reasserted its commitment to free trade through the passage of both the General Agreement on Tariffs and Trade (GATT) and the North American Free Trade Agreement (NAFTA).

See also General Agreement on Tariffs and Trade; North American Free Trade Agreement; Protectionism; Trade Policy.
References Martin Feldstein, ed., *American Economic Policy in the 1980s* (1994); Gary Mucciaroni, *Reversals of Fortune: Public Policy and Private Interests* (1995).

Freedom of Information Act

The 1966 Freedom of Information Act is the nation's most important law regarding public access to government records. Until the passage of this act, there was no law requiring that federal records be made open to the public. The result was that the federal bureaucracy often operated in secrecy, withholding considerable information from the public. In the 1950s, Representative John Moss of California began a concerted effort to enact legislation reducing government secrecy. After more than a decade of effort, Moss's efforts resulted in the passage of the Freedom of Information Act.

Although the act represented an important

first step in opening federal records to the public, access often remained difficult because of resistance within the bureaucracy. In order to overcome this problem, Congress strengthened the act in 1974 to force greater compliance. These revisions have been credited with allowing closer public scrutiny of the federal government and with helping to unveil a number of questionable government activities.

See also Open Record Laws; Sunshine Rules.
References Sam Archibald, "The Early Years of the Freedom of Information Act: 1955 to 1974" (1993); William T. Gormley, Jr., *Taming the Bureaucracy: Muscles, Prayers, and Other Strategies* (1989).

Freund Committee

The Freund Committee was created in 1971 by Chief Justice Warren Burger to propose reforms to reduce the U.S. Supreme Court's workload. In its final report, the committee proposed the creation of a new national court of appeals between the current federal court of appeals and the Supreme Court, which would have the power to screen petitions before they came to the Supreme Court. The committee's proposal, which immediately met strong resistance, is credited with helping to spark the debate in the 1970s and 1980s on the creation of this court.

The Freund Committee was chaired by Professor Paul A. Freund of Harvard University Law School and was formally titled the Study Committee on the Caseload of the Supreme Court.

See also Caseload; Hruska Commission; National Court of Appeals; Supreme Court.
References Henry J. Abraham, *The Judicial Process: An Introductory Analysis of the Courts of the United States, England, and France* (1993); Samuel Estreicher and John Sexton, *Redefining the Supreme Court's Role: A Theory of Managing the Federal Judicial Process* (1986); Richard A. Posner, *The Federal Courts: Crisis and Reform* (1985).

Friedan, Betty (b. 1921)

The publication of Betty Friedan's *The Feminine Mystique* in 1963 is considered a key event in the rise of the contemporary women's movement. Three years later, Friedan became one of the primary founders of the National Organization for Woman as well as the group's first president.

See also Equal Rights Amendment; National Organization for Women; Women's Movement.
References Susan M. Hartmann, *From Margin to Mainstream: American Women and Politics since 1960* (1989).

Friedman, Milton (b. 1912)

Milton Friedman, 1976 Nobel Prize winner in economics, is considered the preeminent leader in monetarist theory, and his writings have had an important influence on the nation's economic policy over the past 30 years. With the selection of Paul Volcker as chair of the Federal Reserve Board during the Carter administration, Friedman's ideas began to shape U.S. monetary policy. Friedman is a strong advocate of the free market system and is also well-known for his past support of a negative income tax as an alternative to traditional welfare.

See also Federal Reserve System; Free Market Economy; Monetarism; Monetary Policy; Negative Income Tax.
References E. J. Dionne, Jr., *Why Americans Hate Politics* (1991); Milton Friedman, *Capitalism and Freedom* (1982); Bruce Miroff et al., *The Democratic Debate: An Introduction to American Politics* (1995).

Frontloading

States' efforts to schedule their presidential primary elections near the beginning of the primary season in order to increase their influence on the selection of the party nominees is referred to as frontloading.

Frontloading has become a much more common practice since the early 1980s.

One type of frontloading that has emerged in recent years is the creation of regional primaries near the beginning of the nomination process. With regional primaries, neighboring states schedule their presidential primary vote on the same day in order to increase the influence of that region of the nation on the nomination process. The most visible regional primary was the 1988 Super Tuesday election in which 14 southern and border states joined together to schedule their primaries on 8 March 1988 as a way to increase the South's influence in selecting the party nominees.

The number of states involved in frontloading reached record levels in the 1996 election when 29 states held primaries in a four-week period following the New Hampshire primary, the traditional kick-off of the nomination process.

See also Presidential Primaries; Super Tuesday.
References Rhodes Cook, "GOP Faces Unchartered Terrain in Wake of Buchanan Upset" (1996); William J. Keefe, *Parties, Politics, and Public Policy in America* (1991); Barbara Norrander, *Super Tuesday: Regional Politics and Presidential Primaries* (1992).

Fullilove v. Klutznick

In its 5–3 decision in support of affirmative action in *Fullilove v. Klutznick* (1980), the U.S. Supreme Court upheld legislation that required the federal government to set aside a 10 percent share of its business for minority contractors. The Public Works Employment Act of 1977 mandated that a particular amount of federal construction business be given to minority contractors. The court ruled that differentiating between the races in that situation was not unconstitutional and that Congress can discriminate by race in certain cases where this may rectify past discrimination. This ruling came after a 1979 Supreme Court decision that allowed a private employer to establish quotas for minorities voluntarily to remedy a racial imbalance. However, in 1984, the Court swung the other way and prohibited an employer from laying off workers who had more seniority than black employees in order to maintain a racial balance.

See also Affirmative Action; *Regents of the University of California v. Bakke;* Reverse Discrimination; *United Steelworkers of America v. Weber; Wards Cove Packing Co. v. Frank Antonio.*
References Donald Altschiller, ed., *Affirmative Action* (1991); Susan D. Clayton and Faye J. Crosby, *Justice, Gender, and Affirmative Action* (1992).

Fund, John

One of the leading proponents of term limits, John Fund wrote an editorial that appeared in the *Wall Street Journal* in October 1990, "Term Limits: An Idea Whose Time Has Come" (a treatise originally written for the Cato Institute), that has been credited with helping to inspire the term limits movement.

See also Term Limits.
Reference Gerald Benjamin and Michael J. Malbin, eds., *Limiting Legislative Terms* (1992).

G

Gambling

One of the ways many states attempted to solve their fiscal problems in the late 1980s and early 1990s was to legalize gambling. Until the early 1980s, only 13 states held lotteries and only 2 permitted casinos. Today, lotteries are held in 37 states and 10 states allow casinos. In addition, many states now permit video poker, keno, bingo, and other forms of legalized betting.

Despite the growing popularity of various forms of legalized gambling, its introduction has been heavily criticized; gambling's opponents argue that it is equivalent to a regressive form of taxation and that it encourages undesirable social behavior. Gambling has also been attacked in recent years because it has not produced as much revenue as anticipated. For instance, lotteries, which tend to be the largest source of gambling revenue, generated only $9.3 billion in state revenue nationwide in 1993. This amount represented less than 4 percent of all tax revenue in those states with lotteries.

A second issue involving gambling has been the rise of American Indian gaming operations in reservations across the United States. As of 1994, Indian tribes in 19 states operated gambling facilities. It has been estimated that the gross revenue from these operations in 1992 was $1.5 billion. These gaming operations have helped the economic position of Indian tribes, but have generated controversy in many states, because the tribes operate these facilities with only minimal government regulation and without having to pay taxes on their earnings.

See also American Indians; Finance, State; Lotteries; Regressive Tax; Taxes.
References Steven D. Gold, "It's Not a Miracle, It's a Mirage" (1994); John J. Harrigan, *Politics and Policy in States and Communities* (1994); Richard L. Worsnop, "Gambling Boom: Will the Gaming Industry's Growth Hurt Society?" (1994).

Garcia v. San Antonio Metropolitan Transit Authority

In the landmark case of *Garcia v. San Antonio Metropolitan Transit Authority,* the U.S. Supreme Court ruled that the Constitution does not set a specific limit on the national government's power to become involved in traditional state government functions, and that if states are dissatisfied with the federal government's actions, they need to seek redress from Congress, and not the courts. The Court's decision gave the federal government broad power to interfere in traditional state functions and reduced the states' constitutional protections. This decision has generated considerable criticism from supporters of states' rights, who argue that it ignored the reserved powers clause of the Tenth Amendment.

Whether the *Garcia* decision will survive is uncertain, but the Supreme Court has shown signs that it is willing to reassert some constitutional protection for the states. In *Gregory v. Ashcroft* (1991), for instance, the Court ruled that the Tenth Amendment can protect state laws governing the formation of state governments. In *United States v. Lopez* (1995), the Court took steps to restrict the federal government's use of the commerce clause to supersede state authority, throwing out a federal law that had banned the possession of firearms near public schools. In *Seminole Tribe of Florida v. Florida (1996),* the court ruled that Congress does not have the power to authorize private lawsuits against state governments, citing the Eleventh Amendment in its decision.

See also Federal-State Relations; *National League of Cities v. Usery; United States v. Lopez.*
References Laurence J. O'Toole, Jr., *American Intergovernmental Relations: Foundations, Perspectives, and Issues* (1993); Michael A. Pagano and Ann O'M. Bowman, "The State of American Federalism, 1994–1995" (1995); David B. Walker, *The Rebirth of Federalism: Slouching toward Washington* (1995).

Gardner, John W. (b. 1912)

John W. Gardner, liberal Republican and former secretary of health, education and welfare under President Johnson, has made a career of advocating government reforms. In 1970 he founded Common Cause, one of the preeminent "good government" groups in the United States. Within a year of the group's founding, it had attracted 230,000 members.

See also Common Cause.
References Jeffrey M. Berry, *The Interest Group Society* (1989); Michael W. McCann, *Taking Reform Seriously: Perspectives on Public Interest Liberalism* (1986).

Garn-St. Germaine Depository Institutions Act

The Garn-St. Germaine Depository Institutions Act of 1982 completed the deregulation of the savings and loan industry that had begun with the Depository Institutions Deregulation and Monetary Control Act of 1980. The act allowed savings institutions to expand the diversity of deposit accounts and loans they could offer the public with minimal federal restrictions. Among the act's most important changes was that it allowed savings and loans to offer money market deposit accounts, which other types of financial institutions had been using to draw investors away from savings institutions. The act was one of several efforts in the late 1970s and early 1980s to reduce the federal government's involvement in the economy. It is considered to have been partially responsible for the savings and loan crisis of the 1980s.

See also Depository Institutions Deregulation and Monetary Control Act; Deregulation; Financial Institutions Reform, Recovery, and Enforcement Act; Savings and Loan Crisis.
References Anthony S. Campagna, *The Economy in the Reagan Years: The Economic Consequences of the Reagan Administrations* (1994); Robert E. Litan, "Financial Regulation" (1994); William A. Niskanen, *Reaganomics: An Insider's Account of the Policies and People* (1988).

Gay Rights Movement

Efforts of reform groups since the late 1960s to end discrimination against and to ensure civil rights for homosexuals are referred to collectively as the gay rights movement. The birth of the movement is generally tied to the 1969 Stonewall riots, in which hundreds of protesters rioted after police raided the Stonewall Inn, a gay bar in New York City. The riots galvanized the gay community, spurring the rise of homosexual civil rights organizations across the United States.

Since the Stonewall riots, these organizations have led the campaign to protect homosexuals' rights. The movement has been particularly influential in a number of major cities, including San Francisco, where gay activists have been successful in both shaping policy and influencing local elections. The movement has had less success at the national level in producing changes in law, though it was able to get homosexuals listed as one of the reference groups in the Hate Crime Statistics Act of 1988.

Among their goals, gay rights groups seek repeal of local and state laws that regulate sexual behavior, an end to government discrimination in military service and immigration regulation, and government protection from discrimination in the private sector. Gay organizations have also been actively involved in lobbying government for increased research spending on acquired immune deficiency syndrome (AIDS).

See also Civil Rights Movement; Clinton, William J.

References Denise L. Baer and David A. Bositis, *Politics and Linkage in a Democratic Society* (1993); Richard J. Hunt, "Gay and Lesbian Politics" (1992).

General Agreement on Tariffs and Trade (GATT)

The General Agreement on Tariffs and Trade (GATT) is a set of international agreements first adopted in 1947 to reduce barriers and encourage free trade among nations. Following the bruising battle over the North American Free Trade Agreement (NAFTA) in 1993, Congress overwhelmingly approved changes in GATT to remove trade barriers and reduce international tariffs. Although it received less public attention and passed more easily through Congress than NAFTA, GATT is expected to have more profound effects on the nation's economy. The agreement, and its subsequent revisions, are considered part of the federal government's effort since the end of the Second World War to promote free trade between the United States and other nations.

See also Free Trade; North American Free Trade Agreement; Preemption; Protectionism; Trade Policy.

References Susan M. Collins and Barry P. Bosworth, *The New GATT: Implications for the United States* (1994); Gary Mucciaroni, *Reversals of Fortune: Public Policy and Private Interests* (1995); Ellen Perlman, "The Gorilla That Swallows State Laws" (1994).

General Revenue Sharing

General revenue sharing was a federal program instituted by President Richard Nixon to give state and local governments greater power in solving societal problems by channeling federal tax funds to these governments with no strings attached. The first proposal for introducing revenue sharing arose in the late 1950s, and the concept soon grew into a popular proposal for restructuring federal-state relations. Nixon championed revenue sharing as part of his New Federalism proposals in the late 1960s, but it was not until 1972 that the program was adopted by Congress. The revenue sharing program allocated $6.1 billion to state and local governments based on a specific distribution formula. In the early 1980s, President Reagan advocated an end to general revenue sharing and reduced the funds allocated to it. The revenue sharing program was discontinued entirely in 1986 as part of the federal government's effort to reduce federal spending.

See also Block Grants; Categorical Grants; Devolution; New Federalism.
References Timothy J. Conlan, *New Federalism: Intergovernmental Reform from Nixon to Reagan* (1988); David B. Walker, *The Rebirth of Federalism: Slouching toward Washington* (1995).

Gerrymandering

Gerrymandering is the drawing of legislative district boundaries to benefit a particular interest or party. Since the 1960s, the problem of gerrymandering has become a major issue for civil rights organizations and political parties that feel they are being denied adequate representation.

The term originated in 1812 after the redrawing of legislative district boundaries in Massachusetts under the direction of Governor Elbridge Gerry. One of the legislative districts that had been drawn to help a Gerry ally was very oddly shaped, and it was depicted in a newspaper cartoon drawn by portraitist Gilbert Stuart in the shape of a salamander. Stuart reportedly referred to Gerry's handiwork as gerrymandering, and the term was born.

There are three main types of gerrymandering: incumbent, party, and racial. In incumbent gerrymandering, district lines are drawn to benefit legislative incumbents, regardless of their party affiliations. Party, or partisan, gerrymandering is designed to help one political party while reducing the electoral prospects of others. Racial gerrymandering is done to dilute the voting power of African-Americans and other minorities; it is considered a form of electoral discrimination.

In the 1962 *Baker v. Carr* case, the U.S. Supreme Court ruled that legislative districting is justiciable, opening a floodgate of suits concerning gerrymandering. Subsequent Court decisions have required the use of an equal population standard in drawing district lines (*Reynolds v. Sims, Wesberry v. Sanders*). The Court has also ruled that both racial and partisan gerrymandering can violate constitutional protections (*Gomillion v. Lightfoot, Davis v. Bandemer*).

See also *Baker v. Carr; Davis v. Bandemer;* Electoral Discrimination; Redistricting; *Reynolds v. Sims;* Voting Rights Act; *Wesberry v. Sanders.*
References Chandler Davidson, ed., *Minority Vote Dilution* (1989); Bernard Grofman and Arend Lijphart, eds., *Electoral Laws and Their Political Consequences* (1986); William J. Keefe and Morris S. Ogul, *The American Legislative Process: Congress and the States* (1993).

Gingrich, Newt (b. 1943)

A Republican congressman from Georgia, Newt Gingrich led the Republican landslide victory in the fall 1994 congressional elections. With sweeping promises to reform government and return the nation to traditional values, Gingrich promoted a "Contract with America" to appeal to voters disgruntled over social problems and big government.

Gingrich criticized liberal social programs, claiming that programs for the poor, such as Aid to Families with Dependent Children, had simply created "a corrupt welfare state" in which poor people had no incentive to improve their lot and crime festered. A former college professor, Gingrich had an ability to communicate and to analyze the issues of the day that helped him leap (in *Time* magazine's words) "from virtual obscurity to the position of virtual president," according to one postelection account. He had been known, however, as a particularly venomous Republican partisan in his persistent campaign to oust Democratic House Speaker Jim Wright in the late 1980s.

Once the Republicans took the majority of seats in Congress in January 1995, Gingrich was promptly elected Speaker of the House, the first Republican to take the seat in 40 years. During his first year as Speaker, he continued to direct Republican efforts to enact the reforms embodied in the Contract with America and to resist President Clinton's more liberal policies. A prolonged budgetary standoff between Gingrich's allies and the Clinton administration in fall 1995 was one example.

See also Clinton, William J.; Contract with America.
References John M. Barry, *The Ambition and the Power* (1989); "Gingrich the Warrior" (1995); Clyde Wilcox, *The Latest American Revolution? The 1994 Elections and Their Implication for Governance* (1995).

Goals 2000
See Education.

Gold Convertibility
After the end of the Second World War, the member nations of the International Monetary Fund agreed to maintain a relatively fixed exchange rate in which the value of each country's currency would be pegged to the country's gold reserves, and the U.S. Dollar. This agreement, known as the Bretton Woods System, allowed a country that had amassed U.S. dollars to exchange those dollars with the U.S. government for gold. The system is generally considered to have worked well until the 1960s, when the United States began to experience a growing trade imbalance that was causing American dollars to accumulate abroad. Fearful that this imbalance would imperil the nation's gold reserves, President Richard Nixon ended the convertibility of dollars into gold, bringing an end to the Bretton Woods System. Since then, the exchange rates between countries have been allowed to float.

See also Trade Policy.
References Lloyd G. Reynolds, *Economics: A General Introduction* (1988); Herbert Stein, *Presidential Economics: The Making of Economic Policy from Roosevelt to Clinton* (1994).

Gore, Albert, Jr. (b. 1948)
Albert Gore, former U.S. senator, presidential contender, and current vice president, has been active in various reform efforts, particularly those involving the environment, telecommunications, and the federal bureaucracy. His leadership and activism are unusual among his vice presidential predecessors. Besides his efforts to ensure environmental protection and a sweeping National Information Infrastructure, Gore was the leader of the National Performance Review task force, which made hundreds of recommendations for streamlining federal agencies, many of which were quickly adopted. Gore has been President Clinton's goodwill ambassador for reforms in several instances. He was instrumental in garnering public support for the North American Free Trade Agreement in 1993 when he appeared in a debate with Ross Perot on the *Larry King Live* television show, for example.

See also Bureaucracy; Clinton, William J.; National Information Infrastructure; National Performance Review; Telecommunications; Vice President.
References Eliza Newlin Carney, "Still Trying To Reinvent Government" (1994); Phil Duncan, "Perot Gores His Own Ox in Debate" (1993); Mike Mills, "Clinton and Gore Hit the Road To Build a Better Bureaucracy" (1993).

Gore Report
See National Performance Review.

Government in Sunshine Act

The Government in Sunshine Act of 1976 required approximately 50 major federal agencies to open their meetings to the public except when discussing specific issues identified in the act. The act applied to agencies headed by collegial bodies, including the Interstate Commerce Commission, the Federal Trade Commission, the Federal Communications Commission, and the National Labor Relations Board. The act has been praised by reformers for making the bureaucracy more accountable. However, exemptions in the act have allowed some federal agencies, including the Federal Reserve Board, to continue to meet in private. Moreover, some critics argue that the primary beneficiaries of this act have been well-financed interest groups, which are more likely to monitor these meetings than are members of the public or the press.

See also Ethics; Sunshine Rules.
Reference William T. Gormley, Jr., *Taming the Bureaucracy: Muscles, Prayers, and Other Strategies* (1989).

Governors

The role of the governor in state politics has changed considerably since the 1950s, when few governors had the resources or talent to lead their states. Political reforms over the past 30 years have enabled governors to become more powerful players in state politics than ever before.

Prior to the 1960s, the position of the governor in state politics was so incidental that Professor Larry Sabato of the University of Virginia has referred to the governors of that period as "good-time Charlies." In the mid-1960s, however, one state after another began to restructure the executive branch to give the governor greater control over the bureaucracy. From 1965 to 1973, 23 states adopted major reorganizations of the executive branch, consolidating agencies and making the bureaucracy more accountable to the governor. Almost all states experienced at least a partial reorganization of the executive branch.

Possibly the most important reorganization to take place during this period was the restructuring of the budget office in many states so that it was directly answerable to the governor, which has given the governor greater financial control of the rest of the executive branch. In addition to reorganizing the executive branch, 22 states gave their governors the power to reorganize the executive branch in the future through the use of the executive order. Many observers of state politics argue that these reorganization efforts were the most important reforms in concentrating power in the governor's office.

However, governors were also helped by increases in the size of their staffs. In 1956, the average governor had only 4 staff members. By the end of the 1970s, that number had risen to 39. Today, the average governor has more than 50 staff members. Most states also created new planning agencies within the governor's office or moved existing ones so that they would be more closely under the governor's control. Increases in staff have allowed governors to play a much more active role in policy making.

In addition to these reforms, many governors saw their veto power increased during this period, including several who were granted the line-item veto. In 1995, North Carolina became the final state to give its governor veto power. In some states, there was also a reduction in the number of statewide executives, which helped concentrate additional power in the governor's office. Over the past 40 years, many states have lengthened the governor's tenure and removed restrictions on the governor's ability to seek reelection. Both of these trends have enabled governors to spend more time on policy making and in developing their expertise. Finally, governors' salaries have increased considerably over the past 30 years, which has made the office much more attractive to many talented politicians.

The results of these reforms have been a strengthening in the position of the governor and improvement in the quality, training, and capability of governors. Despite these gains, many reformers argue that additional changes are needed. In particular, many reformers argue that the number of additional statewide executives besides the governor needs to be reduced, and greater power concentrated in the governor's office. Moreover, many argue that state bureaucracies are still too fragmented, and that further reorganization is needed to make them more accountable to the governor.

See also Administrative Reorganization; Cabinet System, State; Constitutions, State; Fragmented Executive; Gubernatorial Appointments; Legislative Reform Movement; Line-Item Veto; Reorganization Power; Short Ballot; State Renewal; Term Expansion.

References Thad Beyle, "Being Governor" (1993); Larry J. Sabato, *Goodbye to Good-Time Charlie: The American Governorship Transformed* (1983).

Grace Commission

The Grace Commission was created by President Ronald Reagan in 1982 to identify ways to reduce waste in the federal government and to improve the management of the bureaucracy. The commission, which was composed of 161 members and another 2,000 volunteers, is considered one of the most extensive efforts in the nation's history to address management problems in the federal government.

The commission produced nearly 50 separate reports and 2,500 recommendations. In general, these recommendations encouraged the greater use of business practices by the federal government. In addition, the commission argued that if its proposals were adopted, they would save the government $424 billion in three years.

The report was immediately criticized by many political analysts who argued that most of the private sector techniques advocated by the commission were inappropriate for government use. Moreover, others argued that the savings from the reforms would be far smaller than projected. In one of the most cited reports released after the Grace Commission's work was completed, the General Accounting Office argued that the commission's recommendations would at best result in savings of $100 billion, and that even that figure was probably high.

After the commission presented its final report, the Reagan administration began to introduce many of the commission's recommendations. By the end of his presidency, Reagan claimed that he had implemented more than 80 percent of the Grace Commission's recommendations. Many analysts argue, however, that few of the commission's recommendations were actually implemented, and those that were had only minimal effects on the government's operation.

The official name of the Grace Commission was the President's Private Sector Survey on Cost Control. It was more popularly known, however, by the name of its chair, businessman J. Peter Grace.

See also Administrative Reorganization; Bureaucracy; Citizens against Waste; Office of Management and Budget; Reform 88.

References George W. Downs and Patrick D. Larkey, *The Search for Government Efficiency: From Hubris to Helplessness* (1986); Charles H. Levine, ed., *The Unfinished Agenda for Civil Service Reform: Implications of the Grace Commission Report* (1985); Donald J. Savoie, *Thatcher, Reagan, Mulroney: In Search of a New Bureaucracy* (1994).

Gramm, Phil (b. 1942)

Phil Gramm is a Texas senator who has supported conservative budgetary reforms since he gained the spotlight as a political maverick in the early 1980s. Elected to Congress as a Democrat in 1979, Gramm served on the House Budget Committee, but in 1983 the party caucus removed him for working too closely with Republicans on the committee. He then resigned his congressional seat, ran for office again as a Republican, and won. The notoriety he gained from these maneuvers led to his successful campaign for a Senate seat in 1984.

One of Gramm's first actions in the Senate was to cosponsor a landmark act to stop the huge rise in the federal budget deficit. The Balanced Budget and Emergency Deficit Control Act (better known as Gramm-Rudman-Hollings) put strict controls on congressional spending. Riding on his continued popularity as a champion of conservative economic policies, Gramm ran in the 1996 Republican presidential primaries.

See also Gramm-Latta; Gramm-Rudman-Hollings.

References Howard E. Shuman, *Politics and the Budget: The Struggle between the President and the Congress* (1992); Michael Barone and Grant Ujifusa, eds., *The Almanac of American Politics* (1995).

Gramm-Latta

The 1981 Gramm-Latta budget resolution was the first effort by the newly elected Reagan administration to roll back the government's support for social programs. Sponsored by Texas Senator Phil Gramm and Ohio Representative Delbert L. Latta, the resolution forced a $37.7 billion reduction in domestic spending. The resolution had been devised by Gramm and David Stockman, Reagan's budget director.

See also Gramm, Phil; Reagan, Ronald W.; Reaganomics.

References Howard E. Shuman, *Politics and the Budget: The Struggle between the President and the Congress* (1992).

Gramm-Rudman-Hollings

The federal budget began to experience unprecedented deficits in the early 1980s. At the same time, Congress found it increasingly difficult to pass the budget by the October 1 start of the fiscal year. In response to these problems, Congress enacted the Balanced Budget and Emergency Deficit Control Act of 1985. Known by the name of its three sponsors, the Gramm-Rudman-Hollings act attempted to end deficit spending over a six-year period by establishing maximum deficit limits for each fiscal year from 1986 to 1991. If the budget exceeded the yearly limit, the General Accounting Office (GAO) was given the responsibility to institute automatic across-the-board budget cuts on defense and domestic programs. The act also introduced a new budget timetable.

The original intent behind the budget act was to force Congress and the president to make the difficult budget decisions needed to balance the budget. If the two sides were unable to work out an agreement, however, the act ensured that the budget deficit would be reduced.

The act required that the Congressional Budget Office and the Office of Management and Budget (OMB) make an estimate on August 15 of the following year's fiscal deficit. This estimate, or what was sometimes called the "snapshot," would then be passed on to the General Accounting Office.

If the deficit was estimated to go above the yearly maximum established in the act, the GAO would institute the across-the-board cuts, or what is called sequestration. Most defense and domestic programs would be included in the cuts, with the key exceptions of entitlements and interest payments.

In 1986, the U.S. Supreme Court ruled that the use of the GAO to administer such cuts was an unconstitutional violation of the separation of powers, because the GAO was not part of the executive branch, but a legislative agency. Congress reasserted its commitment to Gramm-Rudman-Hollings in 1987 by passing the Balanced Budget and Emergency Deficit Control Reaffirmation Act, which made the OMB responsible for administering the cuts. This second act, which was dubbed Gramm-Rudman-Hollings II, also extended the goal for balancing the budget until 1993 and postponed the need to make serious budget cuts until after the 1988 presidential election.

Although Gramm-Rudman-Hollings promised a reliable mechanism to balance the federal budget, it quickly proved incapable of attaining that goal. One of the main problems was that the president began to rely on overly optimistic economic and fiscal forecasts in developing the budget, which Congress quickly found prudent to accept. These overly optimistic forecasts allowed both branches to avoid making difficult cuts in the budget by use of deception. In addition, members of Congress began to put off approval of some legislation until after the snapshot date, thus ensuring that these figures would not be calculated in the deficit level. The Budget Enforcement Act of 1990, which supersedes Gramm-Rudman-Hollings, was meant to close these loopholes and offer a more realistic mechanism for balancing the budget.

Gramm-Rudman-Hollings was authored by Senators Phil Gramm of Texas, Warren Rudman of New Hampshire, and Ernest F. Hollings of South Carolina. The act is sometimes referred to simply as Gramm-Rudman.

See also Budget Deficit, Federal; Budget Enforcement Act of 1990; Congressional Budget and Impoundment Control Act; Gramm, Phil; Hollings, Ernest F.; Rudman, Warren; Sequestration.

References Daniel P. Franklin, *Making Ends Meet: Congressional Budgeting in the Age of Deficits* (1993); Donald F. Kettl, *Deficit Politics: Public Budgeting in Its Institutional and Historical Context* (1992); Howard E. Shuman, *Politics and the Budget: The Struggle between the President and the Congress* (1992); James A. Thurber, "New Rules for an Old Game: Zero-Sum Budgeting in the Postreform Congress" (1992).

Great Society

The Great Society is the name attached to the broad, sweeping package of social programs championed by President Lyndon Johnson in the 1960s to end poverty and racial injustice in the United States. It grew out of an optimistic belief among members of the Johnson administration that the nation's ills could be solved through more direct and aggressive efforts by the federal government. Social commentators continue to debate the effectiveness of these programs in reaching their goals, but one result of Johnson's efforts is certain: the Great Society created a profound change in the role of the federal government in U.S. society, causing political power to shift to Washington, D.C. Since the Johnson administration, conservative reformers have sought to roll back Great Society programs, to reduce the federal government's role in society, and to return more power to the states.

Some of the major initiatives associated with the Great Society are the Civil Rights Act of 1964, the Economic Opportunity Act of 1964, the Elementary and Secondary Education Act of 1965, the Fair Housing Act of 1968, Head Start, the Jobs Corp, Medicaid, Medicare, the Model Cities Act of 1966, and the Voting Rights Act of 1965.

See also Civil Rights Act of 1964; Community Action Agencies; Creative Federalism; Johnson, Lyndon B.; Medicaid; Medicare; Model Cities Program; New Federalism; Voting Rights Act; War on Poverty.
References Eli Ginzberg and Robert M. Solow, *The Great Society: Lessons for the Future* (1974); Marshall Kaplan and Peggy L. Cuciti, *The Great Society and Its Legacy: Twenty Years of U.S. Social Policy* (1986).

Greater Portland Metropolitan Service District

The Greater Portland Metropolitan Service District, an Oregon planning agency, is considered to be one of the two most developed types of regional government in the United States. Created in 1978, the Service District has the power to set areawide policy on land use and development, and has direct responsibility over a number of specific government services, including waste management, flood control, transportation, and the Washington Park Zoo. Political reformers point to it as an example of how regional government can be structured to overcome the fragmentation of governments that troubles the nation's metropolitan areas.

See also Metropolitan Fragmentation; Regional Government; Twin Cities Metropolitan Council.
References Terry Christensen, *Local Politics: Governing at the Grassroots* (1995); John J. Harrigan, *Political Change in the Metropolis* (1993); David B. Walker, *The Rebirth of Federalism: Slouching toward Washington* (1995).

Gubernatorial Appointments

One of the primary reforms that many analysts argue is needed to make state government more accountable and effective is to give governors greater power to hire and fire major state officials. In particular, reformers argue that the number of statewide elected officials in each state should be reduced and the governor be given the power to appoint individuals to these positions. Reformers also advocate giving governors the power to appoint most state officials who are currently selected by independent boards. Supporters of such reforms argue that giving governors greater power to appoint and remove officials will reduce the independence of the bureaucracy and make these officials more responsive to governors' demands.

See also Governors; Short Ballot.
References Thad Beyle, "Being Governor" (1993); Ann O'M Bowman and Richard C. Kearney, *The Resurgence of the States* (1986); Larry J. Sabato, *Goodbye to Good-Time Charlie: The American Governorship Transformed* (1983).

Guinier, Lani (b. 1950)

Lani Guinier, a law professor at the University of Pennsylvania, has emerged as one of the nation's most visible advocates for the use of alternative types of election systems in order to increase proportional representation in Congress. One example of the kind of election reform she has proposed is "cumulative" voting, which calls for replacing single-member districts with larger multimember ones. Voters would then be allowed to cast the same number of votes as there are seats being filled, which they could either distribute among a few candidates or give to just one. That way, minorities could concentrate their votes on one or two candidates, thus ensuring that more minority candidates would be elected.

Guinier's proposals, outlined in a 1994 book, were at first dismissed as too radical, but the tortuous gerrymandering in North Carolina's 12th Congressional District led to Supreme Court challenges, and Guinier's plan was reexamined as an alternative to ensure that the state's African-American population, 24 percent of the state's total population, would be represented. Guinier is a vocal opponent of racism and sexism, and was President Clinton's nominee for assistant attorney general for civil rights in 1993. Clinton withdrew the nomination when critics asserted that Guinier's politics were too radical.

See also Cumulative Voting; Election Systems; *Shaw v. Reno;* Single-Member Districts.

References Peter Applebome, "Guinier Ideas, Once Seen as Odd, Now Get Serious Study" (1994); Lani Guinier, *The Tyranny of the Majority: Fundamental Fairness in Representative Democracy* (1994).

H

Hansen Committee

The Hansen Committee was created by the House Democratic Party caucus in 1970 to study reforms for democratizing the House's structure and procedures. The committee was brought back together in 1973 and 1974 to continue these efforts. The Democratic Party's adoption of the committee's reform proposals profoundly altered political power in the House of Representatives. The reforms reduced the importance of seniority and the power of committee chairs, strengthened the position of subcommittees and party leaders, and gave rank-and-file Democrats greater control of the House.

There were three sets of Hansen Committee reforms. The first, which was adopted in 1971, allowed House Democrats to vote separately on the selection of a committee chair if ten members requested such a vote. The 1971 reforms also restricted Democrats to serving as only one subcommittee chair and allowed all subcommittee chairs to hire at least one professional staff member.

The second and more sweeping set of Hansen reforms was adopted by the Democratic caucus in 1973. These reforms took the power to distribute subcommittee assignments and select subcommittee chairs away from the committee chairs and gave it to each committee's Democratic caucus. The reforms required that a vote be taken by the House Democratic caucus on all committee chairmanships, and gave the caucus the right to use a secret ballot in the vote if 20 percent of the members agreed. The reforms also placed the Speaker and other party leaders on the Committee on Committees, enhancing the leadership's control over committee assignments. Until then, the Committee on Committees was solely under the control of the House Ways and Means Committee and its powerful chair, Wilbur Mills. Finally, the 1973 reforms included a set of changes that became known as the Subcommittee Bill of Rights. These changes required that the committees develop more specific subcommittee jurisdictions and that bills be sent automatically to the appropriate subcommittee after they are referred to a committee. The bill of rights also gave the subcommittees the power to control their own rules, staffs, and budgets.

The third set of Hansen reforms was enacted in 1974; these reforms were offered as milder substitutes for the structural reforms proposed by the Bolling Committee. The 1974 reforms promised to redistribute committee jurisdictions in a more rational manner, though ultimately they made only minor changes in jurisdictions. The 1974 reform package, which was formally known as the Committee Reform Amendments of 1974, did include a provision, however, allowing the House Speaker to refer bills to multiple committees, a rule change that greatly enhanced the Speaker's powers.

The Hansen Committee was formally known as the Committee on Organization, Study, and Review. It was chaired by Representative Julia Butler Hansen of Washington.

See also Bolling Committee; Congress; House Democratic Steering and Policy Committee; House Rules Committee; Legislative Reorganization Act; Multiple Referrals; Seniority Rule.
References Roger H. Davidson and Walter J. Oleszek, *Congress and Its Members* (1994); Lawrence C. Dodd and Bruce I. Oppenheimer, "The House in Transition: Change and Consolidation" (1981); Leroy N. Rieselbach, *Congressional Reform: The Changing Modern Congress* (1994); David W. Rohde, *Parties and Leaders in the Postreform House* (1991).

Hatch Act Reforms

See Federal Employees Political Activities Act.

Hays, Wayne (1911–1989)

As chair of both the House Administration Committee and the Democratic Congressional Campaign Committee, Wayne Hays was considered one of the most powerful men in Congress in the mid-1970s. Hays was forced to resign in 1976, however, when it was revealed that he kept Elizabeth Ray on his office payroll because she was his mistress. The Hays scandal was considered one of the key events leading to congressional ethics reforms in the late 1970s.

See also Congress; Ethics; Obey Commission.
References Michael Barone, et al., eds., *The Almanac of American Politics 1978* (1977).

Health Care

Health care reform emerged as an important political issue in the early 1990s as private health care costs soared and the demands on government health care programs began to place increasing stress on federal and state budgets. In his presidential campaign, Bill Clinton pledged that as president he would introduce a comprehensive health care reform proposal to reduce these costs and to improve the coverage of the nation's health system. Soon after taking office, Clinton appointed First Lady Hillary Rodham Clinton to chair the newly created Task Force on National Health Care Reform. In October 1993, the task force presented its proposal, the National Health Security Act, to Congress. The proposal provided for universal coverage for all citizens and sought to reduce costs by creating regional health alliances of small businesses that could negotiate prices with health care providers and insurers. The proposal died in Congress, however, in late 1994.

Despite the defeat of Clinton's initiative, the concern for reforming the nation's health care system remains strong because of the high costs and poor service of the current one. Instead of comprehensive reform, as in Clinton's proposal, however, most of the primary reform proposals being discussed in Congress in 1995 offered only minor changes in the current structure.

See also Clinton, William J.; Medicaid; Medicare; Senior Citizens Fairness Act.
References Henry J. Aaron, *Serious and Unstable Condition: Financing America's Health Care* (1991); Charles L. Cochran and Eloise F. Malone, *Public Policy: Perspectives and Choices* (1995); Peter MacPherson, "GOP Revives 1994's Hot Issue: Health Insurance Overhaul" (1995); Joseph A. Pechman and Michael S. McPherson, *Fulfilling America's Promise: Social Policies for the 1990s* (1992).

Heard Commission

In 1961, President John F. Kennedy created a commission to study presidential campaign costs, with Professor Alexander Heard of the University of North Carolina as its chair. Referred to informally as the Heard Commission, the President's Commission on Campaign Costs recommended a series of reforms to improve public participation in presidential campaigns and federal oversight of elections. Although these proposals failed to pass Congress, the commission's work is often cited as the first modern attempt to reform presidential campaign finances.

See also Campaign Finance.
Reference *Congressional Campaign Finances: History, Facts, and Controversy* (1992); Frank J. Sorauf, *Money in American Elections* (1988).

Heritage Foundation

The Heritage Foundation is a conservative policy research institution that promotes studies on free enterprise, limited government, strong national defense, and individual liberty. The group's scholars influenced the economic and social philosophy behind policies instituted during the Reagan administration in the 1980s. Based in Washington, D.C., the foundation boasts a $19 million budget, most of which is derived from corporate sponsors.

Hill, Anita (b. 1956)

Anita Hill is a University of Oklahoma law professor who stirred an unprecedented controversy over the judicial nomination process and was credited with revitalizing the women's movement in the 1990s. In 1991, Hill brought charges that Clarence Thomas, President Bush's nominee for the Supreme Court, had sexually harassed her when she worked for him at the U.S. Department of Education and the Equal Employment Opportunity Commission. Her charges and Thomas's countercharges made in hearings before an all-male Senate Judiciary Committee were played out in dramatic detail on national television. The committee voted to approve Thomas's nomination, sparking even more controversy over sexual ethics in the workplace as well as the nature of the nomination.

The hearings helped to stir a massive influx of women into politics in the 1992 election year, leading it to be dubbed "The Year of the Woman." As a result, a record number of women were elected to Congress. Ethical standards in the workplace and in government changed following the Hill-Thomas case, and new policies against sexual harassment were implemented. The hearings have also been credited with helping to propel the passage of the Civil Rights Act of 1991. The Senate strove to change its white male image in response by appointing two women to the Judiciary Committee, including Carol Moseley-Braun, who is African-American.

See also Civil Rights Act of 1991; Congress; Ethics; Judicial Selection; Thomas, Clarence.
References "Anita Hill" (1995); Roger H. Davidson and Walter J. Oleszek, *Congress and Its Members* (1994); Lawrence C. Dodd and Bruce I. Oppenheimer, "Perspectives on the 1992 Congressional Elections," (1993); Jane Mayer and Jill Abramson, *Strange Justice: The Selling of Clarence Thomas* (1994); Toni Morrison, ed., *Race-ing Justice, En-gendering Power: Essays on Anita Hill, Clarence Thomas, and the Construction of Social Reality* (1992).

Hollings, Ernest F. (b. 1922)

Ernest F. Hollings, Democratic U.S. senator from South Carolina, coauthored the Gramm-Rudman-Hollings bill in 1985. The bill was designed to force Congress and the president to make the difficult budget decisions needed to balance the budget.

See also Gramm-Rudman-Hollings.
Reference Howard E. Shuman, *Politics and the Budget: The Struggle between the President and the Congress* (1992).

Home Rule

In the 1860s, Iowa State Judge John F. Dillon ruled that local governments have only those powers specifically granted to them by the state, those necessarily implied by these powers, and those essential to their purposes for corporation. The judge's ruling, which is known today as Dillon's Rule, has dominated the relationship between state and local governments ever since it was issued, severely restricting local governments' ability to act independently.

During the past few decades, however, many city and county governments have pushed for greater freedom to adopt services and programs as they see fit by asking their state governments for greater home rule. Home rule is a type of government charter that allows local government to operate with only very broad limits by the state government. Since the mid-1960s, 20 states have granted home rule to municipal governments, bringing the total number of states granting this type of discretionary power to 48. Moreover, 23 states granted home rule to county governments during this period. The result of these reforms is that cities and counties have far greater freedom today to implement programs and policy initiatives as they see fit.

See also Mandates, State.
References Charles R. Adrian and Michael R. Fine, *State and Local Politics* (1991); Doyle W. Buckwalter, "Dillon's Rule in the 1980s: Who's in Charge of Local Affairs?" (1982); David B. Walker, *The Rebirth of Federalism: Slouching toward Washington* (1995).

Hoover Institution on War, Revolution and Peace

The Hoover Institution on War, Revolution and Peace is a multimillion-dollar research institute based at Stanford University; it promotes studies based on conservative philosophies. The institution's research on social and economic issues influenced and supported the conservative economic and social policies of the Reagan administration. Much of the organization's funding is derived from major corporations that would benefit from the policy reforms touted by the institution's researchers.

House Banking Scandal

For more than 40 years, the bank that serves the House of Representatives allowed House members to write checks even when they had insufficient funds in their accounts. The service was free, and there was only one main stipulation—overdrafts had to be covered by the member's next paycheck. In 1991, the General Accounting Office released a report critical of this practice that quickly exploded in the press. An investigation by a special prosecutor revealed that 269 House members had written overdrafts between 1988 and 1991, including several who had written more than 100. New York Representative Robert Mrazak led the pack with 920 overdrafts.

The revelation was one of many scandals that plagued Congress in the early 1990s, causing the public approval ratings of Congress to reach record lows and forcing both houses to consider reform. The House bank was soon closed and a number of member perquisites were cut back, including subsidized medical care, free flowers, and inexpensive access to the House gym. The scandal also helped cause the defeat of 25 incumbents who had written overdrafts and encouraged another 50 to step down.

See also Congress; Ethics.
References Roger H. Davidson and Walter J. Oleszek, *Congress and Its Members* (1994); Phil Kuntz, "The History of the House Bank: Scandal Waiting To Happen" (1992); Charles Stewart III, "Let's Go Fly a Kite: Correlates of Involvement in the House Bank Scandal" (1994).

House Democratic Steering and Policy Committee

The House Democratic caucus created the Steering and Policy Committee in 1973 to help the party attain its policy goals. In 1975, the caucus stripped the House Ways and Means Committee of its power to make committee assignments and passed that power on to the Steering and Policy Committee, where the party could exercise greater control over these decisions. This transfer of power was an important step in efforts to democratize the House in the 1970s. The creation of the Steering and Policy Committee was one of the 1973 Hansen Committee reforms.

See also Congress; Hansen Committee.
References Leroy N. Rieselbach, *Congressional Reform: The Changing Modern Congress* (1994); David W. Rohde, *Parties and Leaders in the Postreform House* (1991).

House Post Office Scandal

Since the late 1970s, federal law has banned members of Congress from pocketing money allocated to their offices for the purchase of stamps. Despite this ban, several members of Congress continued to exchange their stamps for cash at the House of Representative's post office. Federal prosecutors launched an investigation into this practice in the early 1990s.

In 1993, the postmaster of the House post office was charged with embezzling funds and allowing members to exchange stamps or stamp vouchers for cash. After the postmaster pled guilty, the investigation began to focus on two members of the House of Representatives, Joe Kolter and Dan Rostenkowski. At the time, Rostenkowski was the chair of the House Ways and Means Committee and considered one of the most powerful men in Congress. Criminal indictments were eventually filed against both members for illegally exchanging stamps and stamp vouchers for cash. In 1996, Rostenkowski pled guilty to corruption charges stemming from the post office scandal and other illegal activities. The charges against Kolter were scheduled to reach the courts in the summer of 1996.

The post office scandal was one of several events in the early 1990s that made the public grow increasingly disillusioned with Congress and helped the Republican Party gain control of both houses in the 1994 election.

See also Congress; Ethics.
References Stephen Gettinger, "Rostenkowski Case: A Question Hovers" (1996); Phil Kuntz, "Stamp Embezzlement Scheme Points to Rostenkowski" (1993).

House Rules Committee

The Rules Committee of the House of Representatives is often considered the most powerful committee in Congress, because it controls changes in the House calendar and the rules governing debate when legislation reaches the House floor. Until the mid-1970s, the Rules Committee enjoyed considerable independence and often ignored the wishes of the majority party. In 1975, however, the House Democratic caucus voted to give the Speaker the power to nominate the chair and other Democratic members of the committee as a way to make the committee more responsive to the party and its leaders. The Democratic caucus was given the power to approve these nominations. This change in Democratic caucus rules strengthened the Democratic Party leadership and gave the party members greater influence in the policy-making process. In fact, congressional scholar Barbara Sinclair writes that this reform may have been the "most vital resource" for the House leaders in causing the emergence of strong party leadership during the 1980s.

See also Bolling Committee; Congress; Hansen Committee.
References Roger H. Davidson and Walter J. Oleszek, *Congress and Its Members* (1994); Lawrence C. Dodd and Bruce I. Oppenheimer, "The House in Transition: Change and Consolidation" (1981); Barbara Sinclair, "The Emergence of Strong Leadership in the 1980s House of Representatives" (1992).

Hruska Commission

The 1972 panel known as the Hruska Commission was created by Congress to consider reforms for the federal appellate system. The commission's most controversial recommendation was a proposal to create a national court of appeals between the current federal appeals courts and the Supreme Court. The new court would have the power to review cases assigned to it by the Supreme Court. After the commission released it report, legislation was introduced in Congress to create a national court of appeals, but it was not enacted.

The commission, which was formally titled the Commission on Revision of the Federal Court Appellate System, was chaired by Roman L. Hruska.

See also Caseload; Freund Committee; National Court of Appeals; Supreme Court.
Reference Samuel Estreicher and John Sexton, *Redefining the Supreme Court's Role: A Theory of Managing the Federal Judicial Process* (1986).

Hughes Commission

The Hughes Commission was the first of several commissions created within the Democratic Party to propose reforms in the presidential nominating process. It grew out of discontent among supporters of Eugene McCarthy who were dissatisfied with the delegate selection process used in the Connecticut state Democratic Party convention. The commission was formally known as the Commission on the Democratic Selection of Presidential Nominees. It was chaired by Iowa Governor Harold Hughes.

The commission's report, which was released immediately before the 1968 Democratic Party National Convention, called for broadening the representation of the party's divergent membership by ending such practices as winner-take-all primaries and the unit rule. The commission's work is considered an important forerunner of the work of the McGovern-Fraser Commission.

See also McGovern-Fraser Commission; Political Parties; Unit Rule.
References Nelson W. Polsby, *Consequences of Party Reform* (1983); Byron E. Shafer, *Quiet Revolution: The Struggle for the Democratic Party and the Shaping of Post-Reform Politics* (1983).

Human Rights

President Jimmy Carter redirected U.S. foreign policy during the 1970s by placing greater emphasis on how other nations treat their citizens and other individuals within their borders. Until the 1970s, the dominant force in shaping U.S. foreign policy was the perceived communist threat, which caused America's leaders to focus on containing the expansion of the Soviet Union. President Richard Nixon made an important change in this policy by trying to reduce the tensions with the

Soviet Union through détente. Carter, in turn, argued that the nation's relationship with other countries should also be concerned with human rights. Although previous presidents had talked about human rights, Carter was the first to make concern for these rights a central feature in his foreign policy efforts. Carter's redirection in foreign policy did not last long, however. The election of Ronald Reagan as president in 1980 brought renewed concern over the potential spread of communism.

See also Carter, James E.; Containment; Détente; Foreign Policy.
References Louis Henkin, *The Age of Rights* (1990); Robert C. Johansen, *The National Interest and the Human Interest: An Analysis of U.S. Foreign Policy* (1980); George Weigel, *Idealism without Illusion* (1994).

Human SERVE

Human SERVE, or the Human Service Employees' Registration and Voter Education Campaign, is a national organization that was founded in 1983 to increase voter registration and reform the U.S. voter registration system. The organization has been actively involved in lobbying cities, states, and the federal government to revise procedures so that citizens can register to vote at many government offices serving the public, including those issuing driver's licenses and those providing social services.

See also National Voter Registration Act; Voter Registration.
Reference Frances Fox Piven and Richard A. Cloward, *Why American Don't Vote* (1988).

Humphrey-Hawkins Act of 1978

Adopted during a period of severe economic stagflation, the Humphrey-Hawkins Act of 1978 reasserted the federal government's commitment to attaining a stable economy and limiting unemployment. To do this, the act required the president to establish a five-year economic plan while directing the government to seek both a 4 percent unemployment rate and no inflation. The act's requirements were considered so unattainable that the act had no meaningful effect on economic policy making. The act was formally known as the Full Employment and Balanced Growth Act of 1978.

See also Economic Policy; Stagflation.
References Campbell R. McConnell and Stanley L. Brue, *Economics: Principles, Problems, and Policies* (1990); Herbert Stein, *Presidential Economics: The Making of Economic Policy from Roosevelt to Clinton* (1994).

Hunt Commission

After the defeat of George McGovern in 1972 and the election of political outsider Jimmy Carter in 1976, one of the most common complaints leveled against the Democratic Party reforms of the 1970s was that they had created a presidential nomination process that selected candidates who either could not win or could not govern. The problem with the reforms, many party officials argued, was that they excluded party leaders from participating in the nomination convention, leaving the process to political amateurs.

The Winograd Commission made an initial effort to rewrite party rules to allow some party leaders to participate in the convention. The Hunt Commission was even more important in bringing party leaders back to the nominating convention. The commission, known formally as the Commission on Presidential Nomination, set aside more than 14 percent of the seats at the 1984 convention for party leaders and elected officials, who were then allowed to vote as they pleased.

Supporters of the Hunt Commission argued that these superdelegates, as they are known, would provide peer review over nominees and allow the party to nominate better candidates. Despite some criticism that the commission's proposal reduced the influence of rank-and-file Democrats, the party has continued to provide for superdelegates since the 1984 election.

The Hunt Commission was chaired by Governor James Hunt of North Carolina.

See also Fairness Commission; Hughes Commission; McGovern-Fraser Commission; Mikulski Commission; National Primary; Political Parties; Presidential Primaries; Winograd Commission.

References William Crotty and John S. Jackson III, *Presidential Primaries and Nominations* (1985); William J. Keefe, *Parties, Politics, and Public Policy in America* (1994).

I

Immigration and Naturalization Service v. Chadha

See Legislative Veto.

Impoundment

When a president refuses to spend money previously appropriated by Congress, this is referred to as impoundment. Several presidents since Thomas Jefferson have withheld expenditures, though the practice has been rare and limited in scope. In the early 1970s, however, President Richard Nixon impounded several billion dollars in funds earmarked for public housing, water treatment facilities, farm subsidies, and several other domestic programs. This unprecedented action infuriated Congress and led to the passage of the Congressional Budget and Impoundment Control Act of 1974 by a nearly unanimous vote in both houses.

The Impoundment Control Act restricts the president's ability to impound funds, allowing for only temporary deferments within the fiscal year. Such a deferment, however, can be overturned by the vote of one house of Congress. The president can also withhold funds entirely when a program has been canceled or in a few other specified circumstances, but after doing so the president must obtain Congress's permission. If both houses of Congress do not agree to the president's actions within 45 days of continuous session, then the action is nullified.

See also Congressional Budget and Impoundment Control Act; Deferral; Legislative Veto; Recission.
References John W. Ellwood and James A. Thurber, "The Politics of the Congressional Budget Process Re-examined" (1981); Howard E. Shuman, *Politics and the Budget: The Struggle between the President and the Congress* (1992).

Income Tax

See Corporate Income Tax; Personal Income Tax.

Incrementalism

Incrementalism is the traditional process used in preparing a government budget. In this process, one year's expenditures are used as a baseline in developing the next year's budget allocations, with slight adjustments made on individual programs. This results in only marginal, or incremental, changes in budgeting from year to year.

Critics argue that incrementalism is an irrational process for dealing with societal problems and creating an effective bureaucracy. The process provides little opportunity for the government to redirect funds to new concerns and to cut back on agencies that no longer serve their purpose.

The process is also seen as creating undesirable behavior within bureaucracies. Among other consequences, it encourages agencies to spend their entire budgets to ensure that their funding is not reduced in the following year. A number of different reforms have been proposed to create a budgeting process that is more effective at channeling government funds where needed and improving the bureaucracy's performance. These include cost-benefit analysis, performance budgeting, program budgeting, and zero-base budgeting.

Supporters of incremental budgeting argue that it is a process that works and one that is desirable, because it limits conflicts among competing political interests, as change comes gradually.

See also Budgeting Techniques; Cost-Benefit Analysis; Performance Budgeting; Program Budgeting; Zero-Base Budgeting.
References Donald F. Kettl, *Deficit Politics: Public Budgeting in Its Institutional and Historical Context* (1992); John L. Mikesell, *Fiscal Administration: Analysis and Applications for the Public Sector* (1991); Aaron Wildavsky, *The New Politics of the Budgetary Process* (1988).

Incumbency Advantage

A major concern of political reformers in the United States today is the high reelection rate of incumbent members of Congress and state legislatures. In any given election, it has become common for more than 90 percent of all legislative incumbents who seek reelection to be returned to office. Moreover, incumbents are winning their reelection campaigns by far greater margins than ever before. Incumbent U.S. senators have not been as successful in attaining reelection as have other legislators, but even they are generally advantaged by their incumbency status.

A variety of explanations have been put forward for the advantage incumbents have in elections. Some electoral scholars argue that the decline of political parties has caused incumbency status to become a new voting cue. Others argue that the increased resources available to legislators, especially greater franking privileges, have improved voter awareness of and, in turn, support for incumbents. Along with franking privileges, incumbents are much better able to raise campaign contributions than are challengers, putting them at a distinct advantage in election campaigns. Finally, some scholars argue that the behavior of legislators themselves has changed, with legislators focusing increasing attention on catering to the personal needs of their constituents, especially through casework.

Reformers argue that the advantages held by incumbents have harmed electoral competition and representation. Several reforms have been proposed to reduce incumbents' advantage, one of the most popular of which is term limits. Term limits would reduce the reelection rate of incumbents by simply limiting the number of terms any individual can serve. Alternatively, some reformers call for changes in the campaign finance system to improve the position of challengers. Among the proposals to improve campaign finance are public financing of legislative campaigns, the use of tax credits to encourage more campaign contributions from individuals, stricter rules governing political action committees, and an increased electoral role for political parties.

See also Campaign Finance; Casework; Congress; Constituency Service; Franking; Off-Year Fund-Raising; Political Action Committees; Political Parties; Public Financing; Tax Credits; Term Limits.
References Gary C. Jacobson, *The Politics of Congressional Elections* (1992); Gary F. Moncrief and Joel A. Thompson, eds., *Changing Patterns in State Legislative Careers* (1992).

Independent Counsel

The Office of Independent Counsel was created in 1978 as part of the Ethics in Government Act to investigate allegations of illegal activity by top federal officials. The office, which was originally called the Office of Special Prosecutor, was established in the aftermath of Watergate to ensure the fair treatment of alleged government crimes by placing investigations into the hands of individuals who are independent from the executive branch. Individual independent counsels are appointed by the federal courts after the courts are informed by the U.S. attorney general that an investigation is warranted. The title of the office was changed in 1983.

See also Ethics; Ethics in Government Act; Watergate; Whistle-Blowing.
References Suzanne Garment, *Scandal: The Culture of Mistrust in American Politics* (1991); Stanley I. Kutler, *The Wars of Watergate: The Last Crisis of Richard M. Nixon* (1990).

Independent Expenditures

Independent expenditures are those expenditures made by individuals or groups to help particular candidates' campaigns without the candidates' cooperation or consultation. Since the Supreme Court's decision in *Buckley v. Valeo* in 1976, independent spending has played an increasingly important role in the financing of federal election campaigns, and has become one of the most difficult problems confronting campaign finance reform.

In *Buckley v. Valeo,* the Court ruled that the government could not limit the amount of money individuals or groups can spend on campaigns, including through independent expenditures. Such limits, the Court maintained, violated the First Amendment right to free speech. Reformers argue that by permitting unlimited independent expenditures, the Court has made the attainment of meaningful campaign finance reform impossible. The Center for Responsive Politics, a nonpartisan research organization in Washington D.C., is one of the leading advocates seeking a reversal of the Court's decision.

See also *Buckley v. Valeo;* Campaign Finance; Center for Responsive Politics; Federal Election Campaign Act.
References Herbert E. Alexander, *Financing Politics: Money, Elections, and Political Reform* (1992); *Congressional Campaign Finances: History, Facts, and Controversy* (1992); David B. Magleby and Candice J. Nelson, *The Money Chase: Congressional Campaign Finance Reform* (1990); Jamin B. Raskin and John Bonifaz, *The Wealth Primary: Campaign Funding and the Constitution* (1994); Frank J. Sorauf, *Money in American Elections* (1988).

Indian Treaty Rights

See American Indians.

Industrial Policy

Efforts to strengthen the U.S. economy against foreign competitors by having the federal government play a more active role in nurturing the nation's industries are referred to as industrial policy. Although there are some important differences among industrial policy proposals, most call for the government to provide support for upcoming industries, particularly those in high-technology. Some proposals also call for the federal government to protect troubled industries. Industrial policy grew increasingly popular in the mid-1980s among Democratic politicians, who saw it as an alternative to traditional big-government activism and a free market economy. The policy proposals generally include tax breaks, federal subsidies or loans, and trade protection for identified industries. Many conservatives, however, view industrial policy as an unnecessary and potentially harmful intrusion of the government into the economy.

Former Colorado senator and presidential candidate Gary Hart is one of the most well-known advocates of industrial policy.

See also Economic Policy; Free Market Economy; Trade Policy.
References Gary Hart, *A New Democracy* (1983); Robert Z. Lawrence, *Can America Compete?* (1984); Robert B. Reich, *The New American Frontier* (1983); Herbert Stein, *Presidential Economics: The Making of Economic Policy from Roosevelt to Clinton* (1994).

Initiative

The initiative process is a type of direct democracy in which citizens circulate petitions to put proposed laws on the ballot for direct popular vote. Originally introduced by Progressive reformers at the turn of the century to circumvent corrupt and intransigent legislatures, the initiative has itself become the focus of recent reform efforts. Today, 24 states allow for the use of initiatives to change state constitutions or statutory law. Initiatives are also used in cities and other local governments.

There are two different types of initiatives: direct and indirect. Under the direct initiative, a proposed law is placed directly on the ballot after a requisite number of signatures are obtained. Under the indirect initiative, the proposed law is sent to the state legislature for consideration after the signatures are gathered. The legislature is then given the opportunity to respond to the proposal before it is presented to the voters.

In recent years, there has been a large increase in the number and complexity of initiatives being put before voters. The rise in the initiative's popularity is often traced to the passage of California's Proposition 13, which reduced the collection of property taxes in the state and spawned a property tax revolt nationwide. The results of these changes, as well as the growing amount of money spent in initiative campaigns, have generated considerable criticism of the initiative process.

Critics assail almost all aspects of the process, from the drafting of initiatives to the forces shaping election outcomes. Unlike in legislative politics, there is little compromise in the drafting of initiatives. Initiative sponsors simply draw up the wording on their own, and then present their proposals to the voters, without offering any alternatives. The signature-gathering process is often criticized because of deceitful tactics used by petition workers and the growing importance of professional signature-gathering firms. Other criticisms are that initiative proposals are too complicated for most voters to understand, that low voter turnout makes the initiative process unrepresentative of the public, that the process discriminates against minorities, and that money has become too influential in shaping initiative results.

A variety of different reforms have been proposed to improve the initiative process. In general, these proposals are designed to increase voter understanding, reduce the influence of money, and instill some element of compromise into the initiative process.

Reformers believe that voter understanding would improve if public hearings were required on ballot initiatives and if more informative voter pamphlets were employed. To reduce the importance of money, a number of states adopted restrictions on contributions and spending in initiative campaigns during the 1970s, but the Supreme Court has since rejected these restrictions, arguing that they violate the First Amendment right of free speech. The primary alternative that has been offered to control spending is the introduction of tighter campaign finance disclosure laws.

Finally, groups such as the National Civic League and the League of Women Voters advocate the increased use of the indirect initiative. The indirect initiative is seen as preferable to the direct initiative because it incorporates the legislature into the process, and thus encourages the development of compromise legislation.

See also National Initiative; Proposition 13; Recall; Referendum.
References Thomas E. Cronin, *Direct Democracy: The Politics of Initiative, Referendum, and Recall* (1989); David Kehler and Robert M. Stern, "Initiatives in the 1980s and 1990s" (1994).

In-Kind Contributions

Instead of making cash contributions, some political action committees (PACs) provide in-kind contributions—that is, goods or services—to help get their favored candidates elected to office. Such services include polling, fund-raising help, advertising production, campaign-training seminars, staff assistance, and other forms of organization support. Critics argue that these in-kind contributions may be even more harmful to the political system than direct monetary contributions, because they give PACs more influence in campaigns and allow them to develop closer ties to elected officials.

See also Campaign Finance; Political Action Committees.
References Michael J. Malbin, ed., *Money and Politics in the United States: Financing Elections in the 1980s* (1984); Larry J. Sabato, *PAC Power: Inside the World of Political Action Committees* (1984); Barbara G. Salmore and Stephen A. Salmore, *Candidates, Parties, and Campaigns: Electoral Politics in America* (1989); Frank J. Sorauf, *Money in American Elections* (1988).

Inspector General Act

The 1978 Inspector General Act created the position of inspector general in a dozen major federal agencies and departments to investigate bureaucratic wrongdoing. The inspector generals report their findings directly to the heads of the agencies or departments and to Congress. The act is considered an important victory in efforts to reduce waste, fraud, and other inappropriate activities within the federal bureaucracy.

See also Whistle-Blowing.
References Suzanne Garment, *Scandal: The Culture of Mistrust in American Politics* (1991); Myron Peretz Glazer and Penina Migdal Glazer, *The Whistleblowers: Exposing Corruption in Government and Industry* (1989).

Institute for Court Management

The Institute for Court Management was created in 1970 to help improve the administration and management of the nation's courts. The institute, which provides training programs for court personnel, was one of several court reforms adopted in the 1970s that have been credited, at least in part, to the work of Chief Justice Warren Burger.

See also Burger, Warren E.; Courts; Federal Judicial Center; National Center for State Courts.
References Philip L. Dubois, *The Politics of Judicial Reform* (1982).

Intercircuit Tribunal

See National Court of Appeals.

Interstate Cooperation

Since the end of the Second World War, and particularly after the 1960s, state governments have made concerted efforts to work together to address mutual problems. One of the primary ways they have accomplished this is through the increased use of interstate compacts. Political scientist

David Saffell reports that in 1940, only 58 interstate compacts had been created. By 1975, the number had reached over 100. Today, more than 170 compacts have been enacted, addressing such diverse issues as economic development, environmental protection, and education. States have also turned frequently to more informal means of cooperation, including the creation of regional commissions, the passage of uniform state laws, and the greater use of existing regional government associations.

References Thad Beyle, "The Governor as Innovator in the Federal System" (1988); David C. Saffell, *State and Local Government: Politics and Public Policies* (1993).

Iran-Contra Affair

The Iran-Contra affair was a political scandal in the Reagan administration that involved the illegal sale of arms to Iran in 1986 to try to gain the release of American hostages held in Lebanon. The profits from the arms sale were then channeled covertly to Contra rebels in Nicaragua, who were trying to overthrow that nation's communist government. The arms sale and transfer of funds had been arranged by members of the National Security Council staff. When the affair became public, it damaged support for Reagan and led to demands for placing new restraints on the president. The affair led to the conviction of National Security Adviser John Poindexter and one of his staff members, Lieutenant Colonel Oliver North. North's conviction was overturned by the courts on the grounds that his testimony before a congressional investigative committee had tainted the evidence against him.

See also Reagan, Ronald W.
References George C. Edwards III and Stephen J. Wayne, *Presidential Leadership: Politics and Policy Making* (1990); Charles W. Kegley, Jr., and Eugene R. Wittkopf, *American Foreign Policy: Pattern and Process* (1991).

Iron Triangles

See Subgovernments.

Isolationism

Until the Second World War, the United States pursued a foreign policy of isolationism, in which it tried to avoid political and military involvement in world affairs. The war pushed the nation out of its isolationist position, however, and into a role of world leader. Although the nation's leaders remain committed to keeping the United States actively involved in world affairs, some political activists on both the left and the right have called for a greatly reduced role now that the Cold War is over, causing them to be labeled neo-isolationists. One of the leading political figures associated with neo-isolationism is former presidential candidate Patrick Buchanan.

See also Buchanan, Patrick J.; Foreign Policy; Multilateralism.
References Charles W. Kegley, Jr., and Eugene R. Wittkopf, *American Foreign Policy: Pattern and Process* (1991); Edward C. Luck, "Making Peace" (1992–1993); George Weigel, *Idealism without Illusion: U.S. Foreign Policy in the 1990s* (1994).

Issue Networks

See Subgovernments.

Item Veto

See Line-Item Veto.

J

Jackson, Jesse (b. 1941)

The Reverend Jesse Jackson is an eminent civil rights leader and advocate of social reforms to benefit the poor and minorities. Active in the civil rights movement as a student in North Carolina during the 1960s, Jackson then moved to Chicago, where he joined in a social program started by Martin Luther King, Jr., called Operation Breadbasket, along with the Southern Christian Leadership Conference (SCLC). Jackson led efforts in the city to provide economic opportunity for African-Americans and to eliminate housing segregation. He was ordained as a Baptist minister in 1968. During the 1970s he left the SCLC to found People United to Serve Humanity (PUSH), a national group dedicated to fighting racial discrimination. He ran unsuccessfully for president in the 1984 and 1988 Democratic primaries, and though he continues his affiliation with the party, he is a strong, left-leaning critic of some of its stances. Jackson founded the Rainbow Coalition in 1984 to promote civil rights, international policies that support human rights, and "progressive" reforms in domestic social programs. He has also been a leading advocate of statehood for the District of Columbia.

See also National Rainbow Coalition.

References Michael Barone and Grant Ujifusa, eds., *Almanac of American Politics* (1995); Allen D. Hertzke, *Echoes of Discontent: Jesse Jackson, Pat Robertson, and the Resurgence of Populism* (1993).

Jarvis, Howard (1902–1986)

Howard Jarvis, a Los Angeles realtor and businessman, was one of the preeminent leaders in the tax revolt of the late 1970s as the architect of California's Proposition 13. The 1978 ballot initiative was the culmination of Jarvis's 15 years of attempted tax reduction initiatives. With cosponsor Paul Gann, Jarvis built a highly organized and well-funded grassroots effort to pass the property tax limitation measure. The timing for the revolt was right, as soaring real estate prices and property taxes left voters more than willing to support Jarvis's proposal. The measure won by a landslide, and discontented taxpayers in other states were quickly led to emulate Jarvis's efforts. In the late 1970s and 1980s, Jarvis sponsored several other important antitax initiatives in California.

See also Proposition 13; Tax Revolt; Taxes.

References Charles G. Bell and Charles M. Price, *California Government Today: Politics of Reform?* (1988); Virginia Gray and Herbert Jacob, eds., *Politics in the American States: A Comparative Analysis* (1996); Arthur B. Laffer and Jan P. Seymour, *The Economics of the Tax Revolt: A Reader* (1979).

Job Creation and Wage Enhancement Act

One of the ten provisions of the Republican Party's Contract with America, the Job Creation and Wage Enhancement Act called for a variety of reforms to encourage economic growth, including a cut in the capital gains tax, a change in how government programs are assessed in order to protect private property rights, and limitations on the use of federal mandates. This has been one of the most successful provisions of the contract, with Clinton signing legislation limiting unfunded mandates and loosening government paperwork restrictions.

See also Capital Gains Tax; Contract with America; Cost-Benefit Analysis; Paperwork; Property Rights Movement; Takings; Unfunded Mandates.
References Donna Cassata, "Paperwork Reduction Bill" (1995); David Hosansky, "Unfunded Mandates Law" (1995); "Republicans' Initial Promise: 100-Day Debate on 'Contract'" (1994); Clyde Wilcox, *The Latest American Revolution? The 1994 Elections and Their Implication for Governance* (1995).

Johnson, Lyndon B. (1908–1973) (36th U.S. President, 1963–1969)

Assuming the presidency after the assassination of John F. Kennedy in 1963, Lyndon Johnson, Texas Democrat and former Senate majority leader, became one of the most active presidents in U.S. history, proposing a sweeping agenda of social and political reforms to fight the nation's ills. His commitment to the war in Vietnam, however, eventually proved his undoing, and in a surprise announcement in March 1968, he broke off his bid for a second full term as president.

Among the legislation and programs that Johnson is credited with helping enact into law are the Civil Rights Act of 1964, the Economic Opportunity Act of 1964, the Elementary and Secondary Education Act of 1965, the Fair Housing Act of 1968, Head Start, the Jobs Corp, Medicaid, Medicare, the Model Cities Act of 1966, and the Voting Rights Act of 1965. Johnson is also considered responsible for concentrating greater political power in Washington, D.C., through his Creative Federalism program.

See also Administrative Reorganization; Civil Rights Act of 1964; Civil Rights Movement; Community Action Agencies; Creative Federalism; Education; Federal-State Relations; Great Society; Medicaid; Medicare; Model Cities Program; Vietnam War; Voting Rights Act; War on Poverty.
Reference Vaughn Davis Bornet, *The Presidency of Lyndon B. Johnson* (1983).

Joint Committee on the Organization of Congress

The Joint Committee on the Organization of Congress has been used on several occasions over the past 50 years to study organizational problems confronting Congress and to propose reforms. The committee was resurrected in 1965, and its work was considered important in the passage of the Legislative Reorganization Act of 1970. In 1992, the committee was resurrected once again to consider reforms to improve Congress's policy output and rebuild its image among the American public. The committee's efforts have been credited with providing important groundwork for the reforms adopted by the Republican majority after the 1994 election.

See also Congress; Legislative Reorganization Act.
References C. Lawrence Evans and Walter J. Oleszek, "The Politics of Congressional Reform: The Joint Committee on the Organization of Congress" (1995); Leroy N. Rieselbach, *Congressional Reform: The Changing Modern Congress* (1994).

Judicial Access

One of the most important reform movements in judicial politics today is the growing effort to ensure greater access to all elements of the judicial system, from increasing the availability of legal information to providing adequate representation for the poor. Many states have begun to examine and adopt court reforms to assist individuals who have disabilities or do not speak English, to reduce bias against the treatment of women and minorities, and to offer alternatives to the traditional courtroom, including the introduction of night court and alternative dispute resolution. Judicial access has also been a concern at the federal level. In 1990, Congress enacted the Civil Justice Reform Act to improve access by trying to cut costs and delays in the federal court system.

See also Alternative Dispute Resolution; Civil Justice Reform Act; Courts; Judicial Improvements and Access to Justice Act; Sentencing.
References Erick B. Low, "Accessing the Judicial System: The States' Response" (1994); Jeffrey J. Peck, "'Users United': The Civil Justice Reform Act of 1990" (1991); Judith Resnik, "Finding the Factfinders" (1993).

Judicial Activism

When judges actively use judicial review to overturn existing laws and to reinterpret public policy according to their personal beliefs, this is referred to as judicial activism. It can be compared with judicial restraint, when judges play a minimal role in changing or overturning public policy.

Conservatives have routinely criticized judicial activism as an inappropriate intrusion of the courts into politics, and have advocated judicial restraint. Many liberals, however, maintain that judicial activism is a legitimate means of bringing about social change and protecting individuals' rights.

Since the 1950s, these competing perspectives on judicial activism have played a major role in shaping debate on the direction of the nation's courts. Under Chief Justice Earl Warren's leadership, the U.S. Supreme Court was very active in the 1950s and 1960s, repeatedly intervening in policy matters to help bring about social change. However, Warren and the Court were heavily criticized by conservatives. After Warren retired in 1969, the Court began slowly to interpret cases from a more conservative perspective. Supporters of the change hailed the Court's new direction, arguing that the Court had become more restrained. Many liberal observers argue, however, that the change in the Court has not been toward judicial restraint, but toward a more conservative form of judicial activism.

See also Supreme Court; Warren, Earl.
References Henry R. Glick, "Policy Making and State Supreme Courts" (1991); William C. Louthan, *The United States Supreme Court: Lawmaking in the Third Branch* (1991).

Judicial Conduct

Both Congress and state legislatures have enacted important reforms over the past 30 years to make it easier to respond to charges of misconduct against judges. Until the 1980s, the primary means available to handle misconduct charges against federal judges was impeachment, which has rarely been used. In 1980, however, Congress enacted the Judicial Councils Reform and Judicial Conduct and Disability Act, which established procedures for filing complaints against and disciplining federal judges. Under the rules of the act, written complaints are filed with the federal appellate court. The chief judge of the circuit in which the complaint has been filed can dismiss the case or lead an investigation. If the investigation determines that a judge has acted inappropriately, the judicial council for that circuit can then take punitive action, including issuing a reprimand or censure. If the judge's actions are particularly egregious, the case may be sent on to the House of Representatives, which has the power of impeachment.

In 1990, Congress created a commission to examine the process for disciplining federal judges and to evaluate additional reforms. In its 1993 report, the commission concluded that the present system works reasonably well, and argued against making any sweeping changes.

Historically, the states have had more tools for handling judges who were charged with misconduct or were unable to perform their functions, but these tools were usually too cumbersome to be effective. The primary approach that was available was to remove unfit judges from the bench altogether, yet this was rarely accomplished. Three methods were used in the states to remove judges: impeachment, recall, and joint action by the state legislature and governor.

Since the 1960s, however, all 50 states have created some form of judicial conduct commission to investigate and help resolve problems involving judicial conduct. These commissions, which are usually composed of judges, lawyers, and appointees from outside the legal profession, have the power to discipline and, in some states, to remove unfit judges. The effectiveness of these commissions has been questioned, however, because commission members have often appeared reluctant to discipline their colleagues.

See also Courts; Judicial Councils Reform and Judicial Conduct and Disability Act; Judicial Selection; National Commission on Judicial Discipline and Removal.
References Henry J. Abraham, *The Judicial Process: An Introductory Analysis of the Courts of the United Stats, England, and France* (1993); Robert A. Carp and Ronald Stidham, *Judicial Process in America* (1993); National Commission on Judicial Discipline and Removal, *Report of the National Commission on Judicial Discipline and Removal* (1993).

Judicial Councils Reform and Judicial Conduct and Disability Act

The Judicial Councils Reform and Judicial Conduct and Disability Act, passed in 1980, gave the federal judicial councils greater control over the courts in their circuits and established procedures for filing complaints against judges. The act also established rules allowing the judicial councils to discipline federal judges.

See also Judicial Conduct.
References Henry J. Abraham, *The Judicial Process: An Introductory Analysis of the Courts of the United States, England, and France* (1993); Robert A. Carp and Ronald Stidham, *Judicial Process in America* (1993).

Judicial Improvements and Access to Justice Act

The Judicial Improvements and Access to Justice Act was one of two major bills enacted by Congress in 1988 to help relieve the caseload burden confronting the federal courts. The act established a federal commission to study federal court operations and to develop long-range plans for the future of the federal judiciary. The act also established an experimental arbitration program and removed the federal courts' jurisdiction over some types of disputes involving state laws.

See also Act to Improve the Administration of Justice; Caseload; Civil Justice Reform Act; Courts.
References Joan Biskupic, "U.S. Judges Turn to the Hill for Help on Pay, Work" (1989); Carl Tobias, "Improving the 1988 and 1990 Judicial Improvements Acts" (1994).

Judicial Restraint

See Judicial Activism.

Judicial Selection

The procedures by which federal and state judges are chosen have generated criticisms in recent years because of the controversial battles over U.S. Supreme Court nominees Robert Bork and Clarence Thomas and the growing importance of money in state judicial elections. These criticisms have led to a number of reform proposals that are meant to address the separate problems in judicial selection at both levels of the court system.

In general, most presidential appointments to federal court positions receive little public attention and are approved by the Senate without controversy. In 1987, however, President Reagan's nomination of Robert H. Bork to the U.S. Supreme Court aroused considerable criticism of the selection process because of the intense lobbying effort made by interest groups to influence Bork's fate. Opposed to Bork's conservative judicial philosophy, a large coalition of civil rights organizations put together a well-orchestrated campaign to defeat his nomination. Conservative groups, in turn, lobbied in Bork's behalf. After three weeks of hearings and widespread public debate, the Senate voted overwhelmingly against approving Bork's nomination.

Four years later, the nomination of Clarence Thomas to the Supreme Court generated more controversy because of Thomas's lack of judicial experience and the Senate Judiciary Committee's handling of information it had received regarding sexual harassment charges against him. These two nominations spurred increased talk of reforming the selection process to reduce the influence of interest groups, ensure better-quality nominees, and improve the Senate's confirmation hearings. Despite the talk, no major changes have been adopted. The Senate did add two women to the Judiciary Committee in 1993 to increase the sensitivity of the committee to issues of particular concern to women, including sexual harassment.

The most important recent effort to reform the selection process for lower federal court positions was the creation during President Jimmy Carter's administration of the Circuit Judge Nominating Commission to help evaluate and make recommendations on prospective judges. The commission, which was dismantled by President Ronald Reagan, was intended to increase the use of merit in the selection process. In addition, several U.S. senators have helped sponsor ad hoc commissions since the late 1970s to evaluate potential nominees for open judgeships in their states. This trend is seen as an important step in improving the quality of judges.

States rely on a variety of different formal procedures for choosing judges, including gubernatorial appointments, partisan and nonpartisan elections, and the merit plan. In recent years, the use of elections has caused controversy because of the increasingly negative tone and growing costs of many judicial campaigns. The rising cost of judicial campaigns is a widespread trend, though in some states it has been especially pronounced. In recent years, state supreme court candidates in Ohio, Texas, and Pennsylvania have spent millions of dollars to ensure their election. Reformers are particularly concerned about the sources of such funding and its potential to corrupt judicial decisions. One of the worst examples of ethically questionable behavior occurred in Texas during the 1980s when both Texaco and Pennzoil gave thousands of dollars in campaign contributions to members of the Texas Supreme Court while the two companies were engaged in a multibillion-dollar court case.

These trends have led to calls for reforms in how judges are selected in the states. At the most extreme, some reformers call for an end to popular election of judges altogether. The most often mentioned alternative is the merit plan, a selection method in which the governor appoints a judge from a list of qualified candidates selected by a judicial nominating commission. A year after the governor makes the appointment, state residents are allowed to vote on whether or not the judge should remain in office. Supporters argue that this plan reduces the corrupting influence of campaign contributions, causes selection of better-qualified judges than would otherwise be the case, and yet still permits some direct public input into judicial selection.

Opponents have attacked the merit plan, saying that there is no evidence that it produces better judges and that it unfairly deprives the public of the right to select judges. Moreover, several recent merit plan elections have themselves been the subject of controversy. One of the most egregious was a battle in California in 1986 over three state supreme court justices in which more than $11 million was spent by both sides.

Other reformers argue that instead of introducing the merit plan, states should create tougher campaign finance rules, establish public funding of judicial candidates, and find means to provide voters with better information about judicial candidates.

See also Circuit Judge Nominating Commission; Hill, Anita; Judicial Conduct; Merit Plan; Thomas, Clarence.

References Henry J. Abraham, *The Judicial Process: An Introductory Analysis of the Courts of the United States, England, and France* (1993); Robert A. Carp and Ronald Stidham, *Judicial Process in America* (1993); Robert F. Utter, "Justice, Money, and Sleaze" (1992); Richard A. Watson, *The Politics of the Bench and the Bar: Judicial Selection under the Missouri Plan* (1969); Tom Watson, "The Run for the Robes" (1991); Amy Young, "In the States" (1990).

Jury Trials

The unexpected verdict in the 1992 police brutality case involving Rodney King helped raise public awareness of the problems associated with jury trials, but legal experts have long discussed the need for jury reform. A litany of criticisms have been lodged against jury trials, among the most common of which are that jury decisions are often irrational and inconsistent, jurors do not understand complex issues and tend to make excessive awards, the juror selection process produces unrepresentative juries, jury trials are too long and expensive, and the nation's dependence on juries has had profound social costs, including boosting insurance rates and forcing individuals and businesses to change behavior to avoid lawsuits.

For each of the problems identified, a multitude of reforms have been proposed. To overcome the irrational and inconsistent decisions of juries, reformers have advocated restricting the discretion of jurors, requiring judges to provide better jury instructions, increasing the size of juries, and depending more on alternative forms of dispute resolution. To help jurors understand complex issues, many legal experts say jurors should be allowed to take notes throughout trials, to discuss the case as it unfolds, and to ask questions of witnesses through the judge. Jurors' abilities to comprehend particular issues may also be helped if judges were to play a more aggressive role in the courtroom, limiting the presentation of evidence and providing jurors with pretrial instructions. Some proposals to improve the jury selection process include requiring greater public participation, narrowing exemptions, and restricting changes of venue. To reduce the high costs and the length of trials, reformers advocate more efficient management of trials by judges and the imposition of higher fees on individuals who want to use jury trials.

Despite the questionable outcome in the Rodney King case and several other well-known recent cases, some legal experts argue that the problems with jury trials are overstated, and that many of the proposed reforms would be unwise. Defenders of the current system argue that desires to make jury decisions more rational and consistent, to increase jurors' technical expertise, and to cut costs should not be the only factors that dictate jury reforms. Instead, the judicial system needs to be structured in such a way that it enjoys widespread public support, produces results that reflect community values, and protects individuals against unreasonable laws. The problem with many of the proposed reforms is that they may detract from these goals.

See also Alternative Dispute Resolution; Courts.
Reference Robert E. Litan, ed., *Verdict: Assessing the Civil Jury System* (1993).

K

Keating Five

In a political scandal in the 1980s, five U.S. senators were charged with violating congressional ethics by trying to influence how federal regulators treated an ailing savings and loan owned by a wealthy campaign contributor. The senators, who became known as the Keating Five, appealed to the Federal Home Loan Bank Board on behalf of Lincoln Savings and Loan Association owner Charles H. Keating, Jr., who had contributed some $300,000 to their reelection campaigns. Of the five, Senator Alan Cranston of California was the only one reprimanded for his actions. The other four senators involved were Dennis DeConcini, John Glenn, John McCain, and Donald Riegle. The scandal is considered one of the key factors leading to the passage of the Ethics Reform Act of 1989.

See also Congress; Ethics Reform Act of 1989; Savings and Loan Crisis.
References Leroy N. Rieselbach, *Congressional Politics: The Evolving Legislative System* (1995); Bruce C. Wolpe, *Lobbying Congress: How the System Works* (1990).

Kemp, Jack R. (b. 1935)

Jack Kemp, former New York congressman and secretary of housing and urban development, first made his mark in the late 1970s as a proponent of tax cuts as a way to build the nation's economy. He was coauthor of the Kemp-Roth Tax Cut, an important 1978 tax reform proposal modeled on supply-side economic principles. According to Kemp, high taxes stifled investment, savings, and innovation, thereby stalling the economy. During the 1980s, he continued to push his tax-cutting agenda despite the economic woes of the Reagan years. Continuing his GOP involvement even after leaving his congressional seat, Kemp led a privately sponsored tax overhaul commission during 1995–1996 and endorsed some of the presidential candidates' calls for a flat income tax. He also warned the party that issues such as immigration and affirmative action policies could prove too divisive.

See also Economic Recovery Tax Act; FAST; Kemp-Roth Tax Cut; Revenue Act of 1978; Supply-Side Economics.
Reference Martin Feldstein, ed., *American Economic Policy in the 1980s* (1994); Arthur B. Laffer and Jan P. Seymour, *The Economics of the Tax Revolt: A Reader* (1979); "Washington Wire: Kemp's Support" (1995); R. A. Saldivar, "Trashing the Tax Code" (1996).

Kemp-Roth Tax Cut

The Kemp-Roth Tax Cut, proposed in the late 1970s, was the first modern attempt to apply supply-side economics to U.S. fiscal policy. Authored by Representative Jack

Kemp of New York and Senator William Roth of Delaware, the bill called for a 10 percent income tax cut in each of three successive years to promote economic growth. The proposal was offered as an amendment to the Revenue Act of 1978, but was defeated on the House floor. It was later resurrected by President Ronald Reagan, and a slightly modified version was incorporated into the Economic Recovery Tax Act of 1981. This version called for a 5 percent cut the first year, followed by 10 percent cuts in both of the next two years. Combined, these three cuts reduced the tax rate by 23 percent.

See also Economic Policy; Economic Recovery Tax Act; Fiscal Policy; Kemp, Jack R.; Revenue Act of 1978; Supply-Side Economics.
References Michael B. Berkman, *The State Roots of National Politics: Congress and the Tax Agenda, 1978–1986* (1993); Arthur B. Laffer and Jan P. Seymour, *The Economics of the Tax Revolt: A Reader* (1979); C. Eugene Steuerle, *The Tax Decade: How Taxes Came To Dominate the Public Agenda* (1992).

Keynesian Economics

The economic theory associated with the writings of British economist John Maynard Keynes dominated U.S. economic policy making from the late 1930s, when Keynes's seminal work *The General Theory of Employment, Interest, and Money* appeared, until the late 1970s.

Initially put forward in the middle of the Great Depression, Keynesian economics is concerned primarily with controlling the detrimental effects of the business cycle. Keynes wrote that the capitalist system does not automatically move toward equilibrium with full employment, but by using fiscal and monetary policies, the government could regulate demand to reduce unemployment. In very general terms, Keynesian economics argues that when the economy is in a recession and employment is down, the federal government should increase spending and reduce taxes to stimulate demand, which will spur economic growth. Conversely, when the economy is experiencing inflation, the government should reduce spending and increase taxes to reduce demand.

During the late 1970s, the nation economy experienced a period of economic stagnation with inflation, which led to growing disillusionment with Keynesian economics. In 1979, the Federal Reserve Board began to rely more on the monetarist ideas put forward by Milton Friedman. After Ronald Reagan was elected president in 1980, he briefly used supply-side economics to guide the nation's fiscal policy. Despite criticism, Keynesian economics continues to play a key role in shaping economic debate in the nation's capital.

See also Economic Policy; Fiscal Policy; Monetary Policy; Reaganomics; Stagflation; Supply-Side Economics.
References Paul A. Samuelson and William D. Nordhaus, *Economics* (1992); Herbert Stein, *Presidential Economics: The Making of Economic Policy from Roosevelt to Clinton* (1994).

King, Martin Luther, Jr. (1929–1968)

The Reverend Martin Luther King, Jr., was a minister who became the preeminent advocate of nonviolent protest during the turbulent civil rights movement of the 1950s and 1960s. The movement peaked with the March on Washington for Jobs and Freedom in August 1963, where King stood at the Lincoln Memorial and mesmerized the 250,000 participants with his now famous "I Have a Dream" speech. King's expressed wish that his children would "not be judged by the color of their skin, but by the content of their character" has been used by conservative reformers in the 1990s against affirmative action policies aimed at increasing minority employment.

King's peaceful demonstrations against racial prejudice were instrumental in the passage of the Civil Rights Act of 1964. The Southern Christian Leadership Conference, of which he was an influential member, also helped promote voting rights legislation, including the Voting Rights Act of 1965. King was assassinated in 1968.

See also Civil Rights Act of 1964; Civil Rights Movement; Southern Christian Leadership Conference; Voting Rights Act.

References Charles W. Eagles, ed., *The Civil Rights Movement in America* (1986); David J. Garrow, *Protest at Selma: Martin Luther King, Jr. and the Voting Rights Act of 1965* (1978).

Koreagate

Koreagate was one of several influence-peddling scandals that stirred up American politics during the 1970s and impelled Congress to enact stricter ethics codes. The scandal, which was exposed in 1977, involved the bribery of U.S. congressmen by South Korean officials. In the end, only one lawmaker was found guilty, but the incident left the American public questioning the ethics of representatives who willingly exchanged their political power for personal gain.

The incident took place after the Nixon administration moved to withdraw some 20,000 troops from South Korea in 1970. The decision was opposed by South Korean President Park Chung Hee, and in the early 1970s, South Korean businessman Tongsun Park began to coordinate lobbying efforts in Congress to halt the withdrawal. Senators and representatives were offered money, trips, and honorary degrees from South Korean universities as rewards for supporting South Korea's interests.

The Justice Department and the Senate's ethics committee began to investigate the scandal after allegations of bribery surfaced in the mid-1970s. By 1977, it was reported that the 115 legislators involved in the scandal attempted to conceal their actions. In congressional testimony that same year, Park admitted to handing over $850,000 to legislators. Several congressmen were indicted, but only one, Richard T. Hanna, a Democrat from California, was found guilty. Three other democratic congressmen were reprimanded for their involvement in the scandal.

As a result of Koreagate and other scandals, Congress tightened its own code of ethics in 1977 and then passed the Ethics in Government Act the following year.

See also Congress; Ethics; Ethics in Government Act; Obey Commission.

References Lawrence C. Dodd and Bruce I. Oppenheimer, "The House in Transition: Change and Consolidation" (1981); Susan Garment, *Scandal: The Culture of Mistrust in American Politics* (1991); George C. Kohn, *Encyclopedia of American Scandal* (1989).

L

Laffer, Arthur B. (b. 1940)

Arthur B. Laffer, a University of Southern California economics professor, produced an economic model on the relationship between tax rates and tax revenues in 1974 that became part of the intellectual foundation of supply-side economic. According to the model, known as the Laffer curve, the relationship between taxes and government revenue is curvilinear, and when taxes become too high, government revenue will actually decline. Laffer first drew the curve on a napkin during a dinner conversation with a *Wall Street Journal* editor. The editor, Jude Wanniski, became convinced of the validity of Laffer's argument, and helped champion its use by the government. Wanniski was the one who named the model the Laffer curve. Laffer's work helped motivate the Kemp-Roth Tax Cut proposal in 1978 and the Economic Recovery Tax Act of 1981.

See also Economic Recovery Tax Act; Kemp-Roth Tax Cut; Laffer Curve; Supply-Side Economics.

References Don Fullerton, "Tax Policy" (1994); Arthur B. Laffer and Jan P. Seymour, *The Economics of the Tax Revolt: A Reader* (1979).

Laffer Curve

The Laffer curve is one of the primary economic models associated with supply-side economics, and a major inspiration in shaping President Ronald Reagan's economic policy. The curve, which was proposed by economist Arthur Laffer, depicts the relationship between tax rates and tax revenues. The curve shows that the same level of tax revenue is attainable by two different tax rates. As tax rate rises, government revenue will increase until it reaches a maximum level. Once the tax rate becomes too high, however, there is a disincentive to work, and tax revenue begins to decline. Thus, for example, when the tax rate is at either 0 or 100 percent, the government will not bring in any revenue.

Laffer and other supply-side economists argued in the late 1970s that the federal tax rate had become too high, and that if the government wanted to stimulate economic growth and increase revenue, it should cut taxes. President Reagan was reportedly heavily swayed by Laffer's argument in deciding to support supply-side economics.

See also Economic Policy; Economic Recovery Tax Act; Fiscal Policy; Kemp-Roth Tax Cut; Laffer, Arthur B.; Reaganomics; Supply-Side Economics.

References Arthur B. Laffer and Jan P. Seymour, *The Economics of the Tax Revolt: A Reader* (1979); Paul A. Samuelson and William D. Nordhaus, *Economics* (1992).

Laissez-Faire Economics

In a laissez-faire economic system, the government plays a minimal role in the marketplace, serving only to protect private property and provide a means to adjudicate legal conflicts. This is commonly referred to as a free market system. The term *laissez-faire* means "to let do" or to leave alone.

See also Free Market Economy; Keynesian Economics.
References Milton Friedman and Rose Friedman, *Free To Choose* (1980); Robert Lekachman, *Greed Is Not Enough: Reaganomics* (1983).

Leadership Conference on Civil Rights

The Leadership Conference on Civil Rights is a coalition of national civil rights organizations that promotes the passage of legislation and enforcement of current laws relating to racial equality. It was founded as the civil rights movement gained force in 1950. During the 1980s it published critiques of the Reagan administration's economic and social policies. It monitors the civil rights-related actions of the U.S. Departments of Justice and Education.

See also Civil Rights Lobby; Civil Rights Movement.

Leadership PACs

Leadership PACs are a type of personal political action committee that are controlled by individual officeholders or candidates, providing these individuals with legal means to raise and distribute campaign contributions to other candidates running for office. These PACs, which are also referred to as leadership campaign committees, are used by officeholders and candidates to improve their party's position in a legislature and their own political clout.

Leadership PACs have been criticized for corrupting the political system by encouraging elected officials to accumulate increasingly large campaign war chests while making interest groups more powerful. Supporters of these PACs argue that they increase electoral competition by channeling funds to candidates who would otherwise receive little support.

See also Campaign Finance; Legislative Caucus Campaign Committees; Personal PACs; Political Action Committees; Transfers.
References *Congressional Campaign Finances: History, Facts, and Controversy* (1992); Anthony Gierzynski, *Legislative Party Campaign Committees in the American States* (1992); David B. Magleby and Candice J. Nelson, *The Money Chase: Congressional Campaign Finance Reform* (1990); Frank J. Sorauf, *Money in American Elections* (1988).

League of United Latin American Citizens (LULAC)

The League of United Latin American Citizens is an organization that promotes voter registration and political involvement among people of Hispanic background. The group actively supports legislation that ensures the civil rights of minorities.

See also Chicano Movement.
Reference Rodolfo Acuña, *Occupied America: A History of Chicanos* (1988).

League of Women Voters

Though founded as a women's organization in 1920, when women gained the vote, the League of Women Voters now includes both men and women among its members. It is a nonpartisan public affairs organization that is especially active during national campaign years. The group promotes voter registration and good citizenship, occasionally taking action on selected political issues while declining to support particular candidates. A strong proponent and sponsor of presidential debates, the League also presses for ethical standards in government, public financing of campaigns, and state constitutional reform.

See also Presidential Debates; Voter Registration.

Learnfare

Learnfare is an experimental welfare reform program introduced in Wisconsin in 1987 that attempts to reduce welfare dependency by requiring the teenage children in welfare families to attend school in order for the family to receive full benefits. If a child drops out of school or misses three days in a month without a valid excuse, the family's benefits from Aid to Families with Dependent Children are reduced. Although the program has been hailed by some welfare reformers as a way to encourage welfare recipients to develop skills, initial studies have found that it has had little effect on school attendance.

See also Aid to Families with Dependent Children; Bridefare; Thompson, Tommy G.; Welfare; Workfare.

Reference Marcus E. Ethridge and Stephen L. Percy, "A New Kind of Public Policy Encounters Disappointing Results: Implementing Learnfare in Wisconsin" (1993).

Legislative Careerism

Growing numbers of state legislators nationwide are devoting their careers to legislative service. Before the 1960s, very few state legislators made legislative service their sole or even primary occupation. Today, however, career legislators can be found across the United States; they are particularly prevalent in legislatures that provide high salaries and are professional in structure.

See also Career Legislators; Professional Legislature; Professional Politicians.

References Alan Ehrenhalt, *The United States of Ambition: Politicians, Power, and the Pursuit of Office (1991);* Gary F. Moncrief and Joel A. Thompson, eds., *Changing Patterns in State Legislative Careers* (1992).

Legislative Caucus Campaign Committees

One of the most important trends in congressional and state legislative elections over the past two decades has been the growing involvement of legislative party caucuses in campaign politics. Until the 1970s, most legislative parties paid little attention to campaign politics, as they focused their efforts instead on the tasks associated with governing.

In the 1970s, however, legislative parties began to create campaign committees to help party candidates. These campaign committees handle many of the roles traditionally associated with political parties, including recruiting and training candidates, raising campaign funds, and providing candidates with political expertise, staff support, and whatever other services the candidates need to attain office. These party committees are unusual, however, in that their membership consists solely of incumbent legislators.

At the national level, four congressional campaign committees exist: the National Republican Congressional Committee, the Democratic Congressional Campaign Committee, the National Republican Senatorial Committee, and the Democratic Senatorial Campaign Committee. Legislative campaign committees also exist in more than a dozen states.

Supporters of these legislative caucus campaign committees argue that they make elections more competitive and improve representation because they provide campaign support to candidates who would otherwise receive little help from traditional campaign contributors.

Opponents argue that the rise of these committees has caused legislators to become more concerned with raising campaign funds than with finding policy solutions to the nation's problems. In California, discontent with the role of legislative parties in elections led state voters to pass Proposition 73 in 1988, banning campaign contributions from the legislative party caucuses. The law, however, was overturned by a federal district court.

See also Campaign Finance; Leadership PACs; Political Parties; Transfers.
References Richard A. Clucas, *The Speaker's Electoral Connection: Willie Brown and the California Assembly* (1995); Anthony Gierzynski, *Legislative Party Campaign Committees in the American States* (1992); Frank J. Sorauf, *Money in American Elections* (1988).

Legislative Reform Movement

When the United States was founded, the legislature was the preeminent branch of state government. By the 1940s, however, the role of state legislatures had changed dramatically, so that most played only a minor role in shaping state policy decisions while being overshadowed by the governor and interest groups. The problem was that state legislatures did not have the time, resources, or independence to address state problems and to consider alternative policy solutions. Most legislatures met for only brief periods every other year, with heavy turnover every session. Legislatures had limited staff support, no research capacity, and minimal office space and supplies for members. Moreover, the members were paid so poorly that in some states they had to rely on interest groups to survive.

After the Second World War and through the 1950s, some states began to take steps to improve the quality of their state legislatures, but it was not until the 1960s and 1970s that major changes were undertaken. The rise of this legislative reform movement is generally tied to the large influx of new members in legislatures across the United States after the *Baker v. Carr* reapportionment decision in 1962, though the movement arrived earlier in some states. California is considered to have been one of the leaders in the reform effort. Beginning in the late 1950s, the California legislature began to take steps to improve its staff support and research capacities. In 1966, state voters approved sweeping constitutional reforms to allow the state legislature to become a professional body. The success of the reform movement in California is often credited to State Assembly Speaker Jesse Unruh, who then went on to help champion the reform effort nationwide.

Over the next few years, numerous legislative and political organizations nationwide began to promote the need for reform. The most important of these groups was the Citizens' Conference on State Legislatures (CCSL). In the early 1970s, the CCSL established a set of criteria that legislatures needed to meet in order to perform their job. It then evaluated and ranked the states on how well they met these separate requirements. When the conference released its ranking in 1971, it generated nationwide attention, spurring state after state to reform its legislature. The reform movement continued in many states through the late 1980s. Some of the reforms enacted included the introduction of annual sessions, the addition of staff, the creation of professional research agencies, the implementation of new internal rules and structure, and increases in the benefits and pay given members.

The reform movement profoundly strengthened the position of legislatures in state politics, allowing them in many states to become a coequal branch with the governor. Alan Rosenthal, who is one of the nation's leading experts on state legislatures, writes that the reform movement has led to the increased capacity and independence of state legislatures. However, the professionalization that has occurred in state legislatures due to the reform movement has been criticized by many who feel the legislatures have grown unresponsive to voters' concerns. The result is that today there is a growing effort to roll back these reforms. The preeminent counterreform measure that has been offered is the introduction of term limits on state legislators.

See also *Baker v. Carr;* Bill Introduction Limit; Citizen Legislators; Citizens' Conference on State Legislatures; Legislative Careerism; Oversight; Professional Legislature; Reapportionment Revolution; State Renewal; Term Limits; Unruh, Jesse.
References Citizens' Conference on State Legislatures, *The Sometimes Governments: A Critical Study of the 50 American Legislatures* (1973); Richard A. Clucas, *The Speaker's Electoral Connection: Willie Brown and the California Assembly* (1995); Alan Rosenthal, *Governors and Legislatures: Contending Powers* (1990); Alan Rosenthal, "The Legislative Institution: In Transition and at Risk" (1993).

Legislative Reorganization Act

The Legislative Reorganization Act was the first major reform package enacted in the 1970s to democratize Congress. The 1970 act arose out of discontent among liberal Democrats who had little influence on the policy-making process despite their growing electoral gains in the 1950s and 1960s. The problem confronting the liberals was that southern Democrats were able to control the powerful committee chair positions because of the seniority rule. The Legislative Reorganization Act included rules changes that reduced the power of the committee chairs and allowed all members greater participation in the process.

To reduce the chairs' power, the act established new procedures allowing committees to move forward in some circumstances without the chair's support, and it included several provisions opening up the decision-making process to greater public scrutiny. Two of the act's most important procedural changes were that it permitted the ranking majority member of a committee to preside if the chair was absent and it allowed a committee majority to move for floor consideration of a bill that has been granted a rule even if the committee chair did not want it heard. Both of these changes reduced the chairs' direct control over legislation. To open up the process, the act allowed members to call for recorded teller votes in the Committee of the Whole, required the disclosure of members' positions in committee roll call votes, and allowed for the presence of television cameras in committee. These actions made it more difficult for committee chairs to pressure members to support their positions. The act also made efforts to improve the position of the minority party by guaranteeing the minority party the right to call witnesses in hearings, increasing the size of staff available to minority members, and ensuring the minority of time for debate on all amendments that had been printed in advance in the *Congressional Record*.

See also Bolling Committee; Congress; Hansen Committee; Joint Committee on the Organization of Congress; Seniority Rule.
References Leroy N. Rieselbach, *Congressional Reform: The Changing Modern Congress* (1994); David W. Rohde, *Parties and Leaders in the Postreform House* (1991).

Legislative Veto

In some legislation, Congress reserves the power to overturn an executive branch decision by a simple majority vote in one or both houses, by an individual congressional committee, or by a committee chair.

Historically, this legislative veto has been used by Congress to exercise oversight on executive branch decisions.

The first legislative veto was created in 1932 when Congress passed a law giving President Herbert Hoover the power to restructure the federal bureaucracy by executive order. The act included a provision that gave either house the power to reject Hoover's actions. Since the 1930s, Congress has sporadically included provisions in legislation giving itself the power to exercise the legislative veto. In the 1970s, Congress began to turn to the veto more frequently as it tried to reassert its power against President Richard Nixon. It has been estimated that as many as 150 laws were enacted during the 1970s that included provisions for the legislative veto. Two of the most prominent of these laws were the War Powers Resolution of 1973 and the Congressional Budget and Impoundment Control Act of 1974.

In 1983, the Supreme Court struck down the use of the legislative veto in *Immigration and Nationalization Service v. Chadha* as a violation of the constitutional requirement that all legislative acts be presented to the president for approval. The Court's actions to some extent reduced Congress's ability to control the executive branch, which led some reformers to call for a constitutional amendment reestablishing this power. Yet the decision did not cause the veto to disappear completely. In some instances, Congress has introduced new procedures to attain the same end, including requiring the passage of a joint resolution before the president's actions can take place. Moreover, on several occasions Congress has simply written provisions for new legislative vetoes into law despite the Court's decision.

The legislative veto has also been used by many state legislatures.

See also Congressional Budget and Impoundment Control Act; Oversight; War Powers Resolution.
References Leroy N. Rieselbach, *Congressional Reform: The Changing Modern Congress* (1994); Steven S. Smith, *The American Congress* (1995); James L. Sundquist, *Constitutional Reform and Effective Government* (1992).

Lieutenant Governor

Historically, the role of lieutenant governor in state politics has been similar to that of the vice president of the United States. Lieutenant governors are ordinarily the next in line to succeed the governor and, at least in name, many serve as president of their state senates. Yet, like the vice presidency, the position of lieutenant governor has long been of little political importance. In recent years, however, many states have attempted to expand the importance of the role by making the lieutenant governor a member of the governor's cabinet and assigning to the office specific responsibilities.

One characteristic that distinguishes the lieutenant governor from the vice president is that most are elected separately from the state's chief executive, which can create a situation in which the governor and lieutenant governor are from different parties. Many states have moved to elect governor and lieutenant governor jointly in recent years to overcome this potential problem. In 1950, only 1 state jointly elected the governor and lieutenant governor; today, 22 do so.

See also Cabinet System, State; Governors.
References Alice Chasan Edelman, "Is There Room at the Top?" (1986); Larry J. Sabato, *Goodbye to Good-Time Charlie: The American Governorship Transformed* (1983); Laura M. Zaremba, "Governor and Lieutenant Governor on Same Ballot" (1994).

Limited Voting

Limited voting is an alternative election system that has been proposed to improve the representation of minority political parties and racial minorities. The system, which is very similar to cumulative voting, works by allowing voters to cast more than one vote in a multimember district election. The total number of votes varies, but is less than the number of seats to be filled in the district. A voter can cast all of his or her votes for one candidate or divide the votes among candidates. By concentrating votes on one candidate, minority parties and racial groups are more likely to elect representatives of their choice than they are in traditional multimember district elections.

This electoral method was introduced in a number of southern states after the Civil War to ensure the representation of minority party candidates. In more recent years, a number of communities in Alabama have introduced limited voting to ensure the representation of African-Americans.

See also Cumulative Voting; Election Systems; Multimember Districts; Single-Member Districts.
Reference Wilma Rule and Joseph F. Zimmerman, eds., *United States Electoral Systems: Their Impact on Women and Minorities* (1992).

Line-Item Veto

The line-item veto is a type of power held by many state governors that allows them to deny passage of specific portions of appropriations bills. It is considered a more powerful weapon than the regular veto, which allows a governor only to reject a bill in its entirety. As with the regular veto, the line-item veto can be overridden by a two-thirds majority in both state houses (some states require only a majority or 60 percent of the members to override).

Presidents since Ulysses S. Grant have requested this power. Since the rise in the federal deficit in the 1980s, the debate over the presidential line-item veto gained increasing attention. During his last term in office, President Reagan repeatedly used the State of the Union Address to call for Congress to grant the president the item veto. The Republican Party's Contract with America in 1994 included a provision for giving the president this power. In March 1996, Congress passed legislation granting the president the power of the line-item veto. However, many constitutional scholars believe the act will be declared unconstitutional. These scholars argue that Congress does not have the power to grant a line-item veto, but that the veto can only be created through a constitutional amendment.

Supporters of the line-item veto argue that it will help curtail the use of legislative riders, control federal spending, and reduce the deficit. Plus, they argue, it is very popular within the states. Opponents maintain that it is more of a political weapon than an effective tool for reducing spending and the deficit, pointing at studies that indicate it has had little effect on balancing state budgets and in some cases has actually encouraged legislators to be more irresponsible in putting budgets together. Moreover, opponents have argued that the adoption of the item veto will give too much power to the president. Finally, some argue that the item veto simply will not work at the national level because the federal budget is structured differently from state budgets and is less detailed in identifying how funds are spent.

The terms *line-item veto* and *item veto* are often used interchangeably, though some scholars argue that the latter term is the more appropriate one to use when discussing national politics, as the federal budget does not include individual lines as state budgets do.

See also Budget Deficit, Federal; Contract with

America; Fiscal Responsibility Act; Omnibus Legislation; Pork-Barrel Legislation; President.
References Robert J. Spitzer, *The Presidential Veto: Touchstone of the American Presidency* (1988); James L. Sundquist, *Constitutional Reform and Effective Government* (1992); Andrew Taylor, "Congress Hands President a Budgetar Scalpel" (1996); Richard A. Watson, *Presidential Vetoes and Public Policy* (1993).

Literacy Tests

In the past, some states required potential voters to pass state-devised literacy tests. The nature and types of these tests varied considerably by state, but in their most extreme form they required citizens to answer detailed questions on the political process and the U.S. Constitution before they were allowed to register to vote. Use of such tests was particularly common in the South, where they were employed to disenfranchise African-Americans. The use of literacy tests to disqualify voters was banned under the 1975 amendments to the Voting Rights Act.

See also Electoral Discrimination; Voting Rights Act.
Reference Chandler Davidson, ed., *Minority Vote Dilution* (1989).

Lobby Disclosure

The requirement that interest group lobbyists regularly file detailed reports on their activities and finances, including information on the distribution of all gifts, campaign contributions, and other expenditures, is referred to as lobby disclosure. This procedure is seen as vital to reduce the influence of special interests in policy making and to restore trust in government. The Federal Regulation of Lobbying Act of 1946 required disclosure information from all individuals lobbying Congress, but the act did not cover other branches of government. The Lobby Disclosure Act of 1995 expanded the list of individuals who must register as lobbyists, including those who lobby the executive branch, and established detailed reporting requirements.

Most states require some disclosure of lobbying activities, but the requirements and effectiveness of state rules vary considerably. The state of Washington is considered to have one of the most effective lobbying laws, requiring disclosure information from almost everyone who attempts to influence government decisions. At the other extreme is Wyoming, which has no lobbying disclosure law at all.

See also Lobbying.
References Common Cause, "Lobby Disclosure Reform in the States" (1994); Ronald J. Hrebenar and Ruth K. Scott, *Interest Group Politics in America* (1990).

Lobbying

Many political observers have long criticized the apparent influence that lobbyists have in Washington, D.C., and in state capitals, yet very few laws have been enacted to regulate the behavior of lobbyists. Critics argue that this lack of regulation allows corruption to flourish, reduces the government's accountability, and produces legislation that is not representative of the people's interests.

The most important federal law governing lobbying activity until 1995 was the Federal Regulation of Lobbying Act, which was enacted as part of the Legislative Reorganization Act of 1946. The act required individuals who had been hired by someone else to lobby Congress to register in the House and the Senate and to file quarterly reports on their lobbying activities. Although the act made a sincere effort to provide more information about lobbyists, it was filled with loopholes, poorly enforced, and limited in scope. The act was imprecise in identifying who had to file disclosure statements and what needed to be disclosed, and it applied only to efforts to lobby Congress.

Over the next three decades, repeated efforts were made to create tougher lobbying laws, but without success. These efforts escalated in the 1970s in the wake of Watergate and other political scandals. The most comprehensive reform effort of this period was the Open Government Act, which was proposed in 1975. This act called for a strengthening of registration laws, more complete financial disclosure, and reporting of all gifts to federal employees exceeding $25. The act included penalties for those who fail to comply and gave enforcement responsibility to the Federal Election Commission. The proposal was highly praised by reformers, but it was ultimately defeated by a broad coalition of interest groups.

Even though Congress did not enact a comprehensive bill to regulate lobbying activities in the 1970s, it adopted various ethics reforms that were designed in part to reduce the influence of interest groups. The Ethics in Government Act of 1978 required executive branch officials to file regular financial disclosure statements on their outside income and established restrictions on the ability of former executive branch officials to lobby the agencies in which they had worked. In 1977, the House adopted the Obey Commission reforms, which set limits on the size of gifts members could received from interest groups and required members to report all gifts and honoraria in annual financial disclosure statements. In 1978, the Senate adopted similar reforms.

Efforts to regulate lobbyists died down in the 1980s, though President Reagan took steps to curtail the lobbying activities of nonprofit groups that received support from the federal government by threatening to cut back the funds flowing to these groups and to remove their nonprofit status. Supporters of this "defunding" effort argue that it is inappropriate for these groups to be involved in lobbying. Critics charge, however, that Reagan's effort was simply a veiled attempt to reduce the influence of liberal interests. In 1989, Congress banned the recipients of federal funds from using these funds for lobbying purposes. The effort to defund nonprofit groups was revived in Congress in 1995, though the proposal met resistance in the Senate and was withdrawn.

Pressure to reform the nation's lobbying laws mounted in the 1990s as the public grew increasingly disillusioned with government. In 1994, House Democrats championed a major reform proposal, but were unable to garner enough votes to get it enacted. The next year, however, Congress enacted strict new disclosure rules that were designed to close the loopholes in the 1946 lobbying law. The Lobby Disclosure Act of 1995 expanded the number of individuals who must register as lobbyists and established more detailed reporting requirements. The law is much more precise than the 1946 act in identifying who is to be considered a lobbyist, and it includes those who lobby the executive branch. The law requires lobbyists to disclose their clients, the issues they are lobbying, and their expenditures.

Along with this new lobbying law, Congress enacted new ethics rules in 1995 that were further designed to reduce the influence of lobbyists. In July, the Senate banned individual gifts of more than $50 and set a $100 annual limit on the amount of gifts that senators and their staffs can receive. These limitations include meals and entertainment. A few months later, the House banned all gifts to House members except for some small home-state goods. Combined, the Lobby Disclosure Act and these new ethics rules represent the most sweeping federal lobbying reform in U.S. history.

As at the national level, the effort to create stricter lobbying laws escalated in the states in the 1970s. California's Political Reform Act of 1974 is considered one of the most comprehensive lobbying reforms in the nation. The act established strict limitations on gifts and required lobbyists to submit regular reports on their lobbying activities and finances. It strengthened the state's campaign finance reporting requirements, imposed conflict-of-interest laws on elected officials, and established the Fair Political Practices Commission to administer it. In 1990, California tightened its lobbying laws even more, banning honoraria, creating stiffer restrictions on gifts, and establishing revolving-door regulations. Although few state laws are as comprehensive as this, today all 50 states require lobbyists to register, and most call for some disclosure of lobbyists' financial activities. The effort to tighten congressional ethics and lobbying laws in 1995 is considered to have spurred similar movements at the state level, including the passage of such strict ethics rules against lobbying gifts that they are referred to as "No Cup of Coffee" Rules.

See also Campaign Finance; Ethics; Ethics in Government Act; Ethics Reform Act of 1989; Federal Election Campaign Act; Keating Five; Koreagate; Lobby Disclosure; Obey Commission; Political Reform Act of 1974; Revolving-Door Restrictions; Subgovernments.

References Charles G. Bell and Charles M. Price, *California Government Today: Politics of Reform?* (1988); Jeffrey M. Berry, *The Interest Group Society* (1989); Common Cause, "Lobby Disclosure Reform in the States" (1993); Ronald J. Hrebenar and Ruth K. Scott, *Interest Group Politics in America* (1990); Jerald A. Jacobs, ed., *Federal Lobbying* (1989); Nancy Lammers, ed., *The Washington Lobby* (1982); Jonathan Rabinovitz, "States Tighten Rules on Lobbyists' Gifts" (1996); Alan Rosenthal, *The Third House: Lobbyists and Lobbying in the States* (1993); Johnathan D. Salant, "Bill Would Open Windows on Lobbying Efforts" (1995); Kay Lehman Schlozman and John T. Tierney, *Organized Interests and American Democracy* (1986); Jack L. Walker, Mobilizing Interest Groups in America: Patrons, Professions, and Social Movements (1991).

Long Ballot

See Short Ballot.

Loser Pays Rules

To reduce the growing caseload burden facing the court system, some court reformers advocate legislation requiring the losers in civil cases to pay all court costs in addition to whatever monetary judgments are made against them. These proposals are referred to as Loser Pays Rules.

See also Caseload; Common Sense Legal Reform Act; Courts.

Lotteries

The recession of the late 1980s and early 1990s put severe stress on state government finances as tax revenues dropped and demand for services rose. To solve their fiscal woes, many states began to look for alternative sources of revenue. One of the primary alternatives introduced was the state-sponsored lottery. From 1980 to 1994, the number of states holding lotteries rose from 13 to 37. Two of the most common types of lottery games that have been introduced are instant winners (scratch cards) and lotto.

Despite their widespread use, lotteries are often criticized as being a regressive form of taxation and as encouraging what many consider to be undesirable social behavior (i.e., gambling). Lotteries have also been attacked because they have not produced as much revenue as anticipated. In 1993, they generated $9.3 billion in state revenue nationwide, which represented less than 4 percent of all tax revenue in those states with lotteries.

See also Finance, State; Gambling; Regressive Tax; Taxes.
Reference Steven D. Gold, "It's Not a Miracle, It's a Mirage" (1994).

LULUs (Locally Unwanted Land Uses)

LULUs, or locally unwanted land uses, are development projects, such as hazardous waste disposal facilities, prisons, and low-cost housing, that are viewed as undesirable by the residents of the areas in which they are planned. The strong activism of NIMBY (not in my backyard) groups and individuals has made it difficult for state and local governments to find sites for many of these projects. One proposal that has been offered to overcome opposition to LULUs is to offer financial benefits to residents in local communities as incentive for accepting these projects. Alternatively, some analysts argue that local residents would be more willing to accept such projects if there were greater public awareness of their importance.

See also NIMBY.
References Terry Christensen, *Local Politics: Governing at the Grassroots* (1995); John J. Harrigan, *Politics and Policy in States and Communities* (1994); Herbert Inhaber, "Of LULUs, NIMBYs, and NIMTOOs" (1992); Albert R. Matheny and Bruce A. Williams, "Strong Democracy and the Challenge of Siting Hazardous Waste Disposal Facilities in Florida" (1988).

M

Majority-Minority Districts

The 1982 amendments to the Voting Rights Act, as well as subsequent court decisions, forced state legislatures to adopt voting procedures that ensured the election of minorities to public office. One of the primary methods states used to accomplish this was by carefully drawing state legislative and congressional district boundaries to create individual districts in which the majority of voters were minority group members.

The use of these majority-minority districts had a profound effect on the 1992 elections, bringing a record number of minorities to Congress and state legislatures. The number of African-Americans in Congress increased from 26 to 40, and the number of Hispanics rose from 13 to 19. At the state level, the percentage of all legislators who were African-American rose from 6 percent to almost 7 percent.

Although the Voting Rights Act has been hailed for opening the political process to African-Americans and other minorities, some critics have attacked the 1982 amendments and these majority-minority districts for moving the nation away from an ideal of a color-blind society and creating a quota system for minority representatives.

See also Electoral Discrimination; *Shaw v. Reno; Thornburg v. Gingles;* Voting Rights Act.

References John R. Cranford, "The New Class: More Diverse, Less Lawyerly, Younger" (1992); Bernard Grofman and Chandler Davidson, eds., *Controversies in Minority Voting: The Voting Rights Act in Perspective* (1992); Karl T. Kurtz, "The 1992 State Legislative Elections in Perspective" (1992); "The Voting Rights Act after *Shaw v. Reno*" (1995).

Management by Objectives

Under administrative and budgeting reforms guided by the philosophy of management by objectives (MBO), government agencies identify specific tasks for themselves and their staffs to accomplish, and then budget decisions are based on how well these objectives are accomplished. Unlike performance budgeting, which focuses on each agency's effectiveness in fulfilling its prescribed function, MBO is more concerned with setting work objectives. President Richard Nixon introduced the use of MBO among federal agencies in 1973, though his interest in it quickly waned. A few agencies continue to use aspects of MBO, as do some state and local governments.

See also Budgeting Techniques; Bureaucracy; Cost-Benefit Analysis; Empowerment; Incrementalism; Performance Budgeting; Program Budgeting; Reinventing Government; Total Quality Management; Zero-Base Budgeting.

References Donald F. Kettl, *Deficit Politics: Public*

Budgeting in Its Institutional and Historical Context (1992); Robert D. Lee, Jr., and Ronald W. Johnson, *Public Budgeting Systems* (1983).

Mandates, Federal

A federal mandate is a national law that requires state or local governments to perform a particular task or service. Since the mid-1980s, the number of federal mandates has increased dramatically, and this has caused them to emerge as one of the most critical concerns among state and local government officials in the 1990s. These officials have been particularly disturbed by the increased use of "unfunded mandates," which require state and local governments to perform specific tasks but do not provide federal funds to help cover the costs.

The federal government first began to use mandates to attain policy goals in the mid-1960s. Until that time, the federal government had been reluctant to force states and local governments directly to take specific actions. There was a slight increase in the use of mandates in the 1970s and early 1980s, before their use exploded in the mid-1980s. In 1991 alone, more than 20 new mandates were enacted, at an estimated cost to states of $15 billion. Some of the more visible mandates enacted in recent years are the Americans with Disabilities Act, the Clean Air Restoration and Standards Act, and the National Voter Registration Act (Motor Voter).

Mandates have become increasingly popular in Washington because they allow Congress to dictate new policies without having to find the funds to pay for them and increasing the federal budget deficit. For state and local governments, however, the increase in federal mandates has worsened their fiscal position while straining their ability to provide other services.

In 1993, state and local government officials began to make a concerted effort to bring reforms in the use of federal mandates. The U.S. Conference of Mayors and the National Association of Counties sponsored a "National Unfunded Mandates (NUM) Day" in October of that year to bring attention to the problems created by federal mandates. The event helped spark increased media attention to the problem and stimulated Congress to take a more serious look at reform.

In 1994, the Republican Party's Contract with America included a provision calling for mandate reform. After the Republican success in the 1994 elections, mandate reform became one of the first concerns of the new Republican majority in Congress. In March 1995, Congress enacted the Unfunded Mandate Reform Act of 1995, banning the creation of new unfunded mandates. The law should make it more difficult for Congress to rely on unfunded mandates, though the ultimate effect of the act is uncertain because it contains a number of important exceptions that may allow Congress to circumvent the law's intent.

See also Americans with Disabilities Act; Balanced Budget Amendment; Budget Deficit, Federal; Contract with America; Federal-State Relations; Job Creation and Wage Enhancement Act; Mandates, State; National Voter Registration Act; Preemption.

References Timothy J. Conlan et al., "Deregulating Federalism? The Politics of Mandate Reform in the 104th Congress" (1995); Martha Fabricus, "More Dictates from the Feds" (1991); David Hosansky, "Unfunded Mandates Law" (1995); Alice M. Rivlin, *Reviving the American Dream: The Economy, the States, and the Federal Government* (1992); David B. Walker, *The Rebirth of Federalism: Slouching toward Washington* (1995).

Mandates, State

One of the biggest concerns among state officials in the 1990s is the federal government's growing use of mandates to force states to perform particular tasks. With many of these demands, the federal government has refused to provide money to the states to help cover the costs, putting additional strain on the states' already stressed fiscal position.

The problem of mandates is not limited to the federal government. Many local officials similarly argue that one of the biggest problems they confront is the growing use of mandates on local governments by the states. As at the state level, the use of mandates is causing increased fiscal strain on local governments while reducing the local governments' ability to provide other services. State mandates are particularly common in the areas of special education programs and solid waste management.

The problem is so severe that many local leaders have pressured state governments to adopt legislation requiring the states to reimburse local governments for programs required by state mandates. Such laws are referred to as mandate-reimbursement requirements. As of 1993, 16 states had adopted these requirements. Moreover, 10 states have rewritten their constitutions banning unfunded mandates.

See also Finance, Local; Home Rule; Mandates, Federal.

References Ann O'M. Bowman and Richard C. Kearney, *State and Local Government* (1993); Kathleen Sylvester, "Mandate Blues," (1989); Linda Wagar, "A Declaration of War" (1995); David B. Walker, *The Rebirth of Federalism: Slouching toward Washington* (1995).

Mandatory Appellate Jurisdiction

Since the passage of the Judiciary Act of 1925, the U.S. Supreme Court has had considerable discretion in choosing the cases it wants to hear, though more than 20 percent of the Court's caseload up through the mid-1980s consisted of cases the Court was required by law to hear. The Judiciary Act reduced what is called the Court's mandatory appellate jurisdiction, but in several classes of appeals, the Court was still required to review cases. This included those situations in which a state court or a U.S. Court of Appeals invalidated a federal law, or when a state court upheld a law that conflicted with federal law.

In the early 1980s, several members of the Supreme Court and judicial scholars began to advocate an end to this mandatory jurisdiction in order to reduce the Court's mounting workload. In 1988, Congress enacted legislation that abolished all mandatory appeals and gave the Supreme Court almost complete freedom to decide what cases it wanted to hear. This legislation is referred to as the Act to Improve the Administration of Justice.

See also Act to Improve the Administration of Justice; Caseload; Supreme Court.

References Samuel Estreicher and John Sexton, *Redefining the Supreme Court's Role: A Theory of Managing the Federal Judicial Process* (1986); William C. Louthan, *The United States Supreme Court: Lawmaking in the Third Branch of Government* (1991).

Marshall, Thurgood (1908–1993)

Thurgood Marshall was one of the most important leaders of the civil rights movement from the 1930s to the 1960s, championing reform through the courts as an attorney and then chief counsel for the National Association for the Advancement of Colored People (NAACP). Marshall was one of the founders and a director of the NAACP Legal Defense and Education Fund. He is credited with winning some of the most important civil rights cases of this period, including *Brown v. Board of Education* (1954).

In 1962, Marshall was appointed to the

U.S. Court of Appeals for the Second Circuit. In 1965, Marshall was named U.S. Solicitor General in the Johnson administration. In 1967, Marshall was appointed to the U. S. Supreme Court, becoming the first African-American to serve on the nation's highest court. After Marshall retired from the Court in 1991, he was replaced by Clarence Thomas.

See also Civil Rights Movement; Supreme Court; Thomas, Clarence.
References "Marshall, Thurgood" (1989); Mark V. Tushnet, *Making Civil Rights Law: Thurgood Marshall and the Supreme Court, 1936–1961* (1994).

McGovern, George S. (b. 1922)

As a Democratic U.S. senator from South Dakota, George McGovern led an effort to reform the Democratic Party following the dissension among delegates at the 1968 national convention. The party selected McGovern as one of the two chairs of the Commission on Party Structure and Delegate Selection (McGovern-Fraser Commission), which rewrote the party's nomination rules prior to the 1972 national convention. The commission reforms radically altered the delegate selection process and made the party more representative of rank-and-file Democrats. These reforms also led to the increased importance of presidential primaries in choosing nominees and marked a shift from party-centered to candidate-centered politics. McGovern won the 1972 presidential primary under the new rules, largely because he gleaned enough delegates sympathetic to his liberal social policy and antiwar proposals. He was defeated in the general election by a landslide to his Republican opponent, Richard Nixon.

McGovern lost his longtime senatorial seat in the Reagan Republican revolution of 1980.

See also McGovern-Fraser Commission; Presidential Primaries.
Reference Byron E. Shafer, *Quiet Revolution: The Struggle for the Democratic Party and the Shaping of Post-Reform Politics* (1983).

McGovern-Fraser Commission

In response to the violent protests at its 1968 national convention in Chicago, the Democratic Party created the Commission on Party Structure and Delegate Selection to propose reforms for opening up the party's delegate selection process. Better known by the names of its chairmen, the McGovern-Fraser Commission developed a list of guidelines to change how states select delegates to the convention. The commission's proposals, which were adopted by the Democratic Party in 1971, profoundly altered the presidential selection process and the role played by political parties in elections.

Until the 1970s, the national nominating conventions were predominantly controlled by party leaders, with only a minority of delegates selected by voters through primary elections. The lack of public input into the selection process brought demands for reform prior to the 1968 election, but the protests on the streets outside the Chicago convention brought the issue to the forefront of political debate. The final straw for many protesters was the Democratic Party's decision to nominate Hubert Humphrey as its presidential candidate that year, even though Humphrey had not run in any primary elections.

The Commission on Party Structure and Delegate Selection was directed to propose changes in party rules to ensure that all Democratic voters had an opportunity to participate in the selection process and to make the convention's decisions more representative of rank-and-file Democrats.

Senator George S. McGovern of South Dakota was appointed to chair the commission. When McGovern resigned to run for president, he was replaced by Representative Donald M. Fraser of Minnesota.

The commission produced 18 different guidelines for changes in party rules. Among the most important, the commission demanded that state parties provide ample public notice of all meetings associated with delegate selection. The commission required that all delegates be selected either through primary elections or in an open system of caucuses, and it banned the automatic selection of party officials. It called for the proportional representation of delegates for all candidates receiving more than 15 percent of the vote in a state. It prohibited the use of the unit rule, in which all delegates were required to vote for the candidate with the majority of delegates. Finally, the commission required that the numbers of minorities and women from each state delegation be reasonably similar to their proportion in the general population.

The result of these reforms was a reduction in the importance of party organizations in selecting candidates and the emergence of more candidate-centered campaigns. The public notice requirements caused many states to remove delegate selection from the caucuses and instead to use primaries for this purpose. The commission did not ban the use of caucuses, but many state party leaders decided it was preferable to choose delegates in separate primaries instead of opening up the caucus system and risking loss of control over the party's other activities. In 1968, only 16 states used primaries to select Democratic Party delegates. Eight years later, 30 states did. The number reached 38 in 1992.

The spread in the use of primary elections has meant that candidates no longer have to appeal to party leaders for support in order to be nominated for president; rather, they must convince voters. This change has made primary elections the central focus of the presidential nomination process. Although the McGovern-Fraser Commission was concerned with reforming the Democratic Party, the Republican Party has similarly increased its use of primary elections to select convention delegates.

After the disastrous nomination of George McGovern in 1972 and the election of political outsider Jimmy Carter in 1976, the Democratic Party instituted a variety of counterreforms to assert greater control by the national party organization in the delegate selection process. Although these counterreforms have increased the number of party officials participating at the national nominating convention, the primary elections remain of preeminent importance in the section of presidential nominees.

See also Candidate-Centered Campaigns; Fairness Commission; Fraser, Donald; Hughes Commission; Hunt Commission; McGovern, George S.; Mikulski Commission; Mississippi Freedom Democratic Party; National Primary; Open Caucuses; Political Parties; Presidential Primaries; Unit Rule; Winograd Commission.

References Larry M. Bartels, *Presidential Primaries and the Dynamics of Public Choice* (1988); James W. Ceasar, *Reforming the Reforms: A Critical Analysis of the Presidential Selection Process* (1982); William Crotty and John S. Jackson III, *Presidential Primaries and Nominations* (1985); Byron E. Shafer, *Quiet Revolution: The Struggle for the Democratic Party and the Shaping of Post-Reform Politics* (1983).

Medicaid

Medicaid is a federal program that provides health insurance to the poor. One of the major innovations of President Lyndon Johnson's Great Society, the program is administered by the states and jointly funded by both federal and state governments. Medicaid has come under increased attack in recent years because of its mounting costs. The total amount spent by the states on Medicaid rose from $27 billion in 1989 to $50 billion three years later, and today the program represents the fastest-growing part of state budgets. A similar trend has been experienced at the federal level, as federal spending on Medicaid has increased by more than 16 percent each year since 1981. Along with Medicare, it is considered by many to be a primary factor in causing the current federal budget deficit. Moreover, if the program is not changed, costs are expected to continue to soar.

As a result of these trends, Medicaid is a primary target of reform today, helping to stimulate President Clinton's health care reform proposal in 1993 and becoming a major focus of debate in the battle to eliminate the federal deficit. Much of the reform effort has taken place at the state level, where government leaders have been trying to reduce the fiscal stress caused by mounting Medicaid costs. One of the most common types of reforms introduced has been managed health care, a system in which the state pays a health care organization to handle an individual recipient. An alternative approach is the decision made by the state of Oregon in 1991 to ration health care benefits to Medicaid recipients.

During the federal budget battle in late 1995, the Republican majority in Congress was championing a proposal to remove Medicaid's status as an "entitlement" program and to turn the program completely over to state government control, with the federal government providing block grants to help fund it. As 1996 began, the fate of this proposal was still uncertain.

See also Big Swap; Budget Deficit, Federal; Entitlements; Finance, State; Great Society; Health Care; Medicare.

References Daniel P. Franklin, *Making Ends Meet: Congressional Budgeting in the Age of Deficits* (1993); Steven D. Gold, *The Fiscal Crisis of the States: Lessons for the Future* (1995); Jackie Koszczuk, "Republicans' Hopes for 1996 Lie in Unfinished Business" (1996); Penelope Lemov, "Climbing Out of the Medicaid Trap" (1991); Joseph A. Pechman and Michael S. McPherson, *Fulfilling America's Promise: Social Policies for the 1990s* (1992); Pauline Vaillancourt Rosenau, ed., *Health Care Reform in the Nineties* (1994).

Medicare

Medicare is the federal program that provides health insurance for the elderly. Created in 1965 as part of President Lyndon Johnson's Great Society, Medicare is an entitlement program that covers hospital and nursing home costs for Americans over 65 years old. An optional program provides coverage on physician charges, diagnostic services, laboratory expenses, and other costs. Funding for Medicare comes from payroll taxes, general revenue, and premiums.

The rising costs of Medicare in recent years have made it the focus of considerable reform efforts in Washington, D.C. From 1981 to 1991, federal spending on Medicare increased nearly 17 percent a year, a rate far exceeding that of any other federal program. Along with Medicaid, it is considered by many to be a primary factor leading to the current national budget deficit. The effect of Medicare on the budget is expected to worsen as the large wave of baby boomers reaches eligibility age, unless substantial reforms are enacted.

The federal government made several efforts to reform Medicare in the 1980s. One of the most important was the passage of legislation in 1983 that established a fixed amount the federal government would pay for specific hospital costs. In

1989, similar legislation was enacted to establish fixed payments for physician services. Despite these efforts, the cost of Medicare continued to rise. The result is that Medicare remains the center of debate in the nation's capital over how best to provide health benefits for the elderly while reducing costs.

Among the primary reforms being discussed today to reduce the costs of Medicare are instituting a higher age for eligibility, placing a tax on Medicare benefits, instituting means tests, rationing benefits, and encouraging greater use of private health insurance. More comprehensive reform proposals call for replacing Medicare with universal health care insurance. Despite the attention given to the budgetary consequences of Medicare, other reformers argue that changes are needed in the program to reduce out-of-pocket costs for poorer recipients and to fill in gaps in coverage.

The battle over Medicare's future was central to the federal budget debate in 1995, forcing a shutdown of the federal government as the new Republican majority in Congress fought with President Clinton over the extent to which Medicare spending should be reduced. Although the shutdown ended, the battle between the two sides had not been resolved as 1996 began.

See also Budget Deficit, Federal; Entitlements; Great Society; Health Care; Medicaid.

References Daniel P. Franklin, *Making Ends Meet: Congressional Budgeting in the Age of Deficits* (1993); Eric R. Kingson and Edward D. Berkowitz, *Social Security and Medicare: A Policy Primer* (1993); Marilyn Moon, *Medicare Now and in the Future* (1993); Joseph A. Pechman and Michael S. McPherson, *Fulfilling America's Promise: Social Policies for the 1990s* (1992); John R. Wolfe, *The Coming Health Crisis: Who Will Pay for Care for the Aged in the Twenty-first Century* (1993).

Merit Plan

The merit plan method for selecting state judges has been strongly advocated by members of the legal profession since the 1930s as a way to improve the quality of judges selected, increase the independence of the judiciary, and provide some, though limited, public input into the selection of judges. The merit plan has remained a popular reform proposal, and it is currently used in more than 20 states.

The most prominent type of merit plan is the Missouri Plan. Under this method, a commission composed of judges, lawyers, and gubernatorial appointees makes nominations to fill vacant judgeships. When a vacancy occurs, the commission reviews the backgrounds of potential nominees and then forwards a list of the most qualified to the governor, who then selects one of the individuals to fill the position. One or two years after the judge is appointed to the bench, state residents are asked to vote on whether the judge should be allowed to remain in that position. No alternative candidates are offered in this election; instead, the voters are simply asked if the judge should be allowed to remain on the bench. If the voters support the appointment, the judge is allowed to remain. If the voters object, the process begins again. After this initial election, the judge's name is put before the voters again every several years.

The California Plan is a well-known alternative to the Missouri Plan. Its primary difference is that it includes one additional step in the selection process. After the governor chooses a person to fill a judicial vacancy, the California State Commission on Judicial Appointments is given the power to veto the selection.

The merit plan is seen as preferable to other forms of nominations because it ensures professional input into the selection of judges. Moreover, it removes the selection of judges from some of the worst excesses of campaign politics that are found in states that rely on either partisan or nonpartisan elections to choose judges. The process, however, still allows citizens to vote on judges, which is not permitted with traditional gubernatorial appointments.

Critics argue that there is no evidence that the merit plan produces better judges, nor does it remove politics from the selection process. In addition, many argue that it deprives the public of its right to select judges and gives too much power to a small, nonelected elite.

See also Judicial Selection.
References Ann O'M. Bowman and Richard C. Kearney, *State and Local Government* (1993); Richard A. Watson, *The Politics of the Bench and the Bar: Judicial Selection under the Missouri Plan* (1969); Tom Watson, "The Run for the Robes" (1991).

Merit System

Under the merit personnel system, government hiring decisions are based on performance and not politics. This system is often compared with patronage systems, in which government jobs are distributed by the party in power to loyal party members. Several recent court decisions as well as changing attitudes about patronage have decreased the use of patronage systems in the past three decades, which has helped expand the use of the merit system.

See also *Elrod v. Burns;* Party Machines; Patronage; *Rutan v. Republican Party of Illinois.*
References Cheri Collis, "Clearing Up the Spoils System" (1990); Ronald N. Johnson and Gary D. Libecap, *The Federal Civil Service System and the Problem of Bureaucracy: The Economics and Politics of Institutional Change* (1994); Jeffrey L. Katz, "The Slow Death of Political Patronage" (1991); Larry J. Sabato, *Goodbye to Good-Time Charlie: The American Governorship Transformed* (1983).

Merit Systems Protection Board

The three-member Merit Systems Protection Board was created by the 1978 Civil Service Reform Act to oversee the treatment of federal employees. The board is responsible for serving as an appeals board for federal employees who feel they have been unfairly treated by their supervisors. The board is also specifically authorized to help protect whistle-blowers from retaliatory action.

See also Civil Service Reform Act of 1978; Whistle-Blowing.
References William T. Gormley, Jr., *Taming the Bureaucracy: Muscles, Prayers, and Other Strategies* (1989); Ronald N. Johnson and Gary D. Libecap, *The Federal Civil Service System and the Problem of Bureaucracy: The Economics and Politics of Institutional Change* (1994); Donald J. Savoie, *Thatcher, Reagan, Mulroney: In Search of a New Bureaucracy* (1994).

Metropolitan Fragmentation

Many reformers believe that the most critical problem confronting the nation's metropolitan areas is that there are too many local governments. Instead of having one centralized government, metropolitan areas are fragmented into multiple governing bodies, with the average area having between 90 and 100 local governments. The primary difficulty confronting these local governments is that major metropolitan problems, from crime to transportation, do not stop at political boundaries, but overlap jurisdictions. Metropolitan reformers argue that the only way these problems can be addressed is through greater regional coordination or the introduction of regional government.

Intergovernmental relations expert David B. Walker has identified 17 different approaches metropolitan governments can introduce to overcome this fragmentation. These range from informal cooperation to the centralization of power into one broad metropolitan government. Each of these individual reforms has its own supporters and detractors. On one extreme, informal cooperation is the easiest to introduce, yet many reformers believe it is not adequate to solve these regional problems. At the other extreme, political pressure from existing governing bodies makes it difficult to create regional governments. Moreover, many critics argue that a single centralized government may be too large to deal effectively with many of these problems, and that such a large government would reduce local control over shaping government policies and services.

See also Annexation; Consolidation; Contracting for Services; Councils of Government; Extraterritorial Jurisdiction; Greater Portland Metropolitan Service District; Private Government; Regional Government; Special Districts; Twin Cities Metropolitan Council.
References Terry Christensen, *Local Politics: Governing at the Grassroots* (1995); John J. Harrigan, *Political Change in the Metropolis* (1993); David B. Walker, *The Rebirth of Federalism: Slouching toward Washington* (1995).

Mexican American Legal Defense and Educational Fund (MALDEF)

Founded in 1968 to "protect and promote the civil rights of over 25 million Latinos living in the United States," the Mexican American Legal Defense and Educational Fund involves itself in civil rights litigation (including several key desegregation cases during the 1970s) and lobbies state legislatures and Congress for antidiscriminatory reforms. The Los Angeles-based organization was actively involved in the campaign against the California anti-immigrant initiative Proposition 187 in 1994. MALDEF has also played a leading role in protecting Mexican-American voting rights, helping to persuade Congress in 1975 to expand the Voting Rights Act to include protection for language minorities.

See also Proposition 187; Redistricting; Voting Rights Act.
Reference Linda Chavez, *Out of the Barrio: Toward a New Politics of Hispanic Assimilation* (1991).

Mikulski Commission

The Mikulski Commission was created by the Democratic Party after the party's presidential nominee, George McGovern, was overwhelmingly defeated by Richard Nixon in the 1972 election. The commission arose out of discontent among party officials who blamed the party's poor showing on the McGovern-Fraser reforms, which had excluded party officials from participating in the 1972 national nominating convention.

The Mikulski Commission's report, which was adopted for the 1976 election, allowed a minor increase in the role of party officials at the convention, but in general limited them to a nonvoting role. In addition, the commission banned winner-take-all primaries, ended the proportional representation of minorities and women at the convention, and required that proportional representation be used in the distribution of delegate seats among competing candidates in states using caucuses and conventions to choose delegates. The commission, which was chaired by Representative Barbara Mikulski of Maryland, was officially titled the Commission on Delegate Selection and Party Structure.

See also Hughes Commission; Hunt Commission; McGovern-Fraser Commission; Winograd Commission.
References William Crotty and John S. Jackson III, *Presidential Primaries and Nominations* (1985); Thomas R. Marshall, *Presidential Nominations in a Reform Age* (1981); Nelson W. Polsby, *Consequences of Party Reform* (1983).

Miller v. Johnson

In *Miller v. Johnson* (1995), the U.S. Supreme Court ruled that electoral redistricting plans may violate the constitutional rights of white voters if race is the "predominant" factor in deciding where to place district boundaries. The Court's decision was its first significant action on voting rights since it began to question the use of race conscious redistricting in the 1993 court case *Shaw v. Reno.*

The *Miller* decision did not ban the use of racial consideration in drawing district lines, but as in the *Shaw* case, it suggested that there are limits to what the Court considers constitutional in promoting minority representation. However, the Court's decision left unanswered the question of how far a state can or must go in considering race when drawing districting boundaries. The Court is expected to address this issue again in the near future.

The Court's decision in the *Miller* case overturned Georgia's congressional redistricting plan.

See also *Shaw v. Reno;* Voting Rights Act.
References Holly Idelson, "It's Back to the Drawing Board on Minority Districts" (1995); Mark E. Rush, "From *Shaw v. Reno* to *Miller v. Johnson:* Minority Representation and State Compliance with the Voting Rights Act" (1995).

Mississippi Freedom Democratic Party

The first modern efforts to reform the Democratic Party are often traced to the 1964 national convention, when members of the Mississippi Freedom Democratic Party challenged the seating of the state's all-white official delegation, which had been chosen through the state's discriminatory election laws. As part of the compromise to end the conflict, the party adopted a resolution banning discrimination in the presidential selection process. The resolution was important because it represented the first effort by the national party to exert its power over how state parties select delegates. The resolution was used in 1968 to deny seats to the official Mississippi delegation to the convention.

See also Hughes Commission; McGovern-Fraser Commission; Political Parties.
References William Crotty and John S. Jackson III, *Presidential Primaries and Nominations* (1985); Austin Ranney, *Curing the Mischiefs of Faction: Party Reform in America* (1975).

Missouri Plan

See Merit Plan.

Model Cities Program

The Model Cities Program was created in 1966 to help solve the social and economic problems confronting the nation's urban core by directing federal resources to selected U.S. cities. Part of President Lyndon Johnson's Great Society, it was one of several initiatives in the 1960s in which the federal government took a much more direct and aggressive role than it had in the past to confront America's social ills. Although the program is considered to have had little success in meeting its goals, it is credited with expanding the role of regional government in metropolitan areas and with helping to strengthen community leadership in the urban core.

See also Councils of Government; Great Society; Regional Government.
References Bernard J. Frieden and Marshall Kaplan, *The Politics of Neglect: Urban Aid from Model Cities to Revenue Sharing* (1975); John J. Harrigan, *Political Change in the Metropolis* (1993).

Model City Charter

Since the late 1800s, the National Municipal League (now known as the National

Civic League) has offered reform proposals on how best to structure city government so that it is both democratic and effective. The proposals are laid out in detail in the League's Model City Charter, which is often used by city government officials as a reference point in restructuring efforts. The National Municipal League has consistently been a strong advocate of the council-manager form of city government, though in recent editions of the Model City Charter it has increasingly recognized the need for flexibility in designing specific government bodies. In cities with mayor-council forms of government, it advocates giving the mayor strong powers.

See also Council-Manager; National Civic League; Strong Mayor.
References David N. Ammons and Charldean Newell, "'City Managers Don't Make Policy': A Lie; Let's Face It" (1988); National Civil League, *Model City Charter* (1989).

Model State Constitution

The National Municipal League (now known as the National Civic League) created what it viewed as an ideal state constitution in 1921. The league's handiwork, known as the Model State Constitution, has served as a guidepost since that time in efforts to reform state constitutions. The model is far shorter than most state constitutions. It includes a bill of rights and provides a general outline for state government structure and operation. The model has been revised five times since it was first put forward, most recently in 1968.

See also Constitutions, State; Governors; Unicameralism.
References Ann O'M. Bowman and Richard C. Kearney, *State and Local Government* (1993); John J. Harrigan, *Politics and Policy in States and Communities* (1994).

Monetarism

Monetarism is an economic theory that gained prominence in the 1970s and has since helped shape conservative economic reform. Monetarists argue that the nation's economy would work more efficiently with limited government intervention and a small, but fixed, increase in the money supply each year. The monetarist argument helped influence the Federal Reserve Board's decision to tighten the money supply in 1979 to reduce inflation. When the nation experienced a recession in 1982, however, the Federal Reserve abandoned the strict monetary policy preferred by monetarists and expanded the money supply to invigorate the economy. Milton Friedman, the 1976 Nobel Prize winner in economics, is often considered the preeminent proponent of monetarist theory.

See also Economic Policy; Friedman, Milton; Monetary Policy; Reaganomics; Volcker, Paul.
References Robert Lekachman, *Greed Is Not Enough: Reaganomics* (1983); Herbert Stein, *Presidential Economics: The Making of Economic Policy from Roosevelt to Clinton* (1994).

Monetary Policy

The federal government's monetary policy is concerned with the use of the money supply and interest rates to regulate the nation's economy. Until the late 1970s, the Federal Reserve used the money supply primarily as a means to help control interest rates. When interest rates rose because of inflation, the Federal Reserve would loosen the money supply to help bring interest rates down. Conversely, when interest rates dropped during an economic downturn, the Reserve would tighten the money supply.

In 1979, however, the board began to use the money supply more directly to control demand and, consequently, the nation's economic growth. The Reserve Board's actions, which came during the chairmanship of Paul Volcker, was considered a major change in Federal Reserve policy. Specifically, the Federal Reserve introduced a strict monetarist policy, restricting the money supply to reduce demand and gain control over the nation's skyrocketing inflation rate. The board stayed with this restrictive policy until 1982, when the recession put pressure on the Federal Reserve to stimulate the economy by loosening the money supply. Since this experiment with monetarism ended, the federal government has been more flexible in its use of the money supply and interest rates to regulate demand and achieve its economic policy goals.

The nation's monetary policy is set by the Federal Reserve Board, a seven-member body appointed by the president with the Senate's approval.

See also Economic Policy; Federal Reserve System; Monetarism; Reaganomics.

References William A. Niskanen, *Reaganomics: An Insider's Account of the Policies and People* (1988); Howard E. Shuman, *Politics and the Budget: The Struggle between the President and the Congress* (1992); Herbert Stein, *Presidential Economics: The Making of Economic Policy from Roosevelt to Clinton* (1994).

Motor Voter

See National Voter Registration Act.

Moynihan, Daniel Patrick (b. 1927)

Daniel Patrick Moynihan is a Democratic senator from New York who first became prominent as a social critic in 1965. His analysis of black urban poverty published in the report *The Negro Family: The Case for National Action* cited "a tangle of pathology" in black families and communities that posed a risk for the nation. The report sparked criticism that it placed the blame for black poverty on family structures rather than on the social and economic conditions of ghetto life. Moynihan's findings were part of the momentum that led to President Johnson's War on Poverty. Moynihan has served in the U.S. Senate since 1976, and is still considered a leading actor on social welfare issues. He was the chief Senate sponsor of the Family Support Act of 1988, which is considered the nation's most important welfare reform in 50 years.

See also Great Society; Welfare.

References Michael Barone and Grant Ujifusa, eds., *The Almanac of American Politics* (1995); Marshall Kaplan and Peggy L. Cuciti, *The Great Society and Its Legacy: Twenty Years of U.S. Social Policy* (1986).

Multilateralism

The effort of several nations to work together to address international problems or for collective security is referred to as multilateralism. Historically, the United States has disdained multilateralism, and has preferred to seek solutions to international problems and security issues on its own. With the collapse of the Soviet Union, many foreign policy experts and political leaders have argued that the United States needs to become more committed to multilateralism to solve world problems. These advocates of multilateralism argue that problems in the nation's economy and the complexity of international issues make it impossible for the United States to continue to forge unilateral policy decisions. President George Bush showed some commitment to multinationalism as he reached out to the United Nations and other countries before sending American troops to fight in the Persian Gulf War in 1991. Many political leaders are wary of placing too much emphasis on multilateral action, however, and would prefer that the United States continue to chart its own course in international affairs. The Republican Party's Contract with America, for instance, advocated severe restrictions on the use of U.S. troops under United Nations command.

See also Foreign Policy; Isolationism.
References Doug Bandow, "Avoiding War" (1992–1993); Edward C. Luck, "Making Peace" (1992–1993); George Weigel, *Idealism without Illusion* (1994).

Multimember Districts

In an electoral system with multimember districts, more than one representative is elected per district to a legislative body. Multimember districts were more common in the past, but they have become a target of recent voting rights reform. Civil rights organizations argue that they make it difficult for African-Americans and other minorities to elect candidates of their choice. The problem with these districts is they can be used to dilute minority groups' voting power by dividing those groups so that their members constitute a small minority in each district. The result is that in states with large minority populations, the minority groups are underrepresented in the state legislatures.

Some recent studies have found evidence that multimember districts can provide better representation of minorities and women than can single-member districts, which has created disagreement among reformers on the best form of electoral system.

The U.S. Supreme Court has not banned multimember districts, but it has forced individual states to replace them. In the 1986 case *Thornburg v. Gingles,* the Court ruled that multimember districts violate the Voting Rights Act if, based on the "totality of circumstances," they are found to deny minority groups access to the political process.

See also At-Large Elections; Election Systems; Electoral Discrimination; Single-Member Districts; *Thornburg v. Gingles;* Voting Rights Act.
References Chandler Davidson, ed., *Minority Vote Dilution* (1989); Bernard Grofman and Arend Lijphart, eds., *Electoral Laws and Their Political Consequences* (1986); Wilma Rule and Joseph F. Zimmerman, eds., *United States Electoral Systems: Their Impact on Women and Minorities* (1992).

Multiple Referrals

The rules of the House of Representatives give the Speaker the power to refer bills to committees after the bills have been introduced. Until the 1970s, the Speaker could refer a bill only to a single committee. In 1974, however, the House adopted a proposal put forward by the Bolling Committee to allow the Speaker to refer bills or parts of bills to more than one committee. The new rules allowed the Speaker to make these multiple referrals so that the separate committees could hear the legislation at the same time or sequentially. Initially, the House Speaker used this newfound power sparingly, but since the late 1970s, multiple referrals have become increasingly common. Congressional scholars argue that this rule change was one of the key factors in strengthening House leadership in the 1980s.

See also Bolling Committee; Congress; Hansen Committee.
References Leroy N. Rieselbach, *Congressional Reform: The Changing Modern Congress* (1994); David W. Rohde, *Parties and Leaders in the Postreform House* (1991).

Murray, Charles (b. 1943)

Charles Murray is a conservative social critic who has called for the repeal of all social programs that have been created since the mid-1960s to help the poor, arguing that these programs have actually had the reverse effect—that is, they have further impoverished the poor. Murray's 1984 book *Losing Ground* has been referred to as the "Bible of the second Reagan administration."

See also Reagan, Ronald W.; Welfare.
References James J. Heckman, "The Impact of Government on the Economic Status of Black Americans" (1989); Christopher Jencks, *Rethinking Social Policy: Race, Poverty, and the Underclass* (1992).

N

Nader, Ralph (b. 1934)

Ralph Nader is an activist who won public admiration when he successfully battled General Motors over automobile safety regulations in the 1960s, resulting in new government regulations on the industry. Nader has been credited with stimulating the creation of public interest groups and increasing their influence on U.S. lawmakers. He continues to champion various grassroots political reforms on issues ranging from campaign finance to trade relations. His group, Public Citizen, promotes issues of direct interest to consumers, including government regulation of industrial emissions, pure food and drugs, and product safety. In 1995, he was nominated for U.S. president by the California Greens Party.

See also Congress Watch; Public Citizen.
References William McGuire and Leslie Wheeler, eds., *American Social Leaders* (1993); Thomas E. Patterson, *The American Democracy* (1990); Ronald G. Shaiko, "More Bank for the Buck: The New Era of Full-Service Public Interest Organizations" (1991).

National Association for the Advancement of Colored People (NAACP)

The National Association for the Advancement of Colored People has played a major role in promoting equal rights for African-Americans since its founding in 1909 by W. E. B. Du Bois and other social reformers. During the civil rights movement of the 1950s and 1960s, the NAACP took the lead in seeking constitutional and other reforms of segregation laws, but the long-standing status of the organization was challenged by more outspoken political action groups. The NAACP continues to wield influence today by working "through the democratic process" and through various social programs designed to assist African-Americans in improving their economic position. The NAACP Legal Defense and Education Fund functions independently, supporting litigation on behalf of African-Americans particularly in the areas of education, employment, voting rights, housing, and other issues. The organization also sponsors a network of voter education and registration programs, particularly in the South.

See also Civil Rights Movement.
Reference Charles W. Eagles, ed., *The Civil Rights Movement in America* (1986).

National Center for State Courts

The National Center for State Courts was created in 1971 to conduct research on the state court system and propose reforms to improve court administration. The center was one of several successful programs that were created in the 1970s to help modernize the nation's court system and that have been credited, at least in part, to the work of Chief Justice Warren Burger. In addition to conducting research and proposing reforms, the center serves as a clearinghouse of information on state court programs.

See also Burger, Warren E.; Courts; Federal Judicial Center; Institute for Court Management.
References Philip L. Dubois, *The Politics of Judicial Reform* (1982).

National Change of Address and Voter Registration

One proposal to improve voter turnout in the United States is to increase the involvement of the U.S. Postal Service in voter registration. Reformers argue that the Postal Service's National Change of Address (NCOA) database should be used to monitor the movement of registered voters, to reregister voters who have moved locally, and to notify voters who have moved outside of their former voting districts to update their registration.

See also Voter Registration.
References Charlotte G. Mullins, *Innovations in Election Administration: Using NCOA Files for Verifying Voter Registration Lists* (1992); Ruy A. Teixeira, *The Disappearing American Voter* (1992).

National Civic League

The National Civic League (NCL), an organization of civic leaders, sponsors projects relating to state and local governance as well as citizen action on a number of issues. It is known for its Model City Charter, the template used by cities across the United States in structuring local government reforms. The NCL serves as a clearinghouse for information on state constitutions (offering a Model State Constitution), legislative apportionments, ethics, campaign finance, and other issues of concern to state and local government. Based in Denver, the organization was founded in 1894 as the National Municipal League.

See also Constitutions, State; Model City Charter; Model State Constitution.
Reference David N. Ammons and Charldean Newell, "'City Managers Don't Make Policy': A Lie; Let's Face It" (1988).

National Commission on Judicial Discipline and Removal

The National Commission on Judicial Discipline and Removal was created by Congress in 1990 to examine the process for disciplining federal judges and to evaluate possible reforms. In its 1993 report, the commission concluded that the present system works reasonably well and argued against making any sweeping changes.

See also Judicial Conduct.
Reference National Commission on Judicial Discipline and Removal, *Report of the National Commission on Judicial Discipline and Removal* (1993).

National Commission on Social Security Reform

See Social Security.

National Commission on the Public Service

See Volcker Commission.

National Commission on the State and Local Public Service

See Winter Commission.

National Court of Appeals

Since the late 1960s, members of the U.S. Supreme Court and judicial scholars have argued that the demands on the Supreme Court have grown so overwhelming that the quality of the Court's work may be suffering. One reform that has been proposed to reduce the burdens on the Court is the creation of a new national court of appeals that would sit between the current federal court of appeals and the Supreme Court.

The movement to create a new national court of appeals emerged in the early 1970s, when two separate commissions were created to study problems confronting the Supreme Court (the Freund Committee) and the federal appellate system (the Hruska Commission). The movement reached a high point in the 1980s after Chief Justice Warren Burger advocated the creation of a national court of appeals in a speech to the American Bar Association. Legislation to enact the new court, or what was titled the Intercircuit Tribunal of the United States Court of Appeals, was introduced into both houses of Congress. Despite these efforts, the court was never created. The proposal has not died, however. In 1992, legislation was introduced in Congress to establish an intercircuit panel in a five-year pilot project.

Advocates of the establishment of a national court of appeals argue that the court is necessary because the current burdens on the Supreme Court have forced the Court to leave many important legal questions unanswered. Opponents argue that the creation of the court might not reduce the Supreme Court's burden; rather, it could actually cause it to increase. Moreover, the creation of an additional tier in the structure of the court system could lead to more incoherence in the interpretation of the law.

See also Caseload; Freund Committee; Hruska Commission; Supreme Court.

References Samuel Estreicher and John Sexton, *Redefining the Supreme Court's Role: A Theory of Managing the Federal Judicial Process* (1986); Richard A. Posner, *The Federal Courts: Crisis and Reform* (1985); "Subcommittee Reports Out Study Committee Bill: Includes JSAS Reforms" (1992).

National Debt

When the federal government incurs a budget deficit, it must borrow money from private and public investors to cover its expenses. The total amount of money the federal government owes to investors through the accumulation of annual deficits is called the national debt. The unprecedented increase in the national debt during the past decade has made the debt one of the nation's most pressing political concerns.

One of the major problems with the expanding debt is that it places growing demands on the federal budget. During the 1980s, interest payments on the debt were among the most rapidly expanding part of the budget, and today they constitute approximately 15 percent of all outlays. With a larger slice of the budget going to interest payment, fewer funds are available to address the nation's problems. Moreover, critics complain that the presence of a large debt has forced the United States to borrow increasingly large amounts from foreign investors, which means that a large proportion of tax revenue is being channeled outside the nation.

Reformers have offered a variety of solutions that they believe will allow the United States to gain better control over federal spending and reduce the debt. These include the presidential line-item veto, a balanced budget amendment, a massive cutback in the federal government's role in society, and increased taxes.

Although debt repayment may represent a growing part of the budget, some economists believe that the debt does not pose as dangerous a threat as some reformers suggest. In particular, many argue that the absolute amount of the debt is not nearly as important as its relative size compared with the economy as a whole. When viewed in relation to the gross national product, the debt is lower today than it was in the 1950s.

See also Balanced Budget Amendment; Budget Deficit, Federal; Line-Item Veto.

References Daniel P. Franklin, *Making Ends Meet: Congressional Budgeting in the Age of Deficits* (1993); Donald F. Kettl, *Deficit Politics: Public Budgeting in Its Institutional and Historical Context* (1992); Alice M. Rivlin, *Reviving the American Dream: The Economy, the States, and the Federal Government* (1992); Howard E. Shuman, *Politics and the Budget: The Struggle between the President and the Congress* (1992).

National Emergencies Act

The National Emergencies Act was one of several laws enacted by Congress in the 1970s to try to limit the power of the president. The act, which was adopted in 1976, attempts to restrain the president's use of emergency powers by requiring him to notify Congress in advance of his intentions when taking emergency action. Moreover, the act also limited emergencies to six months and allowed either branch of government to exercise a legislative veto to halt the emergency.

See also Case Act; Congress; Congressional Budget and Impoundment Control Act; President; War Powers Resolution.

Reference Lance T. Leloup and Steve A. Shull, *Congress and the President: The Policy Connection* (1993).

National Health Security Act

See Health Care.

National Information Infrastructure (NII)

The National Information Infrastructure was a policy initiative championed by the Clinton administration to create a coordinated, universal system for public access to computer telecommunications. Major goals of this initiative, which was spearheaded by Vice President Albert Gore, include the promotion of private sector investment in new communications technologies, extension of universal service so that information is available to all at affordable prices, use of the widest variety of appropriate technologies, and increased access to government information. The National Telecommunications and Information Administration was created within the Department of Commerce to oversee the implementation of NII goals by the year 2000.

See also Electronic Town Meeting; Gore, Albert, Jr.; Telecommunications.

National Initiative

The constitution grants all legislative power to Congress, but since the late 1800s numerous reformers have argued that American voters should be allowed to vote directly on some major legislative issues through either direct national initiatives or referenda. Demands for introducing these reforms rose in the 1960s and 1970s, as voters grew increasingly disillusioned with the nation's leaders.

A national initiative would allow voters to circulate petitions nationwide to place a proposed law on the ballot for a direct popular vote. If a requisite number of signatures were obtained, the proposal would appear on the next national ballot. The proposal would become law if a plurality of citizens voted in support of it. A national referendum would allow either the president or Congress to place a proposed law on the ballot for public approval.

Supporters of the national initiative argue that it would make government decisions more reflective of the popular will, reduce the power of special interest groups, and encourage greater public involvement in politics. Opponents counter that the process is antidemocratic, is open to abuse by well-financed interest groups, would put too much responsibility on uninformed voters, and would dilute the influence of minority opinions. As alternatives, some reformers call for the use of indirect initiatives and advisory referenda. The indirect initiative, which is used in many states, allows the legislature to respond to an initiative proposal before the proposal is placed on the ballot. The advisory referendum would allow Congress to place proposed legislation before voters to express their opinions in a nonbinding election, which Congress could then take into account in making its decision. A third alternative that has been proposed as a way for the public to vote directly on major policy issues is through national electronic town meetings.

In the 1970s, efforts to introduce the national initiative and referendum were led by Initiative America, Ralph Nader, and the People's Lobby. Owing to the efforts of these groups, the National Voter Initiative Amendment was introduced in Congress in the late 1970s. The amendment ultimately failed, but not before it attracted considerable attention after becoming the subject of Senate hearings. Since the early 1980s, there has been little organized effort in support of either a national initiative or referendum, though public opinion polls have found that both proposals continue to enjoy considerable public approval.

See also Electronic Town Meeting; Initiative; Referendum.

References Thomas E. Cronin, *Direct Democracy: The Politics of Initiative, Referendum, and Recall* (1989); People's Lobby, *National Initiative and Vote of Confidence (Recall): Tools for Self-Government* (1974).

National League of Cities v. Usery

In the 1976 case *National League of Cities v. Usery*, the U.S. Supreme Court ruled that the federal government did not have the power to force state and local governments to abide by federal minimum wage requirements and hour restrictions for their employees, which these governments had been required to do under the Fair Labor Standards Act. The Court's decision was important because it restricted the federal government's ability to interfere in functions that had traditionally been reserved for state and local governments. The decision was seen as strengthening the position of state and local governments while decreasing the power of the federal government. In 1985, however, the Court overturned this decision in *Garcia v. San Antonio Metropolitan Transit Authority*.

See also Federal-State Relations; *Garcia v. San Antonio Metropolitan Transit Authority*.

References Laurence J. O'Toole, Jr., *American Intergovernmental Relations: Foundations, Perspectives, and Issues*(1993); David B. Walker, *The Rebirth of Federalism: Slouching toward Washington* (1995).

National Municipal League

See National Civic League.

National Organization for Women (NOW)

The National Organization for Women is a political organization that supports legislation and reforms designed to end discrimination against women. A strong proponent of the Equal Rights Amendment, NOW was also active during the "Year of the Woman" elections of 1992, helping many female Democrats win congressional and state legislative seats. NOW was founded in 1966 and is based in Washington, D.C.

See also Equal Rights Amendment; Friedan, Betty; Women's Movement.

National Performance Review

The National Performance Review was a commission created by President Bill Clinton to propose reforms for improving the operation of the federal bureaucracy. Headed by Vice President Al Gore, the commission put forward a package of reform proposals in 1993 to reduce government costs, make the bureaucracy more accountable, and improve service to the public. The proposals called for the elimination of federal jobs, a reduction in government red tape, and the granting of more discretionary powers to bureaucrats who work directly with the public. The commission's final report, which drew heavily from the ideas of reinventing government put forward by David Osborne and Ted Gaebler, is titled *From Red Tape to Results: Creating a Government That Works Better and Costs Less,* but it is often referred to as the Gore Report.

After the release of this report, President Clinton began to take steps to implement its recommendations, issuing executive orders to reduce the federal government's workforce by 252,000 over the next five years and directing agencies that work directly with the public to develop customer service plans. Clinton also implemented changes in the bureaucracy's management structure and simplified some bureaucratic rules. Despite these actions, many observers remain skeptical of the report's claims that instituting its recommended changes will reduce costs by $108 million and improve the bureaucracy, given the experiences of past bureaucratic reform efforts.

See also Administrative Reorganization; Bureaucracy; Downsizing; Public Service Deregulation; Reinventing Government; Total Quality Management.

References Eliza Newlin Carney, "Still Trying To Reinvent Government" (1994); John J. DiIulio, Jr., ed., *Deregulating the Public Service: Can Government Be Improved?* (1994); Paul Glastris, "Rego a Go-Go: A Reinventing Triumph" (1994); A. C. Hyde, "National Performance Review: On the Path to Management Reform" (1994); Pan Suk Kim and Lance W. Wolff, "Improving Government Performance: Public Management Reform and the National Performance Review" (1994); David Osborne and Ted Gaebler, *Reinventing Government: How the Entrepreneurial Spirit Is Transforming the Public Sector* (1992).

National Primary

Among the major criticisms of the presidential nomination process are that it takes too long and that it does not follow any rational order. As it is now, candidates compete in a series of party caucuses and primaries that begin in Iowa and New Hampshire and then continue without any rational sequence until the eve of the national nominating convention six months later. In the middle of this period, one of the candidates in each party acquires enough delegates to be assured nomination, thus making the remainder of the caucuses and elections irrelevant.

Critics have produced a long litany of complaints against this nomination process, arguing that it denies voters a chance to participate meaningfully in choosing their party's nominee, it makes some states more important than others in determining nominees, it has elevated the role of the media in shaping political outcomes, and it produces poor nominees and presidents.

Several proposals have been introduced in Congress or put forward by party officials to improve the process, including the creation of a national primary in which voters across the nation would cast their ballots for a party nominee on the same day. A variety of national primary proposals have been offered, from amending the Constitution so that Congress can designate a specific day on which states must hold their primaries to far more elaborate plans that dictate all aspects of the primary. Some of these latter proposals detail such factors as how candidates are placed on the ballot, how delegates are proportioned, whether a runoff election will be required if no candidate receives a certain threshold of votes, and whether or not a party convention will still be held.

Aside from a national primary, a number of alternative plans have been proposed to solve the problems associated with the current nomination process. These include creating a series of regional primaries, like Super Tuesday, and simply restricting the time period in which primaries can be held. The McGovern-Fraser Commission made a small effort to control the primary and caucus season in the early 1970s by requiring that the states begin their selection process in the same year as the election. The Winograd and Hunt Commissions tightened this restriction further by requiring that all primaries and caucuses be conducted between March and June, though they made exceptions for both Iowa and New Hampshire.

Finally, some supporters of strong parties advocate a reduction in or elimination of the use of primaries altogether and the increased use of party caucuses or conventions to choose nominees.

See also Frontloading; Hunt Commission; McGovern-Fraser Commission; Party Caucuses; Presidential Primaries; Super Tuesday; Winograd Commission.

References Larry M. Bartels, *Presidential Primaries and the Dynamics of Public Choice* (1988); James W. Ceasar, *Reforming the Reforms: A Critical Analysis of the Presidential Selection Process* (1982); William Crotty and John S. Jackson III, *Presidential Primaries and Nominations* (1985); Robert D. Loevy, *The Flawed Path to the Presidency 1992: Unfairness and Inequality in the Presidential Selection Process* (1995).

National Rainbow Coalition

Founded in 1984, the National Rainbow Coalition coalesced around the presidential campaign of the Reverend Jesse Jackson to promote civil rights, international policies that support human rights, and "progressive" reforms in domestic social programs. Known simply as the Rainbow Coalition until 1986, the organization was active during the 1988 and 1992 election years as well.

See also Democratic Leadership Council; Jackson, Jesse.

National Referendum

See National Initiative.

National Sales Tax

See Sales Tax.

National Security Restoration Act

The National Security Restoration Act, one of the ten provisions of the Republican Party's Contract with America, called for limitations on the deployment of American troops under United Nations command and renewed commitment to defense funding. As of late 1995, the act had passed the House, but had stalled in the Senate.

See also Contract with America; Foreign Policy.
References Carrol J. Doherty, "In Senate, 'Contract' Proposal Survives in Altered Form" (1995); "Republicans' Initial Promise: 100-Day Debate on 'Contract'" (1994); Clyde Wilcox, *The Latest American Revolution? The 1994 Elections and Their Implication for Governance* (1995).

National Taxpayers Union

The National Taxpayers Union, a Washington, D.C.-based organization founded in 1989, is the nation's leading advocate for cutting taxes and reducing government spending. It has 250,000 members and is chaired by James D. Davidson. Along with reducing taxes, some of the political reforms with which the union has been associated include the balanced budget amendment, term limits, and national health insurance.

National Urban League

The National Urban League, a professional social work agency whose members include community service providers, civic leaders, and other professionals, aims to eliminate racial segregation and discrimination in all aspects of American life. The organization provides direct service to communities to increase minority participation in the workplace and in community affairs. It advocated the civil rights reforms of the 1950s and 1960s, but its strength was in negotiating with government officials and white-owned corporations to increase black participation. Based in New York City and with a current budget of $18 million, the National Urban League was founded in 1910 as a merger of several committees representing African-Americans in the city. Today, groups affiliated with the National Urban League are active in every major U.S. city.

See also Civil Rights Movement.
Reference Charles W. Eagles, ed., *The Civil Rights Movement in America* (1986).

National Voter Registration Act

The National Voter Registration Act of 1993 was designed to increase voter registration by requiring states to allow registration through the mail or at government offices serving the public. The act is referred to as the motor voter bill because it requires states to make registration materials available to citizens when they apply for or renew a driver's license. In addition, the act includes safeguards to protect voters from being removed from registration lists except under specified conditions. It also requires states to study the law's effects and designate a specific official to coordinate the state's registration activities.

The impetus for the act arose out of the growing awareness that difficult registration procedures are a major cause of low voter participation. Beginning in the early 1980s, Human SERVE, the League of Women Voters, Common Cause, and a number of other interest groups began to pressure local, state, and national governments to introduce reform to ease the registration process. At the heart of these groups' proposals was the demand to allow voters to register at motor vehicle departments and other government agencies. By the mid-1980s, at least a half dozen states had passed their own motor voter laws. By 1993, more than 25 states had similar laws.

The national motor voter act, which took effect on 1 January 1995, has been criticized by state and local officials because of the costs of implementing the reform and because it was an unfunded mandate.

See also Common Cause; Human SERVE; League of Women Voters; Mandates, Federal; Voter Registration.

References Eugene P. Boyd, "Congressional Actions Affecting Local Governments" (1994); Francis Fox Piven and Richard A. Cloward, *Why Americans Don't Vote* (1988); Richard G. Smolka and Ronald D. Michaelson, "Election Legislation, 1992–93" (1994).

Native Americans

See American Indians.

Negative Campaign Advertising

A negative campaign advertisement is one in which the messages focus entirely on a candidate's opponent, manipulating voters' emotions by highlighting the opponent's character flaws or controversial positions. Since the wealthy industrialist Mark Hanna introduced modern advertising into campaign politics when he directed William McKinley's presidential bid in 1896, candidates have regularly used negative messages against their opponents to win election to office. In recent years, however, the use of negative campaign advertisements has become increasingly widespread, generating demand for reform.

Despite the public's unhappiness with negative campaign advertising, there may be little that can be done to stop its use. Some reformers argue that Congress or the Federal Communications Commission should regulate campaign advertisements. One proposal that has been offered is to restrict television advertisements solely to a "talking heads" format, in which candidates directly address the camera, without using elaborate production techniques. This would not ban negative themes, but it might encourage candidates to focus on the issues or their own qualities. Two problems with federal regulation of advertising, however, are that it is generally opposed by broadcasters and that it may be unconstitutional, violating the First Amendment right to free expression.

Alternatively, some reformers push candidates to refrain voluntarily from using negative advertisements. The problem with voluntary restraints, however, is that negative advertising is very effective in shaping voter opinion, despite the fact that voters say they detest negative ads. As long as negative advertising can affect election results, it is unlikely that candidates will voluntarily refrain from using it.

References W. Lance Bennett, *The Governing Crisis: Media, Money, and Marketing in American Elections* (1992); Barbara G. Salmore and Stephen A. Salmore, *Candidates, Parties, and Campaigns: Electoral Politics in America* (1989); Ruy A. Teixeira, *The Disappearing American Voter* (1992).

Negative Income Tax

The negative income tax is a proposed reform to the nation's welfare system that would eliminate all existing welfare programs and replace them with a government-guaranteed minimum income. This reform is championed as a way to reduce administrative costs and the irrational overlap of government welfare programs while creating a system that uses economic incentives to encourage welfare recipients to work. Proponents say it would encourage welfare recipients to work by allowing them to continue to receive government benefits as their wages grow. Benefit levels do decline as wages rise in a negative income tax system, but at a slower rate than in traditional welfare programs. Thus, for example, if a welfare recipient began to receive $2,000 a year in earned income, the recipient's benefits from the government might drop only $1,000 under a negative income plan. The result is that the more a recipient works, the more money he or she is assured of bringing home.

The concept of a negative income tax is generally attributed to University of Chicago economist Milton Friedman. In the early 1970s, President Richard Nixon included a proposal for the negative income tax in his Family Assistance Plan, but the program was defeated in the U.S. Senate. President Jimmy Carter also supported the negative income tax. Congress has been reluctant to adopt the tax, however, because many current programs enjoy considerable support within the public and among the members of Congress themselves. Moreover, opponents of the negative income tax believe it to be far more expensive than many of its supporters suggest.

In recent years interest in the negative income tax has declined as the nation's leaders have turned away from the use of positive incentives to get individuals off welfare and have looked instead at negative incentives, such as workfare and limits on the benefits themselves.

The earned income tax credit, which was adopted by Congress in 1975, is often considered a type of negative income tax, though there are important differences between the two. Like the negative income tax, the tax credit provides direct cash payments to the poor. The amount of these payments is then slowly reduced as the recipients' wages rise. The primary difference is that the tax credit is only available to wage earners, whereas the negative income tax provides cash to all poor individuals whether or not they have earnings.

See also Friedman, Milton; Welfare; Workfare.

References E. J. Dionne, Jr., *Why Americans Hate Politics* (1991); Saul D. Hoffman and Laurence S. Seidman, *The Earned Income Tax Credit: Antipoverty Effectiveness and Labor Market Effects* (1990); Robert Lekachman, *Greed Is Not Enough: Reaganomics* (1983); Alice M. Rivlin, *Reviving the American Dream: The Economy, the States, and the Federal Government* (1992).

New Deal

The myriad of reform programs introduced by President Franklin D. Roosevelt to stimulate the economy and address the nation's ills during the Great Depression are referred to collectively as the New Deal. The New Deal revolutionized the federal government's role in the United States by encouraging its expansion into all aspects of society. The New Deal produced such laws and federal entities as the Social Security Act, the Securities and Exchange Commission, the National Labor Relations Board, the Farm Credit Administration, the Federal Communications Commission, and the National Industrial Recovery Act.

Many conservative reformers today argue that the New Deal reforms are themselves in need of reform or of complete elimination. These reformers call for a pulling back of the welfare state brought about by the New Deal through the downsizing of the federal government, devolution of federal programs to the states, privatization of many government activities, deregulation of business and industry, and increased emphasis on the free market. Liberal supporters of retaining New Deal programs argue that they remain of vital importance to the nation's social and economic health.

See also Contract with America; Deregulation; Devolution; Downsizing; Federal-State Relations; Free Market Economy; Great Society; Medicaid; Medicare; Privatization; Reaganomics; Social Security; Welfare State.

References Karen O'Connor and Larry J. Sabato, *American Government: Roots and Reform* (1995); Clyde Wilcox, *The Latest American Revolution? The 1994 Elections and Their Implication for Governance* (1995).

New Federalism

The reforms in federal-state relations pursued by Presidents Richard Nixon and Ronald Reagan are referred to as New Federalism, although the two leaders had different policy objectives.

At the heart of Nixon's New Federalism was a desire to place greater responsibility for solving societal problems with the states. Nixon supported an active government role in society, but believed that problems could be addressed more effectively through a devolution of power. He championed a variety of reforms to roll back Lyndon Johnson's Creative Federalism and to reduce the centralization of power in the national government that had developed in the 1960s. One of Nixon's central reforms was the introduction in 1972 of general revenue sharing, in which the federal government collected taxes and then channeled those funds to state and local governments with no strings attached. In addition, Nixon also attempted to merge more than 120 categorical grant programs into six broad block grants in order to give states more flexibility in how they used federal funds.

Ultimately, Nixon's efforts had mixed effects on the relationship between the national and state governments. The introduction of revenue sharing did strengthen the position of state governments, as Nixon desired, but the proposal to create the six block grants met stiff resistance in Congress. In the end, Congress was willing to create only two large block grants while protecting most of the categorical grants. In addition to these efforts to decentralize power, Nixon also oversaw a profound expansion in the federal regulation of state and local governments and an unprecedented increase in direct federal spending to individuals. As a result of these actions, the federal government's power may have actually been enhanced during Nixon's administration, despite the president's concern for strengthening the role of the states.

Ronald Reagan's New Federalism was less concerned with devolving power to the states than it was with simply reducing the role of government in U.S. society. Publicly, Reagan advocated devolution of power to the states, but unlike Nixon, he was unwilling to provide federal funds to help state and local governments handle their growing responsibilities. During his tenure, Reagan eliminated general revenue sharing and approximately 60 categorical grants, and reduced federal grant funds by one-third from 1980 to 1987. In addition, he merged 77 categorical grants into nine new or revised block grants.

As with Nixon's reform proposals, Reagan's efforts had mixed effects. With the reduction in these federal programs and the mounting difficulties in balancing the federal budget during the 1980s, there has been some decline in the federal government's domestic activities, as Reagan wanted. Moreover, the reduction of federal funds flowing to the states has encouraged many states to seek alternative revenue sources to absorb the funding losses. This expansion of state revenue sources, along with recent reforms in the structure of state governments themselves, has helped increase the power and independence of the states. Yet the federal government has not disappeared from the scene. Of particular importance, the federal government began to rely more extensively on use of mandates in the mid- to late 1980s to force state governments to address specific social problems. The increased use of these mandates has meant a continued strong presence of the federal government in domestic policy.

See also Big Swap; Block Grants; Categorical

Grants; Constitutions, State; Creative Federalism; Devolution; Federal-State Relations; General Revenue Sharing; Johnson, Lyndon B.; Legislative Reform Movement; Mandates, Federal; Nixon, Richard M.; Reagan, Ronald W.
References Timothy J. Conlan, *New Federalism: Intergovernmental Reform from Nixon to Reagan* (1988); Martha Fabricus, "More Dictates from the Feds" (1991); Alice M. Rivlin, *Reviving the American Dream: The Economy, the States, and the Federal Government* (1992); David B. Walker, *The Rebirth of Federalism: Slouching toward Washington* (1995).

New Judicial Federalism

The growing activism of state courts in protecting the civil rights and liberties incorporated in state constitutions has been referred to as new judicial federalism. Until the 1970s, state courts gave little attention to state bills of rights in deciding cases. As the U.S. Supreme Court began to play a less active role in protecting civil rights and liberties in the mid-1970s, however, state courts emerged as the new champions of these concerns, basing their decisions on state bills of rights. The nation's federal system of government allows state constitutions to protect additional rights and liberties beyond those spelled out in the U.S. Constitution.

See also Federal-State Relations; Supreme Court.
References John Kincaid, "State Court Protections of Individual Rights under State Constitutions: The New Judicial Federalism" (1988); David B. Walker, *The Rebirth of Federalism: Slouching toward Washington* (1995).

NIMBY (Not in My Backyard)

Opposition to local development projects by nearby residents who fear that the projects will harm the communities or neighborhoods in which they live is often referred to as the NIMBY (for "not in my backyard") syndrome. Waste disposal sites, prisons, low-income housing, factories, and community care facilities are common types of projects that generate NIMBY opposition.

The individuals who oppose such projects, referred to as NIMBYs, are often criticized for selfishly protecting their own self-interests with little concern for broader societal needs, causing some societal problems to be inadequately addressed. One example of the problems associated with NIMBYs is the placement of hazardous waste disposal facilities. Almost everyone agrees that there is a need for more long-term disposal sites for hazardous wastes, but NIMBY opposition has limited their creation. Those who are more sympathetic to NIMBYs, however, argue that it is only rational for local residents to try to protect the communities or neighborhoods in which they live from undesirable projects.

One proposal that has been offered to overcome the problems created by the NIMBY syndrome is the greater use by state and local governments of incentives to encourage local residents to accept undesirable projects, including offering financial benefits to residents for allowing these projects to be placed in their communities. Alternatively, some analysts argue that some of the problems created by NIMBY opposition can be overcome by greater public education regarding the need for particular projects.

See also LULUs.
References Terry Christensen, *Local Politics: Governing at the Grassroots* (1995); John J. Harrigan, *Politics and Policy in States and Communities* (1994); Herbert Inhaber, "Of LULUs, NIMBYs, and NIMTOOs" (1992); Albert R. Matheny and Bruce A. Williams, "Strong Democracy and the Challenge of Siting Hazardous Waste Disposal Facilities in Florida" (1988).

Nixon, Richard M. (1913–1994) (37th U.S. President, 1969–1974)

There may be no figure in recent U.S. history who has been as important in political reform as Richard M. Nixon, who both championed important changes in domestic and foreign policy as president and became the motivator for sweeping reform efforts in the 1970s because of his unethical behavior while in office.

Born in Yorba Linda, California, and educated at both Whittier College and Duke University Law School, Nixon embarked on a political career in the mid-1940s that was repeatedly filled with controversy. Elected to Congress in 1946, he was one of the leading figures in the anticommunist crusade of the period and played a pivotal role in the conviction of Alger Hiss, an alleged communist sympathizer. In 1950, he ran a brutal campaign for the U.S. Senate against Helen Gahagan Douglas, falsely and aggressively accusing her of being a friend of communism. The campaign propelled him into the Senate and drove Douglas from politics. While Nixon was U.S. vice president in the 1950s, his ethics were questioned when allegations were made that he had accepted illegal campaign contributions, a charge he was able to defuse with his famous "Checkers speech." After losing to John F. Kennedy in the 1960 presidential race and to Edmund G. "Pat" Brown in the California gubernatorial race in 1962, Nixon lashed out at the press, declaring that it would no longer have him "to kick around" anymore.

Despite these controversies, Nixon emerged on top in the 1968 presidential election, squeezing by his Democratic opponent, Hubert Humphrey, by a mere 500,000 votes. Elected at a time of great turmoil in the United States, Nixon pledged to restore law and order and to resolve America's conflict overseas. Over the next few years, he championed reforms to return greater responsibilities to the states, introduced general revenue sharing, sought to strengthen the presidency by reorganizing the bureaucracy, expanded affirmative action, and signed into law some of the most sweeping environmental policies in the nation's history. In economic matters, he introduced the use of wage and price controls to bring the nation's inflation rate under control, removed the country from the Bretton Woods System, and proposed a negative income tax as an alternative to welfare. His primary policy legacy, however, was not any of these proposals, but his work in foreign affairs. As the nation became increasingly disillusioned with the war in Vietnam, Nixon began to move away from the policy of containment that had dominated the nation's foreign policy since the end of the Second World War and introduced détente. The result was the opening of the diplomatic door to China and a softening of relations with the Soviet Union.

In the end, however, Nixon's obsession with reelection in 1972 eventually proved his undoing. The investigation into the Watergate burglary in 1972 revealed repeated illegal and unethical activities by Nixon and his associates. When taped conversations from the White House showed that Nixon had conspired to cover up the Watergate break-in, he was forced to leave office. He resigned the presidency on 9 August 1974.

Nixon's unethical behavior as president led to one of the greatest reform periods in U.S. history, as Congress passed new laws regulating campaign finance, tightening the federal government's ethics rules, placing restrictions on the president's powers, and strengthening its own position. The reform movement even reached down into state and local governments as the nation became preoccupied with finding means to obtain good government. As time passed, the reform spirit launched by Nixon's activities slowed, though Nixon's presidency left an indelible mark on the national psyche, leaving Americans increasingly distrustful of government.

See also Administrative Reorganization; Campaign Finance; Congress; Deregulation; Environmental Policy; Federal-State Relations; Foreign Policy; Gold Convertibility; Negative Income Tax; President; Wage and Price Controls; Watergate.
References Fawn M. Brodie, *Richard Nixon: The Shaping of Character* (1981); John Robert Greene, *The Limits of Power: The Nixon and Ford Administrations* (1992); Stanley I. Kutler, *The Wars of Watergate: The Last Crisis of Richard M. Nixon* (1990); Herbert Stein, *Presidential Economics: The Making of Economic Policy from Roosevelt to Clinton* (1994); David B. Walker, *The Rebirth of Federalism: Slouching toward Washington* (1995).

Noble, Lloyd, II

Lloyd Noble II is a prominent Oklahoma businessman who orchestrated the first successful term limits campaign in the 1990s, helping to pave the way for the nationwide term limits movement. With the support of key legislative candidates and Governor Henry Bellman, Noble led a petition drive in Oklahoma to put a term limits initiative on the September 1990 ballot. More than 200,000 signatures were gathered within a few weeks, and State Question 632, limiting terms to 12 years total in either the State House or Senate, was placed on the ballot. Oklahoma voters adopted the proposal by a two-to-one margin. Since that vote, more than 20 other states have adopted laws limiting the terms of state legislators and members of Congress.

See also Term Limits.
Reference Gerald Benjamin and Michael J. Malbin, eds., *Limiting Legislative Terms* (1992).

Nonconnected PACs

Unlike most political action committees, which are controlled by parent or sponsoring organizations, nonconnected PACs are created and overseen by single individuals or groups of individuals. In general, most nonconnected PACs are concerned with championing particular issues or ideological positions. Personal PACs, which are a distinct type of nonconnected PAC, are controlled by officeholders or candidates seeking office. Nonconnected PACs have been among the most rapidly growing type of political action committee since the early 1980s. They are often criticized for their use of negative advertising and independent expenditures, as well as their lack of parent organizations, which, critics argue, reduces their accountability.

See also Campaign Finance; Federal Election Campaign Act; Independent Expenditures; Negative Campaign Advertising; Personal PACs; Political Action Committees.
References Michael J. Malbin, ed., *Money and Politics in the United States: Financing Elections in the 1980s* (1984); Larry J. Sabato, *PAC Power: Inside the World of Political Action Committees* (1984); Frank J. Sorauf, *Money in American Elections* (1988).

Nonpartisan Election

In nonpartisan elections, the candidates' party affiliations are not indicated on the ballot. Nonpartisan elections were introduced at the beginning of the century by progressive reformers to reduce the power of party machines. In recent years, they have been criticized for reducing the influence of minorities and the poor, depressing voter turnout, and increasing the reelection rate of incumbents. More than 70 percent of U.S. cities use nonpartisan elections. Members of the Nebraska Senate are also elected on a nonpartisan basis.

See also Party Machines; Political Parties.

References Ann O'M. Bowman and Richard C. Kearney, *State and Local Government* (1993); Thomas R. Dye, *Politics in States and Communities* (1994); John J. Harrigan, *Political Change in the Metropolis* (1993).

North American Free Trade Agreement (NAFTA)

The 1993 North American Free Trade Agreement was designed to remove barriers and increase trade among the United States, Canada, and Mexico. The agreement was heavily criticized by opponents, who argued that it would eliminate American jobs, harm the environment, and allow international organizations to overturn state regulations. Supporters maintained, however, that the economic benefits to the nation from the agreement would far outweigh its costs, and that the potential harm to the environment and state regulations were overstated. NAFTA is considered a continuation of the federal government's effort since the end of the Second World War to promote free trade between the United States and other nations.

See also Free Trade; General Agreement on Tariffs and Trade; Preemption; Protectionism; Trade Policy.

References Peter M. Garber, ed., *The Mexico-U.S. Free Trade Agreement* (1993); Gary Clyde Hufbauer and Jeffrey J. Schott, *NAFTA: An Assessment* (1993); Gary Mucciaroni, *Reversals of Fortune: Public Policy and Private Interests* (1995); Ellen Perlman, "The Gorilla That Swallows State Laws" (1994).

North, Oliver

See Iran-Contra Affair.

O

Obey Commission

Stung by revelations of unethical behavior among members of Congress, the House of Representatives created a bipartisan commission in the mid-1970s to propose reforms in the House's code of ethics. Chaired by Representative David Obey of Wisconsin, the commission proposed a variety of reforms that were designed primarily to control the influence of money on members' behavior. The commission's proposals were adopted by the House in 1977.

The reforms included a requirement that House members file annual disclosure statements detailing all aspects of their financial histories, from their income and holdings to the gifts and honoraria they receive from interest groups and others. In addition, the commission reforms set limits on members' outside income, the size of gifts members could accept from lobbyists, and the use of frank mail.

Although the commission's reforms introduced some of the strictest ethics regulations in the House's history, they did not solve the problem of unethical behavior, as the Abscam scandal revealed a few years later.

The Obey Commission was formally known as the Commission on Administrative Review.

See also Abscam; Congress; Ethics; Ethics in Government Act; Hays, Wayne; Koreagate.
Reference Lawrence C. Dodd and Bruce I. Oppenheimer, "The House in Transition: Change and Consolidation" (1981).

O'Connor, Sandra Day (b. 1930)

Sandra Day O'Connor, former Arizona attorney, state senate majority leader, and appeals court judge, became the nation's first female U.S. Supreme Court justice in 1981. President Reagan, fulfilling a campaign promise, sought a competent female judge to fill the first vacancy on the court during his tenure. O'Connor's nomination came after years of lobbying by the women's movement for greater inclusion of women in government.

As the first of a string of conservative Reagan appointees, O'Connor has proved fairly consistent in her decisions on the Court. She has shown affinity for feminist concerns in her support of the Court's decision to uphold *Roe v. Wade* in the *Planned Parenthood of Southeastern Pennsylvania v. Casey* decision of 1992 and in cases against sexual discrimination in the workplace.

See also Supreme Court.
References Peverill Squire et al., *Dynamics of Democracy* (1995); Elder Witt, ed., *The Supreme Court and Its Work* (1981).

Office of Management and Budget

The Office of Management and Budget (OMB) was created within the Executive Office of the President in 1970 to provide the president with better oversight of the federal budget and improved management of the bureaucracy. The OMB is considered responsible for some of the executive branch's most important budget and management reforms over the past 30 years, including changes in the civil service, regulatory relief, administrative reorganization, and the use of such budgeting techniques as management by objectives and zero-base budgeting. The OMB replaced the Bureau of the Budget.

Despite the importance of the office in generating reform, it has received considerable criticism over the past two decades for becoming too political, too powerful, and too involved in policy matters. Moreover, the OMB has not played as prominent a role in management as anticipated. These criticisms have led some reformers to advocate the creation of a separate office of management to reduce the OMB's power and give the president better advice on management issues. In the early 1980s, the Grace Commission advocated replacing the OMB with an Office of Federal Management, which would devote more attention than the OMB to management issues.

See also Administrative Reorganization; Budgeting Techniques; Bureaucracy; Deregulation; Grace Commission; Management by Objectives; Zero-Base Budgeting.

References George C. Edwards III and Stephen J. Wayne, *Presidential Leadership: Politics and Policy Making* (1990); William T. Gormley, Jr., *Taming the Bureaucracy: Muscles, Prayers, and Other Strategies* (1989); Donald J. Savoie, *Thatcher, Reagan, Mulroney: In Search of a New Bureaucracy* (1994).

Office of Personnel Management

The Office of Personnel Management is an independent federal agency created by the Civil Service Reform Act of 1978 to replace the Civil Service Commission as the central policy-making body for the federal government's nonmilitary personnel. The Office of Personnel Management is also responsible for the hiring, training, and termination of federal employees. Although the agency was meant to provide neutral guidance of federal personnel, it became heavily politicized during the Reagan administration when Donald Devine served as director. Devine's antagonism toward the bureaucracy was blamed for causing a morale crisis in the civil service in the 1980s and for forcing many talented federal employees to resign.

See also Bureaucracy; Civil Service Reform Act of 1978; Merit Systems Protection Board; Senior Executive Service; Volcker Commission.

References William T. Gormley, Jr., *Taming the Bureaucracy: Muscles, Prayers, and Other Strategies* (1989); Charles H. Levine, ed., *The Unfinished Agenda for Civil Service Reform: Implications of the Grace Commission Report* (1985); Donald J. Savoie, *Thatcher, Reagan, Mulroney: In Search of a New Bureaucracy* (1994).

Official English Movement

The official English movement is a political movement that advocates the adoption of English as the official language of the United States, restricting the use of other languages in most, if not all, government activities. The most extreme proposals involve restricting the use of other languages in the private sector as well. Support for English-only laws has existed since at least the beginning of twentieth century, but the rise of the recent movement is generally associated with efforts to promote bilingual education in the 1960s and 1970s and changes in the nation's immigration patterns.

Senator S. I. Hayakawa of California introduced a constitutional amendment in the U.S. Senate in 1981 to make English the nation's official language. He then helped establish U.S. English, a national interest group dedicated to the passage of official English laws. Unsuccessful in their efforts to get Congress to adopt the constitutional amendment, supporters of the movement turned their attention to state and local governments during the 1980s. By the early 1990s, 14 states and numerous local governments had adopted resolutions declaring English their official language, and many others had considered similar proposals. Most of these resolutions were entirely symbolic, though a few required English to be the sole language used in some government activities. The effects of these laws, however, are considered to be minimal.

Supporters of the movement argue that the adoption of English as the nation's official language is needed to discourage separatism and to compel those who speak other languages to learn English. Opponents argue that the laws are a thinly veiled racist attack on Latinos and other minorities.

See also Chicano Movement; Civil Rights Movement; Proposition 187; Voting Rights Act.
References Linda Chavez, *Out of the Barrio: Toward a New Politics of Hispanic Assimilation* (1991); Jack Citrin et al., "The 'Official English' Movement and the Symbolic Politics of Language in the United States" (1990).

Off-Year Fund-Raising

The growing practice among officeholders of raising campaign funds during years in which there is no election is referred to as off-year fund-raising. Reformers argue that this practice corrupts the political process because contributions made in off years are generally designed to influence policy decisions and not election outcomes. In addition, the practice is seen as reducing electoral competition, making challengers more reluctant to run. Minnesota has adopted legislation to reduce the influence of off-year fund-raising by limiting the amount of money that can be contributed in those years.

See also Campaign Finance; Incumbency Advantage.
References *Book of the States 1994–95* (1994); California Commission on Campaign Financing, *The New Gold Rush: Financing California's Legislative Campaigns* (1985).

Oil Price Shocks

The Organization of Petroleum Exporting Countries (OPEC) abruptly raised the rate of oil prices in both 1973 and 1979. In a short period between late 1973 and early 1974 alone, oil prices quadrupled. These two oil price shocks helped generate the worst inflation the United States had seen in more than 50 years, and in so doing, helped spur the introduction of new and more conservative fiscal and monetary policies. The oil price shocks also encouraged the development of a comprehensive national energy program.

See also Economic Policy; Fiscal Policy; Keynesian Economics; Monetary Policy; Stagflation; Supply-Side Economics.
References Paul A. Samuelson and William D. Nordhaus, *Economics* (1992); George P. Shultz and Kenneth W. Dam, *Economic Policy beyond the Headlines* (1977); Herbert Stein, *Presidential Economics: The Making of Economic Policy from Roosevelt to Clinton* (1994).

Ombudsman

One approach that government bureaucracies have introduced to improve bureaucratic responsiveness to the public is the creation of the position of ombudsman, a person whose job it is to handle complaints and resolve service problems. In the 1970s, many cities and states strengthened the role of ombudsman to cope with problems in particular parts of the bureaucracy. More recently, some congressional reformers have advocated the creation of an ombudsman's office in Congress to reduce the role of Congress members in handling casework. Similarly, some political party reformers have proposed creating ombudsmen within their parties to help citizens deal with local political or government concerns.

See also Bureaucracy; Casework; Political Parties.
References Roger H. Davidson and Walter J. Oleszek, *Congress and Its Members* (1994); William T. Gormley, Jr., *Taming the Bureaucracy: Muscles, Prayers, and Other Strategies* (1989); Larry J. Sabato, *The Party's Just Begun: Shaping Political Parties for Tomorrow's Future* (1988).

Omnibus Legislation

Massive bills that combine several distinct policy initiatives that ordinarily would be considered separately are referred to as omnibus legislation. Over the past two decades, Congress has increasingly turned to omnibus bills as a way to improve the chances for legislation to be enacted into law. Packaging multiple policy initiatives into one massive bill can make it easier to get members of Congress to vote for proposals they might otherwise oppose, as politically unpopular measures are submerged into more popular ones. Omnibus bills also provide Congress with a means to sidestep presidential veto by including proposals that the president opposes in legislation he supports or that must be enacted into law.

Omnibus legislation has become particularly important in the budget process. In the 1980s, Congress repeatedly used omnibus continuing resolutions when it failed to pass the budget on time. Because these resolutions needed to be adopted to keep the government operating, Congress was able to use them to force the president to accept funding decisions he would otherwise have resisted.

Critics argue that the use of omnibus legislation allows major policy proposals to pass through the legislative process without the same degree of scrutiny and debate they would receive if they were packaged separately. Moreover, it allows unpopular bills to be signed into law.

One of the primary reform proposals offered to control omnibus legislation is the line-item veto, which supporters argue would give the president the ability to remove sections of these bills he opposes. In March 1996, Congress enacted legislation granting the president this power. However, many scholars are skeptical of both the constitutionality and effectiveness of the new law. The use of omnibus legislation is also referred to as packaging.

See also Congress; Line-Item Veto.
References Roger H. Davidson and Walter J. Oleszek, *Congress and Its Members* (1994); Leroy N. Rieselbach, *Congressional Reform: The Changing Modern Congress* (1994); Barbara Sinclair, "House Majority Party Leadership in an Era of Legislative Constraint" (1992); Steven S. Smith, *Call to Order: Floor Politics in the House and the Senate* (1989).

Omnibus Reconciliation Act of 1990

See Budget Enforcement Act of 1990.

One Person, One Vote

Until the 1960s, the U.S. Supreme Court was unwilling to intervene in legislative redistricting cases, maintaining that apportionment was a political question and therefore not appropriate for judicial review.

The Court reversed its position in *Baker v. Carr,* when it decided that redistricting was a justiciable concern. Over the next several years, the Court issued a series of rulings on legislative redistricting, at the heart of which was the philosophical principle of one person, one vote. The underlying concept of one person, one vote is that votes for all citizens should carry approximately the same weight in the political system.

Before these Supreme Court rulings, there was great disparity in the populations of state legislative and congressional districts. In *Wesberry v. Sanders* and *Reynolds v. Sims,* the Court ruled that this disparity represented a violation of the equal protection clause of the Constitution because it made some citizens' votes worth more than others. The Court's principle was best articulated in the 1963 case *Gray v. Sanders.* In the *Gray* decision, which banned the use of geographic units such as counties for distributing legislative seats, the Court wrote that "the conception of political equality from the Declaration of Independence, to Lincoln's Gettysburg Address, to the Fifteenth, Seventeenth, and Nineteenth Amendments can mean only one thing—one person, one vote."

The Court's emphasis on one person, one vote has received much praise, though it has also generated some criticism from reformers who believe it has placed too much emphasis on numerical equality, whereas the real question underlying these redistricting cases is how to achieve fair representation. Fair representation can still be denied even with districts of equal population, through gerrymandering and other forms of electoral discrimination.

See also *Baker v. Carr;* Electoral Discrimination; Gerrymandering; Reapportionment Revolution; *Reynolds v. Sims; Wesberry v. Sanders.*

References Gordon E. Baker, *The Reapportionment Revolution: Representation, Political Power, and the Supreme Court* (1966); William J. Keefe and Morris S. Ogul, *The American Legislative Process: Congress and the States* (1993); National Conference of State Legislatures Reapportionment Task Force, *Reapportionment Law: The 1990s* (1989).

Open Caucuses

Many state political parties nominate candidates and choose delegates to the national nominating convention through party caucuses, local meetings of party supporters. The lack of broad public input into the delegate selection process led the Democratic McGovern-Fraser Commission to establish guidelines requiring state parties to open their caucuses to greater participation to rank-and-file party members. Instead of causing caucuses to be opened, however, the McGovern-Fraser Commission reforms led many states to adopt presidential primaries to choose delegates. Removing delegate selection from the caucuses allowed the state parties to keep their caucuses closed and ensured party regulars that they would continue to control local party activities.

See also McGovern-Fraser Commission; Party Caucuses; Political Parties; Presidential Primaries.

References Larry M. Bartels, *Presidential Primaries and the Dynamics of Public Choice* (1988); James W. Ceasar, *Reforming the Reforms: A Critical Analysis of the Presidential Selection Process* (1982); William Crotty and John S. Jackson III, *Presidential Primaries and Nominations* (1985); Byron E. Shafer, *Quiet Revolution: The Struggle for the Democratic Party and the Shaping of Post-Reform Politics* (1983).

Open Meeting Laws

See Sunshine Rules.

Open Primary

An open primary is a type of primary election in which voters decide on which party ballot they want to vote in theprivacy of the polling booth, without having to declare party affiliation publicly. This differs from both closed and blanket primaries. In a closed primary, a voter must publicly state a party affiliation before entering the polling booth, and is then given a ballot for only that party. In a blanket primary, a voter can switch between parties as he or she chooses nominees for each office, so that a person can vote for Democratic nominees for some offices and Republican nominees for others.

Both open and blanket primaries have been criticized by supporters of strong parties because they allow individuals who have only weak ties to a party to vote in that party's primary, which could cause nominees to be selected who do not represent the position of loyal party members.

In the late 1970s, the Democratic Party's Winograd Commission banned the use of open primaries for choosing delegates to the national nominating convention as a way to ensure that the party's nominee closely reflected the preferences of loyal Democrats. The state of Wisconsin fought the party's decision in the courts. In 1981, the Supreme Court ruled in *Democratic Party of the United States of America v. La Follette* that the national party had the right to determine how delegates were selected to the national nominating convention, a decision that forced Wisconsin to abandon its open primary for choosing delegates to the 1984 convention.

Today, 9 states use open primaries to elect nominees to state offices, and 3 states use blanket primaries. Another 11 have "semiopen" primaries, in which voters have to declare party affiliation when they are given a ballot, but do not have to be preregistered for that party.

See also Closed Primary; Political Parties; Presidential Primaries; Primary Elections; Responsible Parties; Winograd Commission.

References John F. Bibby and Thomas M. Holbrook, "Parties and Elections" (1996); William J. Keefe, *Parties, Politics, and Public Policy in America* (1994).

Open Record Laws

Open record laws are laws that permit public access to government records. These laws are designed to reduce government secrecy and to make government actors more accountable for their actions. The nation's first open record law was enacted in Wisconsin in the 1800s. Over the years, other states have followed Wisconsin's lead, and today all 50 states have open record laws on their books. It was not until the 1950s, however, that the federal government began serious consideration of a similar law for federal records. After a decade of struggle, the Freedom of Information Act was enacted in 1966, opening a large portion of federal records to the public. The act was strengthened in 1974 to force greater compliance within the bureaucracy.

See also Bureaucracy; Freedom of Information Act; Sunshine Rules.

References Sam Archibald, "The Early Years of the Freedom of Information Act: 1955 to 1974" (1993); Ann O'M. Bowman and Richard C. Kearney, *State and Local Government* (1993).

Out-of-District Money

A major problem in electoral politics cited by many reformers is the large flow of money into campaigns from outside candidates' own districts and states. The Center for Responsive Politics reports that between 1985 and 1990, most U.S. Senate committee chairs received a majority of their campaign funds from outside their districts, and some senators received more than 90 percent of their funds from out-of-state sources. At the state level, a study on the 1982 California Assembly election found that 92 percent of itemized contributions came from sources outside candidates' districts.

Critics argue that such contributions weaken voters' ability to select candidates of their choice and make elected officials beholden to interests outside their districts. Reformers advocate restricting out-of-district contributions altogether or introducing incentives, such as tax credits for in-district contributors, to encourage candidates to rely more heavily on local contributions.

See also Campaign Finance; Center for Responsive Politics; Tax Credits.

References California Commission on Campaign Financing, *The New Gold Rush: Financing California's Legislative Campaigns* (1985); David B. Magleby and Candice J. Nelson, *The Money Chase: Congressional Campaign Finance Reform* (1990); Michael J. Malbin, ed., *Money and Politics in the United States: Financing Elections in the 1980s* (1984); Frank J. Sorauf, *Money in American Elections* (1988).

Oversight

The effort made by Congress and state legislatures to monitor the performance of the bureaucracy is referred to as oversight. Since the 1970s, there has been an increased effort at both levels of government to improve legislative oversight in order to make the bureaucracy adhere more closely to the legislature's will.

At the national level, Congress has taken a number of different steps to improve its oversight capacities, including increasing staff, creating new legislative agencies, and strengthening old ones. The creation of the Congressional Budget Office in 1974 and the revitalization of the General Accounting Office in 1970 are considered particularly important reforms in strengthening Congress's capacity to monitor the executive branch. With these additional resources to draw upon, Congress has made a more concerted effort to oversee the bureaucracy, holding more investigative hearings than ever before and increasingly demanding that the bureaucracy provide reports explaining its actions. The result of these reforms has been an increase in the flow of information to Congress. During the 1970s, Congress also began to turn to the legislative veto more frequently as a means of controlling the bureaucracy, though this practice was ruled unconstitutional in 1983.

Despite these changes, many congressional scholars argue that Congress's dedication to oversight still remains inconsistent and of less importance than its policy-making and constituency service functions. Moreover, these new activities are seen as having only minimal effects on the bureaucracy's activities.

At the state level, the legislative reform movement of the 1970s is considered responsible for improving the capacity of state legislatures to perform oversight. The reform movement brought growth in the size of legislative staffs, increased the number of support agencies answering to the legislature, and expanded sessions lengths. As a result of these reforms, state legislators today play a much more active role in monitoring how programs are being implemented and state money spent than ever before.

See also Bureaucracy; Congress; Congressional Budget Office; Constituency Service; Legislative Reform Movement; Legislative Veto; Sunset Laws.

References Joel D. Aberbach, *Keeping a Watchful Eye: The Politics of Congressional Oversight* (1990); Leroy N. Rieselbach, *Congressional Politics: The Evolving Legislative System* (1995); Alan Rosenthal, *Governors and Legislatures: Contending Powers* (1990).

P

Pacific Legal Foundation

The Pacific Legal Foundation is a public interest law firm created in 1973 to protect conservative political interests in the courts. The firm has played an active role in championing individual liberties, private property rights, and limited government.

Packaging

See Omnibus Legislation.

PACs

See Political Action Committees.

Paperwork

One of the most common complaints about government among private citizens and bureaucrats is the large amount of paperwork involved in government activities. The federal government has enacted a number of reforms to reduce the amount of paperwork it requires, the most comprehensive effort to date being the Paperwork Reduction Act of 1980. This act was designed to reduce the paperwork demands placed on private citizens, government agencies, and other actors involved in governmental processes. The act also created the Office of Information and Regulatory Affairs within the Office of Management and Budget to monitor paperwork demands and administer the act. The passage of the act has been credited with cutting paperwork and costs, but it has also been criticized for reducing the federal government's collection and dissemination of vital information.

Congress enacted the Paperwork Reduction Act of 1995 to extend and strengthen the earlier act. The 1995 law established paperwork reduction goals through the year 2001 and reauthorized the Office of Information and Regulatory Affairs.

See also Bureaucracy; Job Creation and Wage Enhancement Act; Public Service Deregulation.
References Donna Cassata, "Paperwork Reduction Bill" (1995); Charles R. McClure et al., eds., *United States Government Information Policies: Views and Perspectives* (1989).

Party Caucuses

A party caucus is a type of meeting in which party members gather together to make party policy and to select delegates to the national nominating convention. One of the main complaints about the nomination process in the 1968 election was that many Democrats were denied information on caucus meeting times and rules, and thus were prevented from participating. As part of its efforts to open up the nominating process in the early 1970s, the McGovern-Fraser Commission identified party caucuses that were open to all rank-and-file members as one of two acceptable methods for selecting delegates. Instead of generating more open caucuses, however, the reforms caused an increase in the number of states using presidential primaries.

See also McGovern-Fraser Commission; Open Caucuses; Political Parties; Presidential Primaries; Primary Elections.

References Larry M. Bartels, *Presidential Primaries and the Dynamics of Public Choice* (1988); James W. Ceasar, *Reforming the Reforms: A Critical Analysis of the Presidential Selection Process* (1982); William Crotty and John S. Jackson III, *Presidential Primaries and Nominations* (1985); Byron E. Shafer, *Quiet Revolution: The Struggle for the Democratic Party and the Shaping of Post-Reform Politics* (1983).

Party Machines

During the late 1800s, many states and most of the nation's largest cities were dominated by political machines. These machines were highly centralized organizations that used their control over party nominations and the distribution of patronage to maintain their positions of dominance. Most machines were destroyed by the political reforms introduced by the Progressive movement at the beginning of the century, though a few continued to prosper into the 1970s. Social and political changes over the past two decades, however, have brought an end to most of the remaining party machines, or at least severely curtailed their activities.

The most well-known of the modern-day machines was the one controlled by Mayor Richard J. Daley of Chicago from the 1950s to Daley's death in 1976. In the 1970s, the Daley machine began to fall apart because of increasing dissatisfaction among African-Americans with the workings of the machine and two court rulings that banned the city from hiring and firing employees on political grounds. The election of Harold Washington as Chicago's mayor in 1983 brought what many believed was an end to the machine's rule. Some vestiges of the machine remain, but it does not dominate the city's government as it once did.

See also Patronage; *Shakman v. Democratic Party of Cook County*.

References Anne Freedman, "Doing Battle with the Patronage Army: Politics, Courts, and Personnel Administration in Chicago" (1988); William J. Grimshaw, *Bitter Fruit: Black Politics and the Chicago Machine, 1931–1991* (1992); John J. Harrigan, *Political Change in the Metropolis* (1993).

Party-Centered Campaigns

Party-centered campaigns are those in which political party organizations, and not candidates, dominate the competition. In the past, political parties controlled all aspects of campaign politics, from recruiting candidates and developing campaign strategy to bankrolling campaigns. Over the past four decades, however, party-centered campaigns have been replaced by candidate-centered ones, which some observers argue has created a political system in which officeholders are unrepresentative of their constituencies and incapable of governing.

See also Candidate-Centered Campaigns; Political Parties; Responsible Parties.

References Alan Ehrenhalt, *The United States of Ambition: Politicians, Power, and the Pursuit of Office* (1991); Barbara G. Salmore and Stephen A. Salmore, *Candidates, Parties, and Campaigns: Electoral Politics in America* (1989).

Patronage

The distribution of government jobs, contracts, and other benefits to loyal party members in order to secure their support for party leaders and elected officials is referred to as patronage. The use of patronage was common at national, state, and local levels in the 1800s to help the dominant parties retain control of elected office. It began to decline, however, with the passage of the Pendleton Act of 1883, which introduced the use of the merit system in the federal bureaucracy. Today, less than 1 percent of all federal employees are appointed, leaving few patronage positions available.

After the passage of the Pendleton Act, many states enacted similar reforms, though nearly half of all state employees nationwide were still appointed up through the early 1960s. During the past 30 years, the states have slowly moved to reduce the number of patronage positions in order to improve the effectiveness of their bureaucracies. In addition, many governors have begun to see patronage as more harmful to their positions than helpful.

The reduction in patronage positions has also been caused by a series of court decisions that began in 1970s. The U.S. Supreme Court's first important decision in this area came in the case of *Elrod v. Burns,* where it ruled that state and local employees cannot be fired because of party affiliation. The Court expanded on this decision in *Rutan v. Republican Party of Illinois* in 1989, ruling that no type of government employment decision can be made on partisan grounds. The *Rutan* decision is considered to have severely curtailed the use of government jobs as patronage.

See also *Elrod v. Burns;* Merit System; Party Machines; *Rutan v. Republican Party of Illinois.*

References Cheri Collis, "Clearing Up the Spoils System" (1990); Ronald N. Johnson and Gary D. Libecap, *The Federal Civil Service System and the Problem of Bureaucracy: The Economics and Politics of Institutional Change* (1994); Jeffrey L. Katz, "The Slow Death of Political Patronage" (1991); Larry J. Sabato, *Goodbye to Good-Time Charlie: The American Governorship Transformed* (1983); Frank J. Sorauf, *Party Politics in America* (1984).

Pay-as-You-Go Budgeting

As part of its effort to reduce the federal budget deficit, the Budget Enforcement Act of 1990 included provisions requiring that all increases in direct spending and reductions in taxes through the 1995 fiscal year be offset by corresponding decreases in spending or increases in taxes. This pay-as-you-go provision (or PAYGO) was included in the budget in order to make budget changes deficit-neutral.

The requirements mean that if Congress decides to create new entitlement programs or cut taxes, it must cut other entitlement programs (except Social Security) or find additional revenue to make these changes. In addition, the rules require that all increases in discretionary spending categories (defense, international, and domestic) must be offset by decreases within that same category if the increases cause the category's spending cap to be exceeded. This budget reform has limited Congress's ability to create new entitlement programs, pass additional pork-barrel legislation, and reduce taxes.

See also Backdoor Spending; Budget Deficit, Federal; Budget Enforcement Act of 1990; Discretionary Spending; Entitlements; Pork-Barrel Legislation; Social Security.

References Roger H. Davidson, ed., *The Postreform Congress* (1992); Daniel P. Franklin, *Making Ends Meet: Congressional Budgeting in the Age of Deficits* (1993); Leroy N. Rieselbach, *Congressional Reform: The Changing Modern Congress* (1994).

Payroll Tax

A payroll tax is a government levy placed jointly on employers and employees to pay for social insurance programs, including Social Security, Medicare, and unemployment compensation. Since the 1960s, payroll taxes have grown far more rapidly than any other form of federal tax as the government has tried to pay for the growing demands placed on the nation's social insurance programs. One of the largest increases in payroll taxes came with the passage of the Social Security Amendments of 1983, which brought Social Security from the verge of collapse to a $55 billion surplus in 1990. The Social Security Amendments were considered an important reform in payroll tax policy because they represented the first time the government had tried to create a surplus in order to accommodate future costs in the program.

Despite this increase in revenue, the long-term financial security of the nation's social welfare programs has remained in doubt, which means that the payroll tax continues to be an important political concern in the nation's capital. Currently, there is considerable reluctance to raise payroll taxes further because Social Security taxes are currently producing a surplus and because tax increases are politically unpopular. When the baby boom generation approaches retirement age in the early twenty-first century and the pressures on social welfare programs expand, payroll taxes may once again be increased or reformed.

Conversely, some reformers argue that payroll taxes should be reduced. Part of the complaint against these taxes is that they are regressive in nature. Because wealthier Americans receive larger proportions of their income from sources other than wages, they pay smaller percentages of their income into payroll taxes than do poorer and middle-class Americans. In addition, there is a ceiling on the income used to determine an individual's payroll tax. Earnings above that ceiling are not taxed.

Others argue that payroll taxes should be reduced because the surplus generated by the Social Security Amendments is being used to reduce the federal deficit, which was not the act's intent. Senator Daniel P. Moynihan of New York is one of the leading advocates of this position. Relying on payroll taxes for this purpose, Moynihan has argued, places the weight of balancing the budget on the poor, and uses money to retire the nation's debt that was meant to help the economy in the future.

See also Budget Deficit, Federal; Medicare; Moynihan, Daniel P.; Regressive Tax; Social Security; Taxes.

References Donald F. Kettl, *Deficit Politics: Public Budgeting in Its Institutional and Historical Context* (1992); James M. Poterba, "Budget Policy" (1994); Alice M. Rivlin, *Reviving the American Dream: The Economy, the States, and the Federal Government* (1992).

Pentagon Papers

The Pentagon Papers were the findings from a top-secret government study on the Vietnam War that were illegally made public through a leak to news organizations. The results of the study, which were labeled classified, revealed repeated distortions and political cover-ups by government officials regarding the war. Daniel Ellsberg, a special assistant in foreign affairs at the Pentagon, photocopied the study and carried the documents page by page to a Washington apartment. He later furnished the *New York Times* with the report, which was published in the newspaper beginning 13 June 1971. President Nixon opposed the publication of what came to be known as the Pentagon Papers and began to wiretap administrative offices to prevent the further leaking of information to the press. Claiming that the government could not operate without total secrecy, he supported the suppression of the documents. In *New York Times Co. v. United* States (1971) the Supreme Court ruled that the U.S. Department of Justice could not restrain the

Times from publishing the papers, citing the First Amendment rights of freedom of speech and the press.

The publication of the Pentagon Papers confirmed what critics of the war had been claiming for some time: Presidents Kennedy and Johnson had been denying to the public the nation's involvement in Vietnam while secretly committing the country to war. Public exposure of the documents contributed to the country's increasing distrust of government, helping to set the stage for political reform.

See also Nixon, Richard M.; Vietnam War.
References George C. Herring, *The Secret Diplomacy of Vietnam War* (1983); David W. Levy, *The Debate over Vietnam* (1991); James S. Olson and Randy Roberts, *Where the Domino Fell: America and Vietnam, 1945–1990* (1991).

Performance Budgeting

Performance budgeting is a technique designed to reduce costs and improve government services by basing funding decisions on an agency's ability to produce results. Under performance budgeting, each government agency is expected to establish performance goals, and then funding decisions are based on how well these goals are reached. Advocates of performance budgeting argue that it forces bureaucracies to become more concerned about the services they perform, while offering legislators and other governing bodies a more rational method for distributing funds than is provided by the traditional incremental process. Critics contend that not all types of government activities are suited to performance budgeting, and even for those that are, it is difficult to gauge performance in a fair and rational manner.

Performance budgeting originally emerged before the Second World War, but its popularity diminished in the 1960s. In the past few years, however, there has been a reemergence of interest in performance budgeting, as governments have seen it as a useful tool to improve services and to overcome growing public disillusionment with government. In the early 1990s, some 20 state legislatures adopted performance budgeting regulations.

See also Budgeting Techniques; Cost-Benefit Analysis, Incrementalism; Management by Objectives; Program Budgeting; Zero-Base Budgeting.
References Karen Carter, "Performance Budgets: Here by Popular Demand" (1994); Donald F. Kettl, *Deficit Politics: Public Budgeting in Its Institutional and Historical Context* (1992); John L. Mikesell, *Fiscal Administration: Analysis and Applications for the Public Sector* (1991).

Perot, H. Ross (b. 1930)

H. Ross Perot is a Texas billionaire and political party leader who rose to prominence in the 1992 presidential election campaign, in which he called for a more businesslike approach to governing the nation. Perot built his fortune on computer processing of Medicare claims with his company, Electronic Data Systems Corporation. He talked about running for president on the Larry King Live television talk show in early 1992, and then led the nation's strongest third-party campaign since Theodore Roosevelt ran on the Bull Moose ticket in 1912, receiving 19 percent of the vote.

Perot has urged reforms of the budgetary process, more interparty cooperation, a "reengineering" of Medicare, and a national sales tax. In the 1996 election year, Perot and his organization, United We Stand America, created a new third party, called the Independence or Reform Party, depending on the state, which they hoped would catapult a reform-minded candidate into the White House.

See also United We Stand America.
References Theodore J. Lowi and Benjamin Ginsberg, *Democrats Return to Power: Politics and Policy in the Clinton Era* (1994); H. Ross Perot, *United We Stand: How We Can Take Back Our Country* (1992); H. Ross Perot, *Intensive Care: We Must Save Medicare and Medicaid Now* (1995).

Personal Income Tax

The personal income tax is a type of government levy placed on individuals' earnings. It is the primary source of revenue for the federal government, though states and local governments depend more on sales and property taxes for generating revenue. Currently, 43 states do have some form of personal income tax. This kind of tax is often praised because it is usually more progressive than other forms of taxation.

The federal income tax has been the focus of considerable reform efforts since the late 1970s, as supply-side economists became increasingly vocal in advocating reduction in the tax rate paid by the nation's highest earners to stimulate the economy. Moreover, many taxpayers were growing increasingly unhappy with the income tax system because inflation was pushing them into higher tax brackets, even though their real income levels did not change.

In response to these trends, Congress enacted the Economic Recovery Tax Act of 1981 (ERTA), which reduced personal income taxes by 23 percent and dropped the top tax rate from 70 percent to 50 percent. The act also indexed income tax rates to stop the bracket creep created by inflation. The tax cut did not, however, stimulate the economy as promised, and led to growing complaints that it had placed an unfair burden on poor and middle-income Americans.

After making some minor efforts to increase income taxes in 1982 and 1984, Congress enacted the Tax Reform Act of 1986, which was one of the most comprehensive tax reforms ever enacted. The act limited the income taxes paid by low-wage earners, closed numerous loopholes that benefited corporations and other special interests, and reduced the number of personal income tax brackets from 15 to 3. These changes helped make the federal income tax more progressive, though the tax structure remains more regressive today than it was prior to the passage of ERTA, especially for the middle class.

At the state level, the personal income tax represents a far greater proportion of tax receipts today than it did 30 or 40 years ago. During the 1980s, however, many states reduced their income tax rates in response to a nationwide tax revolt and out of fear that high income taxes were driving skilled workers and businesses to other states. As demands for funds rose during the late 1980s and early 1990s, the states relied more on other forms of taxation to raise additional revenue, including sales taxes and user fees. The result has been a decline in the progressivity of state taxes over the past decade.

See also Corporate Income Tax; Economic Recovery Tax Act; Finance, State; Flat Tax; Progressive Tax; Regressive Tax; Sales Tax; Supply-Side Economics; Tax Reform Act; Tax Revolt; Taxes; User Fees.
References Werner Z. Hirsch and Anthony M. Rufolo, *Public Finance and Expenditure in a Federal System* (1990); "Fiscally Speaking, a Very Good Year" (1995); Joseph J. Minarik, *Making Tax Choices* (1985); Henry J. Raimondo, "State Budgeting in the Nineties" (1993); Howard E. Shuman, *Politics and the Budget: The Struggle between the President and Congress* (1992).

Personal PACs

A personal PAC is a type of nonconnected political action committee that is controlled by a single individual. There are primarily two types of personal PACs: ones used by individuals in exploring a bid for the presidency and ones used by legislators and legislative candidates to channel money to other candidates running for office.

Potential presidential candidates are allowed to create personal PACs as a way to solicit campaign contributions and expend funds prior to making official announcement of their candidacy for office. These PACs are considered to be of increasing importance in presidential primaries, providing candidates with the means to organize the initial steps of their campaigns.

Personal PACs also take the form of campaign committees used by legislators and legislative candidates to channel money to other candidates running for office. These types of committees are also called leadership PACs. Supporters of campaign finance reform often criticize these committees, which are becoming increasingly widespread at both national and state levels, arguing that they corrupt the political system by encouraging elected officials to accumulate increasingly large campaign war chests and by making interest groups more powerful.

See also Campaign Finance; Leadership PACs; Legislative Caucus Campaign Committees; Nonconnected PACs; Political Action Committees; Transfers.

References *Congressional Campaign Finances: History, Facts, and Controversy* (1992); Anthony Gierzynski, *Legislative Party Campaign Committees in the American States* (1992); David B. Magleby and Candice J. Nelson, *The Money Chase: Congressional Campaign Finance Reform* (1990); Frank J. Sorauf, *Money in American Elections* (1988).

Personal Responsibility Act

One of the ten provisions of the Contract with America, the Personal Responsibility Act called for new constraints on federal welfare to discourage out-of wedlock pregnancies, reduce welfare spending, and force recipients to enter the workforce. The act remained under consideration in Congress as of late 1995.

See also Contract with America; Welfare.

References George Hager, "Harsh Rhetoric on Budget Spells a Dismal Outlook" (1995); "Republicans' Initial Promise: 100-Day Debate on 'Contract'" (1994); Clyde Wilcox, *The Latest American Revolution? The 1994 Elections and Their Implication for Governance* (1995).

Planning-Programming-Budgeting System (PPBS)

See Program Budgeting.

Plea Bargaining

A plea bargain is an agreement between a prosecutor and a criminal defendant in which the defendant pleads guilty to a lesser charge in exchange for a more lenient sentence. Plea bargaining is very common in state court systems, and is used to resolve as much as 90 percent of all criminal cases today. Supporters of plea bargaining argue that it helps reduce the growing caseload confronting courts, is less expensive than trials, is more effective than the trial process for rehabilitation, and produces results that are fairly close to what would occur in court. Critics argue that its use should be limited because it inappropriately removes judicial decisions from the courtroom and tends to encourage prosecutors to "overcharge" suspects to give themselves room to negotiate. Moreover, the practice puts the criminal defendant in the position of having to choose between the undesirable options of pleading guilty to one crime or potentially footing the bill for an expensive court case. Finally, some critics argue that the use of plea bargaining often allows criminals to return too quickly to the streets. Several states have attempted to restrict the use of plea bargaining, but with little success.

See also Caseload; Courts; Crime.
References Robert A. Carp and Ronald Stidham, *Judicial Process in America* (1993); William F. McDonald and James A. Cramer, *Plea-Bargaining* (1980).

Political Action Committees (PACs)

Political action committees are legal entities that are used by interest groups to channel campaign contributions to candidates running for elected office. It is illegal for interest groups to give direct contributions to candidates running in federal campaigns, but PACs provide them with a means to contribute money indirectly. By creating a PAC, a group can raise voluntary contributions and redistribute them to a candidate of its choice. Since the passage of the Federal Election Campaign Act of 1971 (FECA), there has been profound growth in the number and importance of these groups in U.S. politics, which has led to proposals to restrict their activities or to ban them altogether.

The first political action committee was created in 1943 by the Congress of Industrial Organization as a way to circumvent federal campaign contribution laws. Over the next two decades, more political action committees arose, a large proportion of which were associated with labor unions. When Congress began to consider revising campaign finance laws in the early 1970s, labor unions pressured legislators to include recognition of political action committees to ensure their legality. The result was that the Federal Election Campaign Act included specific regulation of PACs.

FECA established the legal structure for federal PACs, as well as set limits on their activities. Under FECA, labor unions, corporations, and other groups can use their own funds only for the administration of a PAC. Campaign contributions must come from voluntary contributions given to a PAC. In addition, political action committees can receive only $5,000 a year from any one contributor, and they can contribute only $5,000 per candidate per election. FECA also required PACs to maintain detailed campaign contribution records.

The passage of FECA stimulated the rapid growth of political action committees. Although the primary advocates of legal recognition for PACs were labor unions, other groups have benefited from the FECA reforms. There were 608 registered federal PACs in 1974, most of which were either labor unions or some type of trade or business associations. By the end of 1990, there were more than 4,000 PACs, with labor groups being among the fewest in number. The two most numerous types today are corporate and nonconnected PACs. Corporate PACs are associated with individual businesses, whereas nonconnected PACs are those that have no sponsoring parent organization.

Along with this growth in numbers, political action committees have also become increasingly crucial in providing funds for congressional campaigns. PAC contributions quadrupled from the late 1970s to the late 1980s, rising from less than $35 million in 1978–1979 to $150 million 12 years later.

The growing role played by PACs in these campaigns has led to calls for reform. Three primary reforms have been proposed: reduce the amount of money that PACs can give to individual candidates, limit the total amount of PAC contributions that candidates can receive, or ban PACs altogether. Since the mid-1980s, Congress has considered several bills to accomplish these goals and reduce PAC influence, but partisan differences have led to their downfall.

See also Campaign Finance; Federal Election Campaign Act; In-Kind Contributions; Leadership PACs; Nonconnected PACs; Personal PACs; SunPAC Decision.

References *Congressional Campaign Finances: History, Facts, and Controversy* (1992); Anthony Gierzynski, *Legislative Party Campaign Committees in the American States* (1992); David B. Magleby and Candice J. Nelson, *The Money Chase: Congressional Campaign Finance Reform* (1990); Frank J. Sorauf, *Money in American Elections* (1988).

Political Parties

One of the most important trends in U.S. politics over the past three decades has been the decline in loyalty among Americans to the nation's two major political parties. Disillusioned with these two parties, voters have become more willing to split their votes between them, to support third-party candidates in presidential elections, and to declare themselves independents. The disillusionment has brought repeated talk of reform. For many Americans, the main problem confronting the party system today and over the past few decades has been the lack of choice. Although efforts have been made to create a viable third party, success has remained out of reach.

One area in which the party system has experienced important reform, however, is in the presidential nomination process. In the early 1970s, the Democratic Party adopted a list of reforms proposed by the McGovern-Fraser Commission to open up the party's delegate selection process and democratize the party organization. The adoption of these reforms changed the way the nominees in both parties are selected, reducing the party organization's influence, creating candidate-centered campaigns, and making the presidential primaries the heart of the process. Ever since, the Democratic Party has repeatedly tried to re-reform the selection process and strengthen the party organization, but it has failed to make fundamental change.

Whereas these reforms have weakened the role of the party organizations, there were some changes in the parties in the late 1970s and early 1980s that helped strengthen their role. Most of these changes were not reforms, per se, but changes in behavior. In the late 1970s and early 1980s, the Republican National Committee began to make a concerted effort to rebuild its party organization, orchestrating a massive fund-raising drive to provide support for party candidates. The party's success in the 1980 election helped quickly spur the Democratic National Committee to follow suit. At the same time, the congressional parties, as well as many state parties, were also attempting to build their organizational structure and improve their position in elections.

These efforts to build the parties were helped by one particular reform: the 1979 amendments to the Federal Election Campaign Act. These amendments allowed state and local parties to spend unlimited amounts of money on "party-building" activities. Since then, the national parties have used this provision to channel soft money to state and local campaigns, and this has helped strengthen the entire party system.

These party-building efforts should not be overstated, however. Despite Americans' dislike of the two major parties, the party organizations generally play a subsidiary role in elections today, as campaigns at all levels have become candidate-centered. Since the 1950s, many political scientists have argued that strong parties are essential to democracy, yet American political parties are not strong. Given the public's distaste for party politics, however, it is unlikely that any major reforms will be adopted in the near future to strengthen the party system.

See also Campaign Finance; Candidate-Centered Campaigns; Federal Election Campaign Act; Legislative Caucus Campaign Committees; McGovern-Fraser Commission; Ombudsman; Presidential Primaries; Presidential Selection; Primary Elections; Responsible Parties; Soft Money; Third Parties.

References Paul S. Herrnson, *Party Campaigning in the 1980s* (1988); William J. Keefe, *Parties, Politics, and Public Policy in America* (1994); Byron E. Shafer, *Quiet Revolution: The Struggle for the Democratic Party and the Shaping of Post-Reform Politics* (1983).

Political Reform Act of 1974

The Political Reform Act of 1974, a California law, is considered one of the most comprehensive lobbying reforms in the nation. The act established a $10 monthly limit lobbyists can spend on individual public officials and required lobbyists to submit regular reports on their lobbying activities and finances. It strengthened the state's campaign finance reporting requirements, imposed strict conflict of interest laws on elected officials, and established the Fair Political Practices Commission to administer the new rules.

See also Brown, Edmund "Jerry" Gerald, Jr.; Campaign Finance; Lobbying.

References Charles G. Bell and Charles M. Price, *California Government Today: Politics of Reform?* (1988); Ronald J. Hrebenar and Ruth K. Scott, *Interest Group Politics in America* (1990).

Poll Tax

The poll tax was a fee that prospective voters had to pay in order to register to vote. It became a popular mechanism among southern states after the Civil War to prevent African-Americans from voting. By the early part of the twentieth century, all southern states had introduced poll taxes. Progressive reformers also supported the poll tax, arguing that it reduced voting fraud. Many scholars believe, however, that the progressives supported the tax because they wanted to exclude African-Americans and poor whites from voting.

The use of the poll tax in federal elections was banned in 1964 with the passage of the Twenty-fourth Amendment. The use of the tax in state and local elections was ruled unconstitutional by the Supreme Court in 1966 in *Harper v. Virginia State Board of Elections.*

See also Electoral Discrimination; Voting Rights Act.

References M. Margaret Conway, *Political Participation in the United States* (1991); Chandler Davidson, ed., *Minority Vote Dilution* (1989); Bernard Grofman and Chandler Davidson, eds., *Controversies in Minority Voting: The Voting Rights Act in Perspective* (1992).

Pork-Barrel Legislation

Bills that channel public funds to individual states or districts are referred to as pork-barrel legislation. Such funds are typically provided for dams, highways, military installations, and other local concerns. Pork is often seen as an important resource for helping legislators gain reelection. By "bringing home the bacon," members of Congress and state legislators can claim credit for furthering their constituents' interests, and thus discourage challenges to their reelection.

Critics maintain that restrictions need to be put on pork, arguing that it helps contribute to budget deficits while benefiting only special interests. Supporters contend that legislative politics is inconceivable without pork, because it is essential to building winning coalitions. Moreover, some argue that "one person's pork is another's bread and butter," meaning that while particular projects may seem unnecessary to outsiders, they are usually important to recipients, providing jobs and other benefits that would otherwise not be obtainable.

The line-item veto has been one of the primary proposals offered to reduce pork spending, although some studies in states where this veto power is available indicate that it has not been particularly effective for reaching this goal.

See also Budget Deficit, Federal; Congress; Constituency Service; Line-Item Veto.
References Roger H. Davidson and Walter J. Oleszek, *Congress and Its Members* (1994); Steven S. Smith, *The American Congress* (1995); Robert J. Spitzer, *The Presidential Veto: Touchstone of the American Presidency* (1988).

Pound Conference

The Pound Conference was a meeting held in 1976 in St. Paul, Minnesota, that brought together legal professionals, judicial scholars, and political activists to consider ways to improve the nation's judicial system. Organized by Chief Justice Warren Burger of the U.S. Supreme Court, the conference was considered instrumental in directing greater attention to the need for court reform and in bringing alternative dispute resolution onto the reform agenda in the 1970s and 1980s. The conference's full title was the Roscoe E. Pound Conference on Popular Dissatisfaction with the Administration of Justice.

See also Alternative Dispute Resolution; Burger, Warren; Courts.
References Phillip L. Dubois, *The Politics of Judicial Reform* (1982); Linda R. Singer, *Settling Disputes: Conflict Resolution in Business, Families, and the Legal System* (1990).

Preclearance Provision

When Congress passed the Voting Rights Act in 1965, many lawmakers were concerned that southern states would find ways to circumvent the new law. The preclearance provision was included in Section 5 of the act as a way to protect against this. Section 5 requires state and local governments that have discriminated in the past to obtain the prior approval of the U.S. attorney general or a federal court before they can change election laws or procedures. The inclusion of this preclearance requirement may have been the most significant component of the Voting Rights Act, providing the federal government with the means to combat a wide range of discriminatory electoral practices.

See also Electoral Discrimination; Voting Rights Act.
References Chandler Davidson, ed., *Minority Vote Dilution* (1989); Bernard Grofman and Chandler Davidson, eds., *Controversies in Minority Voting: The Voting Rights Act in Perspective* (1992).

Preemption

When a federal law supersedes a state law, it is referred to as a preemption. Until the 1960s, the federal government rarely passed laws preempting state laws, but over the next three decades more than 275 preemptions were approved as the federal government attempted to expand its powers into policy areas that had traditionally been controlled by the states. Preemptions are often divided into two categories: total and partial. With total preemption, a federal law completely supersedes a state law. With partial preemptions, which are common in environmental regulations, the federal government establishes a minimum standard and then allows the states some flexibility in administering the law if it meets that standard. Some of the primary preemptions have been in the areas of civil rights, environmental control, health and safety, and transportation.

The U.S. Supreme Court has upheld the federal government's use of preemptions as justifiable under the supremacy clause of the Constitution. Critics complain, however, that the use of preemptions has allowed the federal government to become increasingly involved in areas that should be left to the states. Moreover, there have been some instances where powerful economic interests have tried to encourage Congress to pass preemptions to reduce state regulations. Conversely, supporters of preemption argue that it has allowed the federal government to address major problems that states cannot or will not solve on their own, from allowing African-Americans to vote to protecting the environment.

The passage of both the North American Free Trade Agreement (NAFTA) and the General Agreement on Tariffs and Trade (GATT) in 1993 raised new concerns about preemption among some state leaders who feared that these agreements would allow international organizations to overturn state regulations.

See also Federal-State Relations; General Agreement on Tariffs and Trade; Mandates, Federal; North American Free Trade Agreement.
References Ellen Perlman, "The Gorilla That Swallows State Laws" (1994); David B. Walker, *The Rebirth of Federalism: Slouching toward Washington* (1995).

Preferential Voting

See Proportional Representation.

President

The office of president of the United States has been a frequent focus of reform efforts over the past several decades. Many of the reforms that have been proposed have reappeared repeatedly in political debate, whereas others have been put forward to address new political concerns as they have arisen.

Since the Committee on Political Parties of the American Political Science Association (APSA) advocated a responsible party system in the early 1950s, there have been regular calls for strengthening the nation's party system, with the president given a more powerful leadership role. These proposals are designed to make the government more effective, responsive, and accountable. Some of these proposals advocate a British-style parliamentary system, whereas others are simply concerned with changes in electoral rules to tie the fortunes of Congress and the president more closely together. Among these latter proposals are suggestions to require voters to cast their presidential and congressional ballots as a block, thus ensuring direct ties between both offices. Alternatively, some reformers advocate eliminating midterm congressional elections, arguing that this would help encourage, but not require, closer ties between the two branches.

In the early 1970s, reformers turned their attention to restricting the president's power as the Vietnam War and Watergate made many Americans conclude that the president had become too imperial. Congress enacted several reforms to restrain the president's power and reassert its own position. Two of the most important acts to emerge at that time were the War Powers Resolution of 1973 and the Congressional Budget and Impoundment Control Act of 1974. These were designed to strengthen congressional influence over U.S. involvement in foreign wars and the federal budget. In general, the War Powers Resolution is considered to have done little to alter the president's dominance of foreign affairs. However, the Budget and Impoundment Control Act has provided

Congress with greater expertise and more independence in developing the federal budget, which has made it more difficult for the president to dominate the process.

Discontent over Watergate and President Nixon's abuse of power also helped bring Jimmy Carter, a political outsider, into the White House. Carter's weak leadership helped defuse demands for restricting the president's powers. In the 1980s, much of the reform debate began to focus on two of the key issues confronting the nation's leaders: the expanding budget deficit and policy gridlock. The inability of the federal government to balance its budget led many reformers to push for an item veto, which would allow the president to veto portions of appropriations bills. Presidents since Ulysses S. Grant have requested this power, but to no avail until the growing budget deficit brought increased support for it. Until recently, Congress was reluctant to give the president this power, but in April 1996 the line-item veto became law. Many constitutional scholars believe, however, that the veto will be declared unconstitutional.

The public's disillusionment with gridlock in Washington D.C., has recently generated renewed interest in many of the party reforms that have been debated since the release of the APSA report in the 1950s. Many political analysts blame problems of gridlock on the development of divided government, and thus they have advocated changes in the electoral system that would help one party gain control of both branches.

Along with these concerns, other types of reforms relating to the presidency have been championed over the past 30 years. These include proposals to restructure the presidential selection process, to repeal the Twenty-second Amendment, and to strengthen the president's control over the bureaucracy so that it is more accountable for its actions.

See also Administrative Reorganization; Budget Deficit, Federal; Bush, George Herbert Walker; Cabinet; Carter, James E.; Case Act; Congressional Budget and Impoundment Control Act; Divided Government; Ford, Gerald R.; Johnson, Lyndon B.; Legislative Veto; Line-Item Veto; National Emergencies Act; Nixon, Richard M.; Presidential Selection; Responsible Parties; Term Expansion; Twenty-fifth Amendment; Vietnam War; War Powers Resolution; Watergate.
References James W. Davis, *The President as Party Leader* (1992); Charles O. Jones, *The Presidency in a Separated System* (1994); James L. Sundquist, *Constitutional Reform and Effective Government* (1992).

Presidential Debates

The televised campaign debate between John F. Kennedy and Richard M. Nixon in 1960 is considered one of the most widely observed campaign events in the history of presidential elections, attracting an estimated radio and television audience of up to 107 million Americans. The event was so successful that the American Political Science Association created a Commission on Presidential Campaign Debates in 1963 to study the debates and propose recommendations for their future use.

Despite the popularity of the 1960 debates, it was not until 1976 that another presidential campaign debate took place between the Republican and Democratic candidates. It is estimated that almost 160 million Americans watched these debates on television.

The widespread public attention generated by these and subsequent debates has led some reformers to call for making debates a mandatory component of presidential campaigns. James Karayn, director of the presidential debates sponsored by the League of Women Voters in 1976, has argued that Congress should create a national debate commission to organize a series of debates in each election and force candidates to participate. In the early 1990s, a commission created by the Markle Foundation advocated requiring candidates to participate in debates as a precondition of receiving public campaign funds.

See also League of Women Voters; Presidential Selection.
References Bruce Buchanan, *Electing a President: The Markle Commission Research on Campaign '88* (1991); Kathleen Hall Jamieson and David S. Birdsell, *Presidential Debates: The Challenge of Creating an Informed Electorate* (1988); Austin Ranney, ed., *The Past and Future of Presidential Debates* (1979).

Presidential Primaries

Presidential primaries are a type of primary election in which voters select delegates to the parties' national nominating conventions. Until the 1970s, most states relied on party conventions or caucuses instead of primaries to select delegates. The Democratic Party's McGovern-Fraser Commission, however, mandated that state parties use either primaries or open caucuses to select delegates.

Although the commission did not ban the use of caucuses, many state parties decided it was preferable to use primaries for delegate selection instead of opening up the caucus system, which could have resulted in their losing control over the party's other activities. Because the use of primaries is often dictated by state law, the Republican Party was also affected by this change. The result of the McGovern-Fraser Commission's mandate is that presidential primaries have become the main method used to select convention delegates.

See also Closed Primary; Fairness Commission; Frontloading; Hughes Commission; Hunt Commission; McGovern-Fraser Commission; Mikulski Commission; National Primary; Open Primary; Party Caucuses; Political Parties; Primary Elections; Super Tuesday; Winograd Commission.
References Larry M. Bartels, *Presidential Primaries and the Dynamics of Public Choice* (1988); James W. Ceasar, *Reforming the Reforms: A Critical Analysis of the Presidential Selection Process* (1982); William Crotty and John S. Jackson III, *Presidential Primaries and Nominations* (1985); Byron E. Shafer, *Quiet Revolution: The Struggle for the Democratic Party and the Shaping of Post-Reform Politics* (1983).

Presidential Selection

See Campaign Finance; Electoral College; Fairness Commission; Frontloading; Hughes Commission; Hunt Commission; McGovern-Fraser Commission; Mikulski Commission; National Primary; Party Caucuses; Presidential Debates; Presidential Primaries; Public Financing; Super Tuesday; Term Expansion; Winograd Commission.

Presidential Succession

See Ford, Gerald R.; Twenty-fifth Amendment.

President's Reorganization Project

The President's Reorganization Project (PRP) was President Jimmy Carter's sweeping package of reforms to improve the management and effectiveness of the federal bureaucracy. The project included reorganization of the bureaucratic structure, changes in management practices, and regulatory relief. It is considered to have had mixed results. Carter's effort to reorganize the bureaucracy led to the creation of the Departments of Energy and Education, but other restructuring proposals were not adopted, including one to create a Department of National Resources. Carter's proposal to improve bureaucratic management led to the passage of the Civil Service Reform Act of 1978, which created both the Senior Executive Service and the Office of Personnel Management. Both of these enjoyed considerable praise when enacted, but soon confronted severe cutbacks and morale problems. As for regulatory relief, Carter oversaw a reduction in regulations on the banking, natural gas, and trucking industries, and a complete deregulation of the airline industry. However, the amount of regulation in other areas, especially governing the environment, expanded during the Carter administration.

See also Administrative Reorganization; Cabinet; Civil Service Reform Act of 1978; Deregulation; Education; Office of Personnel Management; Senior Executive Service.

References Colin Campbell, *Managing the Presidency: Carter, Reagan, and the Search for Executive Harmony* (1986); Peter Szanton, *Federal Reorganization: What Have We Learned?* (1981).

Primary Elections

Primary elections are the main method used by political parties to select candidates for public office. Individuals who want to run for office as a given party's candidates compete in preliminary elections open only to party members. The winners of these primary elections then compete in the general election, in which the voters decide who will fill particular offices.

Primary elections were introduced by progressive reformers in the early 1900s as a means of stripping party bosses of their power. The popularity of primary elections spread rapidly, and today they are used in all states. Thirteen states, however, retain provisions allowing parties to use nominating conventions under certain specified conditions.

The introduction of primary elections is often considered one of the main reasons for the decline of political parties in the United States. Prior to their use, the party organizations controlled the selection of party nominees, which gave these organizations considerable influence not only in elections but over the direction of government policy. With the spread of primary elections, candidates no longer have to appeal to party leaders for support in order to be nominated, but must instead convince voters. As a result, most candidates today handle all the chores of putting together campaigns themselves, from creating campaign organizations to raising funds.

Although primaries have made the nomination process more democratic, critics argue that the rise of candidate-centered campaigns has produced unrepresentative candidates and reduced the government's ability to function.

These types of elections are also referred to as direct primaries. Presidential primaries are similar except that voters select delegates to represent them at the national nominating convention instead of voting directly on a nominee. The party's presidential nominee is then formally chosen at the convention.

See also Candidate-Centered Campaigns; Closed Primary; Open Primary; Political Parties; Presidential Primaries.

References John F. Bibby and Thomas M. Holbrook, "Parties and Elections" (1996); Alan Ehrenhalt, *The United States of Ambition: Politicians, Power, and the Pursuit of Office* (1991); William J. Keefe, *Parties, Politics, and Public Policy in America* (1994).

Private Government

When private organizations provide services, assess taxes, regulate behavior, and perform other traditional government funcitons, they are referred to as private governments. One of the most common types of private government is the homeowners' association; members pay yearly fees (or taxes), and the association provides such services as landscaping and security. In addition, these associations can regulate behavior, placing restrictions on such activities as land use, structural alterations, and the ownership of pets. Membership in a homeowners' association is often required of residents living within a given association's boundaries.

It is estimated that there are 150,000 private governments in the United States today. Supporters of these governments argue that they give local residents greater control over the communities in which they live, provide services that are not adequately provided by the current local governments, and are more efficient than traditional governments. Critics argue that these governments tend to be unaccountable and undemocratic. Moreover, the growing presence of these governments is seen as contributing to the problem of metropolitan fragmentation.

See also Metropolitan Fragmentation.
References Ann O'M. Bowman and Richard C. Kearney, *State and Local Government* (1993); Terry Christensen, *Local Politics: Governing at the Grassroots* (1995); Mitchell Pacelle, "Block Watch: Not in Your Backyard, Say Community Panels in Suburban Enclaves" (1995).

Private Property

See Property Rights Movement; Takings.

Privatization

The transfer of government responsibilities and assets to the private sector is referred to as privatization. Since the 1970s, privatization has become an increasingly popular reform proposal to improve government efficiency at relatively low costs. Advocates argue that many types of government-provided services, from trash pickup to mail delivery, could be better managed by private companies. Use of private sector service providers forces the delivery of services into the marketplace, which improves their efficiency and causes their costs to come down.

Opponents argue that private business can be just as inefficient as government in fulfilling such responsibilities, and many assert that it is inappropriate to turn some government functions over to the private sector, even if it would reduce costs. These opponents argue that government programs should be concerned with other goals besides delivering services at the lowest cost, including equity in treatment of recipients, citizen involvement in service decisions, and the protection of individual rights. Proposals to privatize corrections systems have been especially criticized as being an inappropriate area for the private sector.

Many members of the Reagan administration were strong advocates of privatization of government responsibilities, but very few federal activities have ultimately been turned over to private companies to handle. One of the most prominent federal privatization acts was the sale of Conrail in 1986. In the past several years, state governments have been turning many responsibilities over to private companies, including tax collection, mental health care, transportation programs, and prison management. Similarly, many cities and counties have been hiring private companies to handle such tasks as trash pickup, street repair, and hospital management.

The primary method state and local governments use to involve the private sector in handling government responsibilities is the contracting out of services, which is the hiring of private companies to handle specific public services. A second method used to privatize government, and one that has generated growing interest, is the use of vouchers. In a voucher system, the government distributes certificates (vouchers) to individuals who need some type of government service, and the individuals can then use those certificates to buy services from suppliers of their choice in the private sector. The use of vouchers has been advocated in recent years by many reformers as a way to improve the nation's education system. Vouchers are also advocated as a better way to provide housing to the poor than through traditional housing projects. A third method of privatization is the sale of a government program to a private company, which then runs the service as it sees fit except where government regulations are imposed.

Reinventing government and public service deregulation are two alternatives to privatization that have been proposed in recent years to improve the delivery and lower the costs of government services.

See also Alternative Service Delivery; Contracting Out; Crime; Education; Finance, Local; Public Service Deregulation; Reinventing Government; School Choice.
References Joan Allen et al., *Private Sector in State Service Delivery: Examples of Innovative Practices* (1989); John R. Miller and Christopher R. Tufts, "Privatization Is a Means to 'More with Less'" (1993); E. S. Savas, *Privatization: The Key to Better Government* (1987); Linda Wagar, "The Tricky Path to Going Private" (1995).

Procurement

Reports of incredibly expensive government purchases and unexpected cost overruns routinely bring demands for reform in how the government purchases goods and services from the private sector. Critics argue that the strict regulations that agencies are required to follow in procuring goods often cause the government to spend its money poorly. One of the major problems associated with the current procurement system is the use of sealed bids in the awarding of contracts. Reformers argue that the use of sealed bids often forces the government to award contracts without giving adequate consideration to the reliability of the proposals or the quality of the bidders' work, especially their past performance.

The main solutions that reformers offer to end procurement inefficiencies are reducing procurement regulations, introducing more competition into the procurement process, giving agencies greater flexibility in making purchasing decisions, and allowing agencies to consider factors other than the amount of bids in making awards, including the bidders' past performance. There have been a few recent efforts to introduce some of these reforms in the federal bureaucracy. In 1993, the Office of Federal Procurement Policy directed all executive agencies to begin using past performance in evaluating bids for most contracts over $100,000. The Department of Defense has also established rules allowing the consideration of positive performance records in the granting of contracts.

Opponents of these reforms argue that increasing the freedom of agencies in procuring goods may open the procurement system to abuse, allowing favoritism to shape government awards.

See also Public Service Deregulation.
References Steven Kelman, *Procurement and Public Management: The Fear of Discretion and the Quality of Government Performance* (1990); Steven Kelman, "Deregulating Federal Procurement: Nothing To Fear but Discretion Itself?" (1994).

Professional Legislators

See Career Legislators; Professional Legislature.

Professional Legislature

Legislative scholars have identified a number of different characteristics that make some state legislatures more "professional" than others. These include the size of the legislative staff, the amount of money legislators are paid, the length of time the legislature is in session, the attitudes that legislators have about making legislative service a career, and the organizational structure of the legislature itself, including its use of committees and the role played by the formal leaders.

The legislative reform movement of the 1970s increased the professional character of most legislatures nationwide, though a handful have remained amateur. The reform movement brought an increase in staff, pay, and the length of time legislatures are in session. It encouraged legislatures to provide members with individual offices and other facilities. It led to the rise of professional or career legislators, and it brought important changes to make the structure and procedures of state legislatures more rational.

These reforms are considered to have increased the power and independence of state legislatures. Scholars have often referred to the changes that have occurred as the professionalization, modernization, or even the congressionalization of state legislatures.

See also Career Legislators; Legislative Reform Movement; State Renewal; Term Limits.
References Ann O'M. Bowman and Richard C. Kearney, *The Resurgence of the States* (1986); Citizens' Conference on State Legislatures, *The Sometimes Governments: A Critical Study of the 50 American Legislatures* (1973); Alan Rosenthal, *Governors and Legislatures: Contending Powers* (1990).

Professional Politicians

Also known as career politicians, professional politicians are those elected officials who make government service their main line of work for most of their professional lives. The power of these professionals and their apparent lack of responsiveness to the voters has led to calls for term limits and other reforms during the 1980s and 1990s.

In the past, most elected officials in the United States maintained outside careers in law, business, farming, or other activities while serving in public office. The only professional politicians were the bosses affiliated with the party machines, but these individuals usually did not hold office themselves. With the decline of political parties during the twentieth century, a new breed of professional has emerged who devotes his or her life to serving in elected office. Professional politicians are found at all levels of government, but most of the public criticism has been lodged against those in Congress and state legislatures.

The rise of professionalism among legislators appeared first in Congress. Until this century, most members of the House of Representatives and Senate served for brief tenures, taking only short breaks, if any, from their primary occupations. Because Congress exercised only limited power and the benefits of service were minimal, most members had little desire to remain in office for long, which meant that turnover was rapid. However, as party machines declined and the power of Congress increased around the turn of the century, House and Senate members increasingly sought reelection. Though they still identified themselves as attorneys, farmers, or businessmen, their real business soon became government.

In state legislatures, the amateur status of legislators was assured for decades by low pay and short sessions. In the 1960s and 1970s, however, the legislative reform movement swept the nation, which called for the revitalization of state legislatures.

Among the movement's goals were the determination to encourage longer tenure and to make legislative work a full-time occupation. Some states resisted the movement and still promote the ideal of part-time legislative service, but most have fostered increased professionalism during the past few decades by offering higher salaries and extending session length. The result is that few state legislators have the time or desire today to pursue careers outside of legislative service.

The trend toward professionalism allows legislators to devote all of their time to governing, which advocates say is necessary if they are to address the increasingly complex nature of legislation and policy issues. In addition, these advocates argue that the move toward professionalism allows for more democratic representation, because it opens legislative service to persons other than the wealthy.

Critics of professional legislatures, on the other hand, contend that entrenched members have lost touch with their constituencies and wield too much power. Political scandals, the budget crises of the 1980s, and growing opposition to big government have led to dissatisfaction with these professionals and brought demands for reform. The result has been a move to set limits on legislative terms and to increase the number of representatives with private sector experience.

Groups such as U.S. Term Limits have led high-profile campaigns to set limits on how long members of Congress and state legislatures can serve in office. The Republican Party's Contract with America includes 12-year limits on House and Senate terms. The goals in these reform efforts are to increase access to legislative seats, improve constituent responsiveness, and reduce the power of individual legislators. Many political observers doubt that term limits will produce these desired results or lead to a reduction in the numbers of professional politicians. They argue that instead of causing a decline in professional politicians, term limits may simply encourage professionals to change offices more often.

See also Amateur Politicians; Contract with America; Legislative Reform Movement; Party Machines; Term Limits; U.S. Term Limits.

References Gerald Benjamin and Michael J. Malbin, eds., *Limiting Legislative Terms* (1992); "Decoding the Contract" (1995); Alan Ehrenhalt, *The United States of Ambition: Politicians, Power, and the Pursuit of Office* (1991); Alan Ehrenhalt, "Power Shifts in State Capitols as Professional Lawmakers Take Over Leadership Spots" (1993); Morris P. Fiorina, *Congress: Keystone of the Washington Establishment* (1977).

Program Budgeting

Program budgeting is a budgeting technique designed to improve bureaucratic efficiency, reduce the overlap of government programs, and instill some rationality into the budget process. Under program budgeting, individual government agencies establish identifiable goals and then design specific programs to attain those goals. The legislature or other government body that oversees the budget then makes its funding decisions based on the needs and effectiveness of individual programs. Instead of having separate categories in the budget for each department and agency, which is traditional, the government's budget is organized so that programs with similar goals are grouped together, regardless of the departments in which they are housed. This budget structure is meant to encourage the government to focus attention on the services it provides and to offer a better foundation for comparing the costs and effectiveness of similar programs. Program budgeting is similar to performance budgeting, with its concern about government outputs, but it asks agencies to develop much more detailed plans for obtaining their goals.

Program budgeting was first introduced by the Department of Defense in 1961 in its planning-programming-budgeting system (PPBS). The success of this experiment caused President Lyndon Johnson to require all federal agencies to adopt this technique in 1965. The program was eliminated in 1971, though some federal agencies continue to use elements of it. In addition, more than 35 states and 300 cities reported using program budgeting in the mid- to late 1980s.

Although program budgeting has been praised by many reformers in the past, its focus on programs rather than agencies has been criticized as incompatible with the current structure of administrative organizations and budget-writing bodies.

See also Budgeting Techniques; Cost-Benefit Analysis; Incrementalism; Management by Objectives; Performance Budgeting; Zero-Base Budgeting.
References Donald F. Kettl, *Deficit Politics: Public Budgeting in Its Institutional and Historical Context* (1992); John L. Mikesell, *Fiscal Administration: Analysis and Applications for the Public Sector* (1991); *The Municipal Year Book 1989* (1989).

Program for Economic Recovery

The Program for Economic Recovery was the economic program unveiled during the first few weeks of President Ronald Reagan's administration that laid out the foundation of what became known as Reaganomics. The program consisted primarily of four goals: reduced government spending, decreased regulation, lower taxes, and stricter monetary policy.

See also Reaganomics.

Progressive Tax

A progressive tax is a government levy in which the tax rate is greater for individuals with higher incomes. It is the opposite of a regressive tax, which require that low-wage earners pay a disproportionate amount of their income on taxes. The federal income tax is often considered among the most progressive taxes in the nation because of its use of higher tax brackets as income levels rise. Sales and property taxes, which are the primary sources of revenue for states and local governments, tend to be more regressive.

Liberal reformers argue that progressive taxes are fairer because they place a greater burden on those who have greater ability to pay. Conservative economists argue, however, that many of the more regressive taxes are preferable because they increase the amount of money in the hands of the wealthy, who are more likely to make investments that will benefit the economy. These economists reason that as the economy grows, everyone will benefit.

During the past two decades, many of the tax reform proposals that have dominated political debate have been regressive in nature. The Economic Recovery Tax Act of 1981, which was based in supply-side economics, was considered one of the most regressive tax reforms in the nation's history, radically reducing the highest tax rate and creating numerous loopholes that benefited the wealthy. Moreover, many of the primary reform proposals being discussed today, including the national sales tax, the value-added tax, and the reduction in capital gains taxes, are all regressive.

Despite the dominant role that conservative economists have played in shaping discourse over tax reform, the nation's tax rate actually became slightly more progressive with the passage of the Tax Reform Act of 1986, which closed numerous tax loopholes and significantly reduced the tax burden on those earning the lowest wages.

See also Benefit Principle; Capital Gains Tax; Consumed-Income Tax; Consumption Tax; Corporate Income Tax; Economic Recovery Tax Act; Flat Tax; Personal Income Tax; Property Tax; Proportional Tax; Reaganomics; Regressive Tax; Sales Tax; Supply-Side Economics; Tax Reform Act; Taxes; Value-Added Tax.

References Werner Z. Hirsch and Anthony M. Rufolo, *Public Finance and Expenditure in a Federal System* (1990); Joseph J. Minarik, *Making Tax Choices* (1985); Howard E. Shuman, *Politics and the Budget: The Struggle between the President and the Congress* (1992).

Property Rights Movement

The property rights movement is a conservative political movement that calls for greater protection of private property, including a decrease in government regulation and restrictions on the use of "takings." In the past few years, legislation has been introduced in more than 40 states and in Congress to reduce government demands on property owners. Supporters of these bills argue that citizens should have greater freedom to do as they please on their private property. Opponents argue that if these bills are enacted they will reduce the power of local governments to control zoning and will harm the nation's environmental policy.

See also Environmental Policy; Job Creation and Wage Enhancement Act; Sagebrush Rebellion; Takings.

References David L. Callies, ed., *After Lucas: Land Use Regulation and the Taking of Private Property Without Compensation* (1993); G. Richard Hill, *Regulatory Taking: The Limits of Land Use Controls* (1993); Richard Moe, "If Men Were Angels . . . Property Rights and the 'Takings' Issue" (1994); Larry Morandi, "Takings for Granted" (1995).

Property Tax

A property tax is any tax levied on the ownership of land and buildings, or what is called real property. This kind of tax is the primary source of revenue for local governments in the United States, although it has attracted considerable criticism over the past 20 years. One of the primary complaints against the property tax is that it is levied against landowners regardless of their ability to pay. It is also considered one of the more regressive forms of taxation, because landowners pass their tax burden on to renters. Finally, the use of property tax allows wealthier communities to obtain better services than can poor ones, which has been a particular concern among education reformers.

The property tax was the focus of considerable reform efforts in the late 1970s and early 1980s, as skyrocketing property values in many states drove taxes upward. A taxpayers' revolt was ignited with the passage of California's Proposition 13 in 1978. During the next five years, more than 40 states are estimated to have adopted laws limiting property taxes or providing property tax relief. Although the revolt reduced the importance of property taxes in generating revenue, they remain the primary source of funds for local governments, accounting for nearly 75 percent of all local government revenue.

The property tax is praised by some analysts because it is more certain than other forms of taxation, including the sales and income tax, both of which are more rapidly affected by economic trends. In addition, some governments have introduced tax credits and other reforms to protect homeowners, especially retirees on fixed incomes, from rapid expansion of property taxes. Education reformers have also had some success in state courts and legislatures in reducing the use of property taxes for funding of public schools.

See also Education; Finance, Local; Personal Income Tax; Progressive Tax; Proposition 13; Regressive Tax; Sales Tax; School Finance; Tax Revolt; Taxes.

References John J. Harrigan, *Politics and Policy in States and Communities* (1994); Werner Z. Hirsch and Anthony M. Rufolo, *Public Finance and Expenditure in a Federal System* (1990); Jeffrey L. Katz, "The Search for Equity in School Funding" (1991); David O. Sears and Jack Citrin, *Tax Revolt: Something for Nothing in California* (1985).

Proportional Representation

One of the problems in electoral politics is how to provide for majority rule and also ensure that minority viewpoints are represented in government. Both of the two most common forms of electoral systems used in the United States—single-member and multimember districts—have been criticized for underrepresenting minority views.

One proposal offered by reformers to improve the electoral system is the use of proportional representation. Two proportional systems have been proposed, both of which are designed to increase minority representation while continuing to allow the majority to rule.

One type of proportional representation is the party list system. Under this type of system, which is common in Europe, voters cast their votes for a list of candidates put forward by a political party. Seats are then distributed among the parties according to the percentage of the vote each list receives.

A second type of proportional system is the single-transferable vote (STV) or preferential voting. Under this system, voters rank their preferences among candidates competing for seats in a multimember district. The ballots are then sorted by each voter's first choice. Candidates who receive above a predetermined percentage of the first-choice votes are automatically elected to office. If no candidate passes this threshold, the candidate with the lowest vote total is eliminated and the second choices from the ballots supporting this candidate are then added to the other candidates' vote tallies.

If any of the seats remain unfilled after this first round of vote counting, the excess votes of winning candidates are transferred to other candidates and a second round of vote counting takes place. The votes are transferred according to the percentage of second-choice votes each candidate receives on the winning candidates' ballots. Thus if a candidate needs only 5,000 votes to be elected but receives 6,000, the additional 1,000 votes are distributed to other candidates based on the percentage of second-choice votes the losing candidates received in all 6,000 of these ballots. Additional rounds of vote counting occur, with more votes transferred until all the positions are filled.

The single-transferable vote system has been used by several city councils and school boards, particularly in New York and Massachusetts. The party list system has been proposed in many cases, but it has not been tried in the United States.

See also Election Systems; Multimember Districts; Single-Member Districts.

References Bernard Grofman and Arend Lijphart, eds., *Electoral Laws and Their Political Consequences* (1986); Wilma Rule and Joseph F. Zimmerman, eds., *United States Electoral Systems: Their Impact on Women and Minorities* (1992).

Proportional Tax

A proportional tax is a tax in which the rate remains the same at all income levels. The flat tax is generally a type of proportional tax, though most flat tax proposals include provisions reducing the rate for the poor.

See also Flat Tax; Progressive Tax; Regressive Tax.

References John L. Mikesell, *Fiscal Administration: Analysis and Applications for the Public Sector* (1991); Joseph J. Minarik, *Making Tax Choices* (1985).

Proposition 13

Proposition 13 was a 1978 California ballot measure that radically reduced property taxes in that state and helped spur a tax revolt across the nation in the late 1970s and early 1980s. Sponsored by conservative real estate developer Howard Jarvis and Paul Gann, the measure amended the California constitution to restrict the maximum property tax rate to 1 percent of a property's 1975–1976 assessed value. It also restricted assessment increases to 2 percent per year and required state and local governments to obtain a two-thirds majority vote to raise taxes.

The amendment attracted widespread support among voters who had grown resentful of rising taxes and disillusioned with government. Despite dire warnings from public officials, "good government" groups, teachers' unions, and others that the measure would adversely affect local government programs, the initiative passed by more than a two-to-one margin.

Nearly overnight, the pressure for property tax relief and reduction in other taxes spread to states across the nation. It has been estimated that more than 40 states enacted some form of local property tax limitation or tax relief plan over the next five years, and many placed restrictions on or approved cutbacks in personal, corporate, and sales taxes. The proposition's success also helped spur a renewed interest in the use of initiative and referendum processes to deal with state and local problems.

In spite of the predictions of its opponents, Proposition 13 did not immediately have severe effects on local government in California, in large part because state funds were used to compensate for the loss of the local property taxes. In the late 1980s and early 1990s, however, Proposition 13 came to be seen as one of the primary factors causing the state's severe fiscal problems.

See also Initiative; Jarvis, Howard; Tax Revolt; Taxes.

References Charles G. Bell and Charles M. Price, *California Government Today: Politics of Reform?* (1988); Thomas E. Cronin, *Direct Democracy: The Politics of Initiative, Referendum, and Recall* (1989); David O. Sears and Jack Citrin, Tax Revolt: *Something for Nothing in California* (1985).

Proposition 187

Proposition 187 was a 1994 proposition on the California ballot designed to deny state social services, public education, and nonemergency medical care to illegal immigrants. The proposition's supporters championed the law as a way to solve the state's social and economic problems. Opponents maintained, however, that the proposition was not a serious effort to address immigration problems, but rather a xenophobic reaction to the large influx of immigrants to the state. The initiative was approved by nearly 60 percent of the state's voters, but its implementation was immediately block by a court restraining order. The passage of the initiative spawned similar measures in other states.

References Nancy H. Martis and A. G. Block, "Proposition 187" (1994); Peter Schrag, "Son of 187" (1995).

Protectionism

Protectionism refers to the use of government restrictions and tariffs to protect American businesses from foreign competition. Since the 1940s, the federal government has generally opposed protectionist policies, and has tried to encourage free trade between the United States and other countries. During the 1980s, however, there was a resurgence of support for protectionist policies to combat what many business and political leaders saw as the unfair trade practices of other nations. The federal government responded by imposing or threatening to impose a variety of restrictions and tariffs on specific foreign goods. This resurgence of protectionism, however, is seen as limited in comparison to the protectionist policies that existed prior to the 1930s. Since the end of the 1980s, support for protectionism has declined, though it has retained enough support that it almost defeated the North American Free Trade Agreement in 1993.

See also Free Trade; General Agreement on Tariffs and Trade; North American Free Trade Agreement; Trade Policy.
References Martin Feldstein, ed., *American Economic Policy in the 1980s* (1994); Gary Mucciaroni, *Reversals of Fortune: Public Policy and Private Interests* (1995).

Public Citizen

Public Citizen is a powerful liberal public affairs group founded by activist Ralph Nader in 1971. Its $7 million budget is used to support the work of "citizen advocates," particularly on issues relating to consumer rights, government regulation of product and workplace safety, environmental protection, industrial and corporate ethics, and government accountability. Public Citizen lobbies government for reforms on these issues and funds litigation through its Public Citizen Litigation Group. It also sponsors public educational campaigns. Public Citizen is the umbrella organization for several reform groups associated with Ralph Nader, including Congress Watch and the Tax Reform Research Group. The organization is considered one of the preeminent "good government" groups in the nation.

See also Congress Watch; Nader, Ralph.
References Ronald J. Hrebenar and Ruth K. Scott, *Interest Group Politics in America* (1990); Michael W. McCann, *Taking Reform Seriously: Perspectives on Public Interest Liberalism* (1986).

Public Financing

For many political reformers, meaningful campaign finance reform must include some form of public financing or funding of candidates. Public financing is seen as an essential tool to increase electoral competition, control escalating campaign costs, and reduce the presence or appearance of corruption in the political system. Proposals to limit campaign spending are often coupled with public financing, in large part because of the U.S. Supreme Court's decision in *Buckley v. Valeo* that spending limits are unconstitutional unless they are part of a public financing program.

At the federal level, the only political office for which there is public financing is the presidency. The 1974 amendments to the Federal Election Campaign Act (FECA) provided for partial funding of presidential primaries and full public funding of the general election for the two major political parties. The act also created a formula to allow independent candidates and third parties to receive some public assistance. In passing FECA, Congress considered providing public funds for congressional campaigns, but the proposal was defeated in the House.

At the state level, many legislatures have adopted public financing of campaigns, though the specific rules vary considerably from state to state. State programs differ primarily in the offices for which public financing is available, the amount of money candidates receive, and whether the support comes directly from state funds or through tax deductions for contributors. According to Professor Frank J. Sorauf of the University of Minnesota, 3 states provide direct public support for candidates in both legislative and some executive races, 6 limit public funds to statewide offices, 18 allow tax deductions or credits to contributors, and 10 provide public funds to political parties.

See also *Buckley v. Valeo;* Campaign Finance; Checkoff Funds; Federal Election Campaign Act; Spending Limits.

References *Congressional Campaign Finances: History, Facts, and Controversy* (1992); Frederick M. Herrmann and Ronald D. Michaelson, "Financing State and Local Elections: Recent Developments" (1994); David B. Magleby and Candice J. Nelson, *The Money Chase: Congressional Campaign Finance Reform* (1990); Frank J. Sorauf, *Money in American Elections* (1988).

Public Funding

See Public Financing.

Public Interest Research Groups (PIRGs)

Public Interest Research Groups are student-led organizations that were first created at many universities in the 1970s to promote government reform, consumer protection, and environmental concerns. Today, there are PIRGs in 25 states. The U.S. Public Interest Research Group in Washington, D.C., serves as the national office for these state groups.

References Katherine Isaac, *Ralph Nader Presents: Practicing Democracy—A Guide to Student Action* (1995); Alan Rosenthal, *The Third House: Lobbyists and Lobbying in the States* (1993).

Public Service Deregulation

Public service deregulation refers to proposals to reduce the number of regulations placed on government bureaucracies in order to give bureaucrats more flexibility in doing their jobs. It has been offered by supporters as an alternative to privatization, reinventing government, and other recent reform efforts to improve the functioning and lower the costs of government administration.

Supporters argue that public service deregulation improves the functioning of government by making the bureaucracy more results oriented and by giving supervisors greater power in making personnel decisions. It is championed as a way to lower costs because it reduces paperwork and allows more flexibility in budgeting and procurement procedures.

Three recent national commissions on bureaucratic reform (the Volcker Commission, the Winter Commission, and President Clinton's National Performance Review) all included proposals for deregulating the public service. In addition, both site management of schools and community-based policing are considered types of public service deregulation.

See also Administrative Reorganization; Bureaucracy; Education; National Performance Review; Paperwork; Privatization; Procurement; Reinventing Government; Volcker Commission; Winter Commission.

References John J. DiIulio, Jr., ed., *Deregulating the Public Service: Can Government Be Improved?* (1994); Frank J. Thompson, "The Challenges Revisited" (1993); James Q. Wilson, *Bureaucracy: What Government Agencies Do and Why They Do It* (1989).

R

Railroad Revitalization and Reform Act of 1976

The Railroad Revitalization and Reform Act of 1976, which loosened restrictions on the railroad industry, is considered the first major legislative effort to reduce government involvement in business and industry after a decade of unprecedented growth of federal regulations. The act made it easier for railroads to change rates and routes, and removed restrictions on mergers.

See also Deregulation.
References Paul L. Joskow and Roger G. Noll, "Economic Regulation" (1994); Gary Mucciaroni, *Reversals of Fortune: Public Policy and Private Interests* (1995).

Rainbow Coalition

See National Rainbow Coalition.

Randolph, Asa Philip (1889–1979)

Asa Philip Randolph was one of the preeminent leaders of the civil rights movement from the 1930s to the 1960s. Originally the head of the Brotherhood of Sleeping Car Porters labor union, he helped establish the Leadership Conference on Civil Rights and organized the March on Washington in 1963, where Martin Luther King, Jr., gave his famous "I Have a Dream" speech.

See also Civil Rights Movement; King, Martin Luther, Jr.; Leadership Conference on Civil Rights.
Reference Charles W. Eagles, ed., *The Civil Rights Movement in America* (1986).

Reagan, Ronald W. (b. 1911) (40th U.S. President, 1981–1989)

When Ronald Reagan, former California governor and Hollywood actor, took office as president in 1981, his vision for a prosperous, militarily strong nation was shared by many Americans. Most of the policies and reforms he introduced related to his belief that the economy would be stimulated only by a reduction in the government's role in society. His mistrust of the "evil empire" (the Soviet Union) also led to the largest peacetime military buildup in U.S. history.

Federal spending priorities changed dramatically during Reagan's tenure. After soaring inflation rates and economic stagnation during the 1970s, voter sentiment turned toward the business-friendly, budget-cutting promises of the Republicans. Reagan captured that sentiment, arguing that cuts in taxes and government spending would lead to economic growth.

The Reagan administration also pushed for government deregulation of industry and a devolution of federal programs to the states.

During his first year in office, Reagan cut social programs and income taxes dramatically, all the while dominating the relationship between himself and Congress. In total, domestic social programs were cut by $37.7 billion for fiscal 1982, and the Economic Recovery Tax Act of 1981 included one of the largest tax cuts in U.S. history. At the same time, military spending was increased from $185 billion in 1982 to nearly $300 million in 1988, the last year of his tenure (and the end of the Cold War era). Among other programs, these funds were used to launch Reagan's expensive Strategic Defense Initiative ("Star Wars") and to provide aid to anticommunist forces in Nicaragua.

Despite his dominance of Washington politics during his first year in office, Reagan's ultimate success in reshaping the direction of government proved limited. By his second year, Congress became more willing to oppose his efforts as the economy sputtered and the public became less enamored of Reagan's proposals. The Reagan tax cuts did not spur economic growth as promised, but instead, they led to historic budget deficits, which came to dominate much of the political debate in the 1980s. Reagan had some initial success at deregulation and devolution, but the growing number of new regulations coming out of Washington soon resumed. Despite the talk of devolution, the federal government found benefits in using unfunded mandates and preemptions to force its will on the states. Finally, Reagan's antipathy toward the Soviet Union also dissipated, and he began to work with Soviet President Mikhail Gorbachev to reduce nuclear arms.

See also Budget Deficit, Federal; Deregulation; Devolution; Economic Policy; Economic Recovery Tax Act; Federal-State Relations; Fiscal Policy; Foreign Policy; Gramm-Latta; Iran-Contra Affair; Laffer, Arthur B.; Mandates, Federal; Monetary Policy; Murray, Charles; Preemption; Reaganomics; Reconciliation; Supply-Side Economics; Taxes.

References Martin Feldstein, ed., *American Economic Policy in the 1980s* (1994); William A. Niskanen, *Reaganomics: An Insider's Account of the Policies and People* (1988); Howard E. Shuman, *Politics and the Budget: The Struggle between the President and the Congress* (1992); Herbert Stein, *Presidential Economics: The Making of Economic Policy from Roosevelt to Clinton* (1994); David B. Walker, *The Rebirth of Federalism: Slouching toward Washington* (1995).

Reaganomics

The conservative economic policies implemented during the Reagan presidential administration are often referred to as Reaganomics. These policies grew out of Reagan's strong ideological beliefs and in response to the economic problems of the 1970s. As Reagan's tenure unfolded, however, he abandoned many of the reform principles associated with Reaganomics to cope with new economic problems and shifting public opinion.

The goals of Reaganomics were initially spelled out in Reagan's Program for Economic Recovery, which he presented to Congress in early 1981. The program consisted primarily of four goals: reduced government spending, fewer regulations, lower taxes, and a stricter monetary policy. These four goals coincided with what most observers believed was Reagan's sincere belief in small government, but his support for them also reflected trends in economic thought in the late 1970s.

During the 1970s, the traditional Keynesian economic principles that had guided U.S. economic policies since the 1930s came under increasing attack as the nation's economy suffered under the weight of stagflation. At the same time Keynes was being criticized, two conservative economic approaches began to enjoy increasing academic and political popularity. These two theories—supply-side economics and monetarism—blamed much of the nation's economic problems on federal interference, though they offered different approaches to making the economy more productive. The supply-siders called for a reduction in federal taxes and deregulation to encourage work, savings, and investment. With more money available for savings and investments, businesses would expand and the economy would grow. The monetarists advocated a reduction in the size of the federal government and an emphasis on the use of monetary policy to produce and sustain economic growth. These two economic theories provided the intellectual foundation of Reaganomics.

Reagan's success in attaining his four goals was mixed. Immediately after taking office, he fought successfully for a reduction in domestic spending of nearly $38 billion in the 1982 budget, the deregulation of several key industries, a major tax cut (the Economic Recovery Tax Act of 1981), and a continuation of the tight monetary policy instituted under the Carter administration. Within a year, however, Reagan's concerns began to change as the nation's economy entered a severe recession and the federal budget started experiencing record deficits. He abandoned supply-side principles and increased taxes in 1982, 1983, and 1984 to try to bring the deficit under control. The Federal Reserve Board loosened the money supply to help stimulate the economy in 1982. As a political backlash began to mount against the deregulation of several industries, Reagan's efforts to reduce regulations elsewhere began to slow. Finally, Reagan also found considerable resistance to further spending cuts, though the high deficits certainly made it more difficult for the federal government to increase spending.

Reaganomics has been credited with reducing the nation's inflation rate, but most economists argue that it did little to stimulate economic growth as the supply-siders promised. It is also seen as one of the primary causes of the unprecedented federal budget deficits in the 1980s.

See also Big Swap; Budget Deficit, Federal; Deficit Reduction Act; Deregulation; Economic Policy; Economic Recovery Tax Act; Fiscal Policy; Gramm-Latta; Keynesian Economics; Laffer Curve; Monetarism; Monetary Policy; Reagan, Ronald W.; Stagflation; Supply-Side Economics; Tax Equity and Fiscal Responsibility Act; Taxes.
References Martin Feldstein, ed., *American Economic Policy in the 1980s* (1994); Charles R. Hulten and Isabel V. Sawhill, eds., *The Legacy of Reaganomics: Prospects for Long-Term Growth* (1984); Bruce Miroff et al., *The Democratic Debate: An Introduction to American Politics* (1995); William A. Niskanen, *Reaganomics: An Insider's Account of the Policies and People* (1988); Herbert Stein, *Presidential Economics: The Making of Economic Policy from Roosevelt to Clinton* (1994).

Reapportionment

Reapportionment is the redistribution of congressional seats among the states after each decennial census, as required by Article I, Section 2, of the U.S. Constitution. Historically, Congress simply added new seats to the House to accommodate population changes, but since 1911 the number of seats has been set at 435. The apportionment of these seats is determined by a specific formula called the Methods of Equal Proportions, which was approved by Congress in 1941.

The reapportionment process is often criticized by states losing seats and by those not gaining as many as they expected. After the 1990 reapportionment, some states began to push for an increase in the number of House members or a change in the formula used to distribute seats. Government officials in Montana were among the most visible actors in seeking reform after the state found itself with only one representative for its two politically distinct regions. The proposal to change the formula was pursued in the courts, and was ultimately rejected by the Supreme Court (*U.S Department of Commerce v. Montana*).

Urban communities have voiced criticism over the census figures that are used in the reapportionment process because the number of residents in urban areas tends to be more difficult to count than in other areas. A number of states pressured the Census Bureau after the 1990 reapportionment to revise its estimates so that they would more accurately capture minority populations. California was one of the most active in pushing for this change, presenting evidence that the census significantly undercounted the state's Mexican-American population. The request for revision was denied by the Commerce Department, and a federal district court later upheld the Commerce Department decision.

The term *reapportionment* is also used synonymously with *redistricting*, although some scholars consider these to be two distinct actions.

See also Redistricting.

References Roger H. Davidson and Walter J. Oleszek, *Congress and Its Members* (1994); Beth Donovan, "Remap Math Doesn't Add Up to One Person, One Vote" (1991); William J. Keefe and Morris S. Ogul, *The American Legislative Process: Congress and the States* (1993).

Reapportionment Revolution

The profound changes in legislative politics that transpired after the U.S. Supreme Court ruled that reapportionment was justiciable in *Baker v. Carr* has been referred to as the reapportionment revolution. Professor Gordon Baker of the University of California, Santa Barbara, writes that within two years of the court ruling, "half of the 50 states had made significant changes in apportionment patterns in at least one legislative house." Within four years, almost all state and congressional districts had met the Court's equal population standard spelled out in *Wesberry v. Sanders* and *Reynolds v. Sims.*

These changes in district lines, in turn, altered political power in Congress and state legislatures. The equal population requirement increased the number of representatives from urban and suburban districts, brought more African-Americans into office, and forced many long-term incumbents into retirement.

See also *Baker v. Carr;* Legislative Reform Movement; Redistricting; *Reynolds v. Sims; Wesberry v. Sanders.*

References Gordon E. Baker, *The Reapportionment Revolution: Representation, Political Power, and the Supreme Court* (1966); Bernard Grofman and Arend Lijphart, eds., *Electoral Laws and Their Political Consequences* (1986).

Recall

The recall is a political process that allows voters to remove an elected official before the end of the official's term. Originally introduced in the United States by progressive reformers to give voters greater control over elected officials, the process itself has generated considerable criticism from those who view it as antidemocratic and open to abuse.

The recall process works by allowing voters to circulate petitions calling for the removal of an elected official. If a requisite number of signatures are obtained, an election is held to decide whether the official will be removed or retained. Currently, 15 states allow the use of the recall to remove state officials, and 36 states provide for its use at the local level.

Although the recall has a long tradition in democratic societies, critics argue that it disrupts the political process, unduly restraining elected officials' actions and providing a weapon to harass officeholders. Critics also charge that the process is too expensive and too burdensome on voters.

A variety of reforms have been proposed to reduce abuses of the recall process, including restrictions on the time frame in which recalls can be used during an official's term, regulations requiring more accessible public records on recall petitioners and their financial backers, and the use of a cooling-off period between the circulation of petitions and the recall election to allow for more reasoned voting.

See also Initiative; National Initiative; Referendum.
References *The Book of the States 1994–95* (1994); Thomas E. Cronin, *Direct Democracy: The Politics of Initiative, Referendum, and Recall* (1989).

Recission

Recission refers to a president's decision to halt spending on a particular program because the program has been canceled or for other reasons. It is one of two types of presidential impoundments defined by the Congressional Budget and Impoundment Control Act of 1974. In order for the president's action to take effect, it must be approved by both houses of Congress within 45 days of continuous session. The recission process has been praised for giving the president the power to force Congress on occasion to reconsider major spending programs.

See also Congressional Budget and Impoundment Control Act; Deferral; Impoundment; Legislative Veto.
References John W. Ellwood and James A. Thurber, "The Politics of the Congressional Budget Process Re-examined" (1981); Daniel P. Franklin, *Making Ends Meet: Congressional Budgeting in the Age of Deficits* (1993); Howard E. Shuman, *Politics and the Budget: The Struggle between the President and the Congress* (1992).

Reconciliation

Reconciliation is the process by which Congress changes existing laws in order to make them meet the federal budget's spending and revenue goals. When Congress passes a Concurrent Budget Resolution establishing its spending and revenue guidelines for the upcoming fiscal year, it provides instructions on the amount of money each congressional committee must cut from the budget in order to meet the resolution's targets. These committees then make recommendations to their houses' Budget Committees on where the part of the budget under their jurisdiction can specifically be cut. These recommendations are rolled into one reconciliation bill that brings previously approved programs in line with the budget goals. Reconciliation was created by the Congressional Budget and Impoundment Control Act of 1974 and is considered one of the major steps of the congressional budget process.

See also Concurrent Budget Resolution; Congressional Budget and Impoundment Control Act.
References Howard E. Shuman, *Politics and the Budget: The Struggle between the President and the Congress* (1992); James A. Thurber, "New Rules for an Old Game: Zero-Sum Budgeting in the Postreform Congress" (1992).

Redistricting

After each decennial census, the states are given the task of redrawing congressional and state legislative district boundaries to adjust for population shifts and changes in the number of congressional seats the states are allocated. This process of redrawing district lines is call redistricting. In most states, the state legislature is primarily responsible for handling redistricting, but in some the governor or an independent commission also plays an important role.

The placement of district boundaries can have important effects on candidates' electoral chances, thus the redistricting process has received considerable scrutiny from minority groups, political parties, and others who want to ensure that they are not underrepresented when new redistricting plans are introduced.

A variety of reforms have been put forward to produce fairer representation or more equitable redistricting plans than is possible in the current electoral system. Some voting rights activists have called for replacing single-member districts, which are the primary electoral structure in the nation, with proportional representation or some other alternative election systems. Common Cause and the National Civic League, on the other hand, argue that the problems of unfair redistricting could be improved if the process was taken away from legislatures and given to independent commissions.

One of the most important trends in redistricting in the 1990s has been the availability of simple computer software programs that allow interested parties to analyze proposed redistricting plans, as well as to help them develop their own alternative plans. The Mexican American Legal Defense and Educational Fund, as well as a number of other civil rights groups, used this technology during the 1990 redistricting process to press for better representation of minorities.

See also Election Systems; Mexican American Legal Defense and Educational Fund; One Person, One Vote; Proportional Representation; Reapportionment; Reapportionment Revolution; Single-Member Districts.

References Bernard Grofman and Arend Lijphart, eds., *Electoral Laws and Their Political Consequences* (1986); William J. Keefe and Morris S. Ogul, *The American Legislative Process: Congress and the States* (1993); National Conference of State Legislatures Reapportionment Task Force, *Redistricting Provisions: 50 State Profiles* (1989).

Reed, Ralph

See Christian Coalition.

Referendum

The referendum is a type of direct democracy that allows or requires voters to approve legislation before it becomes law. Of the forms of direct democracy used in the United States, this is the one that has received the least criticism, though some reforms have been proposed.

The use of the referendum dates to the late 1700s, when Massachusetts and New Hampshire submitted state constitutions to voters for their approval. Today, all states provide for some form of referendum, with the most common being a direct vote on constitutional amendments. Many states also allow legislatures to place proposed statutory changes on the ballot. The citizen petition, which allows voters to request a popular vote on a recently enacted law, is permitted in 23 states.

The referendum tends to receive more support than other forms of direct democracy because it provides for both the involvement of the legislature and a popular vote. As with the initiative process, however, reformers criticize the process for giving too much responsibility to uninformed voters and being open to abuses from well-financed economic interests.

Reformers call for increased financial disclosure in referenda campaigns, more informative voter pamphlets, and greater reliance on advisory referenda, which do not have the force of law, but provide the legislature with input on voter attitudes toward legislative proposals.

See also Initiative; National Initiative; Recall.
References *The Book of the States 1994–95* (1994); Thomas E. Cronin, *Direct Democracy: The Politics of Initiative, Referendum, and Recall* (1989).

Reform 88

Reform 88 was one of two major efforts by the Reagan administration to reform the management of the federal bureaucracy. This 1982 program was designed to reduce waste and fraud in the bureaucracy and to improve government efficiency by introducing new management techniques. In 1984, supporters of the project argued that it had saved the government more than $30 billion, though this figure was questioned by others in the Reagan administration who felt it was significantly overinflated. Today, Reform 88 is viewed as having had minimal effects on improving the bureaucracy's management, and as perhaps having been partially responsible for a decline in morale in the bureaucracy in the 1980s.

See also Budgeting Techniques; Bureaucracy; Empowerment; Grace Commission.
References Colin Campbell, *Managing the Presidency: Carter, Reagan, and the Search for Executive Harmony* (1986); Donald J. Savoie, *Thatcher, Reagan, Mulroney: In Search of a New Bureaucracy* (1994).

Regents of the University of California v. Bakke

The constitutionality of an affirmative action program was brought before the U.S. Supreme Court for the first time in the monumental 1978 case *Regents of the University of California v. Bakke.* The case involved Alan Bakke, a white male who was twice denied admission to the University of California at Davis Medical School even though his admission scores were higher than those of minority students who were accepted into the program. In a 5–4 decision, the Supreme Court ruled in favor of Bakke, overturning the university's use of a quota system in making admissions decisions. Although the ruling restricted the use of quotas, the Court recognized that race could serve as a standard for admission as long as it was considered along with test scores and extracurricular activities.

See also Affirmative Action; *Fullilove v. Klutznick;* Reverse Discrimination; *United Steelworkers of America v. Weber; Wards Cove Packing Co. v. Frank Antonio.*
References Donald Altschiller, *Affirmative Action* (1991); Susan D. Clayton and Faye J. Crosby, *Justice, Gender, and Affirmative Action* (1992); John Charles Daly and William B. Allen, *Affirmative Action and the Constitution* (1987).

Regional Government

One of the primary reforms proposed to overcome the fragmentation of government in U.S. metropolitan areas is the creation of regional governments that would have the power to address problems that currently transcend local government boundaries. Several different approaches have been put forward to create regional governments, including the merger of local governments through either annexation or consolidation. Alternatively, some reformers call for the creation of an additional level of government above cities and counties with its own responsibilities and with the power to overturn the decisions of lower governments. This latter approach would allow cities and counties to continue to provide certain functions.

Supporters argue that regional government would be better able to address such issues as transportation, crime, pollution, and growth than is currently possible through the patchwork efforts made by cities and counties. Unlike councils of government, which are entirely voluntary, a regional government would have the formal power to address such problems. Moreover, the creation of regional governments would allow money from wealthy suburbs to flow to impoverished central cities.

Opponents argue that large central governments can be too big to deal effectively with many urban problems. In addition, the multiplicity of local governments allows local residents greater control in deciding how they want to structure their communities and in making policy choices.

Although regional government may provide a better solution to metropolitan fragmentation than other reforms, it is considered more difficult to adopt because it threatens the political power of current city and county governments.

See also Annexation; Consolidation; Contracting for Services; Councils of Government; Extraterritorial Jurisdiction; Greater Portland Metropolitan Service District; Metropolitan Fragmentation; Special Districts; Twin Cities Metropolitan Council.
References Terry Christensen, *Local Politics: Governing at the Grassroots* (1995); Thomas R. Dye, *Politics in States and Communities* (1994); John J. Harrigan, *Political Change in the Metropolis* (1993); David B. Walker, *The Rebirth of Federalism: Slouching toward Washington* (1995).

Regional Primaries
See National Primary.

Regressive Tax
A regressive tax is one that requires lower-wage earners to pay a greater proportion of their income to the government than do higher-wage earners. It is the opposite of a progressive tax, in which the tax rate rises as an individual's income increases.

See also Progressive Tax.
References Werner Z. Hirsch and Anthony M. Rufolo, *Public Finance and Expenditure in a Federal System* (1990); Joseph J. Minarik, *Making Tax Choices* (1985).

Regulatory Relief
See Deregulation.

Rehnquist, William H. (b. 1924)
William H. Rehnquist is the current chief justice of the U.S. Supreme Court. Under his leadership, the court is considered to have become more conservative. Rehnquist was active in Republican politics during his career as a lawyer in Phoenix, Arizona, and then serving as assistant attorney general in the U.S. Justice Department when President Nixon appointed him to the Court in 1971. Since then, he has built a record as one of the most conservative justices in recent Court history. President Reagan named Rehnquist chief justice in 1986, during a decade when several other political conservatives were nominated to the Court. A "strict constructionist," Rehnquist has said that he does not believe it is the role of the Court to make policy. Instead, he argues, it should adhere to the original intent of the framers of the U.S. Constitution. Critics maintain, however, that rather than leaving policy alone, the Rehnquist Court practices conservative judicial activism.

See also Judicial Activism; Supreme Court.
References John B. Gates and Charles A. Johnson, eds., *The American Courts: A Critical Assessment* (1991); William C. Louthan *The United States Supreme Court: Lawmaking in the Third Branch of Government* (1991).

Reinventing Government
Reinventing government refers to proposals to reform government bureaucracy by

decentralizing decision making, encouraging competition in the delivery of government services, placing greater emphasis on results, and making government agencies more customer oriented. The term *reinventing government* was coined by David Osborne and Ted Gaebler in their 1992 book of that title, and has since been adopted by many reformers. Today, it is often used to refer specifically to the bureaucratic reforms proposed by the National Performance Review in 1993, which drew heavily on Osborne and Gaebler's ideas. Critics argue that the proposals' emphasis on customer service ignores many of the broader roles performed by government in society, and are not applicable to many government operations.

Privatization and public service deregulation are two alternatives to reinventing government that have been advocated in recent years to improve the delivery and lower the costs of government services.

See also Bureaucracy; National Performance Review; Privatization; Public Service Deregulation; Winter Commission.
References Eliza Newlin Carney, "Still Trying To Reinvent Government" (1994); John J. DiIulio, Jr., ed., *Deregulating the Public Service: Can Government Be Improved?* (1994); Richard P. Nathan, "Reinventing Government: What Does It Mean?" (1995); David Osborne and Ted Gaebler, *Reinventing Government: How the Entrepreneurial Spirit Is Transforming the Public Sector* (1992).

Renewing Congress Project

The Renewing Congress Project was a cooperative undertaking between two Washington research institutes in the early 1990s that was designed to identify problems with Congress and propose reforms. The project, which was directed by the Brookings Institution and the American Enterprise Institute, was put together in response to growing public disillusionment with Congress. It produced a comprehensive list of reform proposals, from strengthening campaign finance rules to removing Congress's exemption from federal workplace laws. Although the direct effects of the project in producing reform have been limited, it helped bring greater focus among scholars and reformers on the problems confronting Congress and potential solutions.

See also American Enterprise Institute for Public Policy Research; Brookings Institution; Congress.
Reference Thomas E. Mann, "Renewing Congress: A Report from the Front Lines" (1995).

Reorganization Power

During the past 30 years, many states have granted to governors the power to reorganize the state bureaucracy through an executive order. This trend is part of a nationwide movement to strengthen the governor's position in state politics. By making governors stronger, reformers hope to improve the accountability and effectiveness of state government. Many state executives and political reformers argue that the availability of reorganization power is essential to effective state government because it allows the governor to restructure the bureaucracy when administrative problems arise or new social issues need to be addressed. Today, 22 states grant the governor the power of reorganization. The governor's use of the executive order to reorganize government can ordinarily be overturned by a legislative veto.

See also Administrative Reorganization; Governors.
References Thad Beyle, "Being Governor" (1993); Ann O'M Bowman and Richard C. Kearney, *The Resurgence of the States* (1986); Larry J. Sabato, *Goodbye to Good-Time Charlie: The American Governorship Transformed* (1983).

Responsible Parties

In the responsible parties model of democracy, parties play the central role in the political system. Under this system, each political party presents a platform to the public, spelling out its policy positions. Voters select between the parties depending on their policy preferences. Members of the party that gains control of the government then work to get these policies enacted into law.

Supporters of the responsible party model argue that if it were adopted in the United States it would provide a system in which voters are offered a clear-cut choice at the ballot box and the winning party has the ability to push its proposals into law. Moreover, voters would be able to identify which party to blame when problems occur, or which to credit when they go well. Critics argue, however, that U.S. society is too complex, voters too uninformed, and the parties too decentralized for a responsible party system to be developed.

In 1950, the Committee on Political Parties of the American Political Science Association published *Toward a More Responsible Two-Party System,* which presented a set of proposals to make the U.S. political system closer to this responsible party model. The book immediately stirred spirited debate among scholars on the merits of a strong party system, and has since served as a seminal document in spelling out the potential benefits of party reform.

See also Political Parties.
References Committee on Political Parties of the American Political Science Association, *Toward a More Responsible Two-Party System* (1950); William J. Keefe, *Parties, Politics, and Public Policy in America* (1994); Frank J. Sorauf, *Party Politics in America* (1984).

Revenue Act of 1971

In response to the growing costs of presidential campaigns and increasingly large campaign contributions from private donors, Congress included a section in the Revenue Act of 1971 creating a system for the public financing of presidential election campaigns through federal tax dollars. The act allowed taxpayers to check a box on their federal income tax returns designating one dollar of their taxes to be used for presidential campaigns. The act also detailed how these funds would be distributed among candidates and provided for tax credits for political contributions. In 1974, Congress amended the Federal Election Campaign Act, establishing a broader program for the public funding of presidential campaigns that superseded the Revenue Act. The funding for the current program, however, continues to rely on the tax checkoff plan created by the Revenue Act.

See also Campaign Finance; Checkoff Funds; Federal Election Campaign Act; Public Financing.
References *Congressional Campaign Finances: History, Facts, and Controversy* (1992); David B. Magleby and Candice J. Nelson, *The Money Chase: Congressional Campaign Finance Reform* (1990); Frank J. Sorauf, *Money in American Elections* (1988).

Revenue Act of 1978

Originally conceived as a major effort to reform the federal tax structure, the Revenue Act of 1978 ultimately did little to improve the fairness of the tax code as reformers had hoped. Instead, the act reduced corporate and capital gains taxes and provided protection for the investment tax credit. When the bill reached the floor of the House of Representatives, Representative Jack Kemp of New York offered an amendment to include a 30 percent across-the-board tax cut. His proposal, known as the Kemp-Roth Tax Cut, was defeated, 177 to 240. In 1981, however, the Kemp-Roth plan became one of the main components of the Economic Recovery Tax Act. The Revenue Tax Act of 1978 is considered by many to represent an important turning point in tax policy, when the federal government began to be less concerned with redistributing income and more concerned with providing tax breaks to the wealthy.

See also Economic Recovery Tax Act; Kemp, Jack R.; Kemp-Roth Tax Cut; Supply-Side Economics; Taxes.
References Michael B. Berkman, *The State Roots of National Politics: Congress and the Tax Agenda, 1978–1986* (1993); Thomas Byrne Edsall, *The New Politics of Inequality* (1984); Charls E. Walker, "Tax Policy" (1994).

Revenue Sharing
See General Revenue Sharing.

Reverse Discrimination
The implementation of affirmative action programs that give minorities and women preferential treatment in economic and educational opportunities has led some to call the practice reverse discrimination. Although it has not been proven that reverse discrimination is a widespread occurrence, concern over it has become a rallying point among critics of affirmative action, who argue that these programs unfairly discriminate against whites to obtain civil rights goals.

Reverse discrimination is often associated with quota systems that set aside a specific number of positions in jobs and schools for minorities or women. The Civil Rights Act of 1964, which is the foundation of modern affirmative action laws, did not require employers to hire employees by race, nor was its purpose to set up racial quotas, yet quotas soon began to be used by many to attain the act's goals. Although some early Supreme Court decisions supported these programs, the Court has increasingly sided with those charging reverse discrimination. In 1989, for example, the Court ruled against a program in Richmond, Virginia, that allocated 30 percent of its contracts to minorities. The ruling did not eliminate such "set-asides" completely, but it did limit them only to situations in which there was evidence of discrimination.

Despite the criticisms, affirmative action supporters maintain that quotas are justified to overcome past discrimination and to protect minorities and women from current discriminatory practices.

See also Affirmative Action; *Fullilove v. Klutznick; Regents of the University of California v. Bakke; United Steelworkers of America v. Weber; Wards Cove Packing Co. v. Frank Antonio.*
References Steve Shulman and William Darity, Jr., eds., *The Question of Discrimination: Racial Inequality in the U.S. Labor Market* (1989); Jared Taylor, *Paved with Good Intentions: The Failure of Race Relations in Contemporary America* (1992).

Revolving-Door Restrictions
To many reformers, one of the most troubling problems in interest group lobbying is the large number of government employees who work as lobbyists. This movement from government to lobbying, or what is called the revolving door, is criticized by many who argue that it is potentially unethical for government officials to use the expertise and contacts they have developed working in government to help individual interests within the private sector. Moreover, there is a potential for conflicts of interest among government officials who begin looking for lobbying jobs while still in public service.

Since the 1970s, the federal government and several states have attempted to pass reforms to restrict the lobbying activities of former government employees. The Ethics in Government Act of 1978 forbade executive branch officials in the federal government from lobbying the agencies in which they had worked for one year after leaving their posts. The law also banned these officials from ever lobbying government agencies on matters in which they had been involved both "personally and substantially."

Although the act was praised, many reformers argued that it did not go far enough in restricting the revolving door. One of the major criticisms was that the law did not apply to members of Congress and their staffs. In the late 1980s, pressure mounted on Congress to enact additional restrictions after several prominent Reagan administration officials moved directly into lucrative lobbying positions. At first these efforts were unsuccessful, but in 1989 Congress enacted the Ethics Reform Act. This act extended the revolving-door rules on executive branch officials to limit the lobbying activities of former government officials on behalf of foreign interests. It also placed legal restrictions for the first time on the employment activities of former members of Congress and their staffs.

Efforts to enact similar revolving-door laws at the state level have enjoyed increasing success, and today 35 states have rules regulating the employment activities of those who have left government service.

These restriction are applauded by supporters as a way to ensure more ethical government. Opponents argue, however, that they deter talented workers from taking government jobs and deny government employees the right to seek employment where they choose.

See also Conflict of Interest Laws; Ethics; Ethics in Government Act; Ethics Reform Act of 1989; Lobbying.

References Jeffrey M. Berry, *The Interest Group Society* (1989); Joyce Bullock, "State Lobby Laws in the 1990s" (1994); Ronald J. Hrebenar and Ruth K. Scott, *Interest Group Politics in America* (1990); Jerald A. Jacobs, ed., *Federal Lobbying* (1989); Kay Lehman Schlozman and John T. Tierney, *Organized Interests and American Democracy* (1986).

Reynolds v. Sims

In *Reynolds v. Sims* (1964), the U.S. Supreme Court applied the findings of *Wesberry v. Sanders* to state legislatures, ruling that state legislative districts need to be apportioned based on population. The Court's decision had a profound effect on the structure of state legislative politics and established an important criterion for determining what constitutes a fair redistricting plan.

Prior to the Court's decision, there was considerable population disparity between legislative districts in many states. The problem was particularly severe among state senates, which often distributed seats by county instead of by population. The effect of these state senate districting plans, which were modeled after the U.S. Senate, was that rural districts tended to be far better represented than urban ones.

In the Court's decision, Chief Justice Earl Warren wrote, "Legislators represent people, not trees or acres. Legislators are elected by voters, not farms or cities, or economic interests." Therefore, he concluded, the weight of all citizens' votes must be approximately the same. Districting plans that do not give approximately the same weight to all votes violate the equal protection clause of the Fourteenth Amendment.

The result of *Reynolds v. Sims* was a radical restructuring of state legislatures in the 1960s, as state senates replaced their federal-style plans with ones in which the apportionment was based on population. Since the *Reynolds* decision, population equality has been the primary criterion used in determining the fairness of state redistricting plans.

The decision represented a great victory to reformers from urban districts who sought fairer redistricting practices. Yet some observers have criticized the decision, arguing that it places too much emphasis on numerical equality; the real question underlying these redistricting cases, they say, is how to achieve fair representation. Fair representation can still be denied even with districts of equal population, through gerrymandering and other forms of electoral discrimination.

See also *Baker v. Carr; Davis v. Bandemer;* Electoral Discrimination; Gerrymandering; Reapportionment Revolution; *Wesberry v. Sanders.*
References Gordon E. Baker, *The Reapportionment Revolution: Representation, Political Power, and the Supreme Court* (1966); Bernard Grofman and Arend Lijphart, eds., *Electoral Laws and Their Political Consequences* (1986); William J. Keefe and Morris S. Ogul, *The American Legislative Process: Congress and the States* (1993); National Conference of State Legislatures Reapportionment Task Force, *Reapportionment Law: The 1990s* (1989).

Rightsizing

See Downsizing.

Risk Assessment

See Cost-Benefit Analysis; Job Creation and Wage Enhancement Act.

Rivlin, Alice M. (b. 1931)

Economist Alice M. Rivlin was the first director of the Congressional Budget Office in 1975 and was named director of the powerful federal Office of Management and Budget (OMB) under President Clinton in 1994. The OMB guides the federal bureaucracy by analyzing economic policies and staying with the president's budgetary priorities. Rivlin is a strong advocate for restructuring federal-state relations and has called for more logical distribution of responsibilities among them, a process she dubs "dividing the job." Under her suggested reforms, the states would assume greater responsibility for many domestic programs. In 1996, Rivlin was nominated as vice chairman of the Federal Reserve Board.

See also Common Shared Tax; Economic Policy; Sorting Out.
References Kenneth Janda et al., *The Challenge of Democracy: Government in America* (1995); Alice M. Rivlin, *Reviving the American Dream: The Economy, the States, and the Federal Government* (1992).

Robinson v. Cahill

In the 1973 case of *Robinson v. Cahill,* the New Jersey Supreme Court ruled that the use of the property tax to fund public education violated the education provision of the state's constitution. This case is considered an important landmark in the use of state constitutions to fight financial inequities in public education. When the New Jersey State Legislature refused to follow the court's directive to find an alternative funding source, the state supreme court shut the schools down. Ultimately, the state approved an income tax to overcome the disparities in funding.

See also Education; Property Tax; *Rodriguez v. San Antonio Independent School District;* School Finance; *Serrano v. Priest.*
References John J. Harrigan, *Political Change in the Metropolis* (1993); Jeffrey L. Katz, "The Search for Equity in School Funding" (1991); Richard Lehne, *The Quest for Justice: The Politics of School Finance Reform* (1978); David C. Long, "*Rodriguez:* The State Courts Respond" (1983).

Rodriguez v. San Antonio Independent School District

The U.S. Supreme Court ruled in *Rodriguez v. San Antonio Independent School District* (1973) that the use of property taxes to fund public schools did not violate the equal protection clause of the Fourteenth

Amendment. The Court's decision was considered a blow against education reformers who sought to overcome the inequities in education caused by the reliance on the property tax. Since the Court's ruling, many state courts have found that the use of the property tax violates state constitutional provisions, though the *Rodriguez* decision has allowed vast inequities to continue between school districts in many states.

See also Education; Property Tax; *Robinson v. Cahill;* School Finance; *Serrano v. Priest.*
References John J. Harrigan, *Political Change in the Metropolis* (1993); Jeffrey L. Katz, "The Search for Equity in School Funding" (1991); Richard Lehne, *The Quest for Justice: The Politics of School Finance Reform* (1978); David C. Long, "*Rodriguez:* The State Courts Respond" (1983).

Roe v. Wade

In *Roe v. Wade* (1973), the U.S. Supreme Court severely restricted the government's ability to regulate abortion. The Court ruled that the Fourteenth Amendment to the constitution guarantees a right to privacy, which protects a woman's ability to obtain an abortion. In the 7-2 decision, the Court held that the state cannot regulate or prohibit abortions during the first trimester of pregnancy. The state can place some restrictions on abortions during the final six months of a pregnancy, though even here the government's actions are limited. The court's decision overturned a Texas law that banned abortions except to save the life of the mother.

The decision has been hailed by supporters as the Court's most important action in protecting women's liberty, equality, and health. Opponents argue that human life begins at conception, and thus the decision legalized a form of murder. They also argue that there is no right to privacy in the constitution, but that this right was created by the Supreme Court.

The Supreme Court's decision has had a profound effect on American politics, helping to trigger increased activism among Christian fundamentalist and conservative reformers. The decision has also made abortion one of the most important political issues at all levels of government over the past two decades.

See also Women's Movement.
Reference Jay L. Garfield and Patricia Hennessey, eds., *Abortion: Moral and Legal Perspectives* (1984).

Rudman, Warren (b. 1930)

Warren Rudman, a Republican U.S. senator from New Hampshire, was coauthor of the 1985 Gramm-Rudman-Hollings bill, which was designed to force Congress and the president to make the difficult budget decisions needed to balance the budget.

See also Gramm, Phil; Gramm-Rudman-Hollings.
Reference Howard E. Shuman, *Politics and the Budget: The Struggle between the President and the Congress* (1992).

Rule of Four

The rule of four is the U.S. Supreme Court's custom of accepting those cases for review on which four of the nine justices vote to do so. Some judicial scholars and Supreme Court Justice John Paul Stevens have advocated requiring five justices to agree before a case can be heard as a way to reduce the Court's growing workload. Opponents argue that this approach could cause some important cases to be denied a hearing.

See also Caseload; Courts; Supreme Court.
Reference Samuel Estreicher and John Sexton, *Redefining the Supreme Court's Role: A Theory of Managing the Federal Judicial Process* (1986).

Runoff Elections

In many southern states and communities, a candidate needs to receive an absolute majority of votes in order to be elected. If no candidate receives a majority, a runoff election takes place between the two top vote getters. In single-member districts that do not use runoff elections, a candidate receiving a simple plurality of votes is elected.

Runoff elections, which are used in both primary and general elections, have been criticized by civil rights activists because they tend to reduce the ability of minorities to be elected to office. In districts in which there is racial polarization among voters and whites constitute a majority, the use of runoff elections benefits white candidates. The Reverend Jesse Jackson has been one of the most vocal critics of runoff elections.

See also Election Systems; Electoral Discrimination; Jackson, Jesse; Single-Member Districts.
Reference Wilma Rule and Joseph F. Zimmerman, eds., *United States Electoral Systems: Their Impact on Women and Minorities* (1992).

Rutan v. Republican Party of Illinois

In *Rutan v. Republican Party of Illinois* (1990), the U.S. Supreme Court ruled that government employees could not be hired, promoted, or transferred because of their party affiliations or party activities. Such action, the Court argued, violates the employees' First Amendment rights. The Court's decision in *Rutan* is considered to have severely limited the use of political patronage by elected officials. The case was initiated by five Illinois state employees who argued that they had been denied promotion and employment by the Republican governor because they were not affiliated with that party.

See also *Elrod v. Burns;* Party Machines; Patronage.
References Cheri Collis, "Clearing Up the Spoils System" (1990); Ronald N. Johnson and Gary D. Libecap, *The Federal Civil Service System and the Problem of Bureaucracy: The Economics and Politics of Institutional Change* (1994); Jeffrey L. Katz, "The Slow Death of Political Patronage" (1991); David C. Saffell, *State and Local Government: Politics and Public Policies* (1993).

S

Sagebrush Rebellion

The sagebrush rebellion, a political movement that arose in the western United States in the late 1970s, sought to transfer ownership of federal lands to the states in order to protect the economic interests of ranchers, miners, and other industries that benefit from these lands. Often traced back to earlier efforts by western states to gain control of federal lands, the rebellion was organized by land users who feared that the federal government's growing support for environmentalism threatened their economic security.

Support for the rebellion spread rapidly in 1979 and 1980, leading six states to pass legislation claiming state control over federal lands and encouraging several others to consider similar bills. In 1981, the rebellion gained two important allies in Washington, D.C., with the election of Ronald Reagan as president and the appointment of James Watt as secretary of the interior, both of whom endorsed the rebellion's position. As interior secretary, Watt made a concerted effort to get Congress to sell some federal lands to the states, a move that Congress rejected. Facing growing opposition from environmentalists and with the resignation of Watt in 1983, the rebellion lost momentum and soon receded from national political debate.

See also Deregulation; Property Rights Movement; Takings; Watt, James.

References John G. Francis and Richard Ganzel, *Western Public Lands: The Management of National Resources in a Time of Declining Federalism* (1984); William L. Graf, *Wilderness Preservation and the Sagebrush Rebellions* (1990).

Sales Tax

Sales tax is a type of tax applied to the retail sale of goods. The sales tax is used in 45 states and is the primary source of tax revenue for state governments. Some local governments also rely on the sales tax, though it is far less important for them than the property tax. The federal government does not use a general sales tax, but it does apply excise taxes on the sale of several specific types of goods, including gasoline, alcohol, and tobacco.

Many economists advocate a greater use of the sales tax, including the introduction of a national sales tax, as a mean to discourage consumption and encourage savings. If savings were increased, more money would be available for investments, which would help spur economic growth. The sales tax is criticized, however, because it is a regressive tax that opponents say places an unfair burden on the poor.

Although states have historically relied on the sales tax as their primary source of tax revenue, many have turned to other forms of taxation to supplement their revenue. In particular, many states today rely more on the personal income tax than they did in the past. The personal income tax represented only a minimal amount of state tax revenue in the 1950s, but today it makes up almost one-fourth.

State sales taxes were reduced in more than 20 states in the late 1970s and early 1980s in response to the tax revolt that began with Proposition 13 in California in 1978. As the economy declined in 1982 and again in the late 1980s, many states increased their sales taxes to cope with growing fiscal problems. Others attempted to broaden their sales tax bases by taxing services or increasing the sales tax on selected items, such as gasoline and tobacco.

In order to reduce the regressive nature of sales taxes, most states exclude certain goods, such as food and medicine, from taxation.

See also Finance, State; Personal Income Tax; Progressive Tax; Property Tax; Regressive Tax; Service Tax; Tax Revolt.

References Werner Z. Hirsch and Anthony M. Rufolo, *Public Finance and Expenditure in a Federal System* (1990); Joseph J. Minarik, *Making Tax Choices* (1985); Henry J. Raimondo, "State Budgeting in the Nineties" (1993); Christopher Zimmerman, "Flat Tax, Sales Tax, or VAT?" (1995).

Savings and Loan Crisis

In the late 1970s and early 1980s, the Federal Reserve instituted a tighter monetary policy in order to gain control over the nation's skyrocketing inflation rate. The Fed's policy caused interest rates to soar and encouraged investors to redirect their funds away from traditional savings accounts, which were restricted in the amount of interest they could pay, into more profitable investments, particularly money market mutual funds. The decline of savings deposits raised fears that the savings industry was on the verge of collapse. In order to strengthen the savings industry and make it more competitive with other financial institutions, Congress and the president enacted several reforms reducing government restrictions on savings and loan activities. The two most important reforms to emerge were the Depository Institutions Deregulation and Monetary Control Act of 1980 and the Garn-St. Germaine Depository Institutions Act of 1982. These acts phased out the interest rate ceiling that was placed on savings accounts, expanded the coverage of federal deposit insurance on savings from $40,000 to $100,000, and allowed savings institutions to expand the types of loans and accounts they could offer.

The higher ceiling on deposit insurance and the removal of loan restrictions encouraged many savings and loan companies to authorize a growing number of risky loans. At the same time this was occurring, the Reagan administration was cutting back on the number of savings and loan examiners as part of its effort to reduce government involvement in the economy. The cutback meant that the federal government was not fully aware of the severity of the problem that was emerging within the savings industry because of bad loans. Within a short period, a large portion of the savings and loan industry was collapsing, with several hundred savings institutions becoming insolvent. In 1987 alone, the Federal Savings and Loan Insurance Corporation (FSLIC) oversaw the sale or closure of 200 savings institutions. In 1988, more than 230 savings and loans failed and an estimated 900 were insolvent.

The collapse of the savings industry severely drained the resources of the FSLIC and forced the government to seek a remedy. Congress and President Bush agreed to a plan to bail out the savings and loan industry in 1990 as part of the Financial

Institutions Reform, Recovery, and Enforcement Act of 1989. The plan created new savings regulations and established a federal agency (the Resolution Trust Corporation) to help dispose of some 700 ailing savings institutions. Combined, the cost of this program and the full bailout of the savings and loan industry has been estimated at as much as $500 billion.

The savings and loan crisis has had a profound effect on a number of different reform efforts. The collapse of the savings industry helped decrease political support for deregulation after nearly a decade of conservative efforts to reduce the government's involvement in the economy. The high costs of the bailout helped worsen the federal budget deficit, adding to pressures to bring federal spending under greater control. Finally, the savings and loan crisis helped spawn several political controversies surrounding elected officials who took ethically questionable steps to help individual savings and loans. The most noteworthy was the Keating Five scandal, which led to the criticism of four senators and the reprimand of another. The scandal helped trigger the Ethics in Government Act of 1989.

See also Budget Deficit, Federal; Depository Institutions Deregulation and Monetary Control Act; Deregulation; Economic Policy; Ethics in Government Act; Financial Institutions Reform, Recovery, and Enforcement Act; Garn-St. Germaine Depository Institutions Act; Keating Five; Monetary Policy.
References Anthony S. Campagna, *The Economy in the Reagan Years: The Economic Consequences of the Reagan Administrations* (1994); Robert E. Litan, "Financial Regulation" (1994); William A. Niskanen, *Reaganomics: An Insider's Account of the Policies and People* (1988); Bruce C. Wolpe, *Lobbying Congress: How the System Works* (1990).

School Choice

School choice policies allow parents to choose which schools their children attend. These policies, promoted during the education reforms of the 1980s and 1990s, are thought to improve the educational quality of schools in general because of the increased competition they create.

See also Education; Privatization.

School Finance

Since the early 1970s, the use of the property tax to fund public schools has generated attack from education reformers who argue that this form of funding allows schools in higher-income areas to spend substantially more per student than schools in poor inner cities or rural areas. The results are considerable inequities in terms of facilities, equipment, and programs from school to school.

In 1971, supporters of school finance reform enjoyed an important victory when the California State Supreme Court ruled in *Serrano v. Priest* that the use of the property tax to fund schools violated that state's constitution. Two years later, however, reform efforts were slowed when the U.S. Supreme Court ruled in *Rodriguez v. San Antonio Independent School District* that the use of the property tax did not violate the U.S. Constitution. Despite this setback, a growing number of state courts have found that the use of the property tax to fund schools violates their states' constitutions. One of the most recent cases occurred in 1990, when the Kentucky State Supreme Court ruled the entire state system of education unconstitutional, forcing the state's general assembly to restructure the financing system along with other aspects of school governance.

In addition to fighting for funding equity in the courts, many reformers have pushed for change through state legislatures. One notable success occurred in Wisconsin in 1994, when the state legislature voted to reduce radically the use of the property tax to fund the schools. Recent conservative reformers have also called for the use of vouchers as a way to overcome inequities in school finance.

See also Education; Privatization; Property Tax; *Robinson v. Cahill; Rodriguez v. San Antonio Independent School District; Serrano v. Priest.*
Reference John J. Harrigan, *Political Change in the Metropolis* (1993); Jeffrey L. Katz, "The Search for Equity in School Funding" (1991); Richard Lehne, *The Quest for Justice: The Politics of School Finance Reform* (1978); David C. Long, "*Rodriguez:* The State Courts Respond" (1983).

Seminole Tribe of Florida v. Florida

In *Seminole Tribe of Florida v. Florida* (1996), the U.S. Supreme Court ruled that Congress does not have the constitutional power to authorize private lawsuits against state governments in the federal court.

The Court's decision came in a case involving the Indian Gaming Regulatory Act of 1988. Among its other provisions, the 1988 act granted Indian tribes the authority to file lawsuits against states that were unwilling to negotiate in good faith on the rules governing Indian gambling operations. The Court ruled that this provision violated the Eleventh Amendment, which protects states from unwanted lawsuits. Many constitutional scholars believe that the decision may have a profound effect on federal-state relations, strengthening the position of the states and reducing the federal government's ability to force states to comply with federal laws.

The effect of the Court's action on Indian gambling is uncertain, though some observers believe it may lead to revisions in the Indian Gaming Act.

See also Federal-State Relations; *United States v. Lopez.*
References Jon Felde, "Supreme Court Confirms State Sovereignty" (1996); Holly Idelson, "Indian Gaming Ruling Strikes at Congressional Power" (1996).

Senior Citizens Fairness Act

One of the ten provisions of the Republican Party's Contract with America, the Senior Citizens Fairness Act proposed revisions in Social Security rules to increase the benefits received by wealthier retirees and to encourage the use of private long-term care insurance. As of late 1995, the act had passed through a House and Senate conference committee and awaited final congressional action.

See also Contract with America; Health Care; Social Security.
References George Hager, "Harsh Rhetoric on Budget Spells a Dismal Outlook" (1995); "Republicans' Initial Promise: 100-Day Debate on 'Contract'" (1994); Clyde Wilcox, *The Latest American Revolution? The 1994 Elections and Their Implication for Governance* (1995).

Senior Executive Service

The Senior Executive Service (SES) is an elite group of federal bureaucrats that was established in 1978 to help improve the management of the federal bureaucracy. It was the central component of the Civil Service Reform Act of 1978. The SES was established to create a top group of talented bureaucrats who were to be active in solving problems throughout the bureaucracy and who would be paid according to their performance. The act provided procedures to allow the president to reassign these managers more easily to other agencies than is normally allowed under civil service rules. This provision was designed to enable the president to move talented bureaucrats into various agencies where their skills were needed and to reassign managers who were not performing satisfactorily.

Although the SES was designed to

improve the bureaucracy's performance by sharing expertise and using incentives, the Reagan administration used the new procedures to place political allies in key positions in the SES and to gain greater ideological control over the bureaucracy. Reagan's use of the act was one of several key factors blamed for causing a morale crises in the civil service and for forcing many talented supervisors to leave the SES. Today, the SES has approximately 8,000 members.

See also Bureaucracy; Civil Service Reform Act of 1978; Volcker Commission.
References Patricia Ingraham and Carolyn Ban, eds., *Legislating Bureaucratic Change* (1984); Ronald N. Johnson and Gary D. Libecap, *The Federal Civil Service System and the Problem of Bureaucracy: The Economics and Politics of Institutional Change* (1994); Donald J. Savoie, *Thatcher, Reagan, Mulroney: In Search of a New Bureaucracy* (1994).

Seniority Rule

As members of Congress began to view legislative service as a career in the early 1900s, seniority became of increasing importance in the distribution of political power in the House of Representatives. After the revolt against Speaker Joseph Cannon in 1910, seniority emerged as the rule in determining the distribution of committee assignments and the selection of committee and party leaders.

The use of seniority in distributing these positions allowed long-serving southern Democrats to gain control over key committee chairmanships and to dominate the House's politics. In the late 1950s and early 1960s, the House experienced a large influx of northern liberal Democrats. Limited in their ability to influence policy decisions, many of these liberal Democrats joined together to form the Democratic Study Group to find ways to democratize the House and to get more liberal legislation enacted into law.

In the early 1970s, the northern liberal Democrats began to achieve some success in reforming the House with the passage of the Legislative Reorganization Act of 1970 and the Hansen Committee reforms. Since the adoption of these reforms, the seniority rule has become less important in House politics. One of the most consequential reforms for the seniority rule was a provision allowing the Democratic caucus to vote on the selection of all committee chairmanships. In 1975, the House Democrats exercised this newly gained power to remove three sitting committee chairs.

Although these reforms provided the House with the means to use other criteria besides seniority in distributing power, seniority remains of considerable importance in shaping House politics today.

See also Bolling Committee; Congress; Democratic Study Group; Hansen Committee; Legislative Reorganization Act.
References Roger H. Davidson and Walter J. Oleszek, *Congress and Its Members* (1994); Leroy N. Rieselbach, *Congressional Reform: The Changing Modern Congress* (1994); David W. Rohde, *Parties and Leaders in the Postreform House* (1991).

Sentencing

There are two primary problems associated with court sentencing that have brought demands for reform. One is that the nation's tougher attitudes on sentencing have led to overcrowding in prisons and growing stress on state budgets, without solving the nation's crime problems. The second is that there are often considerable disparities in sentencing from judge to judge, which means that the law is applied differently to different individuals. In particular, critics assert that the race, class, gender, and age of the defendant affects the severity of the sentence.

To reduce the overcrowding of state

prisons and lower the costs of the criminal justice system, many reformers have called for the greater use of alternative types of sentencing. Beyond these practical benefits, advocates of sentencing reform argue that current correction practices are not working, and that alternatives may be more effective at reducing recidivism. The most popular alternative sentencing proposals to emerge in the past few years involve intensive supervision programs that allow convicted criminals to remain in the community, but under the strict supervision of probation officers. In addition, some states have introduced or are considering the use of house arrest, electronic monitoring, boot camps, work release (furloughs), and even community service as alternatives to traditional prison terms. Finally, some advocates call for a return to indeterminate sentencing to ensure that the punishment meted out to criminals fits their crimes.

As for disparity in sentencing, Congress enacted the Comprehensive Crime Control Act of 1984, which, among other provisions, created the U.S. Sentencing Commission to investigate problems in sentencing and to develop guidelines on appropriate sentences for specific crimes. Three years later, the Commission released its list of sentencing guidelines, which the federal courts were expected to follow. The states have also moved to establish sentencing guidelines to avoid disparities among individual court cases.

See also Courts; Crime; Finance, State; Taking Back Our Streets Act.
References Robert A. Carp and Ronald Stidham, *Judicial Process in America* (1993); John J. DiIulio, Jr., "Punishing Smarter: Penal Reforms for the 1990s" (1989); Lois G. Forer, *Unequal Protection: Women, Children, and the Elderly in Court* (1991); Penelope Lemov, "The Next Best Thing to Prison" (1991); Wesley G. Skogan, "Crime and Punishment" (1996).

Sequestration

Sequestration was a process originally established by the Gramm-Rudman-Hollings Act of 1985 whereby the General Accounting Office would institute across-the-board cuts on domestic and defense programs if the federal budget deficit went above certain targets from 1986 to 1991. After the Supreme Court ruled that it was unconstitutional for the General Accounting Office to administer these cuts, Congress passed this responsibility on to the Office of Management and Budget. The Budget Enforcement Act of 1990, which superseded Gramm-Rudman-Hollings, divided discretionary spending into three categories (domestic, defense, and international) and required that across-the-board cuts be made within a category if the spending level in that category went above preestablished targets.

See also Budget Enforcement Act of 1990; Discretionary Spending; Gramm-Rudman-Hollings.
References Howard E. Shuman, *Politics and the Budget: The Struggle between the President and the Congress* (1992); James A. Thurber, "New Rules for an Old Game: Zero-Sum Budgeting in the Postreform Congress" (1992).

Serrano v. Priest

In the 1971 case of *Serrano v. Priest,* the California Supreme Court ruled that the use of the local property tax to fund education violated the equal protection clause of the state's constitution. The case is viewed as a landmark decision in the battle to overcome inequities in public education funding. In 1976, the California Supreme Court reaffirmed this decision in a second court case referred to as *Serrano II.*

See also Education; Property Tax; *Robinson v. Cahill; Rodriguez v. San Antonio Independent School District;* School Finance.
References John J. Harrigan, *Political Change in*

the Metropolis (1993); Jeffrey L. Katz, "The Search for Equity in School Funding" (1991); Richard Lehne, *The Quest for Justice: The Politics of School Finance Reform* (1978); David C. Long, "*Rodriguez:* The State Courts Respond" (1983).

Service Tax

Service taxes are a type of sales tax that are applied to the purchase of services. Currently, most states do not tax services, or, if they do, they exclude many types of services from taxation. As the nation's economy has grown more service based, service taxes have emerged as one of the most prominent forms of taxation being considered by state leaders. Taxes could be collected for the provision of legal and financial advice, advertising, housecleaning, automobile repair, cable television installation, hairstyling, or any other form of service activity.

Several states introduced or expanded their use of service taxes in the late 1980s and early 1990s to help deal with growing fiscal problems. Although there was voter opposition to some of these efforts, most notably in Florida, service taxes are expected to become widely used by states in the near future.

See also Finance, State; Sales Tax.
References Ann O'M. Bowman and Richard C. Kearney, *State and Local Government* (1993); Penelope Lemov, "Is There Anything Left To Tax?" (1993).

Sexual Harassment

See Civil Rights Act of 1991; Ethics; Hill, Anita; Thomas, Clarence.

Shadow Government

See Private Government.

Shakman v. Democratic Party of Cook County

In the 1972 case of *Shakman v. Democratic Party of Cook County,* a federal district judge prohibited the city of Chicago from hiring employees based on political grounds. The court's action is considered one of the key factors in causing the decline of the Chicago party machine that had been led by Mayor Richard Daley since the 1950s. It has been estimated that prior to the ruling the machine controlled more than 35,000 patronage jobs that it could offer loyal party members in exchange for their support of the Democratic Party. In 1979, the court expanded its decision to ban the firing of workers on political grounds, taking away another key component of the machine's power. Combined, these two court cases are referred to as the *Shakman* decisions.

See also Party Machines; Patronage.
References Anne Freedman, "Doing Battle with the Patronage Army: Politics, Courts, and Personnel Administration in Chicago" (1988); William J. Grimshaw, *Bitter Fruit: Black Politics and the Chicago Machine, 1931–1991* (1992).

Shaw v. Reno

In order to comply with the 1982 amendments to the Voting Rights Act, state legislatures began to adopt voting procedures in the 1980s that ensured the election of minorities to public office. One of the primary ways they accomplished this was by carefully drawing state legislative and congressional district boundaries to create individual districts composed of a majority of minority voters. In several cases, these majority-minority districts were extremely irregular in shape.

In *Shaw v. Reno* (1993), the U.S. Supreme Court was asked to consider the legality of North Carolina's congressional redistricting plan, which included a thin, meandering district that stretched across the central part of the state, creating a majority African-American district. Previously, the Court had found (*Thornburg v. Gingles*) that when certain conditions apply, district boundaries must be drawn to allow minorities to elect candidates of their choice. In *Shaw v. Reno,* the Court began to reconsider the use of race-conscious districting because of the bizarre shape of the North Carolina districts. In essence, the Court was asked to consider how far a state must go to ensure the election of minorities to office.

The Court did not ban outright the consideration of race in drawing district lines in *Shaw v. Reno,* but it ruled that in some instances race-conscious districting may violate the Fourteenth Amendment if a district is "so extremely irregular on its face that it rationally can be viewed only as an effort to segregate the races for purposes of voting."

The court returned the North Carolina plan to a federal district court for trial, and demanded that the state show a "compelling governmental interest" to justify the plan. The decision has worried civil rights activists because it threatens the gains minorities have made in representation over the past decade. The Supreme Court decision, however, left unanswered the question of how far a state can or must go in using racial considerations in drawing districting boundaries. The court returned to this question again in *Miller v. Johnson,* but it still has not established firm guidelines for using race in redistricting efforts.

See also Electoral Discrimination; Majority-Minority Districts; *Miller v. Johnson; Thornburg v. Gingles;* Voting Rights Act.
References Bernard Grofman and Chandler Davidson, eds., *Controversies in Minority Voting: The Voting Rights Act in Perspective* (1992); "The Voting Rights Act after *Shaw v. Reno*" (1995).

Short Ballot

Under a short ballot structure, a city or state government allows voters to elect only a limited number of officials. Political reformers began to advocate a shortening of the ballot during the progressive movement at the turn of the century as a means to destroy the party machines. In more recent years, however, state constitutional reformers have been the primary advocates of the short ballot, arguing that its use makes state government more accountable and effective by reducing the number of statewide elected officials and consolidating power in the hands of the governor. Efforts to shorten the ballot have enjoyed some success over the past four decades as the number of state elected officials besides the governor was reduced from 709 in 1956 to 481 in 1990. Despite this reduction, most states today retain a long ballot, and thus constitutional reformers continue to argue that the short ballot is one of the most needed reforms in the executive branch of government.

See also Constitutions, State; Fragmented Executive; Governors.
References Thad Beyle, "Being Governor" (1993); Terry Christensen, *Local Politics: Governing at the Grassroots* (1995); Larry J. Sabato, *Good-bye to Good-Time Charlie: The American Governorship Transformed* (1983); David C. Saffell, *State and Local Government: Politics and Public Policies* (1993).

Single-Member Districts

The primary method through which officials are elected in the United States today is through the use of single-member districts. Under the single-member district structure, a political system is divided up into individual districts or wards. Voters then select a single candidate to represent their district. Representatives to the U.S. House of Representatives, moststatelegislatures, and some city councils are elected through this system.

Historically, many state and local governments have used multimember districts and at-large elections to select candidates for office instead of single-member districts. Since the passage of the Voting Rights Act of 1965, however, there has been considerable pressure on state and local governments from the U.S. Justice Department and the federal courts to replace these electoral systems with single-member districts, which many reformers argue better enable African-Americans and other minorities to elect candidates of their choice.

Single-member districts are themselves a subject of reform efforts. Gerrymandering of these districts is a particular concern among reformers because of its potential to deny representation to minorities and other groups. Single-member districts are also criticized because they reduce the chances for third-party candidates to be elected.

See also At-Large Elections; Election Systems; Electoral Discrimination; Gerrymandering; Multimember Districts; Third Parties; Voting Rights Act.

References Chandler Davidson, ed., *Minority Vote Dilution* (1989); Bernard Grofman and Arend Lijphart, eds., *Electoral Laws and Their Political Consequences* (1986); Wilma Rule and Joseph F. Zimmerman, eds., *United States Electoral Systems: Their Impact on Women and Minorities* (1992).

Single-Transferable Vote

See Proportional Representation.

Slate Mailers

Slate mailers are lists of endorsements for candidates and ballot propositions sent out by political committees to influence voters. In recent years, slate mailers have generated concern because of some unethical practices associated with them. In some instances, organizations have demanded that candidates pay if they want to be endorsed. If the candidates refuse, these organizations endorse their opponents. Mailer sponsors have demanded similar contributions from proposition supporters and opponents for endorsements. Finally, slate mailers are criticized because sponsors have used deceptive organization names to mislead voters into believing the groups represent official party organizations.

Reference Charles G. Bell and Charles M. Price, *California Government Today: Politics of Reform?* (1988).

Social Security

Social Security is an entitlement program created originally by the Social Security Act of 1935 to provide financial support to retired workers. The program was expanded in 1939 to provide support to widows, and in 1956 to aid the disabled. The program has been the focus of reform efforts since the early 1980s, when increasing expenditures and economic troubles created fear that the program was on the verge of collapse.

In 1981, President Ronald Reagan attempted to overcome these problems by changing eligibility requirements and reducing annual cost-of-living increases in Social Security payments. Reagan's efforts were initially unsuccessful, as well-organized senior citizen groups convinced Congress to resist these changes. Reagan responded by creating a bipartisan commission to propose reforms. The National Commission on Social Security Reform came forward with a series of suggested reforms, including raising the retirement age from 65 to 67, reducing cost-of-living increases, increasing Social Security taxes, and expanding the program to cover federal employees and individuals working in nonprofit organizations.

The commission's proposals were approved by Congress with only slight revision as the Social Security Amendments of 1983. These amendments immediately helped improve the program's financial security, bringing it from the verge of collapse to a $55 billion surplus in 1990.

Despite the gains made through these amendments, many reformers believe that additional changes must be made if the program is to survive. It is estimated that the Social Security Trust Fund may go broke before the year 2030, as the baby boom population reaches retirement age. Recent reform proposals include introducing means testing, lowering benefits, raising the eligibility age, and increasing taxes. Reform of the act is difficult, however, because the program enjoys widespread popular support.

See also Budget Deficit, Federal; Entitlements; Payroll Tax; Senior Citizens Fairness Act.

References Donald F. Kettl, *Deficit Politics: Public Budgeting in Its Institutional and Historical Context* (1992); Eric R. Kingson and Edward D. Berkowitz, *Social Security and Medicare: A Policy Primer* (1993); Peter G. Peterson, *Facing Up: How To Rescue the Economy from Crushing Debt and Restore the American Dream* (1993); C. Eugene Steuerle and Jon M. Bakija, *Retooling Social Security for the 21st Century: Right and Wrong Approaches to Reform* (1994).

Soft Money

Campaign contributions that are given to state and local party organizations by individuals, labor unions, corporations, national parties, and other groups in order to circumvent federal campaign finance laws are called soft money. These contributions have become an increasingly important source of funds in federal campaigns, as well as a target for reform, since the passage of the 1979 amendments to the Federal Election Campaign Act (FECA). Prior to the 1979 legislation, federal law placed severe restrictions on contributions to congressional and presidential campaigns, banning direct donations from businesses and unions, and limiting contributions from individuals, political action committees, and parties.

In 1979, Congress revised FECA to allow state and local parties to spend an unlimited amount of money on "party-building" activities. Since then, the national parties have been encouraging contributors to donate funds to state and local party organizations, from which they can then be used to help federal candidates. Because contributions to these party organizations are regulated by state law, the 1979 amendments created a loophole that permits individuals and groups that would otherwise be under federal spending rules to contribute unlimited funds to help federal candidates.

See also Campaign Finance; Federal Election Campaign Act.

References Herbert E. Alexander, *Financing Politics: Money, Elections, and Political Reform* (1992); *Congressional Campaign Finances: History, Facts, and Controversy* (1992); David B. Magleby and Candice J. Nelson, *The Money Chase: Congressional Campaign Finance Reform* (1990); Frank J. Sorauf, *Money in American Elections* (1988).

Sorting Out

Sorting out refers to proposals to redistribute the responsibilities handled by state and national governments in a more rational manner than they are currently distributed. Supporters of these proposals argue that the current federal system is ineffective in solving the nation's ills and that it is difficult to hold the government accountable because state and national governments share responsibilities. A clearer delineation of responsibilities would allow each level of government to handle the tasks it does best, which would improve efficiency and allow voters to know who to blame when social problems are not being resolved.

Economist Alice M. Rivlin, the budget director in the Clinton administration, is one of the most prominent supporters of redistributing responsibilities. She has called for "dividing the job," with the states given control of economic development and most public services, including education, job training, infrastructure, and housing. The federal government, in turn, would concentrate on international affairs, health care, and some social welfare programs. A similar proposal was put forward by the Committee on Federalism and National Purpose in 1985. That committee was chaired by Senators Daniel J. Evans and Charles S. Robb.

The phrase *sorting out* is also used to describe the redistribution of responsibilities between state and local governments. During the late 1980s and early 1990s, many states began to redistribute responsibilities to cope with fiscal problems at both the state and local levels. In some cases, states began to assume responsibilities traditionally handled by local governments because of financial problems at the local level. In others, many states passed responsibilities on to local governments to reduce their own fiscal stress. Opponents have criticized this redistribution because it has been motivated by short-term economic needs and not by any rational analysis of how to improve government services.

See also Big Swap; Devolution; Federal-State Relations; Finance, State; Rivlin, Alice M.
References Timothy J. Conlan, *New Federalism: Intergovernmental Reform from Nixon to Reagan* (1988); Alice M. Rivlin, *Reviving the American Dream: The Economy, the States, and the Federal Government* (1992); Rochelle L. Stanfield, "Forced Federalism" (1991); David B. Walker, *The Rebirth of Federalism: Slouching toward Washington* (1995).

South Carolina v. Katzenbach

In *South Carolina v. Katzenbach* (1966), the U.S. Supreme Court upheld the constitutionality of the Voting Rights Act of 1965, thus protecting the federal government's right to intervene in state and local affairs to ensure the franchise for African-Americans.

See also Voting Rights Act.
Reference Bernard Grofman and Chandler Davidson, eds., *Controversies in Minority Voting: The Voting Rights Act in Perspective* (1992).

Southern Christian Leadership Conference (SCLC)

The Southern Christian Leadership Conference was founded by the Reverend Martin Luther King, Jr., in 1957. Based in Atlanta, Georgia, this group promotes the rights of African-Americans, particularly through legislation, political activism, and educational campaigns. Its origins are in the tumultuous civil rights movement, which resulted in numerous social and political reforms, including an end to legal segregation and the extension of voting rights to African-Americans. The SCLC reflects King's philosophy of nonviolent protest. One important current project of the SCLC is Crusade for the Ballot, which aims to double the black vote in the South through increased voter registration.

See also Civil Rights Movement; King, Martin Luther, Jr.
Reference Taylor Branch, *Parting the Waters: America in the King Years, 1954–1963* (1988).

Southwest Voter Registration Education Project

The Southwest Voter Registration Education Project seeks to increase the voter registration and political participation of Hispanics and Native Americans. Based in San Antonio, Texas, the project is composed of church, civic, labor, and fraternal groups that organize coalitions to register minority voters in southwestern and western states. Their efforts are also focused on reapportionment and gerrymandering of counties and cities to increase minority representation.

See also Electoral Discrimination; Voting Rights Act.

Special Districts

Special districts are a type of local government that provides a specialized service to a local community or to a broad region across a state. In general, these districts are created either to provide services that local residents feel are inadequately provided by the current local government structure or to handle functions that transcend local government jurisdictions. Some of the most common functions performed by special districts are fire protection, parks and recreation, water, sanitation and waste disposal, housing, and flood control.

The growth of special districts in recent years has been both applauded and criticized by local government officials and reformers. These districts are seen as beneficial by many because they provide a direct means to address particular needs that are not currently being met. Moreover, the creation of special districts often offers politically attainable solutions to particular problems, because such districts do little to disrupt the current political structure. On the other hand, critics argue that the growth of these districts is partly responsible for the fragmentation of governments in metropolitan areas. The presence of multiple districts in a given area means that government decisions are spread out, with no one government body looking at the big picture.

Special districts are the most common type of government in the United States.

See also Metropolitan Fragmentation; Regional Government.

References Terry Christensen, *Local Politics: Governing at the Grassroots* (1995); Thomas R. Dye, *Politics in States and Communities* (1994); John J. Harrigan, *Political Change in the Metropolis* (1993).

Specialized Courts

One reform that has been proposed to reduce the caseload burden on the federal courts and to improve the quality of justice is the creation of new courts that specialize in particular legal areas. Advocates argue that these specialized courts may work more efficiently and produce better decisions than general-jurisdiction trial courts because they would have familiarity with the issues being addressed. Critics argue, however, that specialized courts may be less responsive to legislative intent than are nonspecialized courts, and that their creation may allow particular legal camps to dominate court decisions while excluding other legitimate perspectives. Moreover, these critics maintain that there is little evidence that the use of specialized courts would actually reduce the caseload problem. Some types of specialized courts that have been proposed are a science court, an administrative court, and a tax court of appeals.

See also Caseload; Courts.

References Phillip L. Dubois, *The Politics of Judicial Reform* (1982); Richard A. Posner, *The Federal Courts: Crisis and Reform* (1985).

Spending Limits

Many supporters of campaign finance reform argue that one of the best ways to control the growing costs of election campaigns and to make competition more equitable would be to limit the amount of money candidates can spend on elections. Without spending limits, the Center for Responsive Politics argues, it is very easy for a well-funded candidate to drown out the voices of competitors.

In *Buckley v. Valeo,* however, the U.S. Supreme Court ruled that spending limits are unconstitutional because they violate the First Amendment right to free speech. The one exception permitted by the Court is that the government can place expenditure limits on individual campaigns as a condition for the candidate to receive public financing. The Court's decision has meant that spending limits are not a legal option for campaign finance reform unless they are part of a public financing plan.

A number of groups, including the Center for Responsive Politics, advocate a reversal of *Buckley v. Valeo.* Some reformers, however, oppose spending limits because they tend to help incumbents.

See also *Buckley v. Valeo;* Campaign Finance; Center for Responsive Politics; Federal Election Campaign Act; Public Financing.
References Herbert E. Alexander, *Financing Politics: Money, Elections, and Political Reform* (1992); *Congressional Campaign Finances: History, Facts, and Controversy* (1992); David B. Magleby and Candice J. Nelson, *The Money Chase: Congressional Campaign Finance Reform* (1990); Jamin B. Raskin and John Bonifaz, *The Wealth Primary: Campaign Fundraising and the Constitution* (1994); Frank J. Sorauf, *Money in American Elections* (1988).

Stafford-Kennedy Lobby Reform Act

The Stafford-Kennedy Lobby Reform Act was a 1975 proposal that offered one of the most comprehensive efforts to regulate lobbying in Washington, D.C., since the passage of the 1946 Federal Regulation of Lobbying Act. Named after its two Senate sponsors (Senator Robert T. Stafford of Vermont and Senator Edward M. Kennedy of Massachusetts), the act would have established stricter guidelines on the registration of lobbyists and full disclosure of lobbying activities. Like many other modern efforts to regulate lobbying activities, the act was defeated in Congress.

See also Lobbying.
Reference Ronald J. Hrebenar and Ruth K. Scott, *Interest Group Politics in America* (1990).

Stagflation

Stagflation is an economic situation in which stagnation and inflation occur simultaneously. In the mid-1970s, the rapid rise of oil prices produced severe stagflation as output declined and inflation reached the highest levels in more than 50 years. The federal government's inability to solve these problems helped generate disillusionment with Keynesian economics and opened the door to more conservative fiscal and monetary policies.

See also Economic Policy; Fiscal Policy; Humphrey-Hawkins Act of 1978; Keynesian Economics; Monetarism; Monetary Policy; Oil Price Shocks; Reaganomics; Supply-Side Economics.
References Paul A. Samuelson and William D. Nordhaus, *Economics* (1992); Herbert Stein, *Presidential Economics: The Making of Economic Policy from Roosevelt to Clinton* (1994).

State Courts

See Courts.

State Government

See Constitutions, State; Courts; Federal-State Relations; Finance, State; Governors; Legislative Reform Movement; State Renewal.

State Renewal

From the 1930s to the 1960s, the role of state government in U.S. politics had declined to such a meaningless position that some political observers began to question the continued viability of the states. The problem was that neither the executive nor the legislative branch of state government had the capacity or resources to deal with the nation's pressing social problems. Moreover, the discriminatory racial practices of many states made the states appear to be one of America's problems, not part of the solution.

Beginning in the 1960s, however, state leaders moved to revitalize state government and make it an important actor in American politics once again. State after state moved to expand the powers and resources of governors, to professionalize state legislatures, and to channel more resources to state bureaucracies. These reforms helped improve the states' abilities to analyze and address state problems. An increase in federal funds to the states in the 1970s then helped improve the states' financial position. When the federal funds were cut back in the 1980s, the states found ways to cope by improving their own revenue systems.

These changes have caused state governments to reemerge as important actors in the nation's political system. No longer do they simply follow the dictates of the federal government, but today they actively lead the nation in many policy areas, from environmental protection to welfare reform. This renewal of the states has led many reformers to call for an even greater role for the states in shaping American domestic policy in the future.

See also Federal-State Relations; Finance, State; Governors; Legislative Reform Movement.

References Ann O'M. Bowman and Richard C. Kearney, *The Resurgence of the States* (1986); Alice M. Rivlin, *Reviving the American Dream: The Economy, the States, and the Federal Government* (1992); Carl E. Van Horn, *The State of the States* (1993); David B. Walker, *The Rebirth of Federalism: Slouching toward Washington* (1995).

State Reorganization

See Administrative Reorganization.

Stevenson Committee

The Stevenson Committee was created in 1976 to study the Senate's committee structure and propose reforms. The committee's proposals, which were approved by the Senate with slight revisions in 1977, reduced the number of Senate committees from 31 to 24, clarified committee jurisdictions, and instituted fairer rules governing the distribution of committee assignments. The committee reforms also increased the power of the Senate leadership over bill referral and scheduling. The formal name of the committee, which was chaired by Senator Adlai Stevenson of Illinois, was the Temporary Committee to Study the Senate Committee System.

See also Congress.

References Roger H. Davidson, "Two Avenues of Change: House and Senate Committee Reorganization" (1981); Leroy N. Rieselbach, *Congressional Reform: The Changing Modern Congress* (1994).

Strong Mayor

In the strong mayor form of municipal government, considerable formal power is vested in the mayor, who runs the government much as a governor runs a state. The mayor works with a city council, which play a less important role in shaping political decisions. The strong mayor system emerged as a major component of the reform movement to destroy the political party machines at the beginning of the twentieth century. When this change did little to alter the power of the machines, reformers began to view other forms of municipal government as preferable, most notably the council-manager system. In recent years, however, there has been renewed interest in the strong mayor system, which many reformers see as being more responsive to voters' concerns and better able to lead the nation's cities than other types of city government. Opponents argue that the strong mayor system may not be as efficient as the council-manager system, that it concentrates too much power into the hands of one individual, and that it politicizes many local activities that need professional oversight. Moreover, some critics argue that a move to a strong mayor system may deprive minorities of influence at a time when changes in voting rights laws have just increased their representation on city councils.

Under the strong mayor system, the mayor is usually given the power to prepare the city budget, initiate policy proposals, oversee the city administration, fire and hire city personnel, and veto council decisions.

See also At-Large Districts; City Commission; Council-Manager; Model City Charter; Party Machines; Weak Mayor.
References David N. Ammons and Charldean Newell, "'City Managers Don't Make Policy': A Lie; Let's Face It" (1988); Terrell Blodgett, "Beware the Lure of the 'Strong' Mayor" (1994); Terry Christensen, *Local Politics: Governing at the Grassroots* (1995); Rob Gurwitt, "The Lure of the Strong Mayor" (1993); John J. Harrigan, *Political Change in the Metropolis* (1993).

Student Nonviolent Coordinating Committee

One of the most active organizations promoting civil rights for African-Americans during the 1960s, the Student Nonviolent Coordinating Committee (SNCC) was a coalition of white and black student activists who originally worked toward peaceful protest against inequalities. Among the organization's actions were sit-ins and "freedom rides" to force integration of public places in the South. Early members included Marion Barry (later mayor of Washington, D.C.) and Marian Wright Edelman. By 1966, SNCC grew more radical, as Stokely Carmichael led the cry for "black power" and called for greater militancy in response to white injustices. The group lost its momentum by the early 1970s.

See also Civil Rights Movement.
Reference Charles W. Eagles, ed., *The Civil Rights Movement in America* (1986).

Subcommittee Bill of Rights

See Hansen Committee.

Subgovernments

Subgovernments are small groups of legislators, bureaucrats, and lobbyists who work together to dominate government decisions in a narrow policy area to benefit one particular interest. Subgovernments were the focus of increased criticism in the 1970s and 1980s because they were seen as producing government policy with limited public input and little regard for the greater public interest.

Reformers argue that the influence of subgovernments can be reduced by opening up the legislative process and bureaucratic decision making to greater public input, expanding the number of groups that have access to government decision making, and reducing the government's regulation of the economy and society.

In recent years, many political scientists have begun to question the significance of subgovernments, arguing that they are not now, and possibly never were, as prominent as critics maintain. These scholars argue that policy decisions are more likely to be shaped by issue networks, which are broader and more diverse coalitions of lobbyists and government actors than are found in subgovernments. Instead of being linked by shared political goals, as is true in a subgovernment, the members of these groups are seen as being linked by their expertise in given policy areas.

Subgovernments are also referred to as iron triangles.

See also Congress; Lobbying.
References Jeffrey M. Berry, *The Interest Group Society* (1989); Ronald J. Hrebenar and Ruth K. Scott, *Interest Group Politics in America* (1990); Kay Lehman Schlozman and John T. Tierney, *Organized Interests and American Democracy* (1986).

SunPAC Decision

One of the most criticized aspects of the Federal Election Campaign Act (FECA) of 1971 is that it gave legal recognition to political action committees (PACs). After the act was adopted, however, there was considerable uncertainty concerning the rights of businesses and corporations to create PACs. In 1975, the Sun Oil Company asked the Federal Election Commission (FEC) if it could use its general funds to administer a political action committee (SunPAC) and to solicit contributions to the PAC. The FEC ruled that under FECA the Sun Oil Company was legally entitled to take such action. The FEC ruling, which is referred to as the SunPAC decision, led to profound growth in the number and influence of business and corporate PACs throughout the 1970s and 1980s.

See also Campaign Finance; Federal Election Campaign Act; Political Action Committees.
References Herbert E. Alexander, *Financing Politics: Money, Elections, and Political Reform* (1992); *Congressional Campaign Finances: History, Facts, and Controversy* (1992); David B. Magleby and Candice J. Nelson, *The Money Chase: Congressional Campaign Finance Reform* (1990); Frank J. Sorauf, *Money in American Elections* (1988).

Sunset Laws

Sunset laws are laws that authorize particular government programs and also include specific dates on which the programs will end. During the past two decades, state legislatures have relied more extensively on sunset laws as a way to control the growth of the bureaucracy, eliminate programs that are not needed, and improve legislative oversight. The push for sunset laws was particularly strong in the states during the 1970s after Colorado adopted the nation's first major sunset law in 1976, though it has tapered off a bit since then. Advocates argue that sunset laws should be adopted by Congress and used more frequently in the states, because without built-in ending dates, government programs and agencies tend to survive indefinitely, outliving the needs they were created to address. Critics argue, however, that these laws may create a bureaucratic system that is more closely tied to interest groups and that they may actually raise the cost of government operation.

An alternative reform that is often mentioned in tandem with sunset legislation is the use of sunshine provisions. These are rules that require supporters of a new government program to provide strong justification and goals for the program before it can be enacted into law.

See also Oversight.
References Roger H. Davidson and Walter J. Oleszek, *Congress and Its Members* (1994); Karen Diegmueller, "Sunrise, Sunset Cut Costs" (1990); David C. Nice, *Policy Innovation in State Government* (1994).

Sunshine Rules

Sunshine rules are laws or government policies that are designed to open government meetings to greater public scrutiny. Since the 1970s, when the United States was rocked by a series of political scandals, including Watergate, there has been a move at both federal and state levels to adopt sunshine rules to make government officials more accountable to voters.

Some of the most important sunshine reforms have come in Congress. Until the 1970s, Congress often conducted much of its most important business behind closed doors, beyond the reach of the press and public. The first step toward reform was the passage of the Legislative Reorganization Act of 1970, which required that committee roll call votes be made public and for the first time permitted recorded votes in the Committee on the Whole. The act also made provisions allowing television and radio to broadcast from committee chambers.

In the mid-1970s, both the House and the Senate passed reforms requiring that most committee hearings be made open to the press and the public unless a majority of members voted publicly to keep a meeting closed. Public access to congressional floor activity was improved in 1979 when the House allowed C-SPAN to begin television coverage of its general sessions. The Senate opened its doors to C-SPAN in 1986.

These reforms have made formal congressional activities more open to public scrutiny. Some political observers argue, however, that sunshine rules have simply caused legislators to conduct many of their key negotiations and develop compromises in informal meetings outside the view of the public and press. Moreover, some argue that the primary beneficiaries have not been voters, who keep only a sporadic watch on Congress, but full-time lobbyists, who now can keep a closer eye on legislative action.

Sunshine reforms have also been introduced to open up the federal bureaucracy. The most important bureaucratic reform of the past three decades was the Government in Sunshine Act of 1976, which required many of the nation's most important agencies to make their meetings open to the public.

State governments have enacted similar sunshine rules over the past 30 years, opening up state and local meetings to the public. Efforts to enact sunshine laws in the states arose initially in the mid-1960s after the state of Florida enacted such a law in 1967. The reform efforts were then given a big push by the legislative reform movement that swept the states in the 1970s. The Citizens' Conference on State Legislatures argued that open meetings were needed to make legislators more accountable for their actions. The reform movement stimulated many state legislatures to adopt their own sunshine rules. Today, all states have some form of open meeting laws.

In addition to enacting open-meeting laws, both the federal and state governments have enacted a variety of laws to make government records more accessible to the public. The primary federal law governing federal records is the Freedom of Information Act, which was enacted in 1966. The act was then strengthened in 1974 to force greater compliance within the bureaucracy. Today, all 50 states have their own open records laws.

See also Congress; C-SPAN; Ethics; Freedom of Information Act; Government in Sunshine Act; Legislative Reform Movement; Legislative Reorganization Act; Open Record Laws.

References Sam Archibald, "The Early Years of the Freedom of Information Act: 1955 to 1974" (1993); Ann O'M. Bowman and Richard C. Kearney, *State and Local Government* (1993); William J. Keefe and Morris S. Ogul, *The American Legislative Process: Congress and the States* (1993); Leroy N. Rieselbach, *Congressional Reform: The Changing Modern Congress* (1994); Leroy N. Rieselbach, *Congressional Politics: The Evolving Legislative System*

(1995); David W. Rohde, *Parties and Leaders in the Postreform House* (1991).

Super Tuesday

In the early 1980s, Democratic party leaders in the South began to feel that the party would be more successful if southern states joined together to schedule their presidential primaries on the same day. It was hoped that such a change would increase the South's influence on the nomination process and help the party to nominate more moderate candidates.

The result was the creation of Super Tuesday, a date early in the nomination process in which southern and border states would jointly schedule their primary elections. The first Super Tuesday was held in 1984 when three southern and two northern states joined together to hold their primary elections on the same day.

After the defeat of Walter Mondale in the 1984 election, support for Super Tuesday increased throughout the South. In 1988, 14 southern and border states agreed to hold a second Super Tuesday election. The election, held on 8 March, did not produce a clear-cut moderate winner as its organizers had hoped, but helped propel the campaigns of two liberals (Michael Dukakis and Jesse Jackson) and one moderate (Albert Gore). In 1992, only six states participated in Super Tuesday, but the outcome was more in line with the organizers' goals, helping strengthen the candidacy of the moderate governor of Arkansas, Bill Clinton.

Super Tuesday is a type of regional primary. With regional primaries, neighboring states schedule their presidential primary vote on the same day in order to increase the influence of that region of the nation on the nomination process. Since the first Super Tuesday election in 1984, many other states have joined together to form regional primaries, though the 1988 Super Tuesday election is considered the largest such effort.

See also Frontloading; Presidential Primaries; Presidential Selection.
References Robert D. Loevy, *The Flawed Path to the Presidency 1992: Unfairness and Inequality in the Presidential Selection Process* (1995); Barbara Norrander, *Super Tuesday: Regional Politics and Presidential Primaries* (1992).

Superdelegates

See Hunt Commission

Supermajorities

Supermajorities are a type of procedural reform that have been introduced in several state legislatures since the 1970s, and incorporated into the rules of the U.S. House in 1995, to make it more difficult to enact certain types of legislation, particularly tax increases. Supermajority rules or laws require that particular kinds of legislation must receive extra-large majorities in both houses in order to be enacted into law. Many supermajority rules require a 60 percent majority, though the threshold is higher in some states. Supporters argue that supermajorities make it more difficult to pass tax increases and other unpopular legislation. Critics argue that supermajorities are undemocratic because they allow a legislative minority to frustrate the will of the majority. After the Republican Party gained a majority in the House in the 1994 election, it incorporated provisions in the House rules requiring that all legislation involving tax increases must receive more than 60 percent of the vote in order to pass.

See also Congress; Contract with America.
References David S. Cloud, "GOP, to Its Own Great Delight, Enacts House Rules Changes"

(1995); Frank J. Thompson, "Executive Leadership as an Enduring Institutional Issue" (1995).

Supply-Side Economics

Supply-side economic theory, which has enjoyed increased popularity since the late 1970s, laid the foundation for fiscal policy at the outset of the Reagan administration. Supply-side economists argue that the government would be more effective at producing economic growth if it concentrated on the supply or production of goods rather than on demand, which had been the government's primary concern since the 1930s. To increase supply, the government should reduce taxes and deregulate industry, because these actions increase the incentives for work, savings, and investments. Moreover, supply-siders argue that reductions in taxes should actually increase government revenue as a result of economic growth.

Although the principles underlying supply-side economics are not new, its popularity increased after the nation's economy became mired in a combination of economic stagnation and inflation in the 1970s. When Ronald Reagan was elected president in 1980, he attempted to use supply-side economics to guide the nation's fiscal policy. The cornerstone of this effort was the Economic Recovery Tax Act of 1981, which drastically cut personal and corporate income taxes. The act did not generate the economic growth promised by supply-siders, and led to growing skepticism regarding supply-side economics. The recession of 1982 and the unprecedented federal budget deficits forced the president to abandon supply-side theories and turn his attention to deficit reduction. Although Reagan's experiment with supply-side economics proved unsuccessful, many supply-side ideas remain popular among conservative economic reformers.

See also Budget Deficit, Federal; Economic Policy; Economic Recovery Tax Act; Fiscal Policy; Kemp-Roth Tax Cut; Keynesian Economics; Laffer, Arthur B.; Laffer Curve; Reaganomics; Stagflation; Taxes.

References Paul A. Samuelson and William D. Nordhaus, *Economics* (1992); Herbert Stein, *Presidential Economics: The Making of Economic Policy from Roosevelt to Clinton* (1994).

Supreme Court

The U.S. Supreme Court has changed considerably over the past 30 years, moving away from a liberal activist orientation under Chief Justice Earl Warren's leadership in the 1960s to a more conservative stance under William Rehnquist. This change in philosophy has had a profound effect on the Court's role in society, making it far less important in championing equal rights and civil liberties than it was three decades ago.

Although liberal activists decry the Court's move to the right, just as conservatives criticized the Warren Court, most discussion about Supreme Court reform focuses on structural problems, not the Court's philosophy. The most pressing structural issue that has confronted the Supreme Court over the past two decades has been its growing workload. Since the late 1960s, many members of the Supreme Court and judicial scholars have argued that the demands on the Court have grown so overwhelming that the quality of the Court's work may be suffering.

Several proposals have been put forward to reduce this workload. The most dramatic reform that has been proposed is the creation of a national court of appeals between the current federal appeals court and the Supreme Court. This new appeals court would have the power to review cases directed to it by the Supreme Court. Other proposals include ending mandatory appellate jurisdiction, assessing penalties on lawyers who file frivolous appeals, establishing clearer criteria on the petitions the Court will consider, instituting stricter rules on switching venues, creating specialized appeals courts, and altering the rule of four to require five votes for a hearing.

Despite the attention that has been given to the Court's growing workload, few reforms have been adopted. In the early 1980s, Chief Justice Warren Burger came out in support of a new national court of appeals, but the proposal was never enacted. The most important reform to be enacted in recent years was the passage of legislation in Congress in 1988 that abolished the Court's mandatory appellate jurisdiction.

Another area that has sparked talk of reform is the selection process used for Supreme Court justices. After the disruptive nomination battles over Robert Bork in 1987 and Clarence Thomas in 1991, many political commentators discussed the need for reform, especially in the confirmation process. Although both of these confirmation battles generated considerable criticism, no serious effort has been made to change the process.

Along with these proposals to help the Court handle its workload and to reform the selection process, there have been some efforts to find a way to force the Court to reduce its activism. One proposal that has been put forth is for Congress to enact legislation forbidding the Court to exercise judicial review on some legal issues. There is some constitutional support and judicial precedent for such action, but most legal scholars are doubtful it would be upheld by the courts. In addition, most argue that such action would constitute a profound threat to the court system.

See also Burger, Warren; Caseload; Freund Committee; Hill, Anita; Hruska Commission; Judicial Activism; Judicial Selection; Mandatory Appellate Jurisdiction; Marshall, Thurgood; National Court of Appeals; Rehnquist, William H.; Rule of Four; Thomas, Clarence; Warren, Earl.

References Robert A. Carp and Ronald Stidham, *Judicial Process in America* (1993); Samuel Estreicher and John Sexton, *Redefining the Supreme Court's Role: A Theory of Managing the Federal Judicial Process* (1986); William C. Louthan, *The United States Supreme Court: Lawmaking in the Third Branch of Government*(1991).

T

Taking Back Our Streets Act

One of the ten proposals in the Contract with America, the Taking Back Our Streets Act called for the tightening of sentencing laws, new limitations on death penalty appeals, loosening of the exclusionary rule, and cutbacks in federal crime prevention programs in order to fund the construction of more prisons. As of late 1995, the act remained under congressional consideration.

See also Contract with America; Crime; Sentencing.
References David Masci, "Mandatory Victim Restitution OK'd by Senate Judiciary" (1995); "Republicans' Initial Promise: 100-Day Debate on 'Contract'" (1994); Clyde Wilcox, *The Latest American Revolution? The 1994 Elections and Their Implication for Governance* (1995).

Takings

The Fifth Amendment to the U.S. Constitution guarantees that private property will not "be taken for public use without just compensation." The takings clause, as this phrase is called, has come to play an important part in recent battles over the government's role in society. Supporters of private property rights and limited government argue that the takings clause requires the government to provide compensation not only when the government exercises its traditional powers of eminent domain, but on all actions that restrict the use of private property.

In 1992, the U.S. Supreme Court gave some support to this position, ruling in the case of *Lucas v. South Carolina Coastal Council* that the government must pay compensation when its regulations deny a landowner of all economic benefits from the use of his or her land. The Court identified two exceptions: when the proposed activity of the landowner constituted a nuisance or violated a "background principle of the state's" property laws. Two years later, the Court again addressed the takings clause, ruling in *Dolan v. the City of Tigard* that the city's requirement that a hardware store owner set aside part of her land for drainage and a bike trail in order to receive a construction permit was inappropriate.

Legal scholars are uncertain of the full significance of these decisions, but both rulings have caused government agencies to begin to reassess their regulatory and zoning policies. In addition, some political activists fear that the decisions will reduce the power of local governments to control zoning and harm the nation's environmental policy.

The courts have not been the only political body concerned with takings. Several states have enacted legislation requiring government agencies to assess the effects of their programs on property owners and establishing new compensation requirements. Similar proposals have been advocated by members of the new Republican majority in Congress. The Republican Party's Contract with America calls for compensation to private landowners whose property values are affected by the Endangered Species Act, the Clean Water Act, and the Food Security Act.

See also Contract with America; Deregulation; Environmental Policy; Job Creation and Wage Enhancement Act; Property Rights Movement; Sagebrush Rebellion.

References David L. Callies, ed., *After Lucas: Land Use Regulation and the Taking of Private Property Without Compensation* (1993); G. Richard Hill, *Regulatory Taking: The Limits of Land Use Controls* (1993); Richard Moe, "If Men Were Angels . . . Property Rights and the 'Takings' Issue" (1994); Larry Morandi, "Takings for Granted" (1995).

Tax Credits

In order to reduce candidates' dependence on political action committees and to increase electoral competition, many reformers advocate the greater use of income tax credits to encourage more contributions from individuals. The Revenue Act of 1971 allowed individual taxpayers to deduct up to $50 for political contributions from their federal tax returns. The Tax Reform Act of 1986, however, repealed this deduction.

In the 1980s, the Democratic Study Group lobbied Congress to enact a 100 percent tax credit for contributions up to $100 to candidates, and a 50 percent credit for party contributions. Though the group's efforts were unsuccessful, support for reinstituting tax credits remains a major political goal for many reformers. At the state level, 18 states permitted either tax credits or deductions for campaign contributions in the late 1980s.

See also Campaign Finance; Democratic Study Group; Federal Election Campaign Act; Political Action Committees; Public Financing; Revenue Act of 1971; Tax Reform Act.

References *Congressional Campaign Finances: History, Facts, and Controversy* (1992); David B. Magleby and Candice J. Nelson, *The Money Chase: Congressional Campaign Finance Reform* (1990); Michael J. Malbin, ed., *Money and Politics in the United States: Financing Elections in the 1980s* (1984); Frank J. Sorauf, *Money in American Elections* (1988).

Tax Equity and Fiscal Responsibility Act (TEFRA)

The Tax Equity and Fiscal Responsibility Act, passed in 1982, was one of the first of several tax-raising bills that were enacted in the 1980s to overcome the massive budget deficits spawned by the Economic Recovery Tax Act of 1981. Authored by Senator Robert Dole of Kansas, the act was also noteworthy because it was the first major piece of tax legislation authored by a senator, despite the constitutional requirement that all revenue bills must originate in the House.

See also Budget Deficit, Federal; Deficit Reduction Act; Economic Recovery Tax Act; Social Security; Tax Reform Act.

References Timothy J. Conlan et al., *Taxing Choices: The Politics of Tax Reform* (1990); Howard E. Shuman, *Politics and the Budget: The Struggle between the President and the Congress* (1992).

Tax Expenditures

There are two general ways in which the government can channel money to individuals, businesses, and other groups. One is by redistributing funds raised through taxes and other revenue sources to the targeted groups; the other is by creating tax breaks that reduce the amount of money the targeted groups must pay in taxes. This second type of government spending is referred to as tax expenditures.

Tax expenditures are used by the government to protect individual industries, to stimulate economic growth, and to encourage activities that the government sees as desirable. Many types of tax expenditures are broadly praised because of the economic or social benefits they provide. These include tax deductions for home mortgage payments and donations to charity, as well as tax breaks for particular industries that the nation sees as important to nurture. By the mid-1980s, however, the growing number of tax breaks incorporated into the federal tax structure began to generate demands for change from reformers who argued that the use of these breaks had grown out of control, creating a tax system that was unfair, too complicated, and detrimental to the nation's ability to balance the federal budget.

One of the major goals of the Tax Reform Act of 1986 was to reduce the number of tax breaks given to individuals and corporations. Although the final bill disappointed many reformers, it did close a substantial number of loopholes in the tax structure. It has been estimated that the amount of money the federal government lost in tax expenditures prior to the passage of the act was close to 50 percent of what it brought in through taxes. After the passage of the act, the amount of money lost was reduced to approximately one-third of what the government brought in.

Despite these gains, many people remain unhappy with the large number of tax benefits written into the tax code. Supporters of the flat tax have been among the most vocal advocates for ending tax expenditures. Almost all flat tax proposals include provisions for ending most, if not all, tax breaks.

See also Economic Recovery Tax Act; Flat Tax; Tax Reform Act; Taxes.

References Timothy J. Conlan et al., *Taxing Choices: The Politics of Tax Reform* (1990); Howard E. Shuman, *Politics and the Budget: The Struggle between the President and the Congress* (1992); Christopher Zimmerman, "Flat Tax, Sales Tax, or VAT?" (1995).

Tax Reform Act

The Tax Reform Act of 1986 reformed the federal tax system, reducing the burden on low-wage earners, closing numerous loopholes that benefited corporations and other special interests, and reducing the number of tax brackets from 15 to 3. The act grew out of discontent with the Economic Recovery Tax Act of 1981, which had dramatically cut taxes for wealthy individuals and corporations. The passage of the act was considered a remarkable political feat because of the intense pressure that special interests have waged against past tax reform efforts.

See also Capital Gains Tax; Economic Recovery Tax Act; Fair Tax; FAST; Flat Tax; Progressive Tax; Taxes.

References Timothy J. Conlan et al., *Taxing Choices: The Politics of Tax Reform* (1990); Paul J. Quirk, "Structures and Performance: An Evaluation" (1992); Howard E. Shuman, *Politics and the Budget: The Struggle between the President and the Congress* (1992).

Tax Revolt

The antitax movement that swept the nation in the late 1970s and early 1980s has been referred to as the tax revolt. The onset of this revolt has generally been traced to the 1978 passage of California's Proposition 13, which radically reduced the state's property tax rate. During the next five years, the demand for tax relief, especially from property taxes, became a rallying cry for conservative reformers across the United States. It is estimated that more than 40 states enacted some form of local property tax limitation or tax relief plan during this period, and many adopted limits on other forms of taxation as well. These types of legal restrictions are often referred to as tax and expenditure limitations, or TELs. The revolt is said to have died down by the mid-1980s, but it left an important mark on American politics, causing taxes to emerge as one of the foremost issues in shaping government action over the past two decades.

See also Finance, Local; Finance, State; Proposition 13; Taxes.
References Ann O'M. Bowman and Richard C. Kearney, *State and Local Government* (1993); Steven D. Gold, *The Fiscal Crisis of the States: Lessons for the Future* (1995); Werner Z. Hirsch and Anthony M. Rufolo, *Public Finance and Expenditure in a Federal System* (1990); Henry J. Raimondo, "State Budgeting in the Nineties" (1993).

Taxes

Few issues have shaped political debate in the United States during the past two decades as much as taxes. The emergence of taxes as a major political issue began in the mid- to late 1970s, as the nation's economy faltered, tax rates soared, and the public grew increasing distrustful of government. In 1978, these multiple factors conspired to help generate a nationwide tax revolt. Although this revolt has died down since the mid-1980s, taxes have remained one of the most important issues directing government policies and reform efforts. In general, tax reform proposals have focused on four major concerns: tax relief, economic growth, fairness, and deficit reduction. A desire for tax simplification has also stirred calls for reform, though few policy proposals have actually addressed this concern.

The demand for tax relief was at the forefront of reform efforts during the tax revolt of the late 1970s and early 1980s. With the economy slumping and tax rates reaching unprecedented highs, the desire for lower taxes rose. Moreover, inflation was forcing many taxpayers into higher federal tax brackets even though their real income was not changing. The tax revolt is generally considered to have begun in 1978 with the passage of California's Proposition 13, which radically reduced the state's property tax rate. Over the next five years, some 40 states enacted new laws limiting property taxes or providing property tax relief, and many adopted reductions or limitations on other forms of taxation.

At the same time the tax revolt was spreading across the nation, conservative economic theories were beginning to find support among political leaders. In the late 1970s, the ideas of supply-side economics began to supplant tax relief as the preeminent force in shaping much of the debate over tax reform. The supply-siders argued that the tax rate for the highest income levels and for businesses needed to be reduced to improve the nation's economy. Reducing taxes on these groups, they asserted, would increase the amount of funds available for investments, which in turn would spur economic growth. The supply-side argument was first embraced in Congress by the unsuccessful Kemp-Roth Tax Cut proposal in 1978. The Kemp-Roth plan reemerged as part of the Economic Recovery Tax Act of 1981, which slashed federal taxes on wealthy individuals and corporations. Despite the supply-siders' promise, the act did not stimulate economic growth. However, it did lead to two other important consequences. For one, the tax cuts for the wealthy generated a growing demand for economic fairness toward poor and middle-class taxpayers. The act also helped propel the federal budget into the worst deficit in history.

In order to make the tax system fairer

and to reduce the deficit, Congress enacted several tax reforms in the 1980s. The most important of these was the Tax Reform Act of 1986, which reduced the tax burden on low-wage earners, closed numerous loopholes that benefited corporations and other special interests, and reduced the number of tax brackets from 15 to 3.

Since the passage of the 1986 act, the federal government has passed several other tax laws, though none has been as sweeping as the 1986 reform. The two most important tax-related bills were the Budget Enforcement Act of 1990 and the 1994 federal budget, both of which increased taxes as part of an effort to balance the federal budget.

More radical proposals to restructure the nation's tax system began to receive serious attention in the mid-1990s after the Republican Party gained a majority of seats in both houses of Congress. Many of the new Republican leaders are strong advocates of replacing the federal income tax with alternatives that supply-side theory argues will encourage savings and economic growth. These alternatives include the value-added tax, the flat tax, and a national sales tax. There is considerable doubt, however, that any of these sweeping tax reforms will be enacted because of the intense political pressure that is put on members of Congress when tax legislation is debated on Capitol Hill.

At the state level, most of the debate on tax reform since the end of the tax revolt has focused on how to deal with growing fiscal demands while faced with continued public resistance to tax increases. Since the 1980s, states have adopted a variety of tax reforms that allow them to increase taxes without drawing the voters' wrath. In particular, the 1980s saw an increase in user fees, sin taxes, and, in some cases, the sales tax. More recently, many state leaders have begun to focus on taxing business services as a means to raise additional tax revenue. With the nation's economy growing in the mid-1990s, however, state taxes were reduced in the 1995 fiscal year for the first time in ten years.

See also Budget Enforcement Act of 1990; Budget, Federal; Common Shared Tax; Consumed-Income Tax; Consumption Tax; Corporate Income Tax; Deficit Reduction Act; Economic Recovery Tax Act; Finance, Local; Finance, State; Flat Tax; Gambling; Kemp-Roth Tax Cut; Lotteries; Personal Income Tax; Property Tax; Reaganomics; Revenue Act of 1978; Sales Tax; Service Tax; Stagflation; Supply-Side Economics; Tax Equity and Fiscal Responsibility Act; Tax Reform Act; Tax Revolt; User Fees; Value-Added Tax.

References "Fiscally Speaking, a Very Good Year" (1995); Werner Z. Hirsch and Anthony M. Rufolo, *Public Finance and Expenditures in a Federal System* (1990); Penelope Lemov, "Is There Anything Left To Tax?" (1993); Joseph J. Minarik, *Making Tax Choices* (1985); David O. Sears and Jack Citrin, *Tax Revolt: Something for Nothing in* California (1985); C. Eugene Steuerle, *The Tax Decade: How Taxes Came To Dominate the Political Agenda* (1992); Christopher Zimmerman, "Flat Tax, Sales Tax, or VAT?" (1995).

Telecommunications

Governments have instituted reforms and new regulations to ensure public access to the plethora of new technologies for communication. Today, telecommunications encompasses all technologies relating to transmission of information, especially the higher-end transmissions via satellite that now fuel telephone, broadcasting, and computer network communications. With the deregulation of the telephone industry during the 1970s and 1980s, a number of new companies sprang up to deliver services that were once run as a virtual monopoly by the AT&T Bell System. Later, deregulation of cable television led to a similar shake-up of the original television broadcasting networks, and today many households have access to hundreds of television channels through local and national service companies. Local governments and federal regulators struggle with dividing telephone and television service markets among an increasing number of companies.

With the current explosion of personal computer use and the growing importance of communication over the Internet, governments are again looking at ways to encourage entrepreneurship while ensuring public access to information. Various agencies of the federal government (particularly the Federal Communications Commission) and congressional committees are following Vice President Gore's reformist goals for the National Information Infrastructure (NII), which envision coordinated and universal access to information via the Internet. By the year 2000, NII goals state, all citizens should be able harness telecommunications technology for lifelong learning, health care, manufacturing, delivery of government services, and other applications.

In 1996, Congress passed a major reform bill to deregulate local telephone service and cable television. The bill allows companies from each industry to compete for the other's business and dismantles 61 years of regulations that separated telephone and television service providers as distinct industries. Industry experts expect that the deregulation measures will increase competition and consumer choice for these services, but also bring more confusion to the telecommunications field.

See also Clinton, William J.; Deregulation; Electronic Town Meeting; Gore, Albert, Jr.; National Information Infrastructure.

References Jeffrey Berry, *The Interest Group Society* (1989); John Greenwald, "Ready, Willing, Cable" (1995); Kenneth Janda et al., *The Challenge of Democracy: Government in America* (1995).

Teledemocracy

See Electronic Town Meeting.

Term Expansion

One of the most important reform movements in the United States since the early 1990s has been the effort to limit the number of terms elected officials can serve. Over the past 30 years, however, many reformers have argued that the solution to the problem of poor government is not a reduction in the length of terms but an expansion. Where term limits have been offered as a means to make elected officials more responsive to private citizens, term expansion is presented as a way to give elected officials more time to do their jobs instead of constantly worrying about the next election.

Efforts to lengthen terms have occurred at both the state and national levels. State reformers in the 1950s and 1960s argued that governors' terms needed to be increased from two to four years to allow the governors to develop better policy programs and gain greater control over the bureaucracy. Reformers also advocated an end to the restrictive term limits on governors, which in many states denied them the opportunity to serve more than one consecutive term. Similarly, in the late 1960s and 1970s, supporters of the state legislative reform movement advocated improving legislative salaries and benefits as a way to increase members' tenure in office. If members served longer terms, the supporters argued, it would improve their expertise and lead to better public policy.

In large part, both of these reform efforts were quite successful. Since 1955, 18 states have established four-year terms for governors, leaving only 3 that still maintain two-year terms. Moreover, most states now allow the governor to serve at least two terms, and many have no limit whatsoever.

Improved pay and benefits in legislative service have also increased the tenure of state legislators.

The length of terms for federal officials has remained unchanged since the nation's founding, except for the establishment of a two-term limit on the president in 1951. However, many reformers have argued for expanding the terms of both members of Congress and the executive. In particular, some reformers advocate increasing House terms to four years and Senate terms to eight, so that their elections coincide with presidential election years. This reform has been presented as a way to reduce members' obsession with the next election and to encourage greater cooperation between the two branches. In 1966, President Johnson proposed a four-year term for House members. In 1987, the Committee on the Constitutional System advocated extending the terms for House and Senate offices to four and eight, respectively. Opponents argue, however, that frequent elections are needed to make members responsive to the public, and that an eight-year Senate term is simply too long.

A number of reformers have also called for lengthening the president's term to six years, and then denying the president the opportunity to be reelected. This reform has been proposed as a way to reduce the amount of time that sitting presidents spend on campaigning, and to encourage presidents to pursue wiser policy initiatives. Critics argue that instead of improving performance, such a reform would cause a decline in the president's power, because the president would automatically become a lame duck. As an alternative, these critics advocate the repeal of the Twenty-second Amendment. Not only would this overcome the lame-duck problem, they argue, but it would allow voters to continue to reelect a popular president.

See also Divided Government; Governors; Legislative Reform Movement; State Renewal; Term Limits.

References Thad Beyle, "The Governor as Innovator in the Federal System" (1988); Alan Rosenthal, "The Legislative Institution: In Transition and at Risk" (1993); Larry J. Sabato, *Goodbye to Good-Time Charlie: The American Governorship Transformed* (1983).

Term Limits

The idea that elected officials should be allowed to serve for only a limited length of time has found widespread support in recent years as American voters have grown increasingly disillusioned with politics and the apparent unresponsiveness of career politicians to their constituents' concerns. Term limits supporters offer term limits as a solution to many of the nation's political problems, though they place particular emphasis on them as a way to increase electoral competition and make elected officials more responsive to voters. Although the term limits movement has considerable popular support, it has many critics among scholars and other political observers, who are skeptical of both the constitutionality and benefits of term limits laws.

Support for term limits on elected officials has existed in the United States since the nation's founding. When the colonies initially gained independence from England, most of the new states established some form of term limits on their governors, and a few limited the terms of other offices as well. Pennsylvania was considered the most extreme, placing term limits on all state and many local officials. Under the Articles of Confederation, delegates to the National Legislatures were also limited in the number of years they could serve, as was the president of Congress.

Proposals designed to limit terms of

both legislators and the president were strongly supported by many delegates to the Constitutional Convention in Philadelphia in 1787, including Virginia's Edmund Randolph. After several debates, however, the different proposals to limit terms were left out of the Constitution.

Throughout the next century there were no legal restrictions on the number of terms federal officials could serve, but, in practice, most officials served very limited terms. Turnover in Congress was routinely high until the twentieth century, and all presidents beginning with Washington had accepted the norm of serving no more than two terms. Many states, however, retained constitutional limits on the terms of state executives, legislators, and local officials.

There was renewed interest in limiting federal officials' terms in the early 1940s after Franklin D. Roosevelt was elected to his third term as president, breaking the precedent set by George Washington. After several years of debate, the Twenty-second Amendment was ratified in 1951, limiting presidents to two terms.

The recent movement to limit legislative terms is generally considered to have arisen in the early 1990s, after Colorado, Oklahoma, and California passed ballot initiatives limiting the terms of office of state legislators and other officials. Over the next four years, more than 20 states adopted term limit laws regarding state legislators, executives, or members of Congress. The reformers have argued that these limits are needed to remove professional politicians from office, to break the electoral advantage enjoyed by incumbents, and to make the political system more responsive to the needs of the public.

There is no one set of term limit laws and proposals, but rather, they vary from state to state. The laws differ primarily in three areas: the lengths of time the officials are allowed to serve, whether the restrictions apply to individuals' lifetimes or to consecutive service, and whether the laws are retroactive. Some states, such as California, have adopted very strict term limit laws, limiting officials' terms to a few years and banning future service in the same office after a limit is met. Other states, such as Oklahoma, allow for fairly long service, and still others, including Colorado, permit elected officials to return to their former posts after taking a break from those offices.

Many constitutional scholars argue that the congressional term limit laws adopted by individual states are unconstitutional because they represent new qualifications on who can serve in office. These scholars maintain that the only legal means to limit congressional terms is through a constitutional amendment, as was done with the president. In 1995, the U.S. Supreme Court sided with this perspective in the court case *U.S. Term Limits v. Thornton,* ruling that these state-by-state restrictions were unconstitutional. The Court's action, however, did not affect term limit laws regarding state legislatures.

Other scholars have been critical of the promised benefits of congressional and state legislative term limits, arguing that there is no evidence that these laws will achieve their intended goals, and that they may in fact worsen many problems. Term limits, they argue, do nothing to ensure that elected representatives are more attentive to the public's concerns, nor can they make elections more fair. Moreover, they argue that these laws will remove experienced legislators from office, giving more power to interest groups and executives.

See also Amateur Politicians; Career Legislators; Citizen Legislature Act; Fund, John; Incumbency Advantage; Noble, Lloyd, II; Professional

Politicians; U.S. Term Limits; *U.S Term Limits v. Thornton.*

References Gerald Benjamin and Michael J. Malbin, ed., *Limiting Legislative Terms* (1992); Michael A. Pagano and Ann O'M. Bowman, "The State of American Federalism, 1994–1995" (1995).

Third Parties

Most elected officials in state and national politics are members of either the Democratic Party or the Republican Party. In recent years, many Americans have grown disillusioned with these two major parties, which has spurred increased talk of the need for a viable alternative party, or what is referred to as a third party.

Discontent with the two major political parties was so strong in 1992 that Texas businessman H. Ross Perot was able to attract 19 percent of the presidential vote as an independent party candidate. In 1995, Perot began a nationwide effort to launch a new third party, called the Independence or Reform Party, depending on the state. In addition, several leading national politicians who have been known for their independence seriously discussed among themselves the possibility of creating a third party in 1995 that would be socially liberal and economically conservative. These politicians included Paul Tsongas, a moderate Democratic presidential candidate in 1992, Senator Bill Bradley of New York, who is considered a potential presidential candidate in the future, and Governor Dick Lamm of Colorado, who organized the discussions.

Despite this attention, most political analysts remain skeptical of the ability of a third party to succeed because of the constraints placed on such a party by the nation's election laws and tradition. The use of single-member districts to select legislators, the presence of strict ballot access laws in many states, and current federal campaign finance rules all make it difficult for third parties to survive. These legal hurdles are compounded by the reluctance of the news media to pay attention to third-party candidates and of voters to give their support.

Advocates argue that the establishment of a viable third party would provide voters with more choice at the ballot box, improve representation, and force the government to address issues that are currently being ignored. Critics of third parties argue that the current two-party system provides a more stable government and encourages compromise among opposing factions in U.S. society.

Currently, there are many third parties in the United States, though none has emerged to compete effectively with either of the two main political parties. The Libertarian Party has been one of the most successful third parties in recent years, placing its candidate's name on the ballot in all 50 states in the 1992 presidential election.

See also Ballot Access; Campaign Finance; Perot, H. Ross; Political Parties; Proportional Representation; Single-Member Districts.

References Jeffrey H. Birnbaum, "A Plot To Liven Up the Race" (1995); William J. Keefe, *Parties, Politics, and Public Policy in America* (1994); Steven J. Rosenstone et al., *Third Parties in America: Citizen Response to Major Party Failure* (1984).

Thomas, Clarence (b. 1948)

The controversial nomination of Clarence Thomas as the 106th associate justice of the U.S. Supreme Court in 1991 raised widespread public concern over the judicial nomination process and the ethical behavior of government officials. A conservative African-American, Thomas seemed certain to be confirmed when allegations about his past nearly cost him the Supreme Court seat and threw the nation into heated debate about the rights of women in the workplace.

The controversy surrounding Thomas emerged when University of Oklahoma law professor Anita Hill charged that he had sexually harassed her while she worked for him at the U.S. Department of Education and the Equal Employment Opportunity Commission. Hill's testimony before the Senate Judiciary Committee riveted the nation, but ultimately the Senate voted to confirm Thomas's nomination. The Senate's decision led to calls for reform of the nomination process, new standards for ethical behavior among government representatives, and increased involvement of women in the 1992 elections. The public attention given to sexual harassment in the confirmation hearings was also considered partially responsible for the passage of the Civil Rights Act of 1991.

See also Civil Rights Act of 1991; Ethics; Hill, Anita; Judicial Selection; Marshall, Thurgood; Women's Movement.

References Roger H. Davidson and Walter J. Oleszek, *Congress and Its Members* (1994); Lawrence C. Dodd and Bruce I. Oppenheimer, "Perspectives on the 1992 Congressional Elections" (1993); Judith Graham, ed., *Current Biography Yearbook 1992* (1992); Jane Mayer and Jill Abramson, *Strange Justice: The Selling of Clarence Thomas* (1994); Toni Morrison, ed., *Race-ing Justice, En-gendering Power: Essays on Anita Hill, Clarence Thomas, and the Construction of Social Reality* (1992).

Thompson, Tommy G. (b. 1941)

As one of the most visible Republican governors in the United States, Tommy Thompson has shaped the national debate on welfare reform through his welfare experiments in his home state of Wisconsin. Soon after he took the governor's seat in 1986, Thompson called for measures to stem the alleged tide of welfare recipients who traveled north from Chicago for better benefits in Wisconsin. Though he was criticized for racially tinged motives, Thompson's cutbacks were cheered by the state's largely white working-class voters. Later, Thompson implemented several experimental programs, including "Workfare," "Learnfare," and "Bridefare," as a way to break long-term dependency on state aid by requiring recipients to learn a trade, stay in school, or get married. Republicans in Congress and elsewhere have applauded Thompson's efforts. Moreover, Thompson's "tough love" experiments have become models for conservative welfare reform across the nation.

See also Bridefare; Learnfare; Welfare; Workfare.

References Rodney Atkins, "Governor Get-a-Job: Tommy Thompson" (1995); Michael Barone and Grant Ujifusa, eds., *Almanac of American Politics* (1995); Patricia Chargot, "Cut Class, Get a Smaller Check" (1991); "Tommy G. Thompson" (1995).

Thornburg v. Gingles

In the 1986 *Thornburg v. Gingles* case, the U.S. Supreme Court upheld the constitutionality of the 1982 amendments to the Voting Rights Act and established a new criterion for determining discriminatory voting practices. The Court ruled that the Voting Rights Act is violated if racially polarized voting in a district denies a large and compacted minority population the opportunity to elect a candidate of its choice. In establishing this criterion, the Court simplified the requirements needed to determine the lawfulness of an election practice, essentially allowing future cases to focus solely on the statistical relationships among voting patterns, election results, and a district's demographics.

The Court's ruling has encouraged state and local governments to adopt voting procedures that ensure the election of minorities to office, particularly through the use of majority-minority districts.

See also Electoral Discrimination; Majority-Minority Districts; *Shaw v. Reno;* Voting Rights Act; *White v. Regester.*
Reference Chandler Davidson, ed., *Minority Vote Dilution* (1989).

Three Strikes Policies

See Crime.

Total Quality Management (TQM)

Total quality management is a management approach that became increasingly popular among businesses in the 1980s, and has since been championed as an effective reform for government bureaucracies. One of the central goals of TQM is to focus an agency's attention on whether it is meeting the needs of its "customers." TQM also calls for managers to monitor the quality of their agency's services or products continuously to make sure they are meeting these needs, and to make changes when they are not. In addition, TQM calls for increased employee participation in decision making and a greater focus among managers on the operation of the entire system.

Despite TQM's popularity, some analysts question whether it is an appropriate form of management for government agencies because it is difficult to identify who the "customers" are for many programs. Moreover, government agencies cannot be concerned only with the direct beneficiaries of their activities; they must also consider taxpayers, constituents, and other groups within the political system.

See also Budgeting Techniques; Bureaucracy; Empowerment; Management by Objectives; National Performance Review; Performance Budgeting; Program Budgeting; Public Service Deregulation.
References Evan M. Berman et al., "Implementing TQM in the States" (1994); Pan Suk Kim and Lance W. Wolff, "Improving Government Performance: Public Management Reform and the National Performance Review" (1994); James E. Swiss, "Adapting Total Quality Management (TQM) to Government" (1992).

Trade Policy

The federal government has generally promoted liberal trade policies since the end of the Second World War to encourage an open international exchange of goods. As the U.S. economy began to decline in the 1970s and foreign businesses began to compete more effectively with American firms, the federal government became pressured to turn away from this free trade position and focus its efforts on improving the fairness of international trade. Many business leaders felt that foreign laws were restricting their entry into foreign markets and that foreign businesses were dumping goods in the United States. In the 1980s, the federal government imposed or threatened to impose a variety of restrictions and tariffs on specific foreign goods to force open foreign markets and protect American companies from unfair trade practices. With some exceptions, this emphasis on protectionist trade policy lessened in the 1990s as the president and Congress turned away from threatening retaliation and once again concentrated on opening up the international market through trade accords. In 1993, Congress enacted two major free trade laws: the General Agreement on Tariffs and Trade and the North American Free Trade Agreement.

See also Free Trade; General Agreement on Tariffs and Trade; Gold Convertibility; Industrial Policy; North American Free Trade Agreement; Protectionism.
References Martin Feldstein, ed., *American Economic Policy in the 1980s* (1994); Gary Mucciaroni, *Reversals of Fortune: Public Policy and Private Interests* (1995).

Transfers

A spreading practice among elected officials and candidates is to contribute, or transfer, funds from their own campaign accounts to the accounts of other candidates running for office. Critics argue that this practice corrupts the political process, encouraging elected officials to become increasingly concerned with accumulating large campaign war chests and making interest groups more powerful.

Some restrictions have been introduced at both the federal and state levels to reduce the influence of transfers. In federal campaigns, transfers are considered as individual contributions under the Federal Election Campaign Act. Thus officeholders and candidates are limited to transferring $1,000 directly per candidate per campaign. Additional funds can be channeled to candidates through personal PACs, though this money is often considered different from transfers.

There is considerable variation in state laws dealing with transfers. Some states, such as Minnesota and Washington, ban transfers entirely. Others follow the federal model by treating them like individual contributions and placing limits on the amount that can be transferred. Finally, many states, including California, have no restrictions on transfers whatsoever.

See also Campaign Finance; Contribution Limits; Federal Election Campaign Act; Leadership PACs; Legislative Caucus Campaign Committees; Personal PACs.

References California Commission on Campaign Financing, *The New Gold Rush: Financing California's Legislative Campaigns* (1985); Richard A. Clucas, *The Speaker's Electoral Connection: Willie Brown and the California Assembly* (1995); Anthony Gierzynski, *Legislative Party Campaign Committees in the American States* (1992); Frederick M. Herrmann and Ronald D. Michaelson, "Financing State and Local Elections: Recent Developments" (1994); Frank J. Sorauf, *Money in American Elections* (1988).

Twenty-fifth Amendment

Enacted in 1967, the Twenty-fifth Amendment to the U.S. Constitution established procedures for the vice president to become acting president if the president becomes incapacitated. The amendment permits the vice president to assume the presidency if the president declares in writing that he is no longer able to discharge his functions or if the vice president and a majority of the cabinet declare the president unable to do so. The amendment allows the president to return to his duties when he declares in a written message to Congress that he is no longer incapacitated. If the vice president and the cabinet disagree, however, Congress is granted the power to decide the issue.

The amendment also established procedures for selecting a new vice president if that office should become vacant. The amendment calls for the president to nominate a new vice president, who must then be confirmed by a majority vote in both houses of Congresses.

The passage of this amendment allowed Gerald Ford to become vice president after Spiro Agnew resigned that position in 1973. In addition, President Reagan used the amendment in 1985 to pass the powers of the presidency on to George Bush temporarily when Reagan underwent surgery for colon cancer.

See also Ford, Gerald R.

References John D. Feerick, *The Twenty-fifth Amendment: Its Complete History and Earliest Applications* (1976); James L. Sundquist, *The Decline and Resurgence of Congress* (1981); Jules Whitcover, *Crapshoot: Rolling the Dice on the Vice Presidency* (1992).

Twenty-seventh Amendment

The Twenty-seventh Amendment to the U.S. Constitution requires that an intervening election take place between the time a congressional pay raise is approved and the time the raise takes effect. The amendment was originally proposed along with the Bill of Rights in 1789, but it was not finally ratified until 1992. The proposal sat dormant for more than 100 years before generating renewed interest in the late 1970s. Public dissatisfaction with a proposed 51 percent congressional pay raise in 1989 increased support for the amendment. During the next three years, 15 states ratified the amendment, providing enough support for it to become law.

The change in the constitution has been applauded by reformers who see it as a means to stop an undeserving Congress from enacting midsession pay raises. Some constitutional scholars, however, have questioned the legitimacy of the amendment because of the unprecedented length of time taken for its ratification. In order to prevent amendments from lingering on the back burner, Congress today routinely includes a ratification deadline when it proposes constitutional amendments.

See also Congress.
Reference Ruth Ann Strickland, "The Twenty-seventh Amendment and Constitutional Change by Stealth" (1993).

Twenty-sixth Amendment

Enacted in response to the growing unrest of the nation's youth during the 1960s, the Twenty-sixth Amendment to the U.S. Constitution lowered the minimum voting age to give 18-years-olds the right to vote. The amendment was ratified in 1971.

Reference Wendell W. Cultice, *Youth's Battle for the Ballot: A History of Voting Age in America* (1992).

Twin Cities Metropolitan Council

The Twin Cities Metropolitan Council is considered to be one of the two most developed regional governments in the United States. Created in the 1960s to provide regional planning for the Minneapolis-St. Paul area, the Metro Council today sets areawide policy on such issues as transportation, waste management, public housing, development, and parks. The council itself does not provide services, but it has the power to set policy for the underlying local governments. Political reformers point to the council as an example of how regional government can be structured to overcome the fragmentation of government that troubles the nation's metropolitan areas.

See also Greater Portland Metropolitan Service District; Metropolitan Fragmentation; Regional Government.
References Terry Christensen, *Local Politics: Governing at the Grassroots* (1995); John J. Harrigan, *Political Change in the Metropolis* (1993); David B. Walker, *The Rebirth of Federalism: Slouching toward Washington* (1995).

Two-Year Budget Cycle

One proposal that has been offered to make the congressional budget process work more coherently is a two-year budget cycle. Currently, the federal budget is produced annually, with the fiscal year running from October 1 of one year to September 30 of the next. This alternative proposal calls for the president and Congress to prepare a budget every other year that would cover a two-year period. Congress would have the power to make adjustments in the second year of the budget cycle to deal with unanticipated problems, but the entire process itself would not be repeated. Approximately half the states currently use a two-year cycle, and the Pentagon has been producing two-year budget estimates for the past decade.

Supporters argue that a two-year budget cycle would give Congress a break from the continuous demands put on it to produce a budget and allow it to focus on other activities, including better oversight of the bureaucracy. Opponents argue that it is too difficult to estimate budget needs and revenue for a two-year period, and that Congress may ultimately spend the off year of the budget cycle reworking the budget anyway. Moreover, many critics argue that the real problem in the budget is not lack of time, but the political demands placed on representatives to protect local concerns.

See also Budget, Federal; Congress.

References Daniel P. Franklin, *Making Ends Meet: Congressional Budgeting in the Age of Deficits* (1993); Donald F. Kettl, *Deficit Politics: Public Budgeting in Its Institutional and Historical Context* (1992); Howard E. Shuman, *Politics and the Budget: The Struggle between the President and the Congress* (1992).

U

Uncontrollable Spending

The portion of the federal budget that cannot be reduced or increased by Congress through the normal appropriations process, but requires a change in federal law, is referred to as uncontrollable spending. Entitlement programs are one of the most common types of such spending. The amount of money that is spent in any particular entitlement program is determined by the number of people who are eligible to receive benefits, and not by predetermined appropriations levels established by Congress. The only way that Congress can reduce spending in an entitlement program is by rewriting the laws governing eligibility requirements and individual benefits. Conversely, discretionary spending programs are considered controllable because their expenditure levels can be altered simply through changes in the amounts allocated in the federal budget. Approximately three-fourths of the federal budget is considered uncontrollable. The large proportion of the budget devoted to uncontrollable spending programs is considered one of the major impediments in efforts to balance the federal budget.

See also Backdoor Spending; Budget, Federal; Budget Deficit, Federal; Discretionary Spending; Entitlements.
References Daniel P. Franklin, *Making Ends Meet: Congressional Budgeting in the Age of Deficits* (1993); Howard E. Shuman, *Politics and the Budget: The Struggle between the President and the Congress* (1992).

Unfunded Mandate Reform Act

See Mandates, Federal.

Unicameralism

In 1934, progressive reformer and U.S. Senator George Norris helped convince the state of Nebraska to consolidate its legislature into one house. Nebraska is the only state in the nation today that has a unicameral legislature, though some reformers argue that one-house legislatures are more accountable and effective than are traditional bicameral ones. The National Municipal League's Model State Constitution has routinely advocated unicameralism. In the 1970s, former California Assembly Speaker Jesse Unruh, a leader in the nationwide legislative reform movement, called for a move to one house. Yet despite these efforts, the states have given little serious attention to departing from the bicameral tradition. In the early 1990s, some attention was focused on unicameralism again as a means to help states reduce the cost of government.

See also Legislative Reform Movement; Model State Constitution; Unruh, Jesse.
References George S. Blair, *American Legislatures: Structure and Process* (1967); David C. Saffell, *State and Local Government: Politics and Public Policies* (1993); Jesse Unruh, "Unicameralism: The Wave of the Future" (1972); Pat Wunnicke, "Fifty Years without a Conference Committee: Nebraska Unicameral Legislature" (1987).

Unit Rule

The unit rule is a procedure formerly used by the Democratic Party in which all the delegates to the national nominating convention from an individual state were required to vote for the candidate supported by the majority of the state's delegation. The party banned the unit rule in 1971 as part of its efforts to make the presidential nomination process more representative of rank-and-file Democrats.

See also Hughes Commission; McGovern-Fraser Commission.
References William Crotty and John S. Jackson III, *Presidential Primaries and Nominations* (1985); Austin Ranney, *Curing the Mischiefs of Faction: Party Reform in America* (1975).

United States v. Lopez

In *United States v. Lopez* (1995), the U.S. Supreme Court ruled that the Gun-Free School Zones Act of 1990 was an unconstitutional intrusion of the federal government in the traditional function of state governments. The case was important because it marked the first time in nearly 60 years that the court had struck down a federal law as not being justified under the interstate commerce clause. Since 1936, the commerce clause has provided the constitutional foundation for the federal government's increased involvement in all areas of the nation's economic life. In this case, however, the court ruled that there was no economic connection to justify the law. Although the long-term significance of the case is unclear, it may lead to a reduction in federal regulation on other activities for which there are no clear economic ties.

See also Federal-State Relations; *Seminole Tribe of Florida v. Florida.*
References Holly Idelson, "High Court Strikes Down Law Banning Guns Near Schools" (1995); Michael A. Pagano and Ann O'M. Bowman, "The State of American Federalism, 1994–1995" (1995).

United Steelworkers of America v. Weber

In *United Steelworkers of America v. Weber* (1979), an affirmative action case, the U.S. Supreme Court deviated from previous rulings by upholding the constitutionality of the use of quotas to overcome racial discrimination. The Court ruled 5 to 2 in favor of a program used by Kaiser Chemical that reserved 50 percent of its training program spots for racial minorities. The program had been implemented as a way to give African-Americans better opportunities to be placed in jobs traditionally held by white employees. The Court ruled that, because of its voluntary nature, the plan did not violate the antidiscrimination rules of the Civil Rights Act of 1964.

See also Affirmative Action; Civil Rights Act of 1964; *Fullilove v. Klutznick; Regents of the University of California v. Bakke;* Reverse Discrimination; *Ward's Cove Packing Co. v. Frank Antonio;* Women's Movement.
References Susan D. Clayton and Faye J. Crosby, *Justice, Gender, and Affirmative Action* (1992); John Charles Daly and William B. Allen, *Affirmative Action and the Constitution* (1987).

United We Stand America

Presidential candidate and Texas business tycoon H. Ross Perot founded United We Stand America, a political organization, during the 1992 election campaign. Critical of Republican and Democratic squabbling in Congress that led to continual gridlock, Perot and his supporters posed that the government should be run more like a business, and that the president should have more power to push reforms through. Perot and his organization lost the 1992 election, but he gained more votes as a third-party candidate than anyone since Theodore Roosevelt in 1912. During the 1996 elections, United We Stand America was actively involved with Perot in seeking another presidential candidate to promote its reformist agenda.

See also Perot, H. Ross; Third Parties.
Reference Theodore J. Lowi and Benjamin Ginsberg, *Democrats Return to Power: Politics and Policy in the Clinton Era* (1994); H. Ross Perot, *United We Stand: How We Can Take Back Our Country* (1992).

Unruh, Jesse (1922–1987)

As speaker of the California Assembly in the 1960s, Jesse Unruh, a Democrat from Long Beach, championed the modernization of the California legislature. He then played a prominent role in leading the legislative reform movement of the late 1960s and the 1970s. Unruh is also remembered for his advocacy of a unicameral legislature and his involvement in state legislative campaigns. In the 1970s and 1980s, legislative leaders across the nation began to follow Unruh's lead in channeling funds to candidates in legislative campaigns, a trend that has been heavily criticized by campaign finance reformers.

See also Legislative Caucus Campaign Committees; Legislative Reform Movement; Transfers; Unicameralism.
References Lou Cannon, *Ronnie and Jesse: A Political Odyssey* (1969); Richard A. Clucas, *The Speaker's Electoral Connection: Willie Brown and the California Assembly* (1995).

Urban League

See National Urban League.

U.S. Term Limits

U.S. Term Limits, a Washington, D.C.-based organization, is the nation's leading advocate for term limits on members of Congress and on state and local officials. Founded in 1992, U.S. Term Limits currently has 115,000 members. The organization has been involved in term limits campaigns in more than 20 states and numerous communities. It also helped defend term limits in the Supreme Court case of *U.S. Term Limits v. Thornton.* Paul Jacobs is the organization's executive director.

See also Term Limits; *U.S. Term Limits v. Thornton.*

U.S. Term Limits v. Thornton

In the 1995 case *U.S. Term Limits v. Thornton,* the U.S. Supreme Court ruled that individual states could not independently establish term limits on the states' members of Congress. The Court majority argued that states do not have the power to create additional restrictions on legislators beyond those in the Constitution. The decision threw out federal term limit laws that had been enacted in 23 states in recent years. The decision means that enactment of term limits on federal legislators will require the passage of a constitutional amendment.

See also Term Limits.
References Holly Idelson, "States' Rights Loses in Close Vote" (1995); Michael A. Pagano and Ann O'M. Bowman, "The State of American Federalism, 1994–1995" (1995).

User Fees

A user fee is a type of tax that is levied directly on the beneficiary of a government service or program. Charges for toll roads, waste disposal, and city recreational programs are all examples of user fees. Since the 1970s, local and state governments have increasingly employed user fees to compensate for declines in other revenue sources. By 1990, user fees accounted for more than 16 percent of local and state government revenue. Many economists advocate user fees as a relatively efficient form of taxation, because charging such fees forces government programs to compete in a market environment. Others see these fees as fairer than other forms of taxation because people who do not use particular programs or services are not charged. Conversely, user fees are criticized because they are a type of regressive tax; they deny poorer citizens access to particular government programs and services.

See also Benefit Principle; Finance, Local; Progressive Tax; Regressive Tax; Taxes.

References Ann O'M. Bowman and Richard C. Kearney, *State and Local Government* (1993); John L. Mikesell, *Fiscal Administration: Analysis and Applications for the Public Sector* (1991); Henry J. Raimondo, "State Budgeting in the Nineties" (1993).

V

Value-Added Tax (VAT)

The value-added tax is a type of consumption tax that has been championed as an effective form of taxation for increasing investments and generating economic growth. The VAT is similar to the traditional sales tax, but broader in its application. With the sales tax, the government places a levy on final retail sales, but not on all business transactions, including the purchase of services and wholesale goods. Under VAT, however, taxes are levied on transactions made at all stages of production. For a small manufacturer, for example, a levy is placed on the goods and services the manufacturer buys from suppliers in order to make its product as well as on the goods the manufacturer sells to other companies and to the public. The levy is called a value-added tax because the amount of tax that a business has to pay directly to the government reflects only the amount of value the business has added to its product. There is more than one way to construct a value-added tax, but one of the most common proposals allows a business to deduct the taxes it pays when purchasing goods from the amount of taxes it collects from the sale of its product. After making this deduction, the business pays the remainder of what it has collected to the government.

Conservative reformers argue that the VAT is preferable to the income tax because it dampens consumption and encourages individuals to save. With increased saving, there is more money available for investment, which will stimulate economic growth. Other proponents argue that the tax is needed to make American goods more competitive with those produced in Europe, where the VAT is popular. The problem, these proponents argue, is that many European countries apply a VAT to American imports but refund the value-added taxes paid by European exporters, which makes American goods less popular abroad and European imports more attractive in the United States. Detractors argue that the VAT is an unfair regressive tax that falls disproportionately on poor and middle-class citizens. When each step of the production of goods is taxed, the increases in costs are ultimately tacked onto the final purchase prices and are paid for by consumers. As for its effect on American goods, opponents argue that the presence of the VAT in Europe is compensated for by the exchange rate.

See also Consumption Tax; Progressive Tax; Regressive Tax; Sales Tax; Taxes.

References Werner Z. Hirsch and Anthony M. Rufolo, *Public Finance and Expenditure in a Federal System* (1990); Joseph J. Minarik, *Making Tax Choices* (1985); Alan A. Tait, *Value Added Tax:*

International Practice and Problems (1988); Christopher Zimmerman, "Flat Tax, Sales Tax, or VAT?" (1995).

Vice President

Since the late 1970s, the vice presidents have assumed a far greater role in the executive branch than in the past. President Carter relied extensively on Walter Mondale for advice and for his participation in developing policy. President Reagan turned to George Bush to chair a number of key presidential committees, including the National Security Council's Crisis Management Team and the Task Force on Regulatory Relief. More recently, President Clinton has had Al Gore lead the federal government's efforts to reform the bureaucracy and to provide advice on environmental issue.

Along with this change in role, the vice president has also begun to receive greater staff and budget support. George Edwards and Stephen Wayne report that the size of the vice president's staff has tripled over the past 30 years.

See also Administrative Reorganization; Bureaucracy; Cabinet; President; Twenty-fifth Amendment.
References George C. Edwards III and Stephen J. Wayne, *Presidential Leadership: Politics and Policy Making* (1990); Jules Whitcover, *Crapshoot: Rolling the Dice on the Vice Presidency* (1992).

Victims' Bill of Rights

See Crime.

Vietnam War

American involvement in Vietnam started in the early 1950s, when the United States began providing monetary aid, military hardware, and advisers to help the French and South Vietnamese stop the spread of communism. After the passage of the Tonkin Gulf Resolution on 7 August 1964, the U.S. effort began to escalate rapidly. By the time the war ended with the signing of the Paris Peace Accord in 1973, more than 58,000 Americans were dead and another 300,000 wounded.

The effects of the war on American politics have been profound: it helped reshape the direction of foreign and domestic policy, reduce Americans' trust in government, and force reform onto the political agenda.

The war's effects on U.S. foreign policy may be its most direct and long-lasting legacy. Disillusionment with the war led many Americans and foreign policy experts to question the wisdom of the U.S. policy of containment, which had been the cornerstone of the nation's foreign policy since the end of the Second World War. With the public less enthusiastic about military conflict, Nixon began to move away from containment as he reached out to the Soviet Union through a new foreign policy called détente. In addition, Congress's mounting discontent with the war and Nixon's policies led to the passage of the War Powers Resolution in 1973, which was designed to give Congress greater control over U.S. involvement in foreign wars.

Over the long run, the war has made the public and military leaders less willing to use American forces in conflict abroad, or what is called the Vietnam syndrome. Even in such recent foreign military affairs as the Persian Gulf War and the sending of peacekeeping troops to Bosnia in 1995, the nation's political leaders had to assure the public that these events would not lead to "another Vietnam."

The war has had effects in areas other than foreign affairs, however. The exceedingly high cost of the war, along with Congress's unwillingness to pass a tax to support it, has been blamed for destroying the Great Society and other innovative social programs of the 1960s, as it absorbed the funds that otherwise would have flowed to them. It is also been blamed for generating the large increase in inflation in the late 1960s and 1970s that led to Richard Nixon's introduction of wage and price controls in 1972. When the nation's inflation rate could not be controlled through traditional Keynesian economics in the late 1970s, support grew for more conservative economic proposals.

More indirectly, the Vietnam War was one of the key political events over the past three decades that helped create widespread distrust of the nation's political system. Other factors have also generated demands for reform, but this distrust has remained central in Americans' desire to reshape the political system since the 1960s.

See also Containment; Détente; Foreign Policy; Great Society; Johnson, Lyndon B.; Nixon, Richard M.; Stagflation; Wage and Price Controls; War Powers Resolution; Watergate.
References John Robert Greene, *The Limits of Power: The Nixon and Ford Administrations* (1992); George C. Herring, *America's Longest War: The United States and Vietnam, 1950–1975* (1986); Ole R. Holsti and James N. Rosenau, *American Leadership in World Affairs: Vietnam and the Breakdown of Consensus* (1984); James A. Nathan and James K. Oliver, *Foreign Policy Making and the American Political System* (1994).

Volcker Commission

The Volcker Commission was established in the late 1980s to propose reforms to lower the costs and improve the functioning of the federal civil service. The commission's final report, which was issued in 1989, called for a reduction in personnel regulations, better pay, cutbacks in the number of political appointees, and other reforms to improve the morale and productivity of government workers after a decade of bureau-bashing under the Reagan administration. The commission, which was known formally as the National Commission on the Public Service, was headed by Paul A. Volcker, the former chair of the Federal Reserve System.

See also Bureaucracy; Public Service Deregulation.
References Robert E. Cleary and Kimberly Nelson, "The Volcker Commission Report Fades Away: A Case Study in Non-implementation" (1993); Frank J. Thompson, ed., *Revitalizing State and Local Public Service: Strengthening Performance, Accountability, and Citizen Confidence* (1993).

Volcker, Paul A. (b. 1927)

Paul A. Volcker, conservative economist and former undersecretary of the treasury, was appointed chairman of the Federal Reserve Board in 1979, where he introduced the use of a monetarist policy in guiding the U.S. economy. After resigning from the board in 1987, Volcker was appointed chairman of the National Commission on the Public Service, which investigated ways to improve the civil service.

See also Monetarism, Monetary Policy, Volcker Commission.
References Howard E. Shuman, *Politics and the Budget: The Struggle between the President and the Congress* (1992); Frank J. Thompson, ed., *Revitalizing State and Local Public Service: Strengthening Performance, Accountability, and Citizen Confidence* (1993).

Vote by Mail

See All-Mail-Ballot Elections.

Vote Dilution

See Electoral Discrimination.

Voter Registration

One of the primary reasons voter turnout is low in the United States is the nation's voter registration system. In most countries, the national government is responsible for registering voters. In the United States, however, the burden of registration falls entirely on the voters. Moreover, many states have created barriers that make it difficult to register, reducing the ability of citizens to vote. Election studies have found that if voting registration were made easier, the number of citizens who actually vote would increase by as much as 14–15 percent.

Over the past three decades, a variety of reforms have been adopted to open up the voter registration process, including an end to poll taxes and the passage of the Voting Rights Act of 1965. A number of reform groups have advocated further changes in voter registration law in order to encourage greater voter participation. Three of the most prominent reform proposals have been to make registration more convenient, to increase the government's involvement in registering voters, and to allow election-day registration.

To make registration more convenient, reformers have advocated increasing the number of government agencies that can register voters, as well as allowing voters to register by mail. Proposals to use state agencies to register voters are often referred to as motor voter laws, because they allow voters to register when they renew their driver's licenses. Since the mid-1970s, several states have passed motor voter laws allowing citizens to register when they interact with a variety of state agencies. The passage of these laws appears to have increased voter registration in these states. In 1993, the federal government passed its own motor voter law, the National Voter Registration Act. Among other features, the act requires states to allow voters to register by mail and when they apply for driver's licenses. The act took effect in January 1995.

Many reformers believe, however, that the passage of motor voter laws is still not enough to improve the nation's poor voting rate. The problem, these reformers argue, is that the act of registering to vote rests entirely on the initiative of individual citizens. Various reform proposals have been put forward to increase the government's responsibility for registering voters. One of the most prominent proposals calls for the use of the U.S. Postal Service's National Change of Address (NCOA) database to keep voters on the voting rolls after they move. More extreme proposals call for giving the government direct responsibility to ensure that all eligible citizens are registered to vote, as is done in Europe.

A third major reform proposal is to allow election-day voter registration. Most states require that voters register to vote by a certain number of days prior to an election. Various studies have shown that the closer the deadline is to the election, the more people will register and vote. Thus reformers advocate that voters be allowed to register on the election day, as is the case in Maine, Minnesota, and Wisconsin.

Opponents of these various reform proposals argue that they are too expensive and beyond the proper role of the government. Election-day registration, which is the cheapest and least obtrusive reform, is criticized as allowing the possible introduction of voting fraud. Finally, both political parties have voiced opposition to these reforms out of fear that they will alter the nation's party structure.

See also Agency Registration; Electoral Discrimination; Human SERVE; National Change of Address and Voter Registration; National Voter Registration Act; Poll Tax; Voting Rights Act.

References Frances Fox Piven and Richard A. Cloward, *Why Americans Don't Vote* (1988); Ruy A. Teixeira, *The Disappearing American Voter* (1992).

Voting Age

See Twenty-sixth Amendment.

Voting Rights Act

The Voting Rights Act is considered one of the great successes of the civil rights movement, as it extended the right to vote to African-Americans and other politically excluded groups. When passed in 1965, the act was initially designed to force southern states to open up the political process to African-Americans. Subsequent extensions, however, expanded the act's coverage to protect language minorities, individuals with disabilities, and minorities living outside the South.

The ability of citizens to participate freely in the political process has long been considered a fundamental ideal in American democracy, yet historically, vast segments of U.S. society have been excluded from participation. Prior to the Civil War, some states allowed free blacks to vote, but for the most part blacks and other non-European minorities were effectively deprived of the right to vote.

The end of the Civil War brought not only freedom to slaves, but the passage of several federal laws that were designed to ensure the rights of African-Americans to participate in the electoral process. The most important was the Fifteenth Amendment to the U.S. Constitution, which said that citizens could not be denied the right to vote because of their race or color. Along with this amendment, Congress passed several laws designed to enforce the provisions of the Fifteenth Amendment.

Initially, these efforts were quite successful, with African-American males voting and winning elected office throughout the South. The success, however, was short-lived. When Reconstruction ended in the late 1870s, African-Americans' ability to participate in elections ended with it. Over the next decade, the right of African-Americans to vote was taken away through violence, electoral fraud, and the passage of discriminatory state laws that restricted suffrage.

One of the major goals of civil rights groups throughout the twentieth century has been to extend the right to vote to African-Americans. Although African-Americans made some political gains through litigation and in Congress during the 1940s and 1950s, their ability to vote remained severely limited into the 1960s.

In the early 1960s, leading civil rights groups, including the Southern Christian Leadership Conference and the Student Nonviolent Coordinating Committee, began to increase their efforts to force an end to the discriminatory voting practices in the South. The turning point in the battle over voting rights was a protest march from Selma to Montgomery, Alabama, on 7 March 1965. The march provoked nationwide outrage when state and local police violently attacked the protesters after they crossed the Edmund Pettus Bridge.

President Lyndon Johnson responded rapidly to the outrage, sending the Voting Rights Act to Congress on 15 March 1965, a week after the Selma protest. Less than five months later, the act had been overwhelmingly approved by both houses of Congress and signed into law.

The Voting Rights Act was designed to enforce the Fifteenth Amendment to ensure that African-Americans were not denied the right to vote by states and local governments. The act represented an important change from previous civil rights legislation because it provided for direct federal intervention to secure this goal.

Several sections of the act are considered particularly important. Section 2 specifically forbids states and other political subdivisions to use any prerequisite, practice, or procedure "which results in a denial or abridgement of the right of any citizen of the United States to vote on account of race or color."

Section 4 was designed to eliminate the use of literacy tests and similar practices that were used to keep minorities from registering to vote in the South. The act did not ban literacy tests, but outlawed their use as a means to discriminate. Section 4 set up a formula for identifying when literacy tests were being used for discriminatory purposes. If a local or state government was found to discriminate, the U.S. attorney general was given the authority to suspend the use of the tests and send federal examiners to the area to compel the registration of qualified applicants. The formula was carefully crafted so that the act applied to only seven southern states (Alabama, Georgia, Louisiana, Mississippi, South Carolina, Virginia, and parts of North Carolina).

Section 5 may have been the most significant component of the law. This section required state and local governments that had discriminated in the past to obtain the prior approval of the attorney general or a federal court before they could change election laws or procedures. This "preclearance provision" was designed to stop southern states from finding creative ways to circumvent the intent of the act.

The initial effects of the act were dramatic. It has been estimated that by 1970, five years after passage of the act, the number of African-Americans registered to vote in the South had increased by 1 million. Today, African-American voting rates rival those of white Americans, and there are more than 7,500 African-American elected officials nationwide, including more than 3,000 in the seven states originally targeted by the Voting Rights Act.

Since its original passage, the act has been readopted three times, and each time its scope has been expanded. In 1970, a new formula was included to extend the coverage of the act to governments outside the South. An amendment was also added directly prohibiting literacy tests for five years. In 1975, the act was expanded to protect the rights of language minorities, including American Indians, Asian-Americans, and Hispanics. Among other consequences of this revision is that election materials must now be provided in languages other than English. The 1975 revisions also permanently banned literacy tests.

The act was extended again in 1982 for 25 years. One of the major changes in the 1982 revisions was an amendment to Section 2 requiring the use of a "results tests" in determining whether a practice was discriminatory or not. The amendment was added to reverse a Supreme Court ruling that said that the act applies only to practices created with the intent to discriminate. Pressure for this revision came from a broad coalition of civil rights groups, which argued that the Supreme Court interpretation made it unreasonably difficult to protect the right to vote, because it required that plaintiffs prove the government's intent.

One result of this amendment, as well as subsequent court decisions, has been the growing effort of federal officials to ensure the election of minorities to office, particularly through the creation of districts that have large enough majorities of minorities to elect minority officials (majority-minority districts). The amendment has been criticized by conservatives, who argue that it requires the proportional representation of minorities. The 1982 revisions also included protection for illiterate and disabled Americans.

Supreme Court reaction to the act and its later revisions has been mixed. Initially, the Court was very supportive of the act, upholding its constitutionality in *South Carolina v. Katzenbach* and interpreting its coverage very broadly in *Allen v. State Board of Elections* and *White v. Regester*. In the 1970s, the Court began to take a narrower view of the act, culminating in the case of *City of Mobile v. Bolden*. This was the case in which the Court asserted that a government's intent must be taken into account in assessing discrimination claims.

After the passage of the 1982 revisions, the Court initially upheld the new provisions of the act in *Thornburg v. Gingles*. In the early 1990s, however, the Court began to raise new issues about the act. In particular, the Court began to question how far a government must go to ensure minorities are elected to office. In the case of *Shaw v. Reno*, the Court remanded a North Carolina redistricting plan to a federal district court because of the "extremely irregular" shape of the districts that had been drawn to help African-American candidates. In making its decision, the Court questioned the use of race-conscious districting. In *Miller v. Johnson*, the Court ruled that redistricting plans may be unconstitutional if race is the "predominant" factor used in shaping district boundaries. The Supreme Court is expected to return to this question again in the near future, and to establish clearer guidelines on the extent to which the electoral system should be structured to ensure that minorities are elected to office.

See also *Allen v. State Board of Elections; City of Mobile v. Bolden;* Civil Rights Movement; Electoral Discrimination; Johnson, Lyndon B.; Literacy Tests; Majority-Minority Districts; Mexican American Legal Defense and Educational Fund; *Miller v. Johnson;* Preclearance Provision; *Shaw v. Reno; South Carolina v. Katzenbach;* Southern Christian Leadership Conference; Student Nonviolent Coordinating Committee; *Thornburg v. Gingles; White v. Regester.*

References Chandler Davidson, ed., *Minority Vote Dilution* (1989); Bernard Grofman and Chandler Davidson, eds., *Controversies in Minority Voting: The Voting Rights Act in Perspective* (1992); "The Voting Rights Act after *Shaw v. Reno*" (1995).

Voting System Standards

See Election Administration.

Voting Technology

See Election Administration.

W

Wage and Price Controls

Until the 1970s, the primary way in which the federal government attempted to control inflation was to use fiscal and monetary policies to slow down the economy, a strategy that invariably resulted in higher unemployment. When inflation soared in the early 1970s, however, President Richard Nixon sought to find an alternative solution that would reduce inflation, but without the detrimental effect on employment. To do this, he imposed a nationwide three-month freeze on wages and prices beginning in August 1971. The Kennedy and Johnson administrations had established voluntary guidelines for wages and prices in selected industries in the 1960s, but Nixon's actions represented an unprecedented intrusion of the federal government into the private sector. Nixon's action enjoyed widespread popular support at the time, though most economists now argue that it had little to no long-term effect on the inflation rate.

Except for a brief period in 1979 when President Jimmy Carter introduced voluntary controls on wages and prices, there have been no other times when the federal government has attempted to use this type of direct action to control inflation. Wage and price controls are referred to by economists as incomes policy.

See also Economic Policy; Fiscal Policy.
References Lloyd G. Reynolds, *Economics: A General Introduction* (1988); Herbert Stein, *Presidential Economics: The Making of Economic Policy from Roosevelt to Clinton* (1994).

War on Poverty

The War on Poverty consisted of a series of initiatives put forward by Presidents John Kennedy and Lyndon Johnson in the 1960s to reduce poverty in the United States. These initiatives included a tax cut to stimulate investments, an increase in federal funds to individual communities to combat poverty, and the creation of several specific programs to aid the poor. The War on Poverty represented a new, more active role on the part of the federal government in trying to solve the nation's ills.

See also Great Society; Johnson, Lyndon B.
References Eli Ginzberg and Robert M. Solow, *The Great Society: Lessons for the Future* (1974); Marshall Kaplan and Peggy L. Cuciti, *The Great Society and Its Legacy: Twenty Years of U.S. Social Policy* (1986).

War Powers Resolution

With growing public discontent over the Vietnam War and new revelations that President Richard Nixon was secretly bombing the neutral country of Cambodia, Congress attempted to reassert its power to declare war and gain control over the president's use of military force by passing the War Powers Resolution in 1973. Adopted over the president's veto, the resolution contained three major provisions: it required the president to consult with Congress before committing American troops in foreign nations where hostilities were imminent, to report the commitment of U.S. troops within 48 hours, and to withdraw these troops within 60 days if Congress did not declare war or explicitly approve of their mission.

The resolution has been generally considered ineffective in achieving its goals. Most presidents have abided by the reporting requirements when committing troops abroad, and in 1991, President George Bush both asked for and received congressional approval for sending troops to Iraq in accordance with the resolution's requirements. The resolution has not, however, restricted the president's ability to deploy troops as he sees fit.

See also Congress; Foreign Policy; President; Vietnam War.

References Roger H. Davidson, *The Postreform Congress* (1992); Roger H. Davidson and Walter J. Oleszek, *Congress and Its Members* (1994); James L. Sundquist, *Constitutional Reform and Effective Government* (1992).

Wards Cove Packing Co. v. Frank Antonio

In *Wards Cove Packing Co. v. Frank Antonio* (1989), the U.S. Supreme Court placed a greater burden on individuals charging discrimination in the workplace to prove that their treatment was unfair. The Court's ruling was considered a major blow against the nation's affirmative action laws and helped lead to the passage of the Civil Rights Act of 1991.

See also Affirmative Action; Civil Rights Act of 1991; Reverse Discrimination.

References Christopher Jencks, *Rethinking Social Policy: Race, Poverty, and the Underclass* (1992); Julia C. Ross, "New Civil Rights Act" (1992); Jared Taylor, *Paved with Good Intentions: The Failure of Race Relations in Contemporary America* (1992).

Warren, Earl (1891–1974)

Earl Warren was a former California governor who served as chief justice of the U.S. Supreme Court from 1953 to 1969, leading the Court in one of the most active and controversial periods in its history. One of Warren's first actions as chief justice was to help mold the unanimous *Brown v. Board of Education* decision in 1954 that banned racial segregation in education. The decision paved the way for several civil rights reforms affecting African-Americans. The rest of Warren's tenure on the Court brought a string of far-reaching decisions on civil rights and civil liberties involving political dissidents, criminals, minorities, and others. Warren's actions were heavily praised by liberals, and criticized by conservatives.

See also Civil Rights Movement; Judicial Activism; Supreme Court.

References Robert A. Carp and Ronald Stidham, *Judicial Process in America* (1993); William C. Louthan, *The United States Supreme Court: Lawmaking in the Third Branch of Government* (1991).

Watergate

The scandal known as Watergate arose from a break-in at the Democratic National Committee's (DNC) headquarters in the Watergate Hotel in 1972. Watergate was the most important political scandal in U.S. history, forcing the resignation of the president, creating profound distrust of the federal government, and leading to concerted efforts to reform the nation's political system.

The events of Watergate began on 17 June 1972, when five burglars were arrested in the DNC's headquarters, including one who was the security director for President Richard Nixon's reelection organization. When the investigation of the break-in led to other people in the reelection campaign and the White House, Nixon told his chief advisers, "I want you to stonewall it, let them plead the Fifth Amendment, cover-up or anything else, if it'll save the plan." Despite the cover-up effort, the investigation slowly revealed that the break-in was part of a larger covert campaign to reelect Nixon as president. This campaign included the acceptance of illegal campaign contributions and the use of the CIA, FBI, and IRS to embarrass and harass Nixon's opponents. The final turning point of the investigation was when it was disclosed that Nixon had secretly taped his own conversations in the White House. The tapes revealed that Nixon had participated in the cover-up, which led to his resignation on 27 July 1974.

Coming at a time when Americans were already disillusioned with the federal government because of the disastrous war in Vietnam, the Watergate scandal helped compound the growing distrust of the political system and led to demands for reform. Watergate helped compel the federal government to strengthen federal rules governing campaign finance, ethics, and public access to government records. It led to the creation of the position of inspector general to weed out fraud in the bureaucracy, and the Office of Special Prosecutor to investigate charges of misconduct by leading government figures. Watergate also helped stimulate similar reform efforts at the state level.

More important than these specific laws are the effects that Watergate has had on political attitudes in the United States. Even though more than two decades have passed since Nixon's resignation, the public's trust in government has never rebounded. The result is that Americans today remain dissatisfied with the political system and open to promises of political reform.

See also Campaign Finance; Ethics; Ethics in Government Act; Federal Election Campaign Act; Independent Counsel; Inspector General Act; Nixon, Richard M.; Sunshine Rules; Vietnam War.

References Fred Emery, *Watergate: The Corruption of American Politics and the Fall of Richard M. Nixon* (1991); John Robert Greene, *The Limits of Power: The Nixon and Ford Administrations* (1992); Stanley I. Kutler, *The Wars of Watergate: The Last Crisis of Richard M. Nixon* (1990).

Watt, James (b. 1938)

James Watt served in President Ronald Reagan's cabinet as secretary of the interior. He continually challenged the regulatory structure that restricted mining, ranching, and logging activities on federal lands. An attorney from Arizona, Watt had served as president of the Mountain States Legal Foundation, which pushed for greater industrial access to public lands. Lambasted by environmentalists for his policies, Watt set a record in the 1980s for allowing the leasing of federal lands by various private enterprises. Coal and oil exploration of environmentally sensitive areas increased, and very little new land was protected for wildlife. Watt was forced out of office in 1983, not for his environmental policies, but because he had made ethnic slurs against members of a special commission.

See also Environmental Policy; Sagebrush Rebellion.

Reference John G. Francis and Richard Ganzel, *Western Public Lands: The Management of National Resources in a Time of Declining Federalism* (1984); William L. Graf, *Wilderness Preservation and the Sagebrush Rebellions* (1990).

Weak Mayor

In the weak mayor form of municipal government, the mayor has limited power and plays a secondary role to a dominant city council. The weak mayor system has been used by cities since the United States was founded, but near the turn of the century it began to fall into disfavor because it was easily controlled by political machines. Other forms of municipal government became preferred among reformers, especially the council-manager and strong mayor systems. In recent years, however, there has been some effort to revitalize city councils in order to make the councils more independent and capable and to improve representation. Despite these changes, most municipal reformers continue to see a need for a strong mayor or a city administrator to provide leadership and effective administration.

See also City Commission; Council-Manager; Party Machines; Strong Mayor.

References Ann O'M. Bowman and Richard C. Kearney, *State and Local Government* (1993); Terry Christensen, *Local Politics: Governing at the Grassroots* (1995); John J. Harrigan, *Political Change in the Metropolis* (1993).

Welfare

The nation's welfare policies constitute one of the primary battlegrounds today between liberals and conservatives over the proper role of government in U.S. society. In the 1960s, the federal government expanded the welfare system as it attempted to take a more active and direct role in solving the nation's social ills, creating such programs as the Great Society, the War on Poverty, food stamps, and Medicaid. Since the late 1970s, however, conservative opponents of these programs have enjoyed greater success in their campaign to roll back the welfare state.

Welfare is a generic term referring to public assistance programs for the needy. Of all the federal welfare programs, the largest and most controversial is Aid to Families with Dependent Children (AFDC), which is primarily distributed to single women with children. In 1993, more than 14 million Americans were on AFDC, two-thirds of whom were children. The total cost of AFDC, which is shouldered jointly by the federal government and the states, was more than $22 billion that year.

The most comprehensive effort to reform the nation's welfare policy in the past 50 years occurred in 1988 with the passage of the Family Support Act. This act tried to help welfare recipients to enter the workforce by requiring all recipients with children over three years of age to participate in state-run job skills programs. The act required all 50 states to create Job Opportunities and Basic Skills programs for this purpose, and to provide child care and other necessary support to allow recipients to attend.

Despite this reform effort, the demand for additional reforms remains strong. In his presidential campaign in 1992, Bill Clinton pledged to "end welfare as we know it." Two years later, the Republican Contract with America placed welfare reform among its ten goals. Many of the welfare reform proposals being discussed are similar in their desire to get recipients into the workforce, although the methods advocated are often different.

One of the most prominent conservative reforms proposed in recent years is workfare, which requires recipients to work in order to receive benefits. Conservative reformers also advocate placing limits on the number of years recipients can be eligible for AFDC and denying benefit increases to recipients who have additional children while receiving AFDC.

Liberal reformers oppose the punitive nature of these proposals, and argue that if the government is seriously going to try to encourage welfare recipients to work, it will have to provide additional support in helping recipients develop job skills and obtain child care. Finally, some welfare experts argue that instead of focusing simply on welfare recipients, the federal government should try to help both the working and nonworking poor to climb out of poverty. The way to do this is by ensuring health insurance and child support for parents who work in low-paying jobs.

See also Aid to Families with Dependent Children; Bridefare; Contract with America; Great Society; Learnfare; Medicaid; Moynihan, Daniel Patrick; Murray, Charles; Personal Responsibility Act; War on Poverty; Workfare.
References Christopher Jencks, *Rethinking Social Policy: Race, Poverty, and the Underclass* (1992); Jeffrey L. Katz, "Clinton Plans Major Shift in Lives of Poor People" (1994); Joseph A. Pechman and Michael S. McPherson, *Fulfilling America's Promise: Social Policies for the 1990s* (1992).

Wesberry v. Sanders

In *Wesberry v. Sanders* (1964), the U.S. Supreme Court required that all congressional districts within a state must be as close to the same population as is practical. The case set an important precedent in establishing population equality as a primary criterion for determining the fairness of congressional redistricting plans. The Court found that unequal population among districts gives greater weight to some citizens' votes than others, and thus constitutes a violation of the equal protection clause of the Constitution.

See also *Baker v. Carr; Davis v. Bandemer;* Gerrymandering; Reapportionment Revolution; Redistricting; *Reynolds v. Sims.*
References Gordon E. Baker, *The Reapportionment Revolution: Representation, Political Power, and the Supreme Court* (1966); William J. Keefe and Morris S. Ogul, *The American Legislative Process: Congress and the States* (1993); National Conference of State Legislatures Reapportionment Task Force, *Reapportionment Law: The 1990s* (1989).

Whistle-Blowing

Reporting by government employees of illegal or inappropriate practices within their own bureaucracies is referred to as whistle-blowing. Until the 1970s, the federal government had few formal procedures or laws that would encourage whistle-blowing or to protect whistle-blowers from retaliatory action by their superiors. In the 1970s, however, several laws were enacted to strengthen the use of whistle-blowing. The Inspector General Act of 1978 created a specific office to handle reports of wrongdoing made by government employees. The Civil Service Reform Act of 1978 created the Merit Systems Protection Broad, which, among other duties, was given the responsibility to investigate complaints of retaliatory action toward whistle-blowers. The Ethics in Government Act of 1978 created the Office of Special Prosecutor (later renamed Office of Independent Counsel) to investigate allegations of wrongdoing by high-ranking government officials. In addition, several specific regulatory acts, such as the Energy Reorganization Act of 1974, provided protections for employees in private industry who report misconduct.

Although these laws helped encourage and protect whistle-blowers, many reformers argued in the 1980s that the laws were still not strong enough to protect whistle-blowers from retaliation. Moreover, both the Office of Independent Counsel and the Merit Systems Protection Board were criticized for not being diligent enough in protecting whistle-blowers. The result was that in 1988 Congress voted to strengthen the Office of Independent Counsel and to provide greater protection to whistle-blowers.

See also Civil Service Reform Act of 1978; Ethics in Government Act; Ethics Reform Act of 1989; Independent Counsel; Inspector General Act; Merit Systems Protection Board.
Reference Myron Peretz Glazer and Penina Migdal Glazer, *The Whistleblowers: Exposing Corruption in Government and Industry* (1989).

White v. Regester

In *White v. Regester* (1973), the U.S. Supreme Court established a criterion for determining if a particular election procedure or practice violated the Voting Rights Act of 1965. The Court ruled that for a practice to be found unlawful, the plaintiffs must show that minority voters had less opportunity "to participate in the process and to elect representatives of their choice." This criterion, which is referred to as the White Test, offered a very broad interpretation of the Voting Rights Act, incorporating not only the right to vote but also the right to be represented.

The Supreme Court reversed the *White* decision in 1980 in *City of Mobile v. Bolden,* ruling that for a practice to be considered unlawful the plaintiff must prove that the government's intent in adopting the practice was to discriminate. Instead of focusing on intent, the *White* decision had emphasized the importance of examining voting practices within the "totality of circumstances" where they had been adopted. The *Bolden* decision was attacked by civil rights groups because it made it considerably more difficult to find a voting practice unlawful. *White*'s totality of circumstances had allowed the courts to look at election results, whereas *Bolden* said that was not enough.

A large coalition of civil rights groups joined together in lobbying Congress to incorporate the Supreme Court's findings in the *White* case directly into the Voting Rights Act when it came up for readoption in 1982. Congress agreed. The effect of this addition to the Voting Rights Act, along with subsequent Supreme Court decisions, has been to encourage governments to adopt voting procedures that ensure the election of minorities to office, particularly through the use of majority-minority districts.

See also *City of Mobile v. Bolden;* Electoral Discrimination; Majority-Minority Districts; *Shaw v. Reno; Thornburg v. Gingles;* Voting Rights Act.
References Chandler Davidson, ed., *Minority Vote Dilution* (1989); Bernard Grofman and Chandler Davidson, eds., *Controversies in Minority Voting: The Voting Rights Act in Perspective* (1992).

Winograd Commission

The Commission on Presidential Nomination and Party Structure, or the Winograd Commission, was one of several Democratic Party commissions created after the McGovern-Fraser Commission to re-reform the Democratic Party's presidential selection process. The commission's proposals, which were used in the 1980 election, set aside specific delegate seats for state party officials, who had been excluded from participating at the convention since the adoption of the McGovern-Fraser reforms in 1971. The commission also required the equal representation of women among the delegates to the nominating convention. It bound delegates to vote for the candidates they represented on the first convention ballot unless the candidates released them from this obligation. Finally, it ruled that state parties could not use open primaries to select delegates. The commission was chaired by Morley Winograd, the Michigan Democratic Party chairman.

See also Fairness Commission; Hunt Commission; McGovern-Fraser Commission; Mikulski Commission; National Primary; Open Primary; Political Parties; Presidential Primaries.
References William Crotty and John S. Jackson III, *Presidential Primaries and Nominations* (1985).

Winter Commission

The Winter Commission was established in 1991 to propose reforms to lower the costs and improve the delivery of state and local government programs. The commission's final report, which was issued in 1993, called on states to strengthen executive power to allow the governor to play a more important leadership role. At the same time, the commission advocated a reduction in middle managers and bureaucratic regulations to improve the responsiveness and efficiency of government workers. Many of these reforms were inspired by the movement to "reinvent government." The commission, which was known formally as the National Commission on the State and Local Public Service, was headed by Walter F. Winter, former governor of Mississippi.

See also Bureaucracy; Public Service Deregulation; Reinventing Government.
References Richard C. Elling, "The Line in Winter: An Academic Assessment of the First Report of the National Commission on the State and Local Public Service" (1994); Richard P. Nathan, "Reinventing Government: What Does It Mean?" (1995); Frank J. Thompson, ed., *Revitalizing State and Local Public Service: Strengthening Performance, Accountability, and Citizen Confidence* (1993).

Women's Movement

The women's movement generally refers to the efforts since the early 1960s to allow women to participate more fully and equally in U.S. society and politics. Although some of the movement's key goals have not been attained, it has been quite successful in changing the role of women in American society, bringing women into politics, and forcing government to consider the needs of women in public policy debates.

Historically, there have been several women's movements in the United States, dating back to the abolitionist and women's suffrage movements of the nineteenth and early twentieth centuries. The contemporary women's movement is usually tied to the creation of the President's Commission on the Status of Women in 1961 and the publication of Betty Friedan's book *The Feminine Mystique* two years later. Combined, these two events helped bring awareness and concern to the problems confronting women and energized a broad base of middle-class women to seek change.

The women's movement was given a strong organizational boost in 1966, when the National Organization for Women (NOW) was founded, with Friedan as its first president. Since then, NOW has served as the leading advocate for women's rights in the United States, though a number of other groups have been important as well, including the League of Women Voters, the National Federation of Business and Professional Women's Clubs, the Center for Women's Policy Studies, and the Women's Equity Action League.

The women's movement is generally considered to have helped improve the economic and political position of women by forcing Congress to consider the needs of women as it has adopted several major bills over the past three decades. Among the movement's successes was the Equal Pay Act of 1963, which required businesses to pay women the same amount as men when they perform the same duties. Title VII of the Civil Rights Act of 1964 banned discrimination against women in employment. Title IX of the Education Amendments Act of 1972 prohibited discrimination in education. The 1978 Pregnancy Non-discrimination Act outlawed employment discrimination against pregnant women. The Federal Family and Medical Leave Act of 1993 allowed women to take up to 12 weeks of unpaid leave for childbirth or adoption, or to care for family members with serious health conditions. As a result of these successes, the women's movement has helped expand the role women play in U.S. society, removing many social and economic barriers that have limited their career options.

In addition, the women's movement has increased the participation of women in politics, including widely expanding the number who have been able to win elected office. The number of women in statewide or national office prior to the 1960s was minimal. Only two women had served as governors, and the most who had ever served in Congress at any one time was no more than 19. The situation was better at the local level, but women still filled only a small percentage of seats on city councils and other local governing boards. By 1994, however, a woman had served as a vice presidential nominee for one of the major political parties, more than 55 women were serving in Congress, and the numbers of women in state and local offices had soared.

Despite these gains, the women's movement has not been completely successful in attaining its reform agenda. The defeat of the Equal Rights Amendment is often considered the movement's worst failure. In addition, many women continue to face economic and job-related discrimination. Finally, the rising percentage of the poor who are women is often considered one of the most troubling problems confronting the United States today.

See also Civil Rights Act of 1964; Civil Rights Movement; Ferraro, Geraldine; Friedan, Betty; National Organization for Women; O'Connor, Sandra Day; *Roe v. Wade*.
References Denise L. Baer and David A. Bositis, *Politics and Linkage in a Democratic Society* (1993); *The Book of the States 1994–95* (1994); Susan M. Hartmann, *From Margin to Mainstream: American Women and Politics since 1960* (1989).

Workfare

Workfare, a form of welfare that requires recipients to work in order to receive benefits, is one type of change that has been proposed for the U.S. welfare system. Workfare proposals have received increasing support among the public and politicians in recent years as a way to compel welfare recipients to enter the workforce. President Bill Clinton's 1994 proposal to reform the welfare system included specific workfare provisions, as did the Republican Party's Contract with America. Workfare is one of many conservative proposals that have been championed in recent years to lessen the role of government in society. Critics argue that there is no evidence from past studies that workfare reduces the welfare rolls or increases recipients' job skills.

See also Aid to Families with Dependent Children; Contract with America; Welfare.
References Dianna M. DiNitto, *Social Welfare: Politics and Public Policy* (1995); Demetra Smith Nightingale and Robert H. Haveman, eds., *The Work Alternative: Welfare Reform and the Realities of the Job Market* (1995).

Wright, James C., Jr. (b. 1922)

James C. Wright was a U.S. congressman from the state of Texas from 1955 to 1989; he served the last two years of his tenure in Congress as Speaker of the House. Wright's long and highly partisan career ended in scandal when his business dealings and royalties from a book were seen to create a conflict of interest with his public office. Wright's ethics violations drew fire from various groups, including Common Cause, many House Republicans, and some Democrats. Vehement and continued criticism from Republican Newt Gingrich led to a House Ethics Committee investigation and Wright's resignation in May 1989. The controversy over Wright's actions helped worsen public attitudes toward Congress and led to efforts to tighten House ethics rules in the late 1980s and early 1990s.

See also Congress; Ethics; Gingrich, Newt.
Reference Suzanne Garment, *Scandal: The Culture of Mistrust in American Politics* (1991); Leroy N. Rieselbach, *Congressional Reform: The Changing Modern Congress* (1994).

Z

Zero-Base Budgeting (ZBB)

Most government bodies rely on an incremental approach to budgeting, in which one year's allocation of funds serves as the base for the following year's allocation. Zero-base budgeting, however, tells government agencies to assume that their budgeting base is zero dollars and then to be prepared to defend their entire operation. In putting together their budget requests, the agencies are then asked to identify how their programs would be affected at different funding levels below and above the previous year's amount. This budgeting technique is seen as a way to force administrators to reexamine their programs more seriously each year and to give budget writers more insight into the potential effects of their funding decisions than occurs with incremental budgeting.

Techniques that are comparable to zero-base budgeting have been used since around the 1920s. In 1977, President Jimmy Carter introduced the use of zero-base budgeting for federal agencies. This practice ended during the Reagan administration. Some 20 states and 150 cities reported using zero-base budgeting in the mid- to late 1980s.

Zero-base budgeting has been criticized for demanding too much time from administrators and for producing budget decisions that are only marginally different from those produced by incrementalism.

See also Budgeting Techniques; Bureaucracy; Cost-Benefit Analysis; Incrementalism; Management by Objectives; Performance Budgeting; Program Budgeting.

References Donald F. Kettl, *Deficit Politics: Public Budgeting in Its Institutional and Historical Context* (1992); John L. Mikesell, *Fiscal Administration: Analysis and Applications for the Public Sector* (1991); *The Municipal Year Book 1989* (1989).

Chronology

1962 In *Baker v. Carr,* the U.S. Supreme Court rules that legislative apportionment is justiciable. This decision will lead to vast changes in electoral and legislative politics.

1963 Betty Friedan's book *The Feminine Mystique* is published, helping to launch the modern women's movement.

President John F. Kennedy is assassinated; Lyndon B. Johnson becomes president.

1963–1968 Through the Great Society and the War on Poverty, President Johnson leads the federal government into playing a more active role in solving the nation's social ills.

1964 The Twenty-fourth Amendment is ratified, banning the use of poll taxes in federal elections.

In *Wesberry v. Sanders* and *Reynolds v. Sims*, the U.S. Supreme Court establishes population equality as a primary criteria in determining the fairness of congressional and state legislative redistricting.

President Johnson introduces Creative Federalism to give the federal government more direct involvement with local governments in addressing the nation's problems.

The Civil Rights Act of 1964 is enacted.

Congress adopts the Tonkin Gulf Resolution, opening the door to greater U.S. military involvement in Vietnam.

Lyndon B. Johnson is reelected president.

1965 The Elementary and Secondary Education Act is enacted.

Medicare and Medicaid are signed into law, providing health care to the elderly and the poor.

Congress enacts the Voting Rights Act, which ensures African-Americans of the right to vote in southern states.

The Department of Housing and Urban Development is created.

President Johnson issues Executive Order 11246, requiring federal contractors to take "affirmative action" to ensure the employment and fair treatment of minorities.

President Johnson requires all federal agencies to use program budgeting as a way to improve bureaucratic efficiency and the budgeting process.

1966 In *Harper v. Virginia State Board of Elections*, the U.S. Supreme Court rules that the use of a poll tax in state and local elections is unconstitutional.

The Freedom of Information Act is adopted, requiring federal records to be made open to the public.

The National Organization of Women is founded.

The Department of Transportation is created.

The Model Cities Program is enacted to help solve the social and economic problems confronting the nation's urban centers.

1967 The Twenty-fifth Amendment is ratified. It establishes procedures for the vice president to become acting president if the president becomes incapacitated.

The President's Commission on Law Enforcement and Administration of Justice releases a report that calls for the consolidation and centralization of state courts, helping stimulate efforts to reform the court system.

Thurgood Marshall becomes the nation's first African-American U.S. Supreme Court justice.

The Twin Cities Metropolitan Council is created. It becomes a model for regional governments in the nation.

The Federal Judicial Center is created to conduct research on the judiciary and to propose reforms to improve the court's operation and administration.

1968 Martin Luther King, Jr., is assassinated.

The Hughes Commission unveils reform proposals for the Democratic Party's national nominating convention, helping to pave the way for the McGovern-Fraser reforms four years later.

As protests mount outside its convention hall in Chicago, the Democratic Party selects Hubert Humphrey as its presidential candidate even though Humphrey has not competed in any primary elections.

The Office of United States Magistrate is created to help reduce federal trial court caseload.

Richard M. Nixon is elected president.

1969–1974 President Nixon seeks to reduce tensions between the United States and the Soviet Union through a new foreign policy called détente.

1969 President Nixon introduces New Federalism to return greater power to the states.

In *Allen v. State Board of Elections*, the U.S. Supreme Court interprets the scope of the Voting Rights Act to cover not only casting a ballot, but a wide range of electoral practices and procedures.

Warren Burger replaces Earl Warren as chief justice of the U.S. Supreme Court.

The Stonewall riots in New York City spur the rise of the Gay Rights movement.

1970 The first Earth Day is held, helping to launch the environmental movement.

The Office of Management and Budget is created to provide the president with better oversight of the federal budget and improved management of the bureaucracy.

The Voting Rights Act is readopted and its coverage is expanded to include areas outside the South. Literacy tests are prohibited for five years.

Common Cause is founded by liberal Republican John Gardner to lobby for more open and accountable government.

The Legislative Reorganization Act is enacted, helping to democratize Congress. The act reduces the power of committee chairs and allows all members greater participation in the policy-making process.

1971 The House Democratic Party adopts the first set of Hansen Committee reforms, democratizing the House's structure and procedures.

The Citizens' Conference on State Legislatures releases its book *The Sometimes Governments*, helping to stimulate a nationwide movement to modernize state legislatures.

The *New York Times* begins publishing the Pentagon Papers, which reveal repeated distortions and political cover-ups by government officials regarding the war in Vietnam.

The Twenty-sixth Amendment is ratified. It lowers the minimum voting age to give 18-year-olds the right to vote.

President Nixon introduces wage and price controls as a way to reduce inflation but without the detrimental effect on employment.

In *Serrano v. Priest*, the California State Supreme Court rules that the use of the local property tax to fund education violates that state's constitution.

The Revenue Act of 1971 creates a checkoff system that allows taxpayers to earmark one dollar of their tax returns to help fund presidential campaigns.

Congress enacts the Federal Election Campaign Act to reduce spending in federal elections and improve campaign finance disclosure. The act also gives legal recognition to political action committees.

1972 President Nixon makes a historic trip to the People's Republic of China.

In *Shakman v. Democratic Party of Cook County*, a federal district judge prohibits the city of Chicago from hiring employees based on political grounds, helping to weaken the political machine led by Mayor Richard Daley.

Five burglars are arrested for breaking into the Democratic National Committee's headquarters at the Watergate Hotel in Washington, D.C., setting off the most important political scandal in the nation's history.

The McGovern-Fraser Commission proposals are used to select delegates to the Democratic Party's National Nominating Convention. These changes profoundly alter the presidential selection process.

President Nixon ends the convertibility of dollars into gold and allows the dollar's value to drop, which brings an end to the Bretton Woods Economic System.

Congress enacts the Case Act to restrain the president's use of executive agreements with other nations.

President Nixon's proposal for general revenue sharing is adopted by Congress.

Richard M. Nixon is reelected president.

The Freund Committee proposes the creation of a new national court of appeals between the federal court of appeals and the Supreme Court.

1973 House Democrats enact a second and more sweeping set of reforms proposed by the Hansen Committee, further democratizing the House's structure and procedures.

Recognizing a woman's right to privacy, the U.S. Supreme Court limits the government's power to regulate abortions in *Roe v. Wade*.

America's involvement in the Vietnam war ends with the signing of the Paris Peace Accord.

In *Rodriguez v. San Antonio Independent School District*, the U.S. Supreme Court upholds the use of property taxes to fund public schools. The decision strikes a blow against education reform.

President Nixon introduces the use of management by objectives among federal agencies.

In *White v. Regester*, the U.S. Supreme Court establishes broad criteria for determining if a particular election procedure or practice violates the Voting Rights Act of 1965.

The first of two oil price shocks in the 1970s helps generate the nation's worst inflation in more than 50 years.

Congress enacts the War Powers Resolution to reassert its influence over America's involvement in foreign wars.

1974 California enacts the Political Reform Act, a heavily praised package of lobbying reforms.

The Hruska Commission proposes the creation of a national court of appeals between the current federal appeals courts and the Supreme Court.

Congress enacts the Congressional Budget and Impoundment Control Act to reassert its control over the federal budget. The act establishes new budgetary procedures, creates the Congressional Budget Office, and limits the president's power to impound funds.

Richard Nixon resigns as president; Gerald R. Ford becomes the first nonelected president in the nation's history.

House Democrats adopt a final set of reforms from the Hansen Committee that includes an important provision strengthening the power of the House Speaker.

The Federal Election Campaign Act is revised, establishing limits on campaign contributions and expenditures, creating the Federal Elections Commission, and providing for the public funding of presidential elections.

1975 The House Democratic caucus introduces new procedures for making committee assignments to gain better control over the process.

The Indian Self-Determination and Education Assistance Act is enacted, providing for greater tribal self-government and more influence by Indians in the management of the Bureau of Indian Affairs.

The U.S. Senate reduces the threshold of votes needed to end a filibuster to three-fifths of the entire Senate membership.

The Voting Rights Act is readopted and its coverage is expanded to protect the rights of language minorities. Literacy test are permanently banned.

The Federal Election Commission issues the SunPAC ruling, giving clear legal recognition to business and corporate political action committees.

Congress enacts the Overseas Citizens Voting Rights Act, which ensures all U.S. citizens living abroad that they can vote in federal elections.

1976 In *Buckley v. Valeo*, the U.S. Supreme Court strikes down the Federal Election Campaign Act's limitations on campaign expenditures, arguing that they violate the First Amendment right to free speech. The Court also declares the Federal Election Commission unconstitutional.

The Railroad Revitalization and Reform Act is passed, marking the first successful effort to roll back federal regulation of the economy.

The Pound Conference brings together members of the legal profession, judicial scholars, and political activists to consider ways to improve the nation's judicial system.

Congress revises the Federal Election Campaign Act a second time, reconstituting the Federal Election Commission and making a number of minor changes.

In *National League of Cities v. Usery*, the U.S. Supreme Court rules that the federal government does not have the power to force state and city governments to abide by federal minimum wage laws.

In *Elrod v. Burns*, the U.S. Supreme Court rules that state and local employees cannot be fired because of their party affiliation, limiting the use of political patronage.

Congress enacts the Government in Sunshine Act to require federal agencies to open their meetings to the public.

The National Emergencies Act is adopted by Congress to restrict the president's use of emergency powers.

Colorado adopts the nation's first major sunset law to control the growth of the bureaucracy.

James E. Carter is elected president.

1977 President Carter makes human rights a cornerstone of his foreign policy.

The Senate adopts the Stevenson Committee reforms, restructuring the Senate's committee system and instituting fairer rules in the distribution of committee assignments.

The Koreagate scandal is exposed.

President Jimmy Carter introduces the use of zero-base budgeting for federal agencies.

The House of Representatives adopts a new ethics code proposed by the Obey Commission.

The Department of Energy is created.

1978 Oregon creates the Greater Portland Metropolitan Service District, which becomes a model for regional governments in the nation.

California voters adopt Proposition 13, launching a nationwide taxpayers' revolt.

In *Regents of the University of California v. Bakke*, the U.S. Supreme Court restricts the use of quotas in affirmative action programs.

The Televote project, an effort to hold a large-scale electronic town meeting, is tried in Hawaii.

Congress passes the Inspector General Act, creating the position of inspector general in a dozen major federal agencies and departments to investigate bureaucratic wrongdoing.

The Civil Service Reform Act is enacted to help increase the efficiency and effectiveness of the federal bureaucracy. The act creates the Senior Executive Service, the Office of Personnel Management, and the Merit Systems Protection Board.

The Airline Deregulation Act is enacted, marking another important victory for reformers seeking to roll back economic regulation in the late 1970s.

The Ethics in Government Act is adopted. It strengthens the federal government's conflict of interest rules, creates a government ethics office, and establishes new procedures for investigating allegations of government misconduct.

1979 The Cable-Satellite Public Affairs Network (C-SPAN) begins televising congressional proceedings.

The Sagebrush Rebellion emerges in western states, calling for the transfer of federal lands to state ownership.

A second oil price shock helps generate the nation's worst inflation in more than 50 years.

Paul Volcker is named chairman of the Federal Reserve Board. The Board introduces the use of strict monetarist policies to reduce inflation.

A federal district judge bans the firing of workers in Chicago on political grounds, further weakening the Daley machine.

The Department of Education is created.

Congress revises the Federal Election Campaign Act to allow state and local parties to spend unlimited amounts of money in party-building activities, spurring the growth of what is called soft money.

1980 The Abscam investigation becomes public.

The Depository Institutions Deregulation and Monetary Control Act partially deregulates the savings and loan industry, which helps to create the savings and loan crisis of the 1980s.

In *City of Mobile v. Bolden*, the U.S. Supreme Court rules that for an election procedure to be considered unlawful under the Voting Rights Act, the plaintiff must prove that a government's *intent* in adopting the procedure was to discriminate.

The Judicial Councils Reform and Judicial Conduct and Disability Act is enacted, establishing procedures for disciplining and filing complaints against federal judges.

Ronald W. Reagan is elected president.

Congress adopts the Paperwork Reduction Act to reduce federal paperwork demands placed on private citizens, government agencies, and others involved in governmental processes.

1981 President Reagan champions his own version of New Federalism to return power to the states and reduce government spending.

President Reagan's effort to use supply-side economics to stimulate growth is introduced through the Economic Recovery Tax Act. The act cuts taxes on corporations and the nation's wealthiest citizens, and helps create unprecedented federal budget deficits.

The Gramm-Latta budget resolution reduces domestic spending by $37.7 billion, marking the Reagan administration's first effort to roll back the government's support for social programs.

Sandra Day O'Connor becomes the nation's first female U.S. Supreme Court justice.

1982 The Court of Appeals for the Federal Circuit is created.

The Voting Rights Act is extended for 25 years. Revisions to the act require the use of "results tests" in determining whether a practice is discriminatory or not. The act is also expanded to protect illiterate and disabled Americans.

The Equal Rights Amendment fails to be ratified.

The Grace Commission is formed to identify ways to reduce waste in the federal government and to improve the management of the bureaucracy.

The federal debt surpasses $1 trillion.

The Garn-St. Germaine Depository Institutions Act completely deregulates the savings and loan industry, helping to create the savings and loan crisis of the 1980s.

1983 Congress adopts the Social Security Amendments to solve the financial crisis confronting Social Security.

The National Commission on Excellence in Education releases *A Nation at Risk*, which advocates education reform.

In *Immigration and Nationalization Service v. Chadha*, the U.S. Supreme Court strikes down the use of the legislative veto.

For the first time, the nation experiences a federal budget deficit of more than $200 billion.

1984 Five southern and northern states join together to hold their presidential primary elections on the same day, creating the first Super Tuesday election.

The Hunt Commission attempts to improve the presidential nominating process by introducing the use of superdelegates at the Democratic Party's national nominating convention.

Democrat Geraldine Ferraro becomes the first female vice presidential candidate for a major political party.

Congress enacts the Voting Accessibility for the Elderly and Handicapped Act to make absentee ballots more accessible to the elderly and the disabled.

The Comprehensive Crime Control Act creates a commission to investigate problems in sentencing and propose reforms in court sentencing.

Ronald W. Reagan is reelected president.

1985 In *Garcia v. San Antonio Metropolitan Transit Authority*, the U.S. Supreme Court overturns the *National League of Cities v. Usery* decision and profoundly strengthens the federal government's position over the states.

The Gramm-Rudman-Hollings Act is enacted to force Congress and the president to balance the federal budget. The act also creates new budgeting procedures.

1986 The Reagan administration becomes involved in the illegal sale of arms to Iran to gain release of American hostages in Lebanon in what becomes known as the Iran-Contra Affair.

In *Thornburg v. Gingles*, the U.S. Supreme Court upholds the constitutionality of the 1982 amendments to the Voting Rights Act and establishes new criterion for determining discriminatory voting practices.

In *Davis v. Bandemer*, the U.S. Supreme Court rules that partisan gerrymandering is a justiciable concern.

Congress enacts the Uniformed and Overseas Citizens Absentee Voting Act, consolidating the nation's absentee voting laws.

William Rehnquist is named as chief justice of the U.S. Supreme Court.

The federal debt surpasses $2 trillion.

President Reagan ends general revenue sharing.

Congress enacts the Tax Reform Act, one of the most comprehensive tax reform proposals ever enacted.

1987 Five U.S. senators meet with federal banking officials to help a major campaign contributor, leading to the Keating Five scandal.

Wisconsin adopts Learnfare, the first of several programs the state will introduce to reform welfare. Learnfare attempts to reduce welfare dependency by requiring the teenage children in welfare families to attend school.

A second Gramm-Rudman-Hollings bill is enacted to reduce the federal budget deficit with revised deficit targets.

President Reagan nominates Robert H. Bork to the U.S. Supreme Court.

The U.S. Sentencing Commission establishes sentencing guidelines for the federal courts.

1988 Congress enacts the Act to Improve the Administration of Justice, ending most of the U.S. Supreme Court's mandatory jurisdiction.

Congress enacts the Family Support Act, the nation's most important welfare reform in 50 years.

The Department of Veterans' Affairs is created.

George H. W. Bush is elected president.

Congress enacts the Judicial Improvements and Access to Justice Act to help relieve the caseload burden confronting the federal courts.

1989 The Volcker Commission proposes a series of reforms to improve the morale and productivity of government workers after a decade of bureau-bashing under the Reagan administration.

James Wright resigns as Speaker of the House in the wake of an ethics scandal.

The Ethics Reform Act places new ethics rules on members of Congress and the executive branch, while at the same time raising their pay.

Congress enacts the Financial Institutions Reform, Recovery, and Enforcement Act to help the federal government gain control over the savings and loan crisis and deregulate the savings industry.

Congress bans the recipients of federal funds from using those funds for lobbying purposes.

1990 In *Rutan v. Republican Party of Illinois*, the U.S. Supreme Court rules that government employment decisions cannot be made on partisan grounds.

The Americans with Disabilities Act is enacted, protecting the civil rights of individuals with physical and mental disabilities.

Colorado, Oklahoma, and California are the first states in modern times to enact term limits on state legislators, launching the term limit movement.

The federal debt surpasses $3 trillion.

President Bush and congressional leaders work together to pass the Budget Enforcement Act to reduce the federal deficit. The act supersedes the Gramm-Rudman-Hollings Act.

The Civil Justice Reform Act is enacted by Congress to reduce costs and delays in the federal court system and to improve judicial access.

1991 President Bush demonstrates a commitment to multinationalism as he reaches out to the United Nations and other countries before sending American troops to fight in the Persian Gulf War.

Texas enacts the nation's first early voting law.

California confronts a projected $14 billion budget deficit, as a recession places severe stress on state finances across the nation.

The state of Oregon rations health care benefits to Medicaid recipients to help control costs.

An investigation reveals that 269 House members had written overdrafts from the bank that serves the House of Representatives between 1988 and 1991, including several who had written more than 100.

Clarence Thomas is appointed to the U.S. Supreme Court.

Congress enacts the Civil Rights Act of 1991 to reverse a series of Supreme Court decisions that had weakened the nation's affirmative action policies.

1992 The Twenty-seventh Amendment is ratified, restricting congressional pay raises.

In *Lucas v. South Carolina Coastal Council*, the U.S. Supreme Court rules that the government must pay compensation when its regulations deny landowners of all economic benefits from the use of their land. The decision sets an important precedent in government "takings."

The federal debt surpasses $4 trillion.

Texas billionaire H. Ross Perot leads the nation's strongest third-party presidential campaign since 1912.

William J. Clinton is elected president.

The use of majority-minority districts helps bring a record number of minorities to Congress and state legislatures.

1993 The Office of Federal Procurement Policy directs all executive agencies to begin using past performance when evaluating bids for most government contracts over $100,000. The change in policy is seen as a step to improving the way government spends it money.

The National Voter Registration Act ("Motor Voter") requires states to allow registration through the mail or at government offices serving the public.

In *Shaw v. Reno*, the U.S. Supreme Court rules that race-conscious districting that is designed to improve minority representation may violate the Fourteenth Amendment.

The Winter Commission proposes a series of reforms to lower the costs and improve the delivery of state and local government programs.

The National Performance Review puts forward a package of reform proposals (the Gore Report) for improving the operation of the federal bureaucracy.

The Federal Employees Political Activities Act allows federal workers to participate more fully in campaigns and elections.

President Clinton's Task Force on National Health Care Reform, led by First Lady Hillary Rodham Clinton, presents its proposal for universal health care to Congress.

Congress enacts the North American Free Trade Agreement and the General Agreement on Tariffs and Trade to further remove trade barriers.

1994 Congress enacts the Goals 2000: Educate America Act to strengthen the nation's education system.

In *Dolan v. the City of Tigard*, the U.S. Supreme Court expands the use of the "takings" clause, potentially restricting local governments' control over zoning.

Republican congressional candidates unveil a Contract with America that pledges sweeping political reform.

The 1994 election gives the Republican Party control of Congress for the first time in 40 years.

1995 Newt Gingrich is elected Speaker of the House of Representatives.

The House of Representatives adopts a supermajority rule, which requires that all tax increases receive more than 60 percent of the vote in order to pass.

The Congressional Accountability Act extends federal workplace laws to Congress.

North Carolina becomes the final state to grant its governor the veto power.

Congress enacts the Unfunded Mandate Reform Act, banning the creation of new unfunded mandates by the federal government.

Congress enacts the Paperwork Reduction Act of 1995 to extend and strengthen the Paperwork Reduction Act of 1980.

In *United States v. Lopez*, the U.S. Supreme Court restricts the federal government's use of the commerce clause to supersede state authority.

In *U.S. Term Limits v. Thornton*, the U.S. Supreme Court rules that individual states cannot limit the number of terms that their members of Congress can serve in office.

Congress establishes the strictest ethics rules in its history, severely restricting the gifts that members can receive from individuals other than their family and friends.

Congress enacts the Lobby Disclosure Act to strengthen federal lobbying laws.

Oregon becomes the first state to use an all-mail-ballot election for a federal election.

A debate over the federal budget forces a shutdown of the federal government as the new Republican majority in Congress fight with President Clinton over the extent to which Medicare spending should be reduced.

1996 In *Seminole Tribe of Florida v. Florida*, the U.S. Supreme Court rules that Congress does not have the power to authorize private lawsuits against states. The decision is seen as potentially strengthening state sovereignty.

Congress grants the president the power of the line-item veto.

Bibliography

Aaron, Henry J. *Serious and Unstable Condition: Financing America's Health Care.* Washington, DC: Brookings Institution, 1991.

Abbott, David W., and James P. Levine. *Wrong Winner: The Coming Debacle in the Electoral College.* New York: Praeger, 1991.

Aberbach, Joel D. *Keeping a Watchful Eye: The Politics of Congressional Oversight.* Washington, DC: Brookings Institution, 1990.

Abraham, Henry J. *The Judicial Process: An Introductory Analysis of the Courts of the United States, England, and France.* 6th ed. New York: Oxford University Press, 1993.

Acuña, Rodolfo. *Occupied America: A History of Chicanos.* 3d ed. New York: Harper & Row, 1988.

Adrian, Charles R., and Michael R. Fine. *State and Local Politics.* Chicago: Lyceum, 1991.

Alexander, Herbert E. *Financing Politics: Money, Elections, and Political Reform.* 4th ed. Washington, DC: Congressional Quarterly Press, 1992.

Allen, Joan W. *Private Sector in State Service Delivery: Examples of Innovative Practices.* Washington, DC: Urban Institute Press, 1989.

Alter, Jonathan. "Decoding the Contract." *Newsweek,* 9 January 1995, 26–27.

Altschiller, Donald, ed. *Affirmative Action.* New York: H. W. Wilson, 1991.

Ammons, David N., and Charldean Newell. "'City Managers Don't Make Policy': A Lie; Let's Face It." *National Civic Review* 77 (March-April 1988): 124–132.

"Anita Hill." *Current Biography* 56 (September 1995): 32–36.

Applebome, Peter. "Guinier Ideas, Once Seen as Odd, Now Get Serious Study." *New York Times,* 3 April 1994, Sec. 4, 5.

Archibald, Sam. "The Early Years of the Freedom of Information Act: 1955 to 1974." *PS: Political Science and Politics* 26 (1993): 726–731.

Arnold, Peri. *Making the Managerial Presidency: Comprehensive Reorganization Planning: 1905–1980.* Princeton, NJ: Princeton University Press, 1986.

———. "Reform's Changing Role." *Public Administration Review* 55 (September/October 1995): 407–417.

Aronowitz, Stanley and Henry A. Giroux. *Education Still under Siege.* 2d ed. Westport, CT: Bergin & Garvey, 1993.

Arrington, Karen McGill, and William L. Taylor, eds. *Voting Rights in America: Continuing the Quest for Full Participation.* Washington, DC: Leadership Conference Education Fund and the Joint Center for Political and Economic Studies, 1992.

Arterton, F. Christopher. *Teledemocracy: Can Technology Protect Democracy?* Newbury Park, CA: Sage, 1987.

Arthur Young and Company. *Computerizing Elections Administration,* Vol. 1, *Current Applications.* Washington, DC: National Clearinghouse on Election Administration, 1985.

Atkins, Norman. "Governor Get-a-Job: Tommy Thompson." *New York Times Magazine,* 15 January 1995, 22–26.

Babson, Jennifer. "House Rejects Term Limits: GOP Blames Democrats." *Congressional Quarterly Weekly Report* 53 (1 April 1995): 918–919.

Backstrom, Charles, Leonard Robins, and Scott Eller. "Partisan Gerrymandering in the Post-Bandemer Era." *Constitutional Commentary* 4 (1987): 285–318.

Baer, Denise L., and David A. Bositis. *Politics and Linkage in a Democratic Society.* Englewood Cliffs, NJ: Prentice Hall, 1993.

Baker, Gordon E. *The Reapportionment Revolution: Representation, Political Power, and the Supreme Court.* New York: Random House, 1966.

Bandow, Doug. "Avoiding War." *Foreign Policy* 89 (Winter 1992–1993): 156–174.

Banner-Haley, Charles T. *The Fruits of Integration: Black Middle-Class Ideology and Culture, 1960–1990.* Jackson: University Press of Mississippi, 1994.

Barone, Michael, and Grant Ujifusa, eds. *The Almanac of American Politics.* Washington, DC: National Journal, 1990–1995.

Barone, Michael, Grant Ujifusa, and Douglas Matthews, eds. *Almanac of American Politics 1978.* New York: E. P. Dutton, 1977.

Barry, John. "The Collapse of Les Aspin," *Newsweek,* 27 December 1993, 22–25.

Barry, John M. *The Ambition and the Power: A True Story of Washington.* New York: Penguin, 1989.

Bartels, Larry M. *Presidential Primaries and the Dynamics of Public Choice.* Princeton, NJ: Princeton University Press, 1988.

Beer, Samuel H. "Foreword," in John William Ellwood, ed., *Reductions in U.S. Domestic Spending.* New Brunswick, NJ: Transaction, 1984.

Bell, Charles G., and Charles M. Price. *California Government Today: Politics of Reform?* 3d ed. Chicago: Dorsey, 1988.

Benenson, Bob. "Procedural Overhaul Fails after Three Tough Votes." *Congressional Quarterly Weekly Report* 53 (22 July 1995): 2159–2162.

Benjamin, Gerald, and Michael J. Malbin, eds. *Limiting Legislative Terms.* Washington, DC: Congressional Quarterly Press, 1992.

Bennett, W. Lance. *The Governing Crisis: Media, Money, and Marketing in American Elections.* New York: St. Martin's Press, 1992.

Berkman, Michael B. *The State Roots of National Politics: Congress and the Tax Agenda, 1978–1986.* Pittsburgh: University of Pittsburgh Press, 1993.

Berkson, Larry Charles, and Susan B. Carbon. *Court Unification: History, Politics, and Implementation.* Washington, DC: National Institute of Law Enforcement and Criminal Justice, 1978.

———. *The United States Circuit Judge Nominating Commission: Its Members, Procedures, and Candidates.* Chicago: American Judicature Society, 1980.

Berman, David R. "Takeovers of Local Governments: An Overview and Evaluation of State Policies." *Publius: The Journal of Federalism* 25 (Summer 1995): 55–70.

Berman, Evan M., Jonathan P. West, and Michael E. Milakovich. "Portrait of a Management Style as a Young Plan: Implementing TQM in the States." *Spectrum: The Journal of State Government* 67 (Spring 1994): 6–12.

Berns, Walter, ed. *After the People Vote: A Guide to the Electoral College.* Washington, DC: American Enterprise Institute, 1992.

Berry, Jeffrey M. *The Interest Group Society.* 2d ed. Glenview, IL: Scott, Foresman/Little, Brown, 1989.

Beyle, Thad L. "The Governor as Innovator in the Federal System." *Publius: The Journal of Federalism* 18 (Summer 1988): 131–152.

———. "Being Governor," in Carl E. Van Horn, ed., *The State of the States.* 2d ed. Washington, DC: Congressional Quarterly Press, 1993.

———. "The Executive Branch: Organization and Issues, 1992–93," in *The Book of the States, 1994–95.* Vol. 30. Lexington, KY: Council of State Governments, 1994.

Bianchi, Carl F. "Alternative Dispute Resolution: Is the Jury Still Out?" *Journal of State Government* 61 (September–October 1988): 174–176.

Bianco, William T. "Representatives and Constituents in the Postreform Congress: The Problem of Persuasion," in Roger H. Davidson, ed., *The Postreform Congress.* New York: St. Martin's Press, 1992.

Bibby, John F., and Thomas M. Holbrook. "Parties and Elections," in Virginia Gray and Herbert Jacob, eds., *Politics in the American States: A Comparative Analysis.* 6th ed. Washington, DC: Congressional Quarterly Press, 1996.

"Bill Clinton." *Current Biography* 55 (November 1994): 19–22.

Birnbaum, Jeffrey H. "A Plot To Liven Up the Race." *Time,* 4 December 1995, 55.

Biskupic, Joan. "U.S. Judges Turn to the Hill for Help on Pay, Work." *Congressional Quarterly Weekly Report* 47 (3 June 1989): 1322–1326.

———. "Civil Rights Act of 1991." *Congressional Quarterly Weekly Report* 49 (7 December 1991): 3620–3622.

Blair, George S. *American Legislatures: Structure and Process.* New York: Harper & Row, 1967.

Block, Peter. *The Empowered Manager: Positive Political Skills at Work.* San Francisco: Jossey-Bass, 1987.

Blodgett, Terrell. "Beware the Lure of the 'Strong' Mayor." *Public Management* (January 1994), 6–11.

The Book of the States, 1994–95. Vol. 30. Lexington, KY: Council of State Governments, 1994.

Bornet, Vaughn Davis. *The Presidency of Lyndon B. Johnson.* Lawrence: University Press of Kansas, 1983.

Bowman, Ann O'M., and Richard C. Kearney. The Resurgence of the States. Englewood Cliffs, NJ: Prentice Hall, 1986.

———. *State and Local Government.* 2d ed. Boston: Houghton Mifflin, 1993.

Boyd, Eugene P. "Congressional Actions Affecting Local Governments," in *The Municipal Yearbook 1994.* Washington, DC: International City/County Management Association, 1994.

Brams, Steven J., and Peter C. Fishburn. *Approval Voting.* Boston: Birkhäuser, 1983.

Branch, Taylor. *Parting the Waters: America in the King Years, 1954–1963.* New York: Simon & Schuster, 1988.

Brodie, Fawn M. *Richard Nixon: The Shaping of Character.* New York: W. W. Norton, 1981.

Buchanan, Bruce. *Electing a President: The Markle Commission Research on Campaign '88.* Austin: University of Texas Press, 1991.

Buchanan, Patrick J. *Right from the Beginning: An Autobiography.* Boston: Little, Brown, 1988.

Buckwalter, Doyle W. "Dillon's Rule in the 1980s: Who's in Charge of Local Affairs?" *National Civic Review* 71 (September 1982): 399–406.

Bullock, Joyce. "State Lobby Laws in the 1990s," in *The Book of the States, 1994–95.* Vol. 30. Lexington, KY: Council of State Governments, 1994.

California Commission on Campaign Financing. *The New Gold Rush: Financing California's Legislative Campaigns.* Los Angeles: Center for Responsive Government, 1985.

Callies, David L., ed. *After Lucas: Land Use Regulation and the Taking of Private Property Without Compensation.* Chicago: American Bar Association, 1993.

Campagna, Anthony S. *The Economy in the Reagan Years: The Economic Consequences of the Reagan Administrations.* Westport, CT: Greenwood, 1994.

Campbell, Colin. *Managing the Presidency: Carter, Reagan, and the Search for Executive Harmony.* Pittsburgh: University of Pittsburgh Press, 1986.

Cannon, Lou. *Ronnie and Jesse: A Political Odyssey.* Garden City, NY: Doubleday, 1969.

Canon, David T. *Actors, Athletes, and Astronauts: Political Amateurs in the United States Congress.* Chicago: University of Chicago Press, 1990.

Carney, Eliza Newlin. "Still Trying To Reinvent Government." *National Journal* 26 (18 June 1994): 1442–1444.

Carp, Robert A., and Ronald Stidham. *Judicial Process in America.* 2d ed. Washington, DC: Congressional Quarterly Press, 1993.

Carter, Karen. "Performance Budgets: Here by Popular Demand." *State Legislatures* 20 (December 1994): 22–25.

Cassata, Donna. "Paperwork Reduction Bill." *Congressional Quarterly Weekly Report* 53 (6 May 1995): 1263–1264.

Ceasar, James W. *Reforming the Reforms: A Critical Analysis of the Presidential Selection Process.* Cambridge, MA: Ballinger, 1982.

Chafe, William H. "The End of One Struggle, the Beginning of Another," in Charles W. Eagles, ed., *The Civil Rights Movement in America.* Jackson: University Press of Mississippi, 1986.

Chargot, Patricia. "Cut Class, Get a Smaller Check." *State Legislatures* 17 (October 1991): 12–13.

Chavez, Linda. *Out of the Barrio: Toward a New Politics of Hispanic Assimilation.* New York: Basic Books, 1991.

"Child Pornography Bill Heads Back to House." *Congressional Quarterly Weekly Report* 53 (8 April 1995): 1030.

Christensen, Terry. *Local Politics: Governing at the Grassroots.* Belmont, CA: Wadsworth, 1995.

Citizens' Conference on State Legislatures. *The Sometimes Governments: A Critical Study of the 50 American Legislatures.* 2d ed. Kansas City, MO: Citizens' Conference on State Legislatures, 1973.

Citrin, Jack, Beth Reingold, Evelyn Walters, and Donald P. Green. "The 'Official English' Movement and the Symbolic Politics of Language in the United States." *Western Political Quarterly* 43 (September 1990): 535–559.

Clayton, Susan D., and Faye J. Crosby. *Justice, Gender, and Affirmative Action.* Ann Arbor: University of Michigan Press, 1992.

Cleary, Robert E., and Kimberly Nelson. "The Volcker Commission Report Fades Away: A Case Study in Non-implementation." *Policy Studies Review* 12 (Autumn-Winter 1993): 55–73.

Cloud, David S. "GOP, to Its Own Great Delight, Enacts House Rules Changes." *Congressional Quarterly Weekly Report* 53 (7 January 1995): 13–15.

———. "GOP's Balancing Act Gets Tricky as Budget Amendment Sinks." *Congressional Quarterly Weekly Report* 53 (4 March 1995): 671–676.

Clucas, Richard A. *The Speaker's Electoral Connection: Willie Brown and the California Assembly.* Berkeley, CA: Institute of Governmental Studies Press, 1995.

Cochran, Charles L., and Eloise F. Malone. *Public Policy: Perspectives and Choices.* New York: McGraw-Hill, 1995.

Cole, Richard L., Delbert A. Taebel, and Rodney V. Hissong. "American Cities and the 1980s: The Legacy of the Reagan Years," in David C. Saffell and Harry Basehart, eds., *Readings in State and Local Government: Problems and Prospects.* New York: McGraw-Hill, 1994.

Collins, Susan M., and Barry P. Bosworth. *The New GATT: Implications for the United States.* Washington, DC: Brookings Institution, 1994.

Collis, Cheri. "Clearing Up the Spoils System." *State Government News* 33 (September 1990): 6–8.

Committee on Political Parties of the American Political Science Association. *Toward a More Responsible Two-Party System.* New York: Rinehart, 1950.

Common Cause. "Lobby Disclosure Reform in the States," David C. Saffell and Harry Baseharts, ed., *Readings in State and Local Government: Problems and Prospects.* New York: McGraw-Hill, 1994.

Congressional Campaign Finances: History, Facts, and Controversy. Washington, DC: Congressional Quarterly Press, 1992.

Conlan, Timothy J. *New Federalism: Intergovernmental Reform from Nixon to Reagan.* Washington, DC: Brookings Institution, 1988.

Conlan, Timothy J., James D. Riggle, and Donna E. Schwartz. "Deregulating Federalism? The Politics of Mandate Reform in the 104th Congress." *Publius: The Journal of Federalism* 25 (Summer 1995): 23–40.

Conlan, Timothy J., Margaret T. Wrightson, and David R. Beam. *Taxing Choices: The Politics of Tax Reform.* Washington, DC: Congressional Quarterly Press, 1990.

Conway, M. Margaret. *Political Participation in the United States.* 2d ed. Washington, DC: Congressional Quarterly Press, 1991.

Cook, Rhodes. "GOP Faces Unchartered Terrain in Wake of Buchanan Upset." *Congressional Quarterly Weekly Report* 54 (24 February 1996): 438–442.

Cooper, Mary H. "Environmental Movement at 25: Will Congress Weaken Environmental Regulations?" *Congressional Quarterly Researcher* 5 (31 March 1995): 273–296.

Cornell, Stephen. *The Return of the Native: American Indian Political Resurgence.* New York: Oxford University Press, 1988.

Cranford, John. "The New Class: More Diverse, Less Lawyerly, Younger." *Congressional Quarterly Weekly Report* 50 (Supplement to No. 44, 7 November 1992): 7–10.

Cronin, Thomas E. *Direct Democracy: The Politics of Initiative, Referendum, and Recall.* Cambridge, MA: Harvard University Press, 1989.

Cropper, Maureen L., and Wallace E. Oates. "Environmental Economics: A Survey." *Journal of Economic Literature* 30 (June 1992): 675–740.

Crotty, William J. *Political Reform and the American Experience.* New York: Thomas Y. Crowell, 1977.

Crotty, William J., and John S. Jackson III. *Presidential Primaries and Nominations.* Washington, DC: Congressional Quarterly Press, 1985.

Cultice, Wendell W. *Youth's Battle for the Ballot: A History of Voting Age in America.* Westport, CT: Greenwood, 1992.

Cunningham, Patrick M. *Welfare Reform: A Response to Unemployed Two Parent Families.* New York: Garland, 1993.

Daly, John Charles, and William B. Allen. *Affirmative Action and the Constitution.* Washington, DC: American Enterprise Institute for Public Policy Research, 1987.

Davidson, Chandler, ed. *Minority Vote Dilution.* Washington, DC: Howard University Press, 1989.

———. "The Voting Rights Act: A Brief History," in Bernard Grofman and Chandler Davidson, eds., *Controversies in Minority Voting: The Voting Rights Perspective.* Washington, DC: Brookings Institution, 1992.

Davidson, Roger H. "Two Avenues of Change: House and Senate Committee Reorganization," in Lawrence C. Dodd and Bruce I. Oppenheimer, eds., *Congress Reconsidered.* 2d ed. Washington, DC: Congressional Quarterly Press, 1981.

———, ed. *The Postreform Congress.* New York: St. Martin's Press, 1992.

Davidson, Roger H., and Walter J. Oleszek. *Congress and Its Members.* 4th ed. Washington, DC: Congressional Quarterly Press, 1994.

Davis, James W. *The President as Party Leader.* Westport, CT: Greenwood, 1992.

Diegmueller, Karen. "Sunrise, Sunset Cut Costs." *State Government News* 33 (October 1990): 7–9.

DiIulio, John J., Jr. "Punishing Smarter: Penal Reforms for the 1990s." *Brookings Review* 7 (Summer 1989): 3–12.

———, ed. *Deregulating the Public Service: Can Government Be Improved?* Washington, DC: Brookings Institution, 1994.

DiNitto, Dianna M. *Social Welfare: Politics and Public Policy.* 4th ed. Boston: Allyn & Bacon, 1995.

Dinnerstein, Leonard, Roger L. Nichols, and David M. Reimers. *Natives and Strangers: Blacks, Indians, and Immigrants in America.* 2d ed. New York: Oxford University Press, 1990.

Dionne, E. J., Jr. *Why Americans Hate Politics.* New York: Simon & Schuster, 1991.

Dodd, Lawrence C., and Bruce I. Oppenheimer. "The House in Transition: Change and Consolidation," in Lawrence C. Dodd and Bruce I. Oppenheimer, eds., *Congress Reconsidered.* 2d ed. Washington, DC: Congressional Quarterly Press, 1981.

———. "Perspectives on the 1992 Congressional Elections," in Lawrence C. Dodd and Bruce I. Oppenheimer, eds., *Congress Reconsidered.* 5th ed. Washington, DC: Congressional Quarterly Press, 1993.

Doherty, Carrol J. "In Senate, 'Contract' Proposals Survive in Altered Form." *Congressional Quarterly Weekly Report* 53 (25 March 1995): 878–879.

Donovan, Beth. "Remap Math Doesn't Add Up to One Person, One Vote." *Congressional Quarterly Weekly Report* 49 (26 October 1991): 3139–3140.

Downs, George W., and Patrick D. Larkey. *The Search for Government Efficiency: From Hubris to Helplessness.* Philadelphia: Temple University Press, 1986.

Dubois, Phillip L. *The Politics of Judicial Reform.* Lexington, MA: Lexington, 1982.

DuBow, Sy, and Sarah Geer. *Legal Rights: The Guide for Deaf and Hard of Hearing People.* 4th ed. Washington, DC: Gallaudet University Press, 1992.

Duncan, Phil. "Perot Gores His Own Ox in Debate." *Congressional Quarterly Weekly Report* 51 (13 November 1993): 3105.

Dye, Thomas R. *Politics in States and Communities.* 8th ed. Englewood Cliffs, NJ: Prentice Hall, 1994.

Eagles, Charles W., ed. *The Civil Rights Movement in America.* Jackson: University Press of Mississippi, 1986.

Edelman, Alice Chasan. "Is There Room at the Top?" in Thad L. Beyle, ed., *State Government: CQ's Guide to Current Issues and Activities, 1987–1988.* Washington, DC: Congressional Quarterly Press, 1987.

Edsall, Thomas Byrne. *The New Politics of Inequality.* New York: W. W. Norton, 1984.

Edsall, Thomas Byrne, and Mary D. Edsall. *Chain Reaction: The Impact of Race, Rights, and Taxes on American Politics.* New York: W. W. Norton, 1992.

Edwards, George C., III, and Stephen J. Wayne. *Presidential Leadership: Politics and Policy Making* 2d ed. New York: St. Martin's Press, 1990.

Ehrenhalt, Alan. *The United States of Ambition: Politicians, Power, and the Pursuit of Office.* New York: Random House, 1991.

———. "Power Shifts in State Capitols as Professional Lawmakers Take Over Leadership Spots," in John R. Baker, ed., *Readings in American Subnational Government: Diversity, Innovation, and Rejuvenation.* New York: HarperCollins, 1993.

Elling, Richard C. "The Line in Winter: An Academic Assessment of the First Report of the National Commission on the State and Local Public Service." *Public Administration Review* 54 (March-April 1994): 107–108.

Ellwood, John W., and James A. Thurber. "The Politics of the Congressional Budget Process Re-examined," in Lawrence C. Dodd and Bruce I. Oppenheimer, eds., *Congress Reconsidered.* 2d ed. Washington, DC: Congressional Quarterly Press, 1981.

Emery, Fred. *Watergate: The Corruption of American Politics and the Fall of Richard M. Nixon.* New York: Times Books, 1991.

Estreicher, Samuel, and John Sexton. *Redefining the Supreme Court's Role: A Theory of Managing the Federal Judicial Process.* New Haven, CT: Yale University Press, 1986.

Ethridge, Marcus E., and Stephen L. Percy. "A New Kind of Public Policy Encounters Disappointing Results: Implementing Learnfare in Wisconsin." *Public Administration Review* 53 (July-August 1993): 340–370.

Etzioni, Amitai. *Capital Corruption: The New Attack on American Democracy.* New Brunswick, NJ: Transaction, 1988.

Evans, C. Lawrence, and Walter J. Oleszek. "The Politics of Congressional Reform: The Joint Committee on the Organization of Congress," in James A. Thurber and Roger H. Davidson, eds., *Remaking Congress: Change and Stability in the 1990s.* Washington, DC: Congressional Quarterly Press, 1995.

Fabricus, Martha. "More Dictates from the Feds." *State Legislatures* 17 (February 1991): 28–30.

Feerick, John D. *The Twenty-fifth Amendment: Its Complete History and Earliest Applications.* New York: Fordham University Press, 1976.

Feigenbaum, Edward D., and James A. Palmer. *Absentee Voting: Issues and Options.* Washington, DC: National Clearinghouse on Election Administration, 1987.

———. *Ballot Access 1: Issues and Options.* Washington, DC: National Clearinghouse on Election Administration, 1988.

Felde, Jon. "Supreme Court Confirms State Sovereignty." *State Legislatures* 22 (May 1966): 19.

Feldstein, Martin, ed. *American Economic Policy in the 1980s.* Chicago: University of Chicago Press, 1994.

Fineman, Howard. "Gingrich the Warrior," *Newsweek,* 9 January 1995, 28–34.

Fiorina, Morris P. *Congress: Keystone of the Washington Establishment.* New Haven, CT: Yale University Press, 1977.

———. *Divided Government.* New York: Macmillan, 1992.

"Fiscally Speaking, a Very Good Year." *State Legislatures* 21 (October-November 1995): 9.

Forer, Lois G. *Unequal Protection: Women, Children, and the Elderly in Court.* New York: W. W. Norton, 1991.

Francis, John G., and Richard Ganzel. *Western Public Lands: The Management of National Resources in a Time of Declining Federalism.* Totowa, NJ: Rowman & Allanheld, 1984.

Franklin, Daniel P. *Making Ends Meet: Congressional Budgeting in the Age of Deficits.* Washington, DC: Congressional Quarterly Press, 1993.

———. "Downsizing: Is It Aimed at the Right Targets?" *Washington Monthly,* November 1994, 22–27.

Freedman, Anne. "Doing Battle with the Patronage Army: Politics, Courts, and Personnel Administration in Chicago." *Public Administration Review* 48 (September-October 1988): 847–859.

Frieden, Bernard J., and Marshall Kaplan. *The Politics of Neglect: Urban Aid from Model Cities to Revenue Sharing.* Cambridge: MIT Press, 1975.

Friedman, Milton. *Capitalism and Freedom.* Chicago: University of Chicago Press, 1982.

Friedman, Milton, and Rose Friedman. *Free To Choose.* New York: Harcourt Brace Jovanovich, 1980.

Fullerton, Don. "Tax Policy," in Martin Feldstein, ed., *American Economic Policy in the 1980s.* Chicago: University of Chicago Press, 1994.

Fulton, William, and Morris Newman. "The Strange Career of Enterprise Zones." *Governing* 7 (March 1994): 32–34.

Garber, Peter M., ed. *The Mexico-U.S. Free Trade Agreement.* Cambridge: MIT Press, 1993.

Garcia, F. Chris, ed. *Latinos and the Political System.* Notre Dame, IN: University of Notre Dame Press, 1988.

Garfield, Jay L., and Patricia Hennessey, eds. *Abortion: Moral and Legal Perspectives.* Amherst, MA: University of Massachusetts Press, 1984.

Garment, Suzanne. *Scandal: The Culture of Mistrust in American Politics.* New York: Times Books, 1991.

Garnett, James L. "Organizing and Reorganizing State and Local Government," in Harry A. Bailey, Jr., and Jay M. Shafritz, eds., *State and Local Government and Politics: Essential Readings.* Itasca, IL: F. E. Peacock, 1993.

Garrow, David J. *Protest at Selma: Martin Luther King, Jr. and the Voting Rights Act of 1965.* New Haven, CT: Yale University Press, 1978.

Gates, John B., and Charles A. Johnson, eds. *The American Courts: A Critical Assessment.* Washington, DC: Congressional Quarterly Press, 1991.

Gelfand, Mark I. "The War on Poverty," in Robert A. Devine, ed., *Exploring the Johnson Years.* Austin: University of Texas Press, 1981.

Gettinger, Stephen. "Rostenkowski Case: A Question Hovers." *Congressional Quarterly Weekly Report* 54 (20 April 1996): 1090.

Gierzynski, Anthony. *Legislative Party Campaign Committees in the American States.* Lexington: University Press of Kentucky, 1992.

Ginzberg, Eli, and Robert M. Solow. *The Great Society: Lessons for the Future.* New York: Basic Books, 1974.

Glastris, Paul. "Rego a Go-Go: A Reinventing Triumph." *New Republic* 210 (21 November 1994): 14–16.

Glazer, Myron Peretz, and Penina Migdal Glazer. *The Whistleblowers: Exposing Corruption in Government and Industry.* New York: Basic Books, 1989.

Glick, Henry R. "The Politics of Court Reform: In a Nutshell." *Policy Studies Journal* 10 (June 1982): 680–689.

———. "Policy Making and State Supreme Courts," in John B. Gates and Charles A. Johnson, eds., *The American Courts: A Critical Assessment.* Washington, DC: Congressional Quarterly Press, 1991.

Gold, Steven D. "It's Not a Miracle, It's a Mirage." *State Legislatures* 20 (February 1994): 28–31.

———. *The Fiscal Crisis of the States: Lessons for the Future.* Washington, DC: Georgetown University Press, 1995.

Gormley, William T., Jr. "Accountability Battles in State Administration," in Carl E. Van Horn, ed., *The State of the States.* 2d ed. Washington, DC: Congressional Quarterly Press, 1993.

———. *Taming the Bureaucracy: Muscles, Prayers, and Other Strategies.* Princeton, NJ: Princeton University Press, 1989.

Graf, William L. *Wilderness Preservation and the Sagebrush Rebellions.* Savage, MD: Rowman & Littlefield, 1990.

Graham, Hugh Davis. *Civil Rights and the Presidency: Race and Gender in American Politics, 1960–1972.* New York: Oxford University Press, 1992.

Graham, Judith, ed. *Current Biography Yearbook 1992.* New York: H. W. Wilson, 1992.

———, ed. *Current Biography Yearbook 1994.* New York: H. W. Wilson, 1994.

Gray, Virginia, and Herbert Jacob, eds., *Politics in the American States: A Comparative Analysis.* 6th ed. Washington, DC: Congressional Quarterly Press, 1996.

Green, Roy E. *Enterprise Zones: New Directions in Economic Development.* Newbury Park, CA: Sage, 1991.

Greene, John Robert. *The Limits of Power: The Nixon and Ford Administrations.* Bloomington: Indiana University Press, 1992.

Greenwald, John. "Ready, Willing, Cable." *Time,* 31 July 1995, 48–50.

Grimshaw, William J. *Bitter Fruit: Black Politics and the Chicago Machine, 1931–1991.* Chicago: University of Chicago Press, 1992.

Grofman, Bernard, and Chandler Davidson, eds., *Controversies in Minority Voting: The Voting Rights Act in Perspective.* Washington, DC: Brookings Institution, 1992.

Grofman, Bernard, and Arend Lijphart, eds. *Electoral Laws and Their Political Consequences.* New York: Agathon, 1986.

Grossman, Lawrence K. *The Electronic Republic: Reshaping Democracy in the Information Age.* New York: Viking, 1995.

Guinier, Lani. *The Tyranny of the Majority: Fundamental Fairness in Representative Democracy.* New York: Free Press, 1994.

Gurwitt, Rob. "The Lure of the Strong Mayor." *Governing* 6 (July 1993): 36–41.

Guskind, Robert. "Zeal for the Zones." *National Journal* 21 (3 June 1989): 1358–1362.

Hager, George. "Harsh Rhetoric on Budget Spells a Dismal Outlook." *Congressional Quarterly Weekly Report* 53 (9 December 1995): 3721–3725.

Hall, Wayne W., Jr. "State Management and Administration: Doing More with Less," in *The Book of the States, 1992–93.* Vol. 29. Lexington, KY: Council of State Governments, 1992.

Harrigan, John J. *Political Change in the Metropolis.* 5th ed. New York: HarperCollins, 1993.

———. *Politics and Policy in States and Communities.* 5th ed. New York: HarperCollins, 1994.

Hart, Gary. *A New Democracy.* New York: Quill, 1983.

Hartmann, Susan M. *From Margin to Mainstream: American Women and Politics since 1960.* New York: Knopf, 1989.

Heckman, James J. "The Impact of Government on the Economic Status of Black Americans," in Steven Shulman and William Darity, Jr., eds., *The Question of Discrimination: Racial Inequality in the U.S. Labor Market.* Middletown, CT: Wesleyan University Press, 1989.

Henkin, Louis. *The Age of Rights.* New York: Columbia University Press, 1990.

Herring, George C. *The Secret Diplomacy of Vietnam War.* Austin: University of Texas Press, 1983.

———. *America's Longest War: The United States and Vietnam, 1950–1975.* 2d ed. New York: Knopf, 1986.

Herrmann, Frederick M., and Ronald D. Michaelson. "Financing State and Local Elections: Recent Developments," in *The Book of the States, 1994–95.* Vol. 30. Lexington, KY: Council of State Governments, 1994.

Herrnson, Paul S. *Party Campaigning in the 1980s.* Cambridge, MA: Harvard University Press, 1988.

Hertzke, Allen D. *Echoes of Discontent: Jesse Jackson, Pat Robertson, and the Resurgence of Populism.* Washington DC: Congressional Quarterly Press, 1993.

Hess, Stephen. *Organizing the Presidency.* Washington, DC: Brookings Institution, 1988.

Hill, G. Richard. *Regulatory Taking: The Limits of Land Use Controls.* Chicago: American Bar Association, 1993.

Hill, Herbert, and James E. Jones, Jr. *Race in America: The Struggle for Equality.* Madison: University of Wisconsin Press, 1993.

Hirsch, Werner Z., and Anthony M. Rufolo. *Public Finance and Expenditure in a Federal System.* San Diego: Harcourt Brace Jovanovich, 1990.

Hoffman, Saul D., and Laurence S. Seidman. *The Earned Income Tax Credit: Antipoverty Effectiveness and Labor Market Effects.* Kalamazoo, MI: W. E. Upjohn Institute for Employment Research, 1990.

Holmes, Steven A. "The Boom in Jails Is Locking Up Lots of Loot." *New York Times,* 6 November 1994, Sec. 4, 3.

Holsti, Ole R., and James N. Rosenau. *American Leadership in World Affairs: Vietnam and the Breakdown of Consensus.* Boston: Allen & Unwin, 1984.

Hosansky, David. "Unfunded Mandates Law." *Congressional Quarterly Weekly Report* 53 (15 April 1995): 1087.

Hrebenar, Ronald J., and Ruth K. Scott. *Interest Group Politics in America.* 2d ed. Englewood Cliffs, NJ: Prentice Hall, 1990.

Hufbauer, Gary Clyde, and Jeffrey J. Schott. *NAFTA: An Assessment.* Washington, DC: Institute for International Economics, 1993.

Hulten, Charles R., and Isabel V. Sawhill, eds. *The Legacy of Reaganomics: Prospects for Long-Term Growth.* Washington DC: Urban Institute Press, 1984.

Hunt, Richard J. "Gay and Lesbian Politics." *PS: Political Science and Politics* 25 (1992); 220-224.

Hyde, A. C. "National Performance Review: On the Path to Management Reform." *Public Productivity and Management Review* 18 (Fall 1994): 57–58.

Idelson, Holly. "High Court Strikes Down Law Banning Guns Near Schools." *Congressional Quarterly Weekly Report* 53 (29 April 1995): 1181.

———. "Indian Gaming Ruling Strikes at Congressional Power." *Congressional Quarterly Weekly Report* 54 (30 March 1996): 889.

———. "It's Back to Drawing Board on Minority Districts." *Congressional Quarterly Weekly Report* 53 (7 October 1995): 3065–3067.

———. "States' Rights Loses in Close Vote." *Congressional Quarterly Weekly Report* 53 (27 May 1995): 1480.

Ingraham, Patricia and Carolyn Ban, eds. *Legislating Bureaucratic Change: The Civil Service Reform Act of 1978.* New York: State University of New York Press, 1984.

Inhaber, Herbert. "Of LULUs, NIMBYs, and NIMTOOs." *The Public Interest* 107 (Spring 1992): 52–64.

"Is This a Bunch of Lollipops?" *Newsweek,* 16 March 1992, 28.

Isaac, Katherine. *Ralph Nader Presents: Practicing Democracy—A Guide to Student Action.* New York: St. Martin's Press, 1995.

Jackson, Brooks. *Broken Promise: Why the Federal Election Commission Failed.* New York: Priority, 1990.

Jacob, Herbert. "Courts: The Least Visible Branch," in Virginia Gray and Herbert Jacob, eds., *Politics in the American States: A Comparative Analysis.* 6th ed. Washington, DC: Congressional Quarterly Press, 1996.

Jacobs, Jerald A., ed. *Federal Lobbying.* Washington, DC: Bureau of National Affairs, 1989.

Jacobson, Gary C. *The Politics of Congressional Elections.* 3d ed. New York: HarperCollins, 1992.

Jamieson, Kathleen Hall, and David S. Birdsell. *Presidential Debates: The Challenge of Creating an Informed Electorate.* New York: Oxford University Press, 1988.

Janda, Kenneth, Jeffrey M. Berry, and Jerry Goldman. *The Challenge of Democracy: Government in America* 4th ed. Boston: Houghton Mifflin, 1995.

Jehl, Douglas. "Clinton Shuffles His Aides, Selecting Budget Director as White House Staff Chief." *New York Times,* 28 June 1994, 1.

Jelen, Ted, and Clyde Wilcox. "The Christian Right in the 1990s." *Public Perspective* (March-April 1993): 10–12.

Jencks, Christopher. *Rethinking Social Policy: Race, Poverty, and the Underclass.* Cambridge, MA: Harvard University Press, 1992.

Johansen, Robert C. *The National Interest and the Human Interest: An Analysis of U.S. Foreign Policy.* Princeton, NJ: Princeton University Press, 1980.

Johnson, Ronald N., and Gary D. Libecap. *The Federal Civil Service System and the Problem of Bureaucracy: The Economics and Politics of Institutional Change.* Chicago: University of Chicago Press, 1994.

Jones, Charles O. *The Presidency in a Separated System.* Washington, DC: Brookings Institution, 1994.

Jones, Rich. "State Legislatures," in *The Book of the States, 1994–95.* Vol. 30. Lexington, KY: Council of State Governments, 1994.

Joskow, Paul L., and Roger G. Noll. "Economic Regulation," in Martin Feldstein, ed., *American Economic Policy in the 1980s.* Chicago: University of Chicago Press, 1994.

Kaplan, Marshall, and Peggy L. Cuciti. *The Great Society and Its Legacy: Twenty Years of U.S. Social Policy.* Durham, NC: Duke University Press, 1986.

Katz, Allan J. "The Politics of Congressional Ethics," in Joseph Cooper and G. Calvin Mackenzie, eds., *The House at Work.* Austin: University of Texas Press, 1981.

Katz, Jeffrey L. "The Slow Death of Political Patronage." *Governing* 4 (April 1991): 58–62.
———."The Search for Equity in School Funding." *Governing* 4 (August 1991): 20–22.
———. "Clinton Plans Major Shift in Lives of Poor People." *Congressional Quarterly Weekly Report* 52 (22 January 1994): 117–122.
Keefe, William J. *Parties, Politics, and Public Policy in America.* 7th ed. Washington, DC: Congressional Quarterly Press, 1994.
Keefe, William J., and Morris S. Ogul. *The American Legislative Process: Congress and the States.* 8th ed. Englewood Cliffs, NJ: Prentice Hall, 1993.
Kegley, Charles W., Jr., and Eugene R. Wittkopf. *American Foreign Policy: Pattern and Process.* 4th ed. New York: St. Martin's Press, 1991.
Kehler, David, and Robert M. Stern. "Initiatives in the 1980s and 1990s," in *The Book of the States, 1994–95.* Vol. 30. Lexington, KY: Council of State Governments, 1994.
Kelman, Steven. *Procurement and Public Management: The Fear of Discretion and the Quality of Government Performance.* Washington: American Enterprise Institute, 1990.
———. "Deregulating Federal Procurement: Nothing To Fear but Discretion Itself?" in John J. DiIulio, Jr., ed., *Deregulating the Public Service: Can Government Be Improved?* Washington, DC: Brookings Institution, 1994.
Kettl, Donald F. *Deficit Politics: Public Budgeting in Its Institutional and Historical Context.* New York: Macmillan, 1992.
Kim, Pan Suk, and Lance W. Wolff, "Improving Government Performance: Public Management Reform and the National Performance Review." *Public Productivity and Management Review* 18 (Fall 1994): 73–87.
Kincaid, John. "State Court Protections of Individual Rights under State Constitutions: The New Judicial Federalism." *Journal of State Government* 61 (September-October 1988): 163–169.
Kingson, Eric R., and Edward D. Berkowitz. *Social Security and Medicare: A Policy Primer.* Westport, CT: Auburn House, 1993.
Kohn, George C. *Encyclopedia of American Scandal.* New York: Facts on File, 1989.
Koszczuk, Jackie. "Republicans' Hopes for 1996 Lie in Unfinished Business." *Congressional Quarterly Weekly Report* 54 (6 January 1996): 6–52.
Kuntz, Phil. "The History of the House Bank: Scandal Waiting To Happen." *Congressional Quarterly Weekly Report* 50 (8 February 1992): 283–289.
———. "Stamp Embezzlement Scheme Points to Rostenkowski." *Congressional Quarterly Weekly Report* 51 (24 July 1993): 1923–1928.
Kurtz, Karl T. "The 1992 State Legislative Elections in Perspective." *APSA Legislative Studies Section Newsletter* 16 (November 1992): 10–11.
Kutler, Stanley I. *The Wars of Watergate: The Last Crisis of Richard M. Nixon.* New York: Knopf, 1990.
Laffer, Arthur B., and Jan P. Seymour. *The Economics of the Tax Revolt: A Reader.* New York: Harcourt Brace Jovanovich, 1979.
Lamb, Brian. *C-SPAN: America's Town Hall.* Washington, DC: Acropolis Books, 1988
Lammers, Nancy, ed. *The Washington Lobby.* 4th ed. Washington, DC: Congressional Quarterly Press, 1982.
Lawrence, Leslie A., and Cynthia D. Prince. "The National Education Goals Panel: State and National Partnerships in Education Reform," in *The Book of the States, 1994–95.* Vol. 30. Lexington, KY: Council of State Governments, 1994.
Lawrence, Robert Z. *Can America Compete?* Washington, DC: Brookings Institution, 1984.
Lee, Robert D., Jr. and Ronald W. Johnson. *Public Budgeting Systems.* 3d ed. Baltimore: University Park Press, 1983.
Lehne, Richard. *The Quest for Justice: The Politics of School Finance Reform.* New York: Longman, 1978.
Lekachman, Robert. *Greed Is Not Enough: Reaganomics.* New York: Pantheon, 1983.
Leloup, Lance T., and Steve A. Shull. *Congress and the President: The Policy Connection.* Belmont, CA: Wadsworth, 1993.
Lemov, Penelope. "Climbing Out of the Medicaid Trap." *Governing* 5 (October 1991): 49–53.
———. "The Next Best Thing to Prison." *Governing* 5 (December 1991): 34–39.
———. "Tailoring Local Government to the 1990s." *Governing* 6 (July 1992): 28–32.
———. "Is There Anything Left To Tax?" *Governing* 6 (August 1993): 26–30.
"Les Aspin." *New York Times Biographical Service,* May 1995, 764–765.
Levine, Charles H., ed. *The Unfinished Agenda for Civil Service Reform: Implications of the Grace Commission Report.* Washington, DC: Brookings Institution, 1985.
Levy, David W. *The Debate over Vietnam.* Baltimore: Johns Hopkins University Press, 1991.
Litan, Robert E., ed. *Verdict: Assessing the Civil Jury System.* Washington, DC: Brookings Institution, 1993.

———. "Financial Regulation," in Martin Feldstein, ed., *American Economic Policy in the 1980s.* Chicago: University of Chicago Press, 1994.

Loevy, Robert D. *The Flawed Path to the Presidency 1992: Unfairness and Inequality in the Presidential Selection Process.* Albany: State University of New York Press, 1995.

Long, David C. "*Rodriguez:* The State Courts Respond." *Phi Delta Kappan* 64 (March 1983): 481–484.

Longley, Lawrence D., and Alan G. Braun. *The Politics of Electoral College Reform.* New Haven, CT: Yale University Press, 1972.

Louthan, William C. *The United States Supreme Court: Lawmaking in the Third Branch of Government.* Englewood Cliffs, NJ: Prentice Hall, 1991.

Low, Erick B. "Accessing the Judicial System: The States' Response," in *The Book of the States, 1994–95.* Vol. 30. Lexington, KY: Council of State Governments, 1994.

Lowi, Theodore J., and Benjamin Ginsberg. *Democrats Return to Power: Politics and Policy in the Clinton Era.* New York: W. W. Norton, 1994.

Luck, Edward C. "Making Peace." *Foreign Policy* 89 (Winter 1992–1993): 137–155.

MacPherson, Peter. "GOP Revives 1994's Hot Issue: Health Insurance Overhaul." *Congressional Quarterly Weekly Report* 53 (1 April 1995): 944–946.

Madison, Christopher. "Ethics as Usual?" *National Journal* 21 (8 July 1989): 1742–1745.

Magleby, David B., and Candice J. Nelson. *The Money Chase: Congressional Campaign Finance Reform.* Washington, DC: Brookings Institution, 1990.

Malbin, Michael J., ed. *Money and Politics in the United States: Financing Elections in the 1980s.* Washington, DC: American Enterprise Institute for Public Policy Research, 1984.

Mangold, Kirsten. "Affirmative Action and the UC Vote." *California Journal* 26 (September 1995): 32–38.

Mann, Thomas E. "Renewing Congress: A Report from the Front Lines," in James A. Thurber and Roger H. Davidson, eds., *Remaking Congress: Change and Stability in the 1990s.* Washington, DC: Congressional Quarterly Press, 1995.

Marshall, Thomas R. *Presidential Nominations in a Reform Age.* New York: Praeger, 1981.

"Marshall, Thurgood," in Charles Moritz, ed., *Current Biography Yearbook 1989.* New York: H. W. Wilson, 1989.

Martis, Nancy H., and A. G. Block. "Proposition 187." *California Journal* 25 (December 1994): 20–22.

Masci, David. "Mandatory Victim Restitution OK'd by Senate Judiciary." *Congressional Quarterly Weekly Report* 53 (18 November 1995): 3548.

Matheny, Albert R., and Bruce A. Williams. "Strong Democracy and the Challenge of Siting Hazardous Waste Disposal Facilities in Florida." *National Civic Review* 77 (July-August 1988): 323–341.

Mayer, Jane, and Jill Abramson. *Strange Justice: The Selling of Clarence Thomas.* Boston: Houghton Mifflin, 1994.

Mayhew, David. *Divided We Govern: Party Control, Lawmaking, and Investigations, 1946–1990.* New Haven, CT: Yale University Press, 1991.

McCann, Michael W. *Taking Reform Seriously: Perspectives on Public Interest Liberalism.* Ithaca, NY: Cornell University Press, 1986.

McClure, Charles R., Peter Hernon, and Harold C. Relyea, eds. *United States Government Information Policies: Views and Perspectives.* Norwood, NJ: Ablex, 1989.

McConnell, Campbell R., and Stanley L. Brue. *Economics: Principles, Problems, and Policies.* 11th ed. New York: McGraw-Hill, 1990.

McDonald, Laughlin, and John A. Powell. *The Rights of Racial Minorities: The Basic ACLU Guide to Racial Minority Rights.* 2d ed. Carbondale: Southern Illinois University Press, 1993.

McDonald, William F., and James A. Cramer. *Plea-Bargaining.* Lexington, MA: D. C. Heath, 1980.

McGuire, William, and Leslie Wheeler, eds. *American Social Leaders.* Denver, CO: ABC-CLIO, 1993.

McLauchlan, William P. "Courts and Caseloads," in John B. Gates and Charles A. Johnson, eds., *The American Courts: A Critical Assessment.* Washington, DC: Congressional Quarterly Press, 1991.

Meier, August, and Elliott Rudwick. *CORE: A Study in the Civil Rights Movement, 1942–1968.* New York: Oxford University Press, 1973.

Meier, August, Elliott M. Rudwick, and Francis L. Broderick, eds. *Black Protest Thought in the Twentieth Century.* 2d ed. Indianapolis: Bobbs-Merrill Educational, 1971.

Mikesell, John L. *Fiscal Administration: Analysis and Applications for the Public Sector.* 3d ed. Pacific Grove, CA: Brooks/Cole, 1991.

Milkis, Sidney M., and Michael Nelson. *The American Presidency: Origins and Development, 1776–1993.* 2d ed. Washington, DC: Congressional Quarterly Press, 1994.

Miller, John R., and Christopher R. Tufts. "Privatization Is a Means to 'More with Less,'" in John R. Baker, ed., *Readings on American Subnational Government: Diversity, Innovation, and Rejuvenation.* New York: HarperCollins, 1993.

Mills, Mike. "Clinton and Gore Hit the Road To Build a Better Bureaucracy." *Congressional Quarterly Weekly Report* 51 (11 September 1993): 2381–2389.

Minarik, Joseph J. *Making Tax Choices.* Washington, DC: Urban Institute Press, 1985.

Miranda, Rowan, and Karlyn Andersen. "Alternative Service Delivery in Local Government, 1982–1992," in *The Municipal Year Book 1994.* Washington, DC: International City/County Management, 1994.

Miroff, Bruce, Raymond Seidelman, and Todd Swanstrom. *The Democratic Debate: An Introduction to American Politics.* Boston: Houghton Mifflin, 1995.

Moe, Richard. "If Men Were Angels . . . Property Rights and the 'Takings' Issue." *State Legislatures* 20 (November 1994): 33.

Moncrief, Gary F., and Joel A. Thompson, eds. *Changing Patterns in State Legislative Careers.* Ann Arbor: University of Michigan Press, 1992.

Moon, Marilyn. *Medicare Now and in the Future.* Washington, DC: Urban Institute Press, 1993.

Moore, W. John. "Cutoff at Town Hall." *National Journal* 19 (11 April 1987): 862–866.

Morandi, Larry. "Takings for Granted." *State Legislatures* 21 (June 1995): 22–27.

Moritz, Charles, ed. *Current Biography Yearbook.* New York: H. W. Wilson, 1975–1985.

Morrison, Toni, ed. *Race-ing Justice, En-gendering Power: Essays on Anita Hill, Clarence Thomas, and the Construction of Social Reality.* New York: Pantheon, 1992.

Mucciaroni, Gary. *Reversals of Fortune: Public Policy and Private Interests.* Washington, DC: Brookings Institution, 1995.

Mullins, Charlotte G. *Innovations in Election Administration: Using NCOA Files for Verifying Voter Registration Lists.* Washington, DC: National Clearinghouse on Election Administration, 1992.

The Municipal Year Book 1989. Washington, DC: International City/County Management Association, 1989.

Nash, Roderick. *Wilderness and the American Mind.* 3d ed. New Haven, CT: Yale University Press, 1982.

Nathan, James A., and James K. Oliver. *United States Foreign Policy and World Order.* Boston: Little, Brown, 1989.

———. *Foreign Policy Making and the American Political System.* 3d ed. Baltimore: Johns Hopkins University Press, 1994.

Nathan, Richard P. "Reinventing Government: What Does It Mean?" *Public Administration Review* 55 (March-April 1995): 213–215.

National Civic League. *Model City Charter.* 7th ed. Denver: National Civic League Press, 1989.

National Clearinghouse on Election Administration. *Voting Systems Standards.* Washington, DC: National Clearinghouse on Election Administration, 1990.

National Commission on Excellence in Education. *A Nation at Risk: The Imperative for Educational Reform.* Washington, DC: U.S. Government Printing Office, 1983.

National Commission on Judicial Discipline and Removal. *Report of the National Commission on Judicial Discipline and Removal.* Washington, DC: National Commission on Judicial Discipline and Removal, 1993.

National Conference of State Legislatures Reapportionment Task Force. *Reapportionment Law: The 1990s.* Denver: National Conference on State Legislatures, 1989.

———. *Redistricting Provisions: 50 State Profiles.* Denver: National Conference of State Legislatures, 1989.

Neely, Alfred S., IV. *Ethics-in-Government Laws: Are They Too 'Ethical'?* Washington, DC: American Enterprise Institute for Public Policy Research, 1984.

Nelson, Michael, ed. *The Elections of 1984.* Washington, DC: CQ Press, 1985.

Nice, David C. *Policy Innovation in State Government.* Ames: Iowa State University Press, 1994.

Nightingale, Demetra Smith, and Robert H. Haveman, eds. *The Work Alternative: Welfare Reform and the Realities of the Job Market.* Washington, DC: Urban Institute Press, 1995.

Niskanen, William A. *Reaganomics: An Insider's Account of the Policies and People.* New York: Oxford University Press, 1988.

Norrander, Barbara. *Super Tuesday: Regional Politics and Presidential Primaries.* Lexington: University Press of Kentucky, 1992.

O'Connor, Karen, and Larry J. Sabato. *American Government: Roots and Reform.* 2d ed. Boston: Allyn & Bacon, 1995.

Olson, James S., and Randy Roberts. *Where the Domino Fell: America and Vietnam, 1945–1990.* New York: St. Martin's Press, 1991.

Osborne, David, and Ted Gaebler. *Reinventing Government: How the Entrepreneurial Spirit Is Transforming the Public Sector.* Menlo Park, CA: Addison-Wesley, 1992.

O'Toole, Laurence J., Jr. *American Intergovernmental Relations: Foundations, Perspectives, and Issues.* 2d ed. Washington, DC: Congressional Quarterly Press, 1993.

Pacelle, Mitchell. "Block Watch: Not in Your Backyard, Say Community Panels in Suburban Enclaves," in Bruce Stinebrickner, ed., *State and Local Government.* 7th ed. Guilford, CT: Dushkin, 1995.

Pagano, Michael A., and Ann O'M. Bowman. "The State of American Federalism, 1994–1995." *Publius: The Journal of Federalism* 25 (Summer 1995): 1–22.

Patterson, Thomas E. *The American Democracy.* New York: McGraw-Hill, 1990.

Pechman, Joseph A., and Michael S. McPherson. *Fulfilling America's Promise: Social Policies for the 1990s.* Ithaca, NY: Cornell University Press, 1992.

Peck, Jeffrey J. "'Users United': The Civil Justice Reform Act of 1990." *Law & Contemporary Problems* 54 (Summer 1991): 105–118.

People's Lobby. *National Initiative and Vote of Confidence (Recall): Tools for Self-Government.* Los Angeles: People's Lobby Press, 1974.

Perlman, Ellen. "The Gorilla That Swallows State Laws." *Governing* 5 (August 1994): 46–48.

Perot, H. Ross. *United We Stand: How We Can Take Back Our Country.* New York: Hyperion, 1992.

———. *Intensive Care: We Must Save Medicare and Medicaid Now.* New York: Harper Perennial, 1995.

Peterson, Peter G. *Facing Up: How To Rescue the Economy from Crushing Debt and Restore the American Dream.* New York: Simon & Schuster, 1993.

Piven, Frances Fox, and Richard A. Cloward. *Why Americans Don't Vote.* New York: Pantheon, 1988.

Polsby, Nelson W. *Consequences of Party Reform.* New York: Oxford University Press, 1983.

Posner, Richard A. *The Federal Courts: Crisis and Reform.* Cambridge, MA: Harvard University Press, 1985.

Poterba, James M. "Budget Policy," in Martin Feldstein, ed., *American Economic Policy in the 1980s.* Chicago: University of Chicago Press, 1994.

Price, Charles. "The Virtual Primary." *California Journal* 26 (November 1995): 35–39.

Quirk, Paul J. "Structures and Performance: An Evaluation," in Roger H. Davidson, ed., *The Postreform Congress.* New York: St. Martin's Press, 1992.

Rabinovitz, Jonathan. "States Tighten Rules on Lobbyists' Gifts." *New York Times* 5 May 1996, 17.

Raimondo, Henry J. "State Budgeting in the Nineties," in Carl E. Van Horn, ed., *The State of the States.* 2d ed. Washington, DC: Congressional Quarterly Press, 1993.

Ranney, Austin. *Curing the Mischiefs of Faction: Party Reform in America.* Berkeley: University of California Press, 1975.

———, ed. *The Past and Future of Presidential Debates.* Washington, DC: American Enterprise Institute for Public Policy Research, 1979.

Raskin, Jamin B., and John Bonifaz. *The Wealth Primary: Campaign Fundraising and the Constitution.* Washington, DC: Center for Responsive Politics, 1994.

Reich, Robert B. *The New American Frontier.* New York: Times Books, 1983.

"Republicans' Initial Promise: 100-Day Debate on 'Contract.'" *Congressional Quarterly Weekly Report* 52 (12 November 1994): 3216–3219.

Reske, Henry J. "Long-Range Plan Would Cut Federal Cases." *ABA Journal* (February 1995): 22–24.

Resnik, Judith. "Finding the Factfinders," in Robert E. Litan, ed., *Verdict: Assessing the Civil Jury System.* Washington, DC: Brookings Institution, 1993.

Reynolds, Lloyd G. *Economics: A General Introduction.* 5th ed. Homewood, IL: Irwin, 1988.

Rieselbach, Leroy N. *Congressional Reform: The Changing Modern Congress.* Washington, DC: Congressional Quarterly Press, 1994.

———. *Congressional Politics: The Evolving Legislative System.* 2d ed. Boulder, CO: Westview, 1995.

Rivlin, Alice M. *Reviving the American Dream: The Economy, the States, and the Federal Government.* Washington, DC: Brookings Institution, 1992.

Roberts, Robert N. *White House Ethics: The History of the Politics of Conflict of Interest Regulation.* Westport, CT: Greenwood, 1988.

Robinson, Armstead L., and Patricia Sullivan, eds. *New Directions in Civil Rights Studies.* Charlottesville: University Press of Virginia, 1991.

Rohde, David W. *Parties and Leaders in the Postreform House.* Chicago: University of Chicago Press, 1991.

Rosenau, Pauline Vaillancourt, ed. *Health Care Reform in the Nineties.* Thousand Oaks, CA: Sage, 1994.

Rosenfield, Margaret. *Agency Voter Registration Program.* Washington, DC: National Clearinghouse on Election Administration, 1992.

———. *Early Voting.* Washington, DC: National Clearinghouse on Election Administration, 1994.

———. *All-Mail-Ballot Elections.* Washington, DC: National Clearinghouse on Election Administration, 1995.

Rosenstone, Steven J., Roy L. Behr, and Edward H. Lazarus. *Third Parties in America: Citizen Response to Major Party Failure.* Princeton, NJ: Princeton University Press, 1984.

Rosenthal, Alan. *Governors and Legislatures: Contending Powers.* Washington, DC: Congressional Quarterly Press, 1990.

———. "The Legislative Institution: In Transition and at Risk," in Carl E. Van Horn, ed., *The State of the States.* 2d ed. Washington, DC: Congressional Quarterly Press, 1993.

———. *The Third House: Lobbyists and Lobbying in the States.* Washington, DC: Congressional Quarterly Press, 1993.

Ross, Julia C. "New Civil Rights Act." *ABA Journal* 78 (January 1992): 85.

Rule, Wilma, and Joseph F. Zimmerman, eds. *United States Electoral Systems: Their Impact on Women and Minorities.* New York: Praeger, 1992.

Rush, Mark E. "From *Shaw v. Reno* to *Miller v. Johnson:* Minority Representation and State Compliance with the Voting Rights Act." *Publius: The Journal of Federalism* 25 (Summer 1995): 155–172.

Sabato, Larry J. *Goodbye to Good-Time Charlie: The American Governorship Transformed.* Washington, DC: Congressional Quarterly Press, 1983.

———. *PAC Power: Inside the World of Political Action Committees.* New York: W. W. Norton, 1984.

———. *The Party's Just Begun: Shaping Political Parties for America's Future.* Glenview, IL: Little, Brown, 1988.

Saffell, David C. *State and Local Government: Politics and Public Policies.* 5th ed. New York: McGraw-Hill, 1993.

Sahu, Anandi P., and Ronald L. Tracy. *The Economic Legacy of the Reagan Years: Euphoria or Chaos?* New York: Praeger, 1991.

Salant, Johnathan D. "Bill Would Open Windows on Lobbying Efforts." *Congressional Quarterly Weekly Report* 53 (2 December 1995): 3631–3633.

Saldivar, R. A. "Trashing the Tax Code." *Knight Ridder News Service,* 18 January 1996.

Salmore, Barbara G., and Stephen A. Salmore. *Candidates, Parties, and Campaigns: Electoral Politics in America.* 2d ed. Washington, DC: Congressional Quarterly Press, 1989.

Samuelson, Paul A., and William D. Nordhaus. *Economics.* 14th ed. New York: McGraw-Hill, 1992.

Savas, E. S. *Privatization: The Key to Better Government.* Chatham, NJ: Chatham House, 1987.

Savoie, Donald J. *Thatcher, Reagan, Mulroney: In Search of a New Bureaucracy.* Pittsburgh: University of Pittsburgh Press, 1994.

Scammon, Richard. "GOP Counts a 'Contract' Win as Compliance Bill Clears." *Congressional Quarterly Weekly Report* 53 (21 January 1995): 197.

Schlozman, Kay Lehman, and John T. Tierney. *Organized Interests and American Democracy.* New York: HarperCollins, 1986.

Schneider, William. "Clinton: The Reason Why." *National Journal* 26 (12 November 1994): 2630–2632.

Schor, Juliet B. *The Overworked American: The Unexpected Decline of Leisure.* New York: Basic Books, 1991.

Schrag, Peter. "Son of 187." *New Republic* 212 (30 January 1995): 16–19.

Schulzinger, Robert D. *Henry Kissinger: Doctor of Diplomacy.* New York: Columbia University Press, 1989.

Sears, David O., and Jack Citrin. *Tax Revolt: Something for Nothing in California.* Cambridge, MA: Harvard University Press, 1985.

Seelye, Katharine Q. "Bob Dole: Pragmatic, Proven." *New York Times News Service,* 15 January 1996.

Serafini, Marilyn Werber. "No Strings Attached." *National Journal* 27 (20 May 1995): 1230–1234.

Shafer, Byron E. *Quiet Revolution: The Struggle for the Democratic Party and the Shaping of Post-Reform Politics.* New York: Russell Sage Foundation, 1983.

Shaiko, Ronald G. "More Bank for the Buck: The New Era of Full-Service Public Interest Organizations," in Allan J. Cigler and Burdett A. Loomis, eds., *Interest Group Politics.* 3d ed. Washington, DC: Congressional Quarterly Press, 1991.

Shapiro, Joseph P. *No Pity: People with Disabilities Forging a New Civil Rights Movement.* New York: Times Books, 1993.

Shulman, Steve, and William Darity, Jr., eds. *The Question of Discrimination: Racial Inequality in the U.S. Labor Market.* Middletown, CT: Wesleyan University Press, 1989.

Shultz, George P., and Kenneth W. Dam. *Economic Policy beyond the Headlines.* New York: W. W. Norton, 1977.

Shuman, Howard E. *Politics and the Budget: The Struggle between the President and Congress.* 3d ed. Englewood Cliffs, NJ: Prentice Hall, 1992.

Sinclair, Barbara. "The Emergence of Strong Leadership in the 1980s House of Representatives." *Journal of Politics* 54 (August 1992): 657–683.

———. "House Majority Party Leadership in an Era of Legislative Constraint," in Roger H. Davidson, ed., *The Postreform Congress.* New York: St. Martin's Press, 1992.

Singer, Linda R. *Settling Disputes: Conflict Resolution in Business, Families, and the Legal System.* Boulder, CO: Westview, 1990.

Skogan, Wesley G. "Crime and Punishment," in Virginia Gray and Herbert Jacob, eds., *Politics in the American States: A Comparative Analysis.* 6th ed. Washington, DC: Congressional Quarterly Press, 1996.

Slaton, Christa Daryl. *Televote: Expanding Citizen Participation in the Quantum Age.* New York: Praeger, 1992.

Smith, Steven S. *Call to Order: Floor Politics in the House and the Senate.* Washington, DC: Brookings Institution, 1989.

———. *The American Congress.* Boston: Houghton Mifflin, 1995.

Smolka, Richard G., and Ronald D. Michaelson. "Election Legislation, 1992–93," in *The Book of the States, 1994–95.* Vol. 30. Lexington, KY: Council of State Governments, 1994.

Sorauf, Frank J. *Party Politics in America.* 5th ed. Boston: Little, Brown, 1984.

———. *Money in American Elections.* Glenview, IL: Scott, Foresman, 1988.

"Special Report: A Summary of Legislative Action: Economics and Finance." *Congressional Quarterly Weekly Report* 53 (2 September 1995): 2627–2633.

Spitzer, Robert J. *The Presidential Veto: Touchstone of the American Presidency.* Albany: State University of New York Press, 1988.

———. *President and Congress: Executive Hegemony at the Crossroads of American Government.* New York: McGraw-Hill, 1993.

Squire, Peverill, James M. Lindsay, Cary R. Covington, and Eric R. A. N. Smith. *Dynamics of Democracy.* Madison, WI: Brown & Benchmark, 1995.

Stanfield, Rochelle L. "Forced Federalism." *National Journal* 23 (14 December 1991): 3020–3023.

Stein, Herbert. *Presidential Economics: The Making of Economic Policy from Roosevelt to Clinton.* 3d ed. Washington, DC: American Enterprise Institute for Policy Research, 1994.

Steuerle, C. Eugene. *The Tax Decade: How Taxes Came To Dominate the Public Agenda.* Washington, DC: Urban Institute Press, 1992.

Steuerle, C. Eugene, and Jon M. Bakija. *Retooling Social Security for the 21st Century: Right and Wrong Approaches to Reform.* Washington, DC: Urban Institute Press, 1994.

Stewart, Charles, III. "Let's Go Fly a Kite: Correlates of Involvement in the House Bank Scandal." *Legislative Studies Quarterly* 19 (November 1994): 521–535.

Strickland, Ruth Ann. "The Twenty-seventh Amendment and Constitutional Change by Stealth." *PS: Political Science and Politics* 26 (December 1993): 716–722.

"Struggling for Standards." *Education Week,* 12 April 1995, special report.

"Subcommittee Reports Out Study Committee Bill: Includes JSAS Reforms." *The Third Branch* 24 (April 1992): 2.

Sundquist, James L. *The Decline and Resurgence of Congress.* Washington, DC: Brookings Institution, 1981.

———. *Constitutional Reform and Effective Government.* Rev. ed. Washington, DC: Brookings Institution, 1992.

Swiss, James E. "Adapting Total Quality Management (TQM) to Government." *Public Administration Review* 52 (July-August 1992): 356–362.

Sylvester, Kathleen. "Mandate Blues." *Governing* 2 (September 1989): 26–30.

Szanton, Peter. *Federal Reorganization: What Have We Learned?* Chatham, NJ: Chatham House, 1981.

Tait, Alan A. *Value Added Tax: International Practice and Problems.* Washington, DC: International Monetary Fund, 1988.

Taylor, Andrew. "Senate May Give in on Line-Item Veto." *Congressional Quarterly Weekly Report* 53 (11 November 1995): 3446.

———. "Bill Curbing Investor Lawsuits OK'd by Veto-Proof Margins." *Congressional Quarterly Weekly Report* 53 (9 December 1995): 3729.

———. "Congress Hands President a Budgetary Scalpel." *Congressional Quarterly Weekly Report* 54 (30 March 1966): 864–867.

Taylor, Jared. *Paved with Good Intentions: The Failure of Race Relations in Contemporary America.* New York: Carroll & Graf, 1992.

Teixeira, Ruy A. *The Disappearing American Voter.* Washington, DC: Brookings Institution, 1992.

Thompson, Dennis F. *Ethics in Congress: From Individual to Institutional Corruption.* Washington, DC: Brookings Institution, 1995.

Thompson, Frank J. "The Challenges Revisited," in Frank J. Thompson, ed., *Revitalizing State and Local Public Service: Strengthening Performance, Accountability, and Citizen Confidence.* San Francisco: Jossey-Bass, 1993.

———, ed. *Revitalizing State and Local Public Service: Strengthening Performance, Accountability, and Citizen Confidence.* San Francisco: Jossey-Bass, 1993.

———. "Executive Leadership as an Enduring Institutional Issue." *State and Local Government Review* 27 (Winter 1995): 7–17.

Thompson, Jake H. *Bob Dole: The Republicans' Man for All Seasons.* New York: Donald I. Fine, 1994.

Thurber, James A. "New Rules for an Old Game: Zero-Sum Budgeting in the Postreform Congress," in Roger H. Davidson, ed., *The Postreform Congress.* New York: St. Martin's Press, 1992.

Thurber, James A., and Roger H. Davidson. *Remaking Congress: Change and Stability in the 1990s.* Washington, DC: Congressional Quarterly, 1995.

Tobias, Carl. "Improving the 1988 and 1990 Judicial Improvement Acts." *Stanford Law Review* 46 (July 1994): 1589–1634.

"Tommy G. Thompson." *Current Biography* 56 (July 1995): 53–56.

Tushnet, Mark V. *Making Civil Rights Law: Thurgood Marshall and the Supreme Court, 1936–1961.* New York: Oxford University Press, 1994.

Tweedie, Jack. "Changing the Face of Welfare." *State Legislatures* 21 (December 1995): 14–21.

U.S. Commission on Civil Rights. *Indian Tribes: A Continuing Quest for Survival.* Washington, DC: U.S. Government Printing Office, 1981.

Unruh, Jesse. "Unicameralism: The Wave of the Future," in Donald G. Herzberg and Alan Rosenthal, eds., *Strengthening the States: Essays on Legislative Reform.* Garden City, NY: Anchor, 1972.

Utter, Robert F. "Justice, Money, and Sleaze." *State Government News* 35 (March 1992): 14–15.

Van Horn, Carl E., ed. *The State of the States.* 2d ed. Washington, DC: Congressional Quarterly Press, 1993.

Vaughn, Robert G. *Conflict-of-Interest Regulation in the Federal Executive Branch.* Lexington, MA: Lexington, 1979.

"The Voting Rights Act after *Shaw v. Reno.*" *PS: Political Science and Politics* 28 (March 1995): 24–56.

Wagar, Linda. "A Declaration of War," in Bruce Stinebrickner, ed., *State and Local Government.* 7th ed. Guilford, CT: Dushkin, 1995.

———. "The Tricky Path to Going Private," in Bruce Stinebrickner, ed., *State and Local Government.* 7th ed. Guilford, CT: Dushkin, 1995.

Walker, Charls E. "Tax Policy," in Martin Feldstein, ed., *American Economic Policy in the 1980s.* Chicago: University of Chicago Press, 1994.

Walker, Charls E., and Mark A. Bloomfield, eds. *The Consumption Tax: A Better Alternative?* Cambridge, MA: Ballinger, 1987.

Walker, David B. *The Rebirth of Federalism: Slouching toward Washington.* Chatham, NJ: Chatham House, 1995.

Walker, Jack L. *Mobilizing Interest Groups in America: Patrons, Professions, and Social Movements.* Ann Arbor: University of Michigan Press, 1991.

Walters, Jonathan. "The Downsizing Myth," in Thad Beyle, ed., *State Government: CQ's Guide to Current Issues and Activities, 1994–95.* Washington, DC: Congressional Quarterly Press, 1994.

"Washington Wire: Kemp's Support." *Wall Street Journal,* 11 August 1995, Sec. A, 1.

Watson, Richard A. *The Politics of the Bench and the Bar: Judicial Selection under the Missouri Plan.* New York: John Wiley, 1969.

———. *Presidential Vetoes and Public Policy.* Lawrence: University Press of Kansas, 1993.

Watson, Tom. "The Run for the Robes." *Governing* 4 (July 1991): 49–52.

Weigel, George. *Idealism without Illusion.* Washington, DC: Ethics and Public Policy Center, 1994.

Whalen, Charles, and Barbara Whalen. *The Longest Debate: A Legislative History of the 1964 Civil Rights Act.* Cabin John, MD: Seven Locks, 1985.

Whitcover, Jules. *Crapshoot: Rolling the Dice on the Vice Presidency.* New York: Crown, 1992.

Wilcox, Clyde. *The Latest American Revolution? The 1994 Elections and Their Implication for Governance.* New York: St. Martin's Press, 1995.

Wildavsky, Aaron. *The New Politics of the Budgetary Process.* Glenview, IL: Scott, Foresman, 1988.

Wilkinson, Charles F. *American Indians, Time, and the Law: Native Societies in a Modern Constitutional Democracy.* New Haven, CT: Yale University Press, 1987.

Wilson, James Q. *The Amateur Democrat.* Chicago: University of Chicago Press, 1966.

———. *Bureaucracy: What Government Agencies Do and Why They Do It.* New York: Basic Books, 1989.

Wilson, Robin. "Bennett's Tenure: Prominence for the Education Dept., but Alienation on Capitol Hill and the Campuses." *Chronicle of Higher Education,* 21 September 1988, A24–A25.

Witt, Elder, ed. *The Supreme Court and Its Work.* Washington, DC: Congressional Quarterly Press, 1981.

Wolfe, John R. *The Coming Health Crisis: Who Will Pay for Care for the Aged in the Twenty-first Century.* Chicago: University of Chicago Press, 1993.

Wolpe, Bruce C. *Lobbying Congress: How the System Works.* Washington, DC: Congressional Quarterly Press, 1990.

Worsnop, Richard L. "Gambling Boom: Will the Gaming Industry's Growth Hurt Society?" *Congressional Quarterly Researcher* 4 (18 March 1994): 241–264.

Wunnicke, Pat. "Fifty Years without a Conference Committee: Nebraska Unicameral Legislature." *State Legislatures* 13 (October 1987): 20–23.

Young, Amy. "In the States." *Common Cause Magazine,* July-August 1990, 41.

Zaremba, Laura M. "Governor and Lieutenant Governor on Same Ballot." *First Reading* 9 (January 1994): 1.

Zimmerman, Christopher. "A Devolution Revolution?" *State Legislatures* 21 (March 1995): 21.

———. "Flat Tax, Sales Tax, or VAT?" *State Legislatures* 21 (October-November 1995): 16–22.

Index